Defending Japan's Pacific War

Often wrongly accused of being fascists, the wartime Kyoto philosophers were among the first non-White thinkers to brood on the secrets of effective national action. They believed, with Marx, that the point of philosophy is to change the world. They exploited a sophisticated idea of history, borrowed partly from Ranke, partly from Hegel, to develop a Japanese understanding of rational self-mastery. This is the first study based on a meticulous examination of the primary sources in Japanese, which clarifies who these forgotten intellectuals were while challenging the orthodox prejudices that explain why we do not know more about them. In their published writings and hitherto secret anti-Tojo seminars of 1940–44, the philosophers of the Kyoto School took the first soundings of the post-White age that will define our tomorrow. They offered us the philosophy of our future.

The wartime Kyoto School made philosophy with a hammer. The resulting sparks illuminate the moral and metaphysical horizon of political science, US history and Japan studies, from Heidegger's encounter with Nazism and Ernst Nolte's call for 'deep revisionism' to the consolidation of American empire and the decay of the White Republic.

David Williams is one of Europe's leading thinkers on modern Japan. Born in Los Angeles, he was educated in Japan and at UCLA, and has contributed for many years to the opinion section of the *Los Angeles Times*. He has taught at Oxford, where he took his doctorate, Sheffield and Cardiff Universities. During twelve of his twenty-five years in Japan, he was an editorial writer for *The Japan Times*. He is the author of *Japan: Beyond the End of History* (Routledge) and *Japan and the Enemies of Open Political Science* (Routledge).

Other *Routledge* books by David Williams

Japan: Beyond the End of History

Japan and the Enemies of Open Political Science

Defending Japan's Pacific War

The Kyoto School philosophers and post-White power

David Williams

RoutledgeCurzon
Taylor & Francis Group
LONDON AND NEW YORK

First published 2004
by RoutledgeCurzon
2 Park Square, Milton Park, Abingdon, Oxon OX14 4RN

Simultaneously published in the USA and Canada
by RoutledgeCurzon
270 Madison Avenue, New York, NY 10016

RoutledgeCurzon is an imprint of the Taylor & Francis Group

© 2004 David Williams

Typeset in Times in by Taylor & Francis Books Ltd
Printed and bound in Great Britain by Antony Rowe Ltd,
Chippenham, Wiltshire

British Library Cataloguing in Publication Data
A catalogue record for this book is available from the British Library

Library of Congress Cataloging in Publication Data
A catalog record for this book has been requested

ISBN 0-415-32314-2 (hbk)
ISBN 0-415-32315-0 (pbk)

To Robin Reilly

Now therefore, that my mind is free from all cares, and that I have obtained for myself assured leisure in peaceful solitude, I shall apply myself seriously and freely to the general destruction of all my former opinions.

Descartes, *First Meditation*

Contents

Prologue: the final sorrows of empire – a Vietnam elegy xi
The book in brief xvi
Acknowledgments xviii
The doomed fleets sail: the Pacific War for beginners xxii
Japanese usage and style xxv

Rise and fall **1**

1 Roman questions: American empire and the Kyoto School 3

2 Revisionism: the end of White America in Japan studies 14

The decay of Pacific War orthodoxy **27**

3 Philosophy and the Pacific War: Imperial Japan and
   the making of a post-White world 29

4 Scholarship or propaganda: neo-Marxism and the decay
   of Pacific War orthodoxy 46

5 Wartime Japan as it really was: the Kyoto School's struggle
   against Tojo (1941–44) 61

In defence of the Kyoto School **77**

6 Taking Kyoto philosophy seriously 79

7 Racism and the black legend of the Kyoto School:
   translating Tanabe's *The Logic of the Species* 92

8 When is a philosopher a moral monster?
Tanabe versus Heidegger versus Marcuse   106

Nazism and the crises of the Kyoto School   **127**

9 Heidegger, Nazism and the Farías Affair:
the European origins of the Kyoto School crises   129

10 Heidegger and the wartime Kyoto School:
after Farías – the first paradigm crisis (1987–96)   141

11 Nazism is no excuse: after Farías – the Allied Gaze
and the second crisis (1997–2002)   151

After America, philosophy   **165**

12 Nothing shall be spared: a manifesto on the future of
Japan studies   167

Appendix: translations of two texts by Hajime Tanabe   **179**

'The Philosophy of Crisis or a Crisis in Philosophy:
Reflections on Heidegger's Rectoral Address' (1933)   181

'On the Logic of Co-prosperity Spheres: Towards a
Philosophy of Regional Blocs' (1942)   188

Notes   200
Select bibliography   220
Index   231

Prologue

The final sorrows of empire – a Vietnam elegy

To stand at the Vietnam War Memorial in Washington, tracing one's fingers over the engraved names of the dishonoured dead of my generation of Americans, is to be shaken, even now, by the humiliation of defeat, the fury of betrayal and full-blooded sorrow at the death of the national myth. This book is an attempt to transcend these emotions. Only transcendence can open the door towards a peaceful transition to a new post-White America. But, contrary to the patriotic faith, Americans cannot be reborn in freedom unless we are reborn in truth. We must resolve, therefore, to pay the price that remains to be paid if the United States is to master her unmastered past.

This book is a reluctant exercise by a most unlikely *soixante huitard*, to use the language of the French rebels of 1968. I did not rebel in 1968. Rather, I clung on, to the disbelief and sometimes disgust of my UCLA classmates, to the myth of American righteousness in the face of the military disaster of Tet and all that followed that grim year. In holding fast, my instincts were sound. To turn against American policy in Vietnam was to embrace, more or less consciously, more or less irrevocably, a momentous change in the national character. It was to begin to die as one kind of American and to be reborn as another.

With its nearly 60,000 names, 'The Wall' memorialises the murderous encounter of my generation with the truth about America's real place in the world. Only battlefield defeat – decisive, blatant and unforgiving – could have finally stripped away the unyielding faith in New World greatness that has defined all previous generations of White Americans, from the Puritan conquerors of the Pequots to the Pacific victors of 1945. Visitors to The Wall claim that when they close their eyes within reach of that black marble, they can hear the chopper blades slash the jungle air; but what they really hear is the bitter drop of history's curtain. The fall of Saigon in 1975 destroyed the cherished vision of a national destiny forever in ascent. This is the source of the negative gravity of The Wall, and its unrivalled power to disturb, for it is the first and only unambiguous shrine to an American future lived in truth in this city of marmoreal effigies and bronze monuments to a now dead and deceiving past.

Nowhere are these deceptions more powerfully on display than in the Iwo Jima Memorial. To the pre-Vietnam generation, this epic recreation of the moment when a handful of Marines raised 'Old Glory' on Mt Suribachi commemorates an unbroken tradition of American virtue demonstrated by invincibility in war. Prisoners of this past, the generation that rejoiced in the American 'high' of 1945, proceeded to water the ice fields and rice paddies of East Asia with the blood of their sons and daughters in desperate military ventures that risked the nation's sense of its unique greatness. Despite the racial humiliations of Pearl Harbour, Corregidor and Bataan, the Iwo Jima Memorial proclaims the bold promise of unchallengeable American suzerainty over Asia, a continent that the generation of 1945 neither understood nor respected.

The Iwo Jima Memorial proposes a final grand salute to the Roman invincibility of the White Republic. This martial prowess had been demonstrated decade after decade, century after century, by the defeat of the French, the Indians, the British, the Mexicans, the Confederacy, the Spanish, the Germans and the Japanese. But the debacles of Tet, Khe Sang and Saigon transformed the meaning of the Iwo Jima Memorial, reducing it to a folly dedicated to national blindness and self-deception. Deceived by such monumental hubris, the generation of 1945 – whom Tom Brokow, trapped in the dream of Iwo Jima nostalgia, has unconscionably called 'the greatest generation' – gambled away the nation's belief in its providential destiny by blundering in Korea and failing in Vietnam.

Only five years of dramatic events separate the confident heroism of the bronze conquistadors of Mt Suribachi from the numbing horror that threatens to overwhelm the American patrol portrayed in the new Korean War Memorial in Washington. Despite the soldiers' wary forward motion, they have the stench of fear in their nostrils. Death is near, and the patrol knows it. Bitter truths, recklessly paid in young lives at the imperious insistence of blind old men, roam these stricken groves of remembrance. The candour of the Korean War Memorial is unthinkable without The Wall and the experience of Asian defeat that stands behind it.

These two monuments to America's humiliation at the hands of aroused East Asia compel us to look back to the six months in 1941–42 when Japanese power almost effortlessly overran America's Pacific empire. The secret iconography of the Korean Memorial derives from the Bataan Death March, a tragic style that the bronze rhetoric of the Iwo Jima Memorial obscures. But the unmemorialised rout of 1941–42 foretold the military disasters of Korea and Vietnam in ways that reduce the Iwo Jima Memorial to a lie. Regardless of what I find, and regardless of what my fellow countrymen and women make of my research, America's truth, its past no less than its future, lives at The Wall.

At frontier's end

Two momentous changes in the national character, both with roots in the Pacific War, will confront all Americans during the next half-century. One is the ethnic-racial revolution that is rapidly eroding the country's White majority, and will replace it, perhaps around mid-century, with a post-White majority of mainly Latin and Asian descent. Not even the Civil War achieved a greater racial revolution because this new change will signal the demographic end of the White Republic as we have known it.

Where demographics lead, power will follow. This truth will stand as long as the United States remains a democracy. The hopeful view holds that the country will probably not face a sudden colonial-style handover. We have time (or think we do). This period of grace is vital because the business of producing what in Roman Catholicism is called 'a native clergy' is not proceeding anything like rapidly enough. It is not only that America will need an army of non-White, particularly Latin, business leaders, politicians, judges, bishops, scientists and bureaucrats almost overnight, but, because this new majority will be the country, in the way Whites are the country now, we will need the Latins and Asians to make the society work. Because it will be theirs.

From the ranks of our emerging non-White majority will be drawn, sometime soon, all of our presidents and most of our governors and Supreme Court judges, the bulk of the Cabinet, the majority of the Senate and House, as well as, *mutatis mutandis*, the presidents of Microsoft and Harvard, the cardinal archbishops of New York and the chairmen of the Federal Reserve Board. This revolution will demand the mobilisation of non-White talent on an unprecedented scale.

At every stage of this revolution, Max Weber's classic meditation on ethos or ethic, that is the value systems and institutional arrangements that foster or discourage effective action in the political, economic, social and scientific realms, should figure prominently. With the decay of the White Republic, the challenge of nurturing non-White agency, the post-White subject, what the Japanese call '*shutaisei*', that is individual and collective self-mastery, must be met if the society is to continue to work, and only if it works for the whole society will we outflank the final sorrows of empire.

The current debate over reverse discrimination, race-sensitive job hiring and admissions to higher education, the multicultural curriculum, and the issue of fairness to minorities generally is in danger of being overtaken by events because all of these approaches assume that the current racial status quo will last. Not only is the status quo not going to last; it is rapidly being swept away. None of these administrative strategies reflect the required sense of urgency. Furthermore, any acceleration of the implied transfer of power to a post-White authority will almost certainly force American policy-makers, at all levels of public administration, to do a quick study of the British experience of rapid colonial handovers. The partition of British India, for example, was a debacle largely because there was insufficient time to manage the process smoothly. Smooth transitions of power are one art form for which history has not prepared Americans.

I am confident that this national handover will be successful. But when peaceful, and thus successful, such political revolutions are subtle, achieved as often as not in the privacies of the home and the heart as in any form of exposed public dialogue. In the 1960 presidential election, the historic battle between John F. Kennedy and Richard M. Nixon, we confronted the prospect of a dramatic but less fraught handover of power, from the Protestant native stock to the Catholic scions of the Irish Diaspora. Here is Theodore H. White's sage assessment of the resistance Kennedy faced as the country's first successful Roman Catholic candidate for president:

> [Kennedy had] to stir the nation with a sense of anticipation strong enough to overcome the hidden and unspoken reluctance of millions of Americans to abandon their past – and not only the past of religion, but the pride of the Anglo-American peoples who had fought the Civil War, who had built America's industry, had cleared the plains, who found themselves still unable to recognise in the third or fourth generation of the immigrant hordes those leadership qualities that run in the tradition of Lincoln, Roosevelt, Adams, Hay, Wilson, Roosevelt, Stimson.[1]

Do most American Whites recognise leaders such as Colin Powell and Condoleezza Rice as the plausible heirs of Lincoln and Theodore Roosevelt, Kennedy and Reagan? Many White Americans do. Such generous recognition is indispensable to the first phase of this racial-ethnic transition. But African-Americans are, even more than White women (and, therefore, White feminism), a declining demographic force, not least because of the 'Tiger Woods effect', so such recognition will only buy us time to prepare for a more testing task: learning to recognise such leadership qualities in the Latin community.

Where are the Latin leaders? What will the declining Anglo majority make of them? What will the political heirs of Simón Bolívar (1783–1830) and Lázaro Cárdenas (1895–1970) feel about the Anglo traditions they will inherit when they sit in the Oval Office? These are the questions we must brood on now if we are to be ready in time.

Inevitably, the whole enterprise turns on the vulnerable psychology of the American experiment. Again, White, in *The Making of the President 1960*, elaborates the conundrum of American identity with elegance and force:

> Britons and Frenchmen, Russians and Germans, Arabs or Chinese, can pass through the uncadenced measure of time and history, swinging from greatness to nothingness and back again – yet still remain Britons, Frenchmen, Russians, Germans, Arabs and Chinese. But America is a nation created by all the hopeful wanderers of Europe, not out of geography and genetics, but out of purpose – by what men sought in fair

government and equal opportunity. If other nations falter in greatness, their people still remain what they are. But if America falters in greatness and purpose, then Americans are nothing but the off-scourings and hungry of other lands.[2]

Confronted with Kennedy's Irish Catholic gauntlet, America's White Protestant majority of 1960 retained the power to choose. It was they who Kennedy had to solicit, persuade and appease. By mid-century, the ability of Whites to veto political change, even if we all vote as a bloc, will be substantially reduced. Power will be draining into other hands. Our Latin and other non-Anglo successors may indeed embrace the full panoply of our institutions and values with the kind of conviction that will ensure that this handover of power and responsibility is seamless and civilised. But the choice of which values and institutions persist will be theirs, not ours. Our adventure may well be drawing to its inevitable close. The end of the frontier is upon us.

Notes

1 Theodore H. White, *The Making of the President 1960*, New York: Atheneum House, 1961, p. 401.
2 *Ibid.*, p. 422.

The book in brief

This book is organised like a set of Russian dolls, one set of problems snugly fitting inside the body of another, and that in turn contained inside a third. The innermost of my three problems was, on the face of it, the simplest: how to read a wartime text by a Japanese philosopher. Surely all that was involved was removing sixty years of dust from an age-spotted tome, making sure one had an excellent philosophy dictionary to hand, and then to begin turning the pages. But, almost at once, a second set of problems intruded.

Supposedly, illiberal thinkers who had taken the morally wrong position at the worst possible of times wrote all of these wartime texts. At least, this is what many of my colleagues in Japan studies insisted was the case. And, initially at least, I believed them. After all, I, like them, had been deeply influenced by the orthodox interpretation of the Second World War. This orthodoxy had been learned at my father's knee and he had fought in the Pacific War. If this were not enough, there were almost endless repeat broadcasts of such triumphs of Hollywood 'agitprop' as *Victory at Sea* and *Air Power* that I had greedily devoured as a child every Saturday afternoon sitting in front of the television. Finally, there were the almost irresistible verbal seductions of such magnificent defences of the Allied cause as Sir Winston Churchill's *The Second World War*, another childhood favourite.

Under the impact of this formidable set of 'true tales', a one-sided orthodoxy imbibed when I was most susceptible to other people's opinions, what chance would my simple task, the one I set for myself almost forty years later, of reading a wartime Japanese philosophic text with objectivity and understanding, have of succeeding? Almost none is the short answer.

But here my third doll, the outermost of the three, came to my rescue. This third set of problems drew its focus from the fact and ideology of American empire. The reaction of the administration of George W. Bush to the events of 11 September 2001 destroyed the last of my childhood illusions about the use and abuse of American power in the modern world. One insight seems irresistible. The road to '9/11' began with the Pacific War because the titanic clash of arms between Imperial Japan and Roosevelt's White Republic was decisive to the rise and consolidation of American empire. To reach this unsettling conclusion was to free oneself from the trammels of Second World War orthodoxy. Thus liberated, I allowed myself to peruse, for the first time with less blindness and prejudice, the political writings of the Kyoto School philosophers.

How I responded to the destruction of my childhood illusions is set out in the Prologue and Chapter 1. The impact of this blow on my under-standing of Pacific War orthodoxy is described in Chapter 2. As the weight of orthodox opinion eased, my ability to appreciate the intellectual horizon of Kyoto philosophy improved, and the first fruits of this new freedom are set forth in Chapter 3. Thus prepared, I began to probe the factual and interpretational foundations of the Western bias against the Kyoto School and found it wanting. Chapter 4 is an exercise in the deconstruction of orthodox opinion. In Chapter 5, I am finally able to begin the simple task of reading closely my heroes among the second generation of the Kyoto School, the ones who came to notorious prominence during the Pacific War.

Chapters 1 to 5 are the product of the bloody aftermath of the monstrous events of 9/11. In the next six chapters, 6–11, I turn to the past in order to lay siege to the Allied mythology of the Pacific War, indeed to Second World War orthodoxy as a whole. The result is a sometimes uncompromising settling of accounts with the philosophic wing of Japan studies, both the religious student of Zen and the moral victims of what I call the 'Allied Gaze'. I have offered no quarter and taken no prisoners.

In Chapter 12, I urge a paradigmatic revolution in Japan studies; one fuelled by the classic critical spirit of Europe, in order to allow us to rethink, in a radical way, the intellectual contours of our world. A post-nationalist vision of America's post-White destiny is elaborated with the aid of Kyoto philosophy. Finally, in translations of two essays by Hajime Tanabe, my favourite among all Japanese philosophers, I come home, at last, to my orig-inal task of reading the wartime work of the Kyoto School. There is no way of more closely reading a text than by translating it.

Acknowledgments

This book has taken shape slowly. A decade of occasional writings, both scholarly and journalistic, stands behind the arguments developed here (and in a companion volume now in preparation: *The Kyoto School's War with Tojo: A Translation, with Commentary, of 'The Standpoint of World History and Japan'*, translated by David Williams, with an introductory essay by Ryōsuke Ōhashi, London and New York: Routledge, forthcoming). My debts are many and varied. The problem that I address in these pages first presented itself to me when preparing opinion pieces for the *Los Angeles Times*, and I would like to thank Marvin Said, the late Art Seidenbaum and Jack Miles for what, in another context, I have called 'the privilege of writing about Japan for one of America's largest and most sophisticated readerships about Asian affairs'.

My years as an editorial writer for *The Japan Times* deepened my doubts about the orthodox interpretation of the Pacific War. During the First Gulf War (1990–91), I argued passionately for Japan to support the Allied cause. This turned out to be my final Churchill–Roosevelt moment, the last time I endorsed 'good war' idealism. Writing editorials for the Japanese media on the various 50th anniversaries of the key events of the Pacific War proved decisive. I am grateful to Yutaka Mataebara, chief editorial writer of Japan's leading English-language daily, for the opportunity to free myself from the blindness of what I now call the Allied Gaze.

The role of critic has not come easily to me. I have a weakness for orthodoxies, for living and thinking inside the pages of a classic text. But to sit alone in a small room writing every day focuses the mind in a unique way. Nevertheless, perspective may be lost as the force of one's ideas grows. The public lecture has been indispensable to this radicalising project. I have needed to see how my words have registered on the faces of my audience. Many have been shocked. I am therefore grateful to all those who allowed me to scandalise the *bien-pensants* among many distinguished audiences.

I owe a special word of thanks to Tae-Chang Kim of the Kyoto Forum, Institute for the Integrated Study of Future Generations, who encouraged me to be bold when I presented my first paper on the Kyoto School, 'Overcoming Whiteness: Tanabe Hajime as an Intellectual in the Public Sphere' in 1998.

Thanks are also due to Ken Ruoff (Oregon State) who invited me to test some of my revisionist ideas about the Kyoto School at a panel that he organised, and which Andy Gordon (Harvard) skilfully chaired, for the annual meeting of the Association of Asian Studies held in Chicago in 2000.

I would like to express gratitude to the organisers of the 2001 annual meeting of the Japan Politics Group (UK) where I gave an early version of the paper that became 'Revisionism: The End of White America in Japan Studies', and to the Royal Institute of International Affairs for inviting me to lecture on 'Global Diplomacy and Post-White America: The Implications of Demographic Revolution for Japanese and British Foreign Policy' at Chatham House in 2002.

Rikki Kersten (Leiden) gave me the chance to reassert the relevance of the classic European idea of subjectivity, as interpreted by the wartime Kyoto School, before a superb student audience in Holland in 2002. She and Axel Schneider then invited me back to Leiden in 2003 to deliver a short version of 'Racism and the black Legend of the Kyoto School' at a workshop in historical consciousness in modern China and Japan. This provoked many interventions, some of them critical but all of them extremely useful for my work, from Fred Wakeman (Berkeley), Susanne Weigelin-Schwiedrzik (Vienna), Kevin Doak (Georgetown) and Christian Ulm (Heidelberg).

Arthur Stockwin (Oxford) cajoled me into giving a talk that became 'A Manifesto on the Future of Japan Studies' at the 2002 annual meeting of the Japan Politics Group held at Oxford on the first anniversary of the destruction of the World Trade Center.

Early versions of 'Philosophy and the Pacific War' and 'Scholarship or Propaganda' appeared in the pages of *Japan Forum*, the official publication of the British Association of Japan Studies (BAJS). I would like to thank Mark Williams, the senior editor, Sue Townsend and Caroline Rose, editors, as well as Chris Jones, reviews editor, for their cooperation and support. I am also very grateful for prompt action by Glenn Hook, president of BAJS, to secure copyright permission for the *Japan Forum* version of 'Philosophy and the Pacific War' to appear in Japanese in *Kyōtō-gakuha no Shisō* (Kyoto: Jinbun Shoin), edited by Ryōsuke Ōhashi.

Since high school, I have been a great admirer of the German intellectual tradition, feelings that have been deepened by regular meetings with Helmut Wagner of the Free University Berlin. He was there almost from the very beginning of my career as a scholar. This 'good European' exemplifies all the best features of the post-war German mind. It was Wagner who arranged for me to meet Ernest Nolte, the controversial historian. We have talked only once, when I interviewed him for *The Japan Times*, but it was one of the most stimulating encounters of my entire life as a writer and thinker. He, as much as anyone, taught me to reject all and every form of *Denkverbot*. He encouraged me to become my own kind of revisionist, and I salute him.

Among Japanese scholars, Ryōsuke Ōhashi has influenced my work more than any Japanese thinker since the death of Hisao Ōtsuka, my teacher. At every turn of my encounter with the Kyoto School, Ōhashi's influence has been decisive. Among Kyoto School experts, email discussions with Agustin Jacinto Zavala (Mexico) were very helpful when my book took a decisive textual turn. As for Graham Parkes (Hawaii), his pioneering research about the Kyoto School and decisive criticism of the Western reception of Kyoto thought have left a profound mark on my labours. His advice and counsel have been invaluable. In navigating the stormy seas of revisionist controversy, it has been very encouraging to know that Ben-Ami Shillony (Hebrew University) has been making a similar voyage.

In America, there is Chalmers Johnson. As in my earlier books on Japan, here I find myself once again sailing in the wake of Johnson, the *enfant terrible* emeritus of modern Japan studies. In *Blowback*, Johnson announced his *tenkō*, or ideological apostasy, from Pacific War and Cold War orthodoxy. Andy Gordon has observed that if most Japanese *tenkō* tend to be from left to right, Johnson has moved from right to left. I have followed a similar trajectory, and as a result, both of us now find ourselves, quite unexpectedly, within shouting distance of that moral-political realm that Noam Chomsky has made his own. As an American *tenkō-ka* who has begun his own unanticipated ideological journey from right to left, I am in very good company.

As for Rikki Kersten, there is no pleasure greater for a teacher than to be taught so much by one of his students. This book is my attempt to respond to the challenge she posed when she declared that 'Today Japan studies must begin all over again'.

This is my third monograph for RoutledgeCurzon, and Peter Sowden has been once again looking after me. When I delivered the most controversial lecture of my career so far – my Chatham House talk on the foreign policy implications of America's racial demographic revolution – Peter not only insisted on being there, he also gathered me up after the rather testy Q & A session and took to me to tea at The Ritz. Working with him has always been a pleasure. As an author, I have benefited, once again, from an excellent production team at RoutledgeCurzon, and special thanks are due to Dorothea Schaefter for her help with the cover design, and to Mark Ralph who did a superb job as copy-editor.

This book is at many points an exercise in the close reading of difficult political and philosophical texts. Burning the midnight oil while grappling with texts by Tanabe and Nishitani inevitably led to late nights discussing the finer points of Heideggerian philosophy with translators such as John Svitek in Freiburg. But before any reading or discussion, one must find the texts at issue. Locating, copying and comparing editions of the relevant

Japanese texts has been an arduous business. Professor Kenneth Jones of Teikyō University, a fellow Californian and fellow graduate of International Christian University, has made an invaluable contribution to this effort. He has played Engels to my Marx, and I shall always be grateful.

Finally, this book is dedicated to Robin Reilly, to whom I owe more than I can say.

D.W.
July 2003
Somerset and Cardiff

The doomed fleets sail
The Pacific War for beginners

In the spring of 1940, President Roosevelt ordered the Pacific Fleet based in West Coast ports to sail for Hawaii. In projecting American power across the Pacific to curb Japanese expansion, if possible by pressure alone, or to solicit a Japanese attack, if that expansion could not be curbed, Roosevelt set a momentous change in American society in motion. Prime Minister Churchill's decision to stand firm with the United States in the Pacific no less than Premier Tojo's determination to challenge Anglo-American hegemony also placed their societies at risk. All the great fleets that sailed at the beginning of the 1940s were dispatched by nations doomed to change as the result of these naval decisions. What kind of conflict were they embarking on?

The three phases of the Pacific War

The Pacific War (1941–45), or, if you will, the Pacific Theatre of the Second World War (1939–45), unfolded in three phases. The first phase began with the Japanese attack on the ground and naval forces of the United States and the British Empire. The Japanese air assault on Pearl Harbour, in the Hawaiian Islands, on 7 December 1941 (8 December in Japan), inflicted the greatest defeat ever on the United States Navy. The capture in February 1942 of Singapore, the strategic British naval base in Southeast Asia, was one of the blackest days in British military history.

Between December 1941 and the Battle of Midway (June 1942), Japan swept all before it, overrunning some of the principal colonial possessions of Britain (Hong Kong, Malaya and Burma), the United States (the Philippines) and Holland (the Dutch East Indies, or Indonesia). Throughout this phase, and indeed the entire Pacific War, Japan was still at war with China, and it was there that the bulk of its troops were committed. Japanese brutality was unrestrained.

By the time of Midway, Japan had occupied the bulk of Southeast Asia and dominated the Western Pacific. During the second phase, roughly from the summer of 1942 until the summer of 1944, the Allies blunted and then threw back this Japanese advance. The main battlefronts were in the Southern Pacific, New Guinea and Burma. Nearly half a million Australian troops were committed to the defence of New Guinea. The Allied navies, mainly American, had previously fought the Japanese to a standstill in the Coral Sea, opening the way for the Allied capture of the Gilbert and Marshall Islands. The British consolidated their position in Burma in anticipation of later gains.

The decisive and third phase began with the capture of the island of Saipan in July 1944 because from this island the air war against Japan's cities was launched. The principal ground battles were Burma, the Philippines and the outlying home islands of Japan (the struggle continued in China, and the Soviet Union invaded Manchuria at the end of the war). The firebombing of Tokyo in March 1945 killed 80,000 civilians, and left some 10 million injured, homeless or displaced. Atomic bombs killed 100,000 civilians at Hiroshima and another 35,000 at Nagasaki in August 1945. The hostilities ended on 15 August. Japan officially surrendered unconditionally on 2 September 1945.

Pacific War controversies

The Pacific War powerfully shaped the international order we still live under. Historians have now quarrelled for over half a century about its causes and consequences. The main controversies focus on the first and third phases of the struggle. Could President Roosevelt have anticipated the attack on Pearl Harbour, or did he in fact seek to trick the Japanese into starting a war they could not win? Was the atomic destruction of Hiroshima and Nagasaki necessary? How many people, to reach back to the Sino-Japanese roots of the conflict, perished during the 1937 Japanese Rape of Nanjing? Was it 50,000 or 300,000?

Today, fresh questions need to be addressed. Did the Japanese commit the only war crimes? Did the Pacific War open the way for the demographic decay of the United States as a White Republic? Can events such as the destruction of the World Trade Center be traced back to the consolidation of American empire in the wake of the Pacific War? How can historians from all the nations involved in the conflict achieve an understanding of the facts of the Pacific War that will satisfy all but the most dogmatic and unforgiving members of their societies?

The controversy that erupted in 1995 over plans for a modestly revisionist exhibition – originally called 'Crossroads: The End of World War II, the Atomic Bomb, and Origins of the Cold War' – to accompany the display of part of the B-29 *Enola Gay* at the Smithsonian Institute in Washington DC illustrates the moral and factual difficulties at issue.[1]

The materials and commentary of the *Enola Gay* exhibition were largely conventional in character, but the issue of whether the bombing was necessary was raised and evidence of the scale and horror of the atomic bombings was to be exhibited. In angry reaction, veterans groups mobilised their political allies on Capitol Hill, and forced the organisers of the exhibition to remove the controversial evidence of the destructive effects of the bombing. Unsettling remarks, such as those by wartime American leaders, that called into doubt the necessity of the dropping of the atomic bombs, were also excluded. At the Smithsonian, this great public forum of the republic, no debate of the facts of the war, however responsibly researched, was to be tolerated. Patriotism was judged more important than the truth. With this conclusion, no responsible historian can be content.

What assumptions stoked the Smithsonian controversy? A simple schema may provide the answer:

Our high ideals vs. Their base conduct

Our base conduct vs. Their high ideals

During the past half-century, the orthodox interpretation of the Pacific War in the former Allied powers has concentrated, not exclusively but essentially, on the first pairing. We have consistently contrasted our high democratic ideals with the barbaric conduct of our Japanese opponents. Today, this self-serving interpretation is becoming increasingly untenable under the pressure of careful revisionist research. Take, for example, the moral and legal implications of the slaughter of more than 600,000 Japanese civilians, to say nothing of the millions of casualties suffered, in 'the Japanese Holocaust' inflicted from the sky by American air power. The mass murder of civilians may be justified in numerous ways – military necessity, national revenge and corrective punishment – but none of them is ethical. Just wars must be fought justly because ends do not justify means. In short, a liberal may not endorse the Japanese Holocaust and remain a liberal.

Nevertheless, not even the moral indictments arising from the Japanese Holocaust have forced the liberal revisionist to abandon an understanding of the Pacific War grounded in the contrast between our high ideals and base Japanese conduct. Rather, he insists that our contrasting pair (our base conduct vs. Japanese high ideals) be also examined without prejudice and with proper attention to the facts of the case. The careful examination of *both* sides to the conflict is assumed when the orthodox position is criticised in this book.

Note

1 For a thorough and dispiriting analysis, with many important documents, see Kai Bird and Lawrence Lifschultz (eds), *Hiroshima's Shadows: Writings on the Denial of History and the Smithsonian Controversy*, Stony Creek, CT: The Pamphleteer's Press, 1998.

Japanese usage and style

Throughout this book, I have followed the style employed at *The Japan Times*, in which Western and Japanese names are given in English order, that is personal name followed by family name. This departs from the conventions of Japan studies, and my reasons for doing so are as follows. First, attempting to reproduce the Japanese convention of family name first, personal second, works against the natural order of English, thus producing horrors such as 'Mishima Yukio's novels', where Yukio is the Japanese novelist's personal name. Secondly, confronted with 'Ōtsuka Hisao', Western readers without Japanese often conclude, quite understandably, that this distinguished economic historian's family name is Hisao. Thirdly, and even more disconcerting, one discovers that undergraduate students of the Japanese language often make the same mistake well into their courses. Finally, the attempt to reproduce Japanese usage in English is largely to blame for the typographical nightmare that is the English side of the Japanese business card where one confronts a chaos of font sizes and faces. All this trouble could be eliminated if we would follow the style of *The Japan Times*. I propose that we return to it.

Macrons have been reluctantly employed for all Japanese words except for 'Tokyo', 'Kyoto' and 'Tojo' (the last looked distinctly odd with macrons).

The line and the circle

The ancient Greeks taught us to think in straight lines, to pursue our logical quarry directly. The Japanese take a different approach; they circle. The Japanese mind tends to work in spirals, slowly tightening the pressure of fact, of reason, of insight, until, like a break in the bolt of cloth that is closed by threads pulled from every direction or angle, the job is done: in the words of Graham Parkes, 'Each return is at a different level, and so is not a simple repetition'.[1] The Kyoto School thinkers were, in this specific sense, very Japanese. To sit with these Japanese texts has been to fall, unconsciously, into these rhythms. Although written in English, this text circles and spirals. The reader may find the path uneven, as in a classical Japanese garden, where a stepping stone may have been placed to force one to slip and thus catch an unexpected vantage.

Note

1 Graham Parkes, personal communication.

Rise and fall

1   Roman questions

American empire and
the Kyoto School

All great things perish by their own agency, by an act of self-cancellation.

Nietzsche

At the beginning of the third millennium of the Christian era, the United States of America reached the summit of its powers. Friend and foe alike concede that the American people have now achieved, for good or evil, unchallengeable ascendancy over the rest of the world in war, commerce, science, technology and many branches of culture. The global hegemony of the American Republic makes it the natural heir to the prestige of the Roman Imperium and the British Empire. That all this has been achieved in just two and a quarter centuries of independent national existence makes this American enterprise one of the epic tales of human history.

The Roman and British precedents to American hegemony offer a warning. The epic tale is a story not only of the rise but also of the fall. Our understanding of the American experience of empire will be naïve and incomplete if we choose to dwell exclusively on the birth, expansion and consolidation of the power of the United States. The greatness of America's beginnings gives no assurance as to its end. Decay comes to all – even Americans.

If the United States now embodies the majesty and imperiousness of global domination, any meditation on the new republican face of empire must confront certain classical anxieties. Thus, as the world marvels at the confident noon point in the trajectory of American will, the dangers of hubris come to mind. At the summit of Roman power and the peak of its virtues, the imperial legions of Varus were slaughtered in the dark woods of Teutoburg. In the middle of the nineteenth century when the splendour of British civilisation reached its apogee, the Sepoy Mutiny almost shattered the nascent Raj.

Can the final destiny of America's blood-dimmed crusade for global mastery be prophesied from the lessons of an ancient imperium and an Asiatic satrapy? Can supreme power ever be total power, let alone ever-lasting power? Such Roman questions stand behind this exploration of a provocative set of twentieth-century Japanese philosophic ideas concerning world history, and what these ideas tell us about the century-old struggle of the United States to add the whole of Asia to its sphere of domination. Among all non-White thinkers who have dwelled on the nature and consequences of the planetary hegemony of the White West, Japanese philosophers have a unique place.[1] They even proposed a cure for Western hegemony. Their insights are as unforgiving as they are indispensable at this decisive hour in the destiny of the American Republic.

Hubris and the domination of Asia

Was the destruction of the World Trade Center our Teutoburg? The ambush of Varus and the annihilation of his three legions shocked and humbled Rome. This military catastrophe did not compel the Romans to abandon their imperial ambitions, but it did teach them a brutal lesson in caution. A certain wariness about German tribesmen and the Rhine frontier resulted. Over the next two centuries, Rome reached out to encompass what Gibbon eloquently called 'the fairest part of the earth, and the most civilised portion of mankind', but a savage warning about the dangers lurking beyond the reach of Roman power had been administered. It would haunt the Roman mind until AD 476 when, with the sack of Rome, the enemies of empire washed their blades in the Tiber itself.

Outraged and humiliated by the events of 11 September 2001, the imperialists in the administration of Bush *fils* have rejected the counsels of prudence. Our immediate response to this monstrous but effective terrorist assault on the heart of the American imperium has been to plunge into two fresh wars against Asia and threaten even more. Realistic answers to the question 'Why was the United States attacked?' have been avoided. Initiatives to reduce the impression of American interference in the Middle East, to discourage al-Qaeda recruitment by addressing the Israeli-Palestinian deadlock or to reduce our dependence on the oil that waters the Islamic holy places have been either delayed or implemented in such a way as to avoid facing the central issue: the intrusive impact of American power on the non-White world.

If President Bush *père* the diplomat built a grand coalition of nations in 1990–91 to fight the First Gulf War, Bush *fils* the warrior has sought to subdue a wide compass of Asian foes, beginning with 'the Axis of evil' composed by Iraq, Iran and North Korea. Extremists with the ear of the president seek to impose 'regime change' even on Saudi Arabia, Syria and the Palestinian people. Pakistan has apparently been threatened with dismemberment if it does not do the administration's counter-terrorist bidding. When it is recalled that Bush *fils* entered the White House set on humbling not militant Islam but a resurgent China, one realises how crucial the reduction of Asia is to the administration's determination to establish an ascendancy over the entire globe that will outlast, because it will remain militarily irresistible, even the imperial legacy of Rome.

Such vaulting ambition tempts one to dispense with the prudent calculation of power and its limits. In the wake of the Sepoy Mutiny of 1857–58, Britain radically rethought its approach to the administration of India. But the American imperialist regards al-Qaeda as an Islamic rabble. The almost effortless overthrow of the Taleban regime in Afghanistan and the relentless pursuit of the al-Qaeda terrorist across the desolate wastes of the Northwest Frontier and along fringes of the Saudi peninsula conjure images in the mind of the American imperialist not of the forest of Teutoburg but of the barren hills to which the Sioux retreated after their Pyrrhic victory over George Custer at the Little Bighorn in 1876. The main difference is that Sitting Bull knew that the American response to his slaughter of Custer's cavalry would seal the fate of the Sioux as an independent nation, while Osama bin Laden's supporters fight on with divine conviction to win a place in their paradise.

The ease of the initial American triumphs in Afghanistan and Iraq may deceive, as the difficulties in winning the peace in both countries show. Furthermore, the war that weighs most heavily on the deliberations of the president, his military planners and foreign advisers (as the interviews gathered in Bob Woodward's *Bush at War* make clear)[2] is not some glorious military feat from the recent past but the debacle of Vietnam. Memories of that jungle quagmire explain not only the Pentagon's caution over the prospect of fresh Asian adventures but also the determination of the ultra-nationalists in the administration to wage as many foreign conflicts as it takes to bleach away the humiliation of the fall of Saigon in 1975. In this sense, the war on terror is a war on Vietnam-induced caution; prudence may be its principal casualty.

So granted, terrorism is central to this American struggle to dominate the Middle East. So is oil. But the psychology is driven by something very different: an almost irresistible compulsion to re-experience the 'American high' of 1945. This can only be achieved by recapturing the unspoiled pre-Vietnam innocence of the American psyche that revelled in the prospect of an unchallengeable hegemony over a prostrate planet. That was the sweetest fruit of our crushing victory over Imperial Japan and Nazi Germany. This is the paradise we would now regain.

AMERICAN EMPIRE AND THE BALANCE OF POWER

> And the end of the fight is a tombstone white,
> with the name of the late deceased, and the epitaph drear:
> 'A fool lies here who tried to hustle the East'.
>
> *The Naulahka*, 1892

Rudyard Kipling has not figured prominently enough in the bedtime reading of American presidents. Coming after the Spanish–American War (1898), the Philippine Insurrection (1899–1901), the Pacific War (1941–45), the Korean Conflict (1950–53), the struggle in Indochina, that is Vietnam, Laos and Cambodia (1965–75), and the First Gulf War (1990–91), the US invasion of Afghanistan and the Second Gulf War (2003) may be counted as the seventh and eighth wars we have had to wage to establish and confirm our ascendancy over Asia. No province of American global influence has taken longer to secure. If commercial penetration defined our strategy towards the fabled wealth of the world's largest and most populous continent during the nineteenth century, our hegemony today over the Orient – from Turkey to Japan, Uzbekistan to the Indian Ocean – is the unambiguous product of the sword.

Only the wilfully blind can now ignore the fact and substance of US power. Thus, it is not only American perceptions of their place in the world that have altered since the autumn of 2001, but also the world's perception of America. Furthermore, it is not the attacks on New York and Washington in September 2001 that have transformed the world's view of the United States; it is how America has reacted to this terrorist provocation. Our national posture – how we talk about ourselves and the rest the world, the new way we throw our weight around, our very gait – has undergone a metamorphosis. Hitherto, the fact of American hegemony has been, more or less, artfully concealed, and thus softened. But now the mask has slipped. The reality of America's unilateral domination over the globe has suddenly and momentously been revealed for all to see. The larger portion of mankind has been forced to awaken to the fact that the entire planet now lives by virtue of military compulsion, real or potential, under the eagle's wing.

The naked fact of American hegemony confronts national elites outside the United States with the most unsettling geopolitical revelation of our time, but one that Americans find difficult to appreciate because we wish to avert our gaze from the fact and price of our empire (the slaughter on Lower Manhattan was part of that price). Bathing in the rhetoric of republican nobility is so much more comforting. But our unshakable assumption that Americans are a good and decent people conspires against understanding the unease the rest of globe may feel when confronted with the blatant reality of America's 'full spectrum domination' of the military sphere.

The former 'free world' is being reduced to an object of imperial American administration and manipulation. The full weight of this bitter truth was captured by Matthew Parris, the British conservative commentator and former Tory MP, when he wrote in *The Times*, the most thoughtfully pro-American of all British newspapers,

> I am not afraid that this war [the Second Gulf War] will fail. I am afraid that it will succeed. I am afraid that it will prove to be the first of an indefinite series of American interventions. I am afraid that it is the beginning of a new empire; an empire that I am afraid Britain may have little choice but to join.'[3]

Has Britain laboured for much of the past century to cultivate a special relationship with the United States only to be reduced to the status of an American protectorate?

Rebalancing the imbalance

One of the central ideas of our Constitution – the doctrine of checks and balances – may serve to highlight the sources of the anxiety the world feels when confronted with the realities of American military supremacy. Since the earliest days of our republic, it has been the ruling conviction of national political life that uncontained power is unacceptable, no matter how wisely or generously the holders of that power may exercise it. This doctrine was a response to the centralised nature of the British state and a well-cultivated dread of Catholic monarchical absolutism.

Power itself is suspect. That is why all branches of American government – federal, state and local – are constrained by an elaborate system of checks and balances. The subplot of almost every episode of the television drama *West Wing*, for example, turns on the constraints of this system. But note that the new American assertion of global hegemony promulgated most recently by the administration of George W. Bush not only celebrates the fact of American power but also insists that no future challenge to this hegemony will be permitted. America's leaders are thus claiming absolute power in the global sphere and defending this unilateral domination by arguing that the world should accept this imbalance because the United States will use its power wisely and benignly. In other words, Americans seek to impose on the world a doctrine of power that they would never accept at home.

The distinction between 'home' and 'abroad' is crucial. In the century-old American discourse on empire that began with the Spanish–American War (1898), the challenge of imperialism has almost always been perceived as a threat not to the world but to American domestic liberty. In the first presidential election after McKinley had stripped Spain of the bulk of her colonial possessions (Cuba, the Philippines and Puerto Rico), the Democratic Party raised the cry 'Republic or Empire?' Sixty years later, a former general and Republican president, Dwight D. Eisenhower, warned of the dangers of the military-industrial complex to the vitality of US democracy. Since the Pacific War, influential American intellectuals, from Charles Beard, the historian and author of *Roosevelt and the Coming of Pearl Harbor* (1948), to Gore Vidal, the writer and neo-isolationist polemicist, have produced forceful jeremiads against expansion abroad. It is the rare critic – Noam Chomsky, Edward Said and Chalmers Johnson are excellent examples – who has stressed the potential for our overseas domain to strike back at the American homeland. On 11 September, it did.

Churchill's dilemma

For Americans, therefore, the question is whether democracy within can be squared with imperialism without. For the rest of the world, the problem is different. American hegemony violates the central doctrine of modern diplomacy: the balance of power. A hegemonic power that towers above all its potential military opponents poses a threat to the liberty of the rest of the world. *The imbalance is of itself unacceptable.*

The emergence of the United States as world history's first 'hyper power' (Hubert Védrine) resurrects what might be called 'Churchill's dilemma'. After the fall of France in 1940, Hitler offered Britain an armistice. He regarded Britons as Aryans and he exhibited a profound admiration for the British Empire. The German dictator ordered his forces to halt their irresistible advance at Dunkirk to avoid humiliating the British. It was Hitler who created the opportunity for the 'miracle of Dunkirk'. Despite all this, Churchill refused to conclude an armistice with Germany because Hitler's victory over France had unacceptably transformed the balance of power in Western Europe. German hegemony itself, whatever the character of the Nazi regime, was unacceptable. But should Britain risk its independence by continuing to resist superior German might? This was Churchill's dilemma.

Because of the *Shoah* (the fitting Hebrew term for the Jewish Holocaust) and the other crimes of the Third Reich, one tends to neglect Churchill's power calculation. An over-powerful Germany compelled Britain to accept alliances with any anti-Nazi regime, however repellent, even Stalin's Russia. As Churchill told his private secretary, John Colville: 'If Hitler invaded Hell, I would at least make a favourable reference to the Devil.'[4] The collapse of the Soviet Union and the surge in US expenditure on defence since the fall of the Berlin Wall mean that the balance of power between America and the rest of the world has decisively altered in a way that no thinking person, American or otherwise, should accept.

To repeat: the imbalance itself is wrong. No American democrat would agree to such a condition within the US system of government; no responsible citizen of the world should surrender to this condition on a planetary scale. Furthermore, if the United States will not unilaterally disarm to restore the relative balance between itself and the rest of the planet, Churchill's dilemma may return with a vengeance. One day soon Western Europe, Russia, Japan, China and the rest of the globe may have to consider how they might be able to contain the American juggernaut.

The hitherto unthinkable may have to be thought. An audit of non-American military and economic assets may have to be undertaken. This will require casting a hard eye over the state of Europe's conventional military forces, Russia's nuclear arsenal, Japan's financial leverage over the US Treasury, and the capabilities of China's ground and air forces. America's dependence on Middle Eastern oil will be a factor in this sober calculation to determine how the rest of the world might be able to compel America, peacefully, to ease the fetters of its global domination.

The implied alliance of Europeans, Russians, Japanese, Chinese and the rest would be as unholy as it is necessary. But the hope must be that the shock of such a diplomatic initiative might encourage the United States to slash its nuclear arsenal and substantially reduce its military spending. Failing this, the fundamental global imbalance of power may have to be addressed in still other ways. The odd rogue state here or there is irrelevant to this larger question. So is Islamic terrorism.

The overwhelming power of the United States means that the world may be threatened by any group of ambitious ultra-nationalists who can seize and hold the levers of power in Washington. Anatol Lieven of the Carnegie Institute has argued that extremists in the Bush White House, the so-called neo-conservatives, or 'neo-cons', form such a junta, one whose aggressive plans have provoked striking forms of resistance from the rest of the world, be it in the United Nations Security Council or the streets of London or the suburbs of Baghdad, thus suggesting that the military policies of George W. Bush may represent something much more radical than a mere break with the multilateralist stance of the Clinton era.[5] According to Lieven, the reactionaries in the Bush administration seek to roll back recent liberal gains in order to return to the conservative social order of the 1950s. To restore the White, Protestant, suburban ascendancy of the immediate post-war period demands that drug-fuelled populist decadence be curbed, the more grating forms of feminism be tamed, the offensive excesses of gay liberation be routed, and, most importantly, the political impact of the racial-ethnic demographic revolution now engulfing urban life – the so-called 'Hispanic flood', or 'Browning' of America – be deflected, even if that means sustaining some form of White minority government after states lose their White majorities.

The neo-con crusade to reshape politics, at home and abroad, is nothing if not bold. Liberal opposition to the neo-con agenda is to be outflanked by a crusade of nationalist assertion abroad to enthral the working classes. An ambitious programme of regime change should be pursued in the Middle East to smash the nests of Islamic terrorism while securing US oil supplies and consolidating Israeli regional hegemony. Modelled on the post-war occupation of Japan, regime change might be pursued across the Middle East to encourage pro-American governments, or at least nominally democratic protectorates, again on the Japanese model. An alliance between Washington and the Israeli Likud Party forms the geopolitical heart of this strategy. Detaching Jewish voters from the Democratic Party is another goal. Finding a right-wing home for the Jewish-American intelligentsia would be another.

Consolidating American hegemony defines neo-con ambitions in the wider international community. The US threat to impose regime change anywhere Washington sees fit applies to any government that voices serious opposition to American hegemony. To invade Afghanistan, defeat Iraq, humiliate the Palestinians or threaten Saudi Arabia is to warn India and

Brazil, Russia and China that a similar fate awaits them should they attempt to resist American domination of their regions. Japan and the European Union are expected also to draw the correct conclusions.

This is the double-edged threat contained in the Bush doctrine of pre-emptive strikes against the enemies of freedom. Here is to be found what future historians may conclude to be the most important geopolitical consequence of al-Qaeda's air assault on Manhattan: the jolting discovery that American power is all but irresistible, and that this global suzerainty can be legally and practically constrained, so most Americans insist, only by the American voter. Apparently, the people of the United States, a tiny fraction of the world's population, reserve the right, in the neo-con vision, to take the entire planet hostage whenever its suits American will. Hence the philosopher's proposition: all imperial destinies end in self-cancellation; that all great things – and surely the United States is one of Nietzsche's great things – perish by their own agency.

ENTER JAPAN

Near the end of his long controversial life, Jun Etō, the right-wing Japanese intellectual, was asked to write the prestigious cover article for the New Year issue of *Bungeishinjū* (January 1998), one of the most influential of Japan's mass-circulation magazines of general opinion (*sōgō zasshi*). In his essay, 'Japan's Second Defeat' ('Dai ni haiboku'), he directed his nationalist ire at the accord that Tokyo had recently signed with Washington to enhance military cooperation between the two nations. Etō dismissed the agreement as one-sided, leaving Japan in a state of unacceptable military dependence on its old wartime adversary. Defeated and occupied in 1945, Japan was once again yielding, this time of her own volition, to the excessive and self-serving demands of the world's self-proclaimed policeman and *de facto* hegemonic power.

What Etō would have made of the events of 11 September 2001 will never be known. He died before the attack on Manhattan. But the revolution in world perceptions of American power provoked by our response to the al-Qaeda onslaught has transformed his bitter critique of American hegemony into something just short of global common sense. Whatever his intentions – Etō's perceptions were often as subtle as they were unnerving – his rubric of 'defeat' brings the argument over the use and abuse of American power into disturbing focus. Regardless of what other framework of historical understanding we may exploit to understand either the assault on Pearl Harbour in 1941 or al-Qaeda terrorism today, both incidents may be seen as violent forms of resistance to American imperial hegemony. Whatever the theoretical origins of the new Bush doctrine of pre-emptive strikes, to the degree that this military strategy arises from the American *experience* of history, this new strategic logic can be traced back to Japan's surprise attack on Hawaii. In short, the Bush administration has finally embraced, out of imperial necessity, the tactics and ethics of America's Imperial Japanese opponent of 60 years ago. Tojo would be proud.

Etō's conundrum

During the past century, the United States has repeatedly defeated its Asian opponents. The first year of the Pacific War, the murderous stalemate in Korea and our humiliation in Vietnam have been the exceptions. But the almost unbroken record of US military superiority over Asia encourages one to probe the causes of the collapse of Asian resistance more closely. This is because Asian weakness is the outward sign of an inward failure.

Asian failure has global implications. If non-Americans are to run the world in America's place, they must be able to run it. And this requires, among other things, that they free their minds of the reactionary values and flawed ideas that might keep them from running it. It is here that Etō and his ideological allies have consistently faltered because, like so many Asian, African and Latin American intellectuals, these Japanese critics of US hegemony have refused to probe, in the name of national self-regard, the root causes of the comprehensive failure of the non-Western world (Japan is the unique exception) finally to overcome the West by surpassing the achievements of Western modernity. The classic choice between Western-style modernisation and the defence of national identity defines Etō's conundrum. A conclusive solution still eludes the non-White world.

Enter the Japanese philosopher. The metaphysical cure for non-Western defeat resides in the idea of subjectivity (*shutaisei*), that is rational self-mastery, a complex set of values, practices and institutions without which the planet cannot be properly managed or, in the language of the Kyoto School of philosophy, history cannot be made. In short, if one is going to criticise American hegemony, one must propose a remedy, and the only effective remedy is the achievement by non-Americans of mature subjectivity. How this formidable challenge might be met forms the overarching concern of the wartime Kyoto School: the need for subjectivity, the challenge of acquiring it, and the constant demonstrations to oneself and to others that one truly possesses *shutaisei*. The frustrations and rewards of trying to master oneself, as an individual and as a nation, dominate the pages of every Japanese philosophic text that will be examined in this book.

While it is true that an irrational, self-serving and myth-ridden form of Manichean nationalism may inspire the global hegemony of the United States, American domination is grounded in rational self-mastery, that is in subjectivity. Thomas Jefferson's 'empire of liberty' is unthinkable without *shutaisei*. Even today, American subjectivity is far from perfect (modernity is a constantly moving target), but it is relatively superior to that of any other nation. On this topic, Ernst Jünger, the conservative German revolutionary, was uniquely penetrating. Reflecting on the causes of Germany's defeat in the First World War in his famous 1930 essay 'Total Mobilisation', Jünger

first touches on the sources of French military morale in the First World
War and then turns to the foundations of American power:

> Likewise, in the United States with its democratic constitution, mobi-
> lization could be executed with a rigor that was impossible in Prussia,
> where the right to vote was based on class. And who can doubt that
> America, the country lacking 'dilapidated castles, basalt columns, and
> tales of knights, ghosts and brigands,' emerged the obvious victor of
> this war? *Its course was already decided not by the degree to which a state
> was a 'military state,' but by the degree to which it was capable of total
> mobilization.*
>
> Germany, however, was destined to lose the war, even if it had won
> the battle of the Marne and submarine warfare. For despite all the care
> with which it undertook partial mobilization, large areas of its strength
> escaped total mobilization, for the same reason, corresponding to the
> inner nature of its armament, it was certainly capable of obtaining,
> sustaining, and above all exploiting partial success – but never a total
> success.[6]

Jünger's assertion may be applied with equal force to the inability of
Hitler and Tojo to achieve total mobilisation. During the Second World
War, it was Britain, the Soviet Union and, pre-eminently, the United States
that successfully waged total war because of the relative superiority of their
ability and willingness to mobilise totally in ways unmatched by any of the
Axis powers. The expression 'total mobilisation' is of German origin
precisely because Imperial Germany desperately needed policies to help it
marshal national energies and material more effectively against opponents
who had proved able to mobilise more completely. If Jünger's analysis is
sound, it would appear that the totalitarian society may be incapable of
waging total war precisely because it is totalitarian, or, to reverse the proposition, it is totalitarian precisely because it lacks the potential for total
mobilisation implied in the very idea of subjectivity. The Soviet Union
under Stalin is the exception that proves the rule; the ultimate fate of Lenin's
state permits no other conclusion.

Jünger offers us one of the most pregnant observations to emerge from
Europe's century of total war. This insight, and the logic behind it, decisively
influenced, as we shall see, the Kyoto School's assessment of Japan's war
aims as elaborated in *The Standpoint of World History and Japan*, one of the
most important neglected texts in modern world philosophy (see Chapters 4
and 5).[7] The Kyoto School's response to Jünger offers a fundamental challenge to the reigning orthodox interpretation of the Second World War.

Jünger's argument is best read alongside the sociology of Max Weber, the
founder of modern social science. In *The Spirit of Capitalism and the
Protestant Ethic* and his controversial studies of the strengths and weaknesses of commercial and scientific cultures of Asia, Weber sought to

explain the decisive importance of rationality and subjectivity in the rise of Europe and the relative failure of the non-Western world to match Western success in the political-economic-social sphere. To read Weber in the light of the 'Jünger–Kyoto School' understanding of the military superiority of British, French and American capitalism (West-of-the-Rhine capitalism) is to exploit Etō's idea of defeat in a powerful and compelling way because it appears to explain not only why the Third World's struggle with modernisation has been so fitful but also why Germany was defeated in two world wars and why Japan was vanquished in the Pacific War.

To link war and subjectivity is to stand on the shoulders of the great thinkers such as Weber. This offers a bold new understanding of the role of America and Japan in world history. Rational self-mastery on a national scale contributed decisively not only to Japan's post-war miracle and the recent economic rise of East and Southeast Asia but also to America's global hegemony. Viewing the trajectory of American empire from the world-historical standpoint of Japanese philosophy may provide conclusive answers to our Roman questions.

2 Revisionism

The end of White America
in Japan studies

The voice of the intellect is a soft one, but it does not rest till it has gained a hearing.

Sigmund Freud[1]

A spectre is stalking Japan studies – the spectre of Pacific War revisionism. As memories of the savage conflict inaugurated by the Japanese attack on Pearl Harbour recede, the factual and ethical foundations of the Allied interpretation of the war in the Pacific, our 'good war', are crumbling on three fronts. First, the Hollywood propaganda film version of the Pacific War (the version that most Americans believe) is being quietly undermined by academic historians who are discovering new continents of fact that undermine the orthodox position. These discoveries make it clear that if historians are to understand the Pacific War 'as it really was' (Leopold von Ranke), the orthodox Allied interpretation of the war must be radically rethought. Wartime propaganda was a form of rhetoric. Its goal was to rally us to the colours, to persuade men and women to die for our cause, not to explain the facts or to weigh evidence objectively. The academic defence of this wartime discourse, a defence which is rife with bias and prejudice, persuasive definitions and value claims, does not qualify as scholarship.

Secondly, a deepening ethical crisis threatens Pacific War orthodoxy. For those who still believe that the Second World War was a noble defence of liberal civilisation, the revisionist challenge is brutally simple: can a war be won with morally indefensible means, and still be just? When the historian Sadao Asada concludes that the Pacific War 'dehumanised victor and vanquished alike', he is not being elegiac; he is delivering a blast at the moral complacency of Pacific War orthodoxy.[2] One has only to strip away one's orthodox blinkers to see that the Allied descent into barbarism during the final phase of the Pacific War – what I call 'the Japanese Holocaust' – has the makings of a liberal crisis of conscience. Here, as elsewhere, holocaust denial is ethically beyond the pale.

Thirdly, the Pacific War helped to make our world, but in ways that this orthodoxy cannot explain. The Pacific War not only laid the foundations for America's post-war oceanic hegemony but also set in motion the demographic revolution that is gradually sweeping away America's White majority, and with it the White Republic itself. Long neglected, this double consequence must now define the principal thrust of Pacific War research. The aftermath of '9/11' and the way it has exposed the true scope of US military supremacy over the rest of the world has drawn fresh attention to the importance of the Pacific War in the rise and consolidation of American hegemony. But if it accelerated the growth of American empire, the Pacific War started a racial demographic earthquake at home. This new revolution of immigrants and birth rates, set in motion by foreign hands, matters far more to the destiny of the United States than Islamic terrorism or any number of *coups d'état* by neo-conservative intellectuals in Washington. In the demographic demise of the nation's very own *Herrenvolk*, the scholar of Asia must now confront a new momentous theme: the end of the White Republic.

Imperial Japan and the fate of the White Republic

This factual and moral crisis was probably inevitable. Westerners have always changed their minds about the past. Revisionism is, as Ernst Nolte has observed, 'as old as history itself'.[3] What he went on to say about why we rethink the past defines the labours of the liberal revisionist who writes about the Pacific War:

> Revisionism ... begins with Herodotus and Thucydides. Indeed, revisionism and critique may be the same thing. Nevertheless, revisionism has a special content, and I do not know if the term 'revisionism' existed before the American Civil War. After that struggle, there arose a form of revisionism which sought to do justice to the Southern states. These revisionists were not only Southerners, but included some Northerners, too. They said, 'There is too much war propaganda in the writings on the Civil War today. We must change this. We must criticise this, without attempting to re-establish the Southern point of view.'[4]

Nolte's final point is crucial. Pacific War revisionism, in the Western liberal mode, does not seek to re-establish the imperial Japanese point of view; it offers no quarter to the deniers of mass murder, be the horror in question the slaughter of Chinese civilians at Nanjing, the firebombing of Dresden or the atomic destruction of Hiroshima. But it does aim to transcend the growing limitations, both factual and ethical, of 'good war' orthodoxy. It aims to stamp firmly on the propagandist who pretends to be a scholar.

These limitations are as easy to illustrate as they are difficult to accept. Liberal revisionist historians of the Second World War are in the business of exposing these difficulties, but they must also recognise how painful, offensive and indeed shocking their factual research and interpretations may be for the general public in the former Allied powers, particularly in the democracies. The impact of Pacific War orthodoxy has been immense not only in the United States but also in Australia, Britain, Canada and New Zealand precisely because it has been so deeply influenced by the propagandist, the myth-maker and the unofficial censor. It is the story we have wanted to hear. As George Orwell warned, in the unpublished preface to *Animal Farm*: 'censorship in free societies is infinitely more subtle and pernicious than in totalitarian states because unpopular ideas can be silenced, and inconvenient facts kept dark, without any need for an official ban'.

Revisionist historians must proceed, therefore, with patience and tact if they are to educate free peoples in the truth about the Pacific War. It has been the duty of the intellectual, since Emile Zola accused the French state and society of moral cowardice and anti-Jewish bigotry in the Dreyfus Affair (1894–1906), to assault the pernicious and self-serving myths of progressive societies. Our first duty, as historians, is to create a meticulous factual record of the events of the Pacific War. Our second duty is to challenge the moral hubris of defenders of 'good war' mythologies. In this struggle, no quarter will be given. Nothing will be spared.

Deep revisionism

The revisionist seeks to shatter illusions. This is a painful business, but without it there can be no progress in the study of history. If the example is war revisionism, the historian will demand that we re-examine the complaints of the old enemy – the one we have defeated – in search of that profundity of interpretative insight that alone can achieve what Nolte calls 'deep revisionism'. It is the search for deep revisionism that urges one to consider afresh the argument made by the Japanese intellectual Yoshimi Takeuchi, in his famous 1959 essay titled 'Overcoming Modernity', that the Pacific War was a two-edged struggle: a war of Japanese expansion, no doubt, but also a struggle against Western imperialism in Southeast Asia.[5] This insight can be improved on. Pacific War orthodoxy dishonestly insists that we set Allied ideals against Japanese moral failure. There has been a consistent refusal even to consider the Japanese case against Western hegemony and at the same time a pronounced determination either to leave Allied war crimes unexamined or to apply the brakes to any criticism of Allied battlefield barbarism because this might smack of so-called 'moral relativism'. Moral relativism, the notion that both sides committed war crimes, is often criticised as ethically suspect, but it may be the only effective cure for moral hypocrisy.

The Pacific War was double-edged for both sides. The battlefield crimes of the Imperial Japanese forces and the brutal treatment of Allied prisoners were war crimes. But we committed terrible deeds as well. It is time we admitted our faults rather than concentrating so resolutely on theirs. It is time to stop deceiving ourselves about what we did.[6] Thousands of war crimes were committed against Japanese soldiers and civilians, crimes that remain unpunished to this day. This fact undermines the legitimacy of the Tokyo War Crimes Tribunal because it appears to endorse the indefensible contention that the Japanese and their allies alone committed all of the sins of the Pacific War. As for the American air war against urban Japan, no moral defence is possible. Nothing the Japanese did to America justified this one-sided massacre of hundreds of thousands of civilians. Our continued silence on this subject reduces much of recent Japanese studies to a form of holocaust denial.

The Japanese had ample reason for violently resisting Western hegemony in the Pacific. The Kyoto School's defence of the attack on Pearl Harbour was coherent, rational and credible. Its main failing was its over-estimate of the strength of Japanese subjectivity. But the claim that the Allies were fighting to defend their empires as well as liberal civilisation will stand.

Only when we have cleared the moral fog of Pacific War orthodoxy will it be possible to understand the real stakes in the Pacific War. Whatever Tojo risked in 1941, the West risked even more. Japan survived the war; European colonial rule in Southeast Asia did not. Less widely recognised but perhaps even more important in the long term was the impact of the Pacific War on the United States. Over the course of its century-old thrust across the Pacific into the East Asian heartland since the 1890s, the United States has acquired a vast sphere of influence. The empire we inherited from the Japanese became our empire in the Pacific and Southeast Asia. This was our ambition; we wanted pre-eminence in the Pacific. To achieve it was one of the reasons why the Roosevelt administration 'provoked' a war with Japan.

Projecting American power into Asia was risky in the extreme. The United States, or, more precisely, the White Republic, risked its hitherto manifest destiny when it emerged from the confines of the New World to confront not fresh versions of the feeble resistance of Native Americans or the Mexican Republic but the armies of the formidably disciplined civilisations of Japan, Korea, China and Vietnam. In a way that America's more recent easy triumphs over the Islamic world could never have done, East Asian resistance taught White Americans the limits of their ability to reshape the world by military force. The prudence and restraint that has made the post-war hegemony of the United States so effective had to be learned, and this bloody learning curve began with the Pacific War.

When the end of White hegemony over the Pacific and Indian Oceans finally comes, historians will trace the origins of this racial fading to the military disasters inflicted on the United States by Imperial Japan between 1941 and 1942. The destruction of the World Trade Center on 11 September 2001 was not a repeat of Pearl Harbour but a mere echo of it. It offered White Americans a refresher course in diplomatic prudence and the limits of our power. Recent headlines of military glory over a prostrate Islamic world must not be allowed to obscure a central truth. Demographically doomed, White global hegemony is in retreat. The various Middle East struggles of recent years may mark not only the apogee of White American power but also its last hurrah.

Defending Japan's Pacific War

In their published writings of 1940–42, the philosophers of the Kyoto School took the first soundings of the post-White age that will define our tomorrow. They offered us the philosophy of our future. If Whiteness is to be overcome, and that is what the expression 'overcoming modernity' really means, White subjectivity must be matched by non-White subjectivity. This is the decisive challenge. During the next century, non-Whites will have to not only master the whole range of skills and knowledge but also assimilate, comprehensively and decisively, the subjectivist values that underpin Eurocentric competence and command. The wartime Kyoto philosophers were among the first non-White thinkers to brood on the challenge of subjectivity. They used a sophisticated idea of world history, borrowed partly from Ranke, partly from Hegel, to develop a Japanese understanding of this challenge. Who were these forgotten intellectuals, and why do we not know more about them?

An impressive list of thinkers and scholars, spread over several generations, has been associated with the Kyoto School of philosophy. Here attention will be focused on five of the most important members of the Kyoto School. Hajime Tanabe (1885–1962) was one of the two founders of the Kyoto School and, for the purposes of this analysis, the representative thinker of the first generation. The remaining four – Iwao Kōyama (1905–93), Shigetaka Suzuki (1907–88), Masaaki Kōsaka (1900–69) and Keiji Nishitani (1900–90) – were prominent voices in the second generation of the Kyoto School. As Kyoto philosophers tend to live remarkably long lives, here only the wartime labours of these thinkers, roughly the period from 1931 to 1946, will be assessed, with special attention given to the crucial period between 1941 and 1943.

Amid the tide of publications – journal articles, lectures, monographs and occasional pieces – produced by the Kyoto philosophers, four works will be given close attention here. The first has already been mentioned: *The Standpoint of World History and Japan* by Kōyama, Suzuki, Kōsaka and Nishitani. The edited transcripts of these three round-table discussions or symposia appeared between January 1942 and January 1943 in the pages of *Chūō Kōron*, the intellectual monthly, a weighty Japanese cross between the influence of *Der Spiegel* and the seriousness of the *New York Review of Books*. The remaining three works are all by Tanabe: his response to Heidegger's controversial rectoral address of May 1933 that appeared in three parts in the *Asahi* newspaper in the autumn of 1933; his secret lecture of 1942 on the philosophy of co-prosperity spheres, which was part of Tanabe's intellectual alliance with the Imperial Navy to resist Tojo's policies; and Tanabe's magnum opus, *The Logic of the Species*, that appeared in thirteen parts between 1934 and 1946.

Focusing only on these thinkers during the Great East Asian War (1931–45) and on these four works alone means that other influential members of the Kyoto School, all thinkers of distinction and influence, have been relatively neglected, but their names will inevitably appear in one or more of the chapters below. These include D.T. Suzuki (1870–1966), the populariser of modern Zen, Kitarō Nishida (1870–1945), co-founder with Tanabe of the Kyoto School and the greatest modern Japanese philosopher, Kiyoshi Miki (1897–1945), another star of the second generation, and Jun Tosaka (1900–45), author of *The Japanese Ideology* and the most prominent 'insider' who became a Marxist 'outsider' critic of the Kyoto School. Miki and Tosaka died in prison.

Why these thinkers and why these texts? Tanabe was instrumental, in the late 1920s and early 1930s, in the *Kehre*, or 'turn', in Kyoto thought away from an exclusive focus on religious and metaphysical concerns to history and politics. This is why *The Logic of the Species* is so important. But because the charge of fascism has been so frequently and so carelessly made against Tanabe, his criticism of Heidegger in 'The Philosophy of Crisis or a Crisis in Philosophy', among the very earliest critiques by a great philosopher of Heidegger's famous 1933 rectoral address, 'The Self-assertion of the German University', merits a closer look. To this end, a translation of this text, the first ever in English, appears in the Appendix to this book. For similar reasons, Tanabe's hitherto unknown lecture, 'On the Logic of Co-prosperity Spheres', part of *The Ōshima Memos*, a recently discovered cache of secret wartime papers which document, directly and indirectly, Tanabe's campaign of intellectual dissent from the Tojo regime, has been translated here for the first time, and also appears in the Appendix.[7] Finally, there is *The Standpoint of World History and Japan*. An English translation of this key text is now underway and will appear as a separate companion volume to this book.

Of all these writings, *The Standpoint of World History and Japan* has been the most widely discussed because of its 'notorious' place in Japanese wartime thought. Just before and immediately after the outbreak of the Pacific War, Kōyama, Suzuki, Kōsaka and Nishitani, emboldened by the writings of Tanabe and the example of Nishida, proposed a reasoned justification for their country's titanic struggle with the United States and the British Empire. In the hundreds of pages of analysis and reflection contained in *The Standpoint of World History and Japan*, only two specific battles figure prominently: the attack on Pearl Harbour and the siege of Singapore.

Even now, a defence of the surprise attack on Pearl Harbour or a justification of the events that led to the horrors of the Burma Railway is a moral provocation. One bridles. In the face of the transcendent claims of ethics, why spend hours reading these wartime writings or urge others to do the same? The answer is plain and unsettling: the moral case for our 'good war' against Imperial Japan has been allowed to overwhelm the historical record, the facts about this savage struggle. For motives high and not so high, we have learned how to deceive ourselves about many aspects of the Second World War. For anyone nursed on the Allied myths of the Pacific War, the wartime texts of the Kyoto philosopher offer an exercise in truth-telling.

The main goal of this book is to uncover these inconvenient facts. But this perusal of the Kyoto School's defence of the Pacific War is more than an exercise in muckraking. In ways suspected by few, then or now, the humbling of Imperial Japan opened, as has been argued above, a kind of Pandora's Box: our victory over the Japanese gave us a vast Pacific realm while setting in motion the one transformation the Civil War did not achieve: the overthrow of America's racial hierarchy.

The Pacific War opened a door on a future few Americans imagined, and the arrival of this future will irresistibly overturn the orthodox understanding of our national past. It is beyond the scope of the traditional rubrics of American history – nationalist, liberal and radical – to account for the strange lingering death of the White Republic. It is our uncertain imperial destiny that explains why these long-neglected Japanese books, essays and discussions demand, today more than ever, what Henry James called 'the deep breathing fixity of total regard'.

These Kyoto School thinkers are remarkable not only for what they argued and how they argued (the method they brought to their thinking) but also for the way they encourage us to elaborate, enrich and deepen their arguments. This is what Ryōsuke Ōhashi rightly calls 'the potential of the Kyoto School'.[8] Tanabe and the second generation of the Kyoto School did not complete a train of thought; they set one in motion for us to complete. More concretely, these Japanese thinkers erected a framework of ideas that illuminate in a new and powerful way not only the character of the Pacific War but also the post-war trials of the non-White world and America's rise to global ascendancy.

The power of this Japanese philosophic discourse is grounded in reason. In the rush to judge the Kyoto School, this decisive truth has been lost sight of. Contrary to the claims of the neo-Marxist critics of the Kyoto School – few of whom have actually read the texts in question – the five Japanese thinkers who dominate these pages were rational thinkers in a sense that any educated European will find plausible. This is what makes the Kyoto School thinker so formidable and therefore so disturbing to any proponent of Pacific War orthodoxy.

This brings us to the greatest failure of the Western critic of the wartime Kyoto School. In the eyes of the Kyoto philosopher, the war against Anglo-American hegemony had to be fought with rational means for rational ends; otherwise, it was wrong metaphysically and would not succeed practically. But because the Tojo regime pursued the war for other than rational ends and insisted on fighting it with less than rational means, the assessment of the war effort by the Kyoto School may qualify as among the most important expressions of public criticism (admittedly oblique) of the government's military strategy to appear in print in Japan between 1941 and 1945.

The Standpoint of World History and Japan was a reasoned, demythifying and secularising assault on the obscurant ideas of the Japanese ultra-right and the militarist clique that surrounded Tojo. Although the original transcripts were carefully edited to eliminate the kinds of remarks that would have got the authors arrested, the version that appeared in the pages of the magazine *Chūō Kōron* had to be edited again before the book version appeared in 1943. The Army censors were still unappeased. Further editions of *The Standpoint of World History and Japan* were banned, the publisher eventually shut down and the participants felt threatened by arrest or worse. Such concerns were not idle; Miki and Tosaka, as noted above, would die in prison. Such official hostility encourages the conclusion that *The Standpoint of World History and Japan*, and the parallel secret conspiracy concocted by Tanabe and the other members of the second generation of the Kyoto School in cooperation with the Yonai faction of the Imperial Navy to bring down the Tojo Cabinet (see Chapters 4 and 5), should transform the reputation of these so-called fascists into something approaching enlightened heroes of the Japanese wartime resistance. This is the stuff of revisionist revolution in the liberal mode.

The neo-Marxist critics of Japan have repeatedly dismissed Tanabe as a fascist, but the grounds for their accusations are improbable and the evidence all but non-existent. The liberal revisionist rejects such charges out of hand. The offending article of faith is Pacific War orthodoxy. It hobbles every effort to understand Kyoto School thought as philosophy. Neo-Marxism lacks both empirical and conceptual rigour. Indeed, the general impression is that the word 'fascism', as used by neo-Marxists, is comparable to a house of cards that can withstand not the faintest breath of critical probing. The term '*Tennō-sei* fascism' (the putative fascism of the emperor system) is, more often than not, as emotionally charged as it is scientifically vacuous. Grievous crimes were committed in the name of the emperor, but this does not permit one to label Imperial Japan as a fascist regime. As for Tanabe, the accusation of fascism made against him does not bear serious examination on either empirical or ethical grounds. It is simply not true.

By providing a rock against which the critique of wartime fascist Japan shatters, the Kyoto School demonstrates its political uses. What then does the liberal revisionist make of the Kyoto School's supposed complicity in the Pacific War? Examining only the most influential documents written by the more prominent members of the second generation of Kyoto School thinkers between 1941 and 1944, it is clear that what is original and remarkable about these books, essays and discussions is not their general patriotic endorsement of the war (this is hardly exceptional) but rather their insistence that only Japanese subjectivity (*shutaisei*) fully achieved could break the global reign of the West, thus opening the door to a multicultural world. For them, Pearl Harbour as 'the event' announced the dawn of the age after Europe.

For the Kyoto School, the creation of a new order in East Asia offered the supreme test of Japanese national character because if (White) Western hands could not be relied upon to manage the Western Pacific, only East

Asian subjectivity, competent and mature, would suffice to replace it. But these thinkers were Hegelian realists. They accepted the reverse proposition as well. If Imperial Japan failed to demonstrate the requisite degree of national subjectivity, and therefore failed in its crusade against the West, the United States, as the supreme contemporary force of Western subjectivity, would rightly and necessarily continue to govern the Western Pacific.

This is the most plausible way of understanding the Kyoto School's post-war endorsement of the Japan–United States security alliance. But in the context of the Great East Asian War (1931–45), this insistence on the pivotal role of Japanese rational self-mastery links the arguments made by Tanabe in his *Logic of the Species* with the challenge of making world history that concentrated the minds of the second generation of the Kyoto School during the Pacific War. *The Standpoint of World History and Japan* as well as *The Ōshima Memos* demonstrate the truth of this claim. Looking back now to the events of 1941–45, it is clear that the wartime Kyoto School thought harder and more incisively about this ethnic-metaphysical-techno-logical challenge than any school of non-White political thought. Although they did not think in racial terms, these philosophers, and they alone, grasped the true historical significance of Pearl Harbour.

War revisionism and racial demography

As a theme in planetary thinking, the mission to overcome Whiteness has become ever more urgent because of the contemporary revolution of racial demography. It is demographic change that gives the ideas of the liberal revisionist their irresistible force. Population experts now predict, with reasonable confidence, that the United States will lose its White majority by around 2050.[9] Demography is an inexact science, and predictions by demographers have to be treated with caution. Nevertheless, it is a fact that three American states – Hawaii, New Mexico and California – have already lost their White majorities. By 2015, Texas may follow suit, with Arizona, New York, Nevada, New Jersey and Maryland projected to do the same before mid-century.

This racial transition will affect other 'White' societies. The United Kingdom, for example, may follow suit as early as 2060. This social revolution will inevitably affect the racial psychology of the remaining societies with White majorities, notably Australia and Canada, among the former Allied powers. Even New Zealand's Anglo-Maori compact will take on a different air by mid-century.

Can Pacific War orthodoxy survive this demographic change? The principal English-speaking nations that fought and won the Pacific War – the United States, Britain, Australia and Canada – were overwhelmingly White societies. This fact is so obvious that historians have rarely dwelt on it. But revisionists have gradually begun to stress the racial character of the battle for Pacific hegemony. Here the reactionary Japanese revisionist has had a point. Until Imperial Japan's emergence on the global scene, every inch of territory washed by the waters of the Pacific Ocean was subject, either directly or indirectly, to the weight and power of a vast White ascendancy, from Alaska to Chile, from Siberia to New Zealand. When Perry sailed into Edo Bay in 1853, China was prostrate; Japan was impotent; the Pacific was a White lake.

From that momentous date in 1552 when Magellan first sailed into the Pacific, this White ascendancy was nearly 400 years in the making. It took three horrific episodes of East Asian resistance – the Pacific War, the Korean Conflict and the Vietnamese/Indo-Chinese Wars – to deflect, to transform and to begin to undermine it. The White will to rule the Pacific would never have been impaired without East Asian victories on the battle-field. These wars of resistance transformed the nature, pace and impact of post-war decolonisation across the former Third World. Furthermore, demographic change in the United States will make the victims of White American expansion – Native Americans, Blacks, Latins and Asians – into the new majority. The history of White expansion across North America and the Pacific War will one day have to be written in ways regarded as unthinkable now. The kind of radical revisionism being advocated here is a significant first step towards preparing the grounds for America's new majority to re-conceive the national past in post-White terms.

Demographic change will fuel ethical revisionism. During the past century, White liberals have allied themselves, intentionally or otherwise, with the Asian nationalist in the struggle to sap the White imperialist will. The decisive battle for decolonisation was a battle for hearts and minds on the home front (Ho Chi Minh acted as if he regarded the American elec-torate as the decisive battlefield in the struggle against US imperialism). The liberal victory in this American domestic battle of conscience, particularly during the Vietnam War, has ensured that any notion of the Pacific War as 'a good war' becomes fraught with moral difficulty. The *long durée* at work in the dissolution of White power – demographically, psychologically and morally – reduces the post-war re-branding of American hegemony in the Pacific as an anti-communist crusade or today's war on terrorism either to comforting diversions or secret accelerators of the long-term trends or to the circling of wagons in a kind of racial-ethnic last stand.

The decay of the élan and confidence of the White Republic, and its mystique of racial supremacy, both at home and abroad, is a phenomenon of great historical interest. Almost all commentators stress its irresistible character. What was a White American liberal to do when confronted with the facts about wartime discrimination against Latins, American Indians and Chinese-Americans, the segregation of blood supplies for Blacks in the American armed forces, the illegal incarceration in concentration camps of thousands of Japanese-Americans at home, to say nothing of the fire-bombing of more or less defenceless Japanese cities? The indiscriminate use of napalm, Agent Orange, search-and-destroy tactics and carpet bombing in

Vietnam intensified the noise of the same ethical alarm bells. These facts, *taken together*, have become the stuff of a moral powder keg. With the perennial tactlessness of truth-tellers, liberal revisionists such as John Dower have now lit the fuse.[10] But this is not, finally, a matter of praise or blame, but historical inevitability.

After four centuries of racial-ethnic expansion and hegemony, the moral and policy options available to White Americans to place Japanese-Americans in camps in 1942, to open the floodgates on non-White immigration in 1965 or to round up suspect Arab-Americans in 2001–02 will now close. The domestic victims and the manipulated of the Pacific War will be the racial majority in post-White America. They will have little time for 'good war' rhetoric and the racial hubris that accompanies it. This may explain why the ultra-nationalists in the administration of Bush *fils* are so desperate to delay the political impact of the 'Browning' of America. But calmness and generosity in the face of irresistible change may be the most sensible posture. The liberal revisionist seeks to encourage this kind of generosity.

Pearl Harbour and the birth of post-White America

The passing of the wartime generation and the end of White majority rule in the United States would have altered how we understand our world and the role of the Pacific War in the making of that world even if the horrors of 11 September 2001 had never occurred. Among all the revisionist findings and interpretations, no suggestion may be more arresting than the idea that the White Republic, in winning the Pacific War, prepared the way for its own demise. This demographic trend has far greater implications for the future trajectory of the American empire than any number of military adventures in the Middle East.

Take, for example, non-White immigration. Once China became an ally of the United States in 1941, the racist barriers against Chinese immigration became indefensible, and were abandoned the following year. At the same time, Mexican immigration was 'expanded and legalized by an agricultural guest-worker programme in 1942 to help with wartime labour shortages'.[11] By the time the programme was scrapped in 1964, some 4.5 million had 'learned the way north'. A hundred years after the White Republic had stripped Mexico of a vast portion of its national territory, the Latin recon-quest had effectively begun.

Again, the decay of inner form may be decisive. Certainly, this demo-graphic revolution could not have unfolded without sparking a revolution in morality. Race subverts the very notion of the Second World War as a 'good war'. How was it possible to fight Hitler and Tojo and still systematically discriminate against Black American soldiers? How long could Afro-Americans be ordered to fight and die for 'Jim Crow'? In a notorious episode, one repeated as often as it was felt necessary by threatened Whites, a Negro veteran returned to the South and refused to sit in the back of a segregated bus after serving his country in war. He was dragged off the bus and beaten nearly to death. After the Atlantic Charter, after Roosevelt's repeated pleas to all Americans to rally to the defence of freedom, how long could this go on?

Racial hypocrisy was not the only poison in the 'good war' rhetoric. For the post-war generation, nursed on Roosevelt's spellbinding language of moral idealism, a rhetoric that canonically derived from Lincoln, how could the United States wage a bad war after it had won a good one? 'Give us a Hitler, and we will defeat him' became the Vietnam draft resister's cry. The new moral certainties cut deep; Ho Chi Minh was no Hitler. The resulting erosion of the White racial will to dominate the earth helped to ensure American defeat in Vietnam. It was during the Vietnam War that federal immigration law was revamped, almost without opposition, in ways that opened the doors to massive non-White immigration, thus dooming America's founding White majority. In such facts and interpretations is to be found the heart of the revisionist history of the Pacific War.

In his second inaugural address as president, Ronald Reagan famously observed that 'A settler pushes west, and sings his song, that's our heritage, that's our song'. A French play, published more than thirty-five years before, about the decay of segregation in the American South, powerfully dramatised Reagan's Hollywood conceit. In the final scene, Fred Clarke, the scion of a local White dynasty, wantonly murders an innocent Negro. Aroused by the moral horror of this killing, the White man's White mistress threatens to shoot him in turn. Facing the barrel of a gun, Fred Clarke saves his skin with the kind of self-serving bourgeois rhetoric that Sartre so despised:

> The first Clarke cleared a forest with his own hands; he shot sixteen Indians before being killed himself in an ambush. His son built nearly the whole of this town; he was Washington's friend and died at Yorktown, fighting for the independence of the United States. His great-grandfather was a Vigilante in San Francisco; he saved twenty-two lives during the great fire. My grandfather came to live here; he dug a canal to the Mississippi and was Governor of the state. My father is a senator; I shall be a senator after him; I am his only male heir and the last of my name. We have made this country and its story is our story. There have been Clarkes in Alaska, in the Philippines, in New Mexico. Dare you shoot the whole of America?[12]

'We have made this country and its story is our story.' The arrival of post-White America spells the end of this 'we' and the end of 'our story'. The road to this ending took a decisive turn at Pearl Harbour. The resulting irony is worthy of Tacitus, the great historian of Roman ironies. In 1941,

Tojo gambled and threw away an expanding but still modest empire; Roosevelt gambled and doomed the White Republic itself. Here is to be found not the end of the beginning but the beginning of the end of the White Republic in Japan studies. *Tora, tora, tora.*

The decay of Pacific War orthodoxy

3 Philosophy and the Pacific War

Imperial Japan and the making of a post-White world

The future will, in all reasonable probability, be what coloured men make it.

W.E.B. du Bois[1]

A people (*minzoku*) in itself is meaningless. When a people acquires subjectivity, it becomes a nation-state. A people without subjectivity, ... that is a people that has not transformed itself into a nation (*kokumin*), is powerless.

Masaaki Kōsaka[2]

Is philosophy the final home of the European spirit? After all the batterings of the old century, Europe even now retains its philosophic centrality. Thus, France may have lost the bulk of her empire, but in the kingdom of the mind, much of the world remains a suburb of Paris. This centrality has prompted Naoki Sakai to observe that Japanese writers on the intellectual history of their country are haunted by a presence that is almost always an absence: the Western reader.[3] For the ambitious Japanese thinker, it is the European reader who has, by tradition, embodied the highest standards.

If knowledge is power, philosophy's power lies in its ability to deconstruct power. It is only in this sense that today, Eurocentrism is still about power. This insight gave the wartime Kyoto philosopher his point of departure. This is why Europe was indispensable to the labours of the Kyoto School during the Pacific War and why Europe remains the last great hope of many Japanese intellectuals, because they recognise that America's hegemony cannot be resisted without Europe and its tradition of radical criticism.

Philosophers at war

In 1941, at the time of the attack on Pearl Harbour, the challenge to the Kyoto philosopher was unambiguous. If East Asia was to master itself, to achieve effective and comprehensive subjectivity, the ability to deconstruct Western power was the one metaphysical skill that East Asians had to acquire because power lay in non-Asian hands. Without this skill, Western power could not be deflected, let alone matched. But to deconstruct power is to understand power, and to understand power is to learn how to foster power. Without the ability to foster power, any effort to achieve shared prosperity for all East Asians would necessarily end in failure. Genuine shared prosperity: this is what the Kyoto School thought the concept of a Greater East Asian Co-prosperity Sphere had to mean. Otherwise, as the authors of *The Standpoint of World History and Japan* argue convincingly, the idea was doomed from the outset.

The wartime Kyoto School was a humanism. It was a subjectivist philosophy in which man and his works occupied centre stage. The Kyoto philosopher learned how to deconstruct power (that of others) in order to construct power (for oneself). This turn to the subjective may explain why Kitarō Nishida, although the father of the Kyoto School and the figure who dominated its first phase (c. 1917–c. 1927), was not the leading thinker in the wartime or middle phase of the Kyoto School (c. 1927–c. 1945). Tanabe exercised that role. Nishida's ambivalence towards Tanabe and the second generation of the Kyoto School derives in part from his preference for objectivism, and we need to keep this fact in mind when we brood on the accusations of 'ultra-nationalism' made against him. But Nishida's fundamental nihilism put him at odds with the central thrust of Kyoto thought between the Manchurian Incident (1931) and the fall of Saipan (July 1944), when all but the most stubborn members of the Japanese establishment, philosophical and otherwise, realised that the war was lost.

The subjectivist cast of wartime Kyoto School thought made, in essence, a philosophy of agency. Kōyama may have shared Nishida's opposition to intellectualism (*shuchishugi*), his preference for 'facts' (*koto*) over 'rationalism' (*ri*) and his fundamentally anti-humanist stance, but only up to a point.[4] The wartime Kyoto School was committed to a non-Western form of modernity. It was not a passive school of anti-Western cultural criticism. The wartime Kyoto thinker sought to change Japan, not to elaborate a defence of a primordial national identity.

The Kyoto thinker's commitment to *shutaisei*, that is his metaphysical subjectivism, sets him apart from many other forms of Japanese nationalist reflection. He has no time for the Japan Romantic School's rejection of modernisation. The Kyoto philosopher believes that 'overcoming modernity' means transcending Western modernity with an East Asian form of modernity that is genuinely modern. It is here that the suggestion that Nishitani introduced the idea of 'subjectivity' into Japanese thought comes into its own. Without close attention to the idea of *shutaisei*, one cannot make sense of *The Standpoint of World History and Japan*.

Any serious engagement with Japanese philosophy during the Great East Asian War (1931–45) requires a rubric of thought that can encompass the reality of power as well as the power of thought. Cornel West, the Black American philosopher, locates this rubric in the moment of post-modernity. For West, three historic transitions define this moment: the end of 'the Age of Europe', the advent of American global domination, and the decolonialisation of Asia and Africa.[5] It is my thesis that no school of non-White philosophy rivals the power and potential of the Kyoto School to rethink the importance and meaning of these three transitions. The decolonialisation of Asia and Africa between 1946 and 1975 was, for example, only one of four critical hours of anti-White resistance during the twentieth century. The three which West neglects are the Russo-Japanese War, Imperial Japan's Southeast Asian and Pacific offensive between 1941 and 1942 (the crucial rehearsal for the Korean and Vietnam conflicts), and the economic rise of East Asia, orchestrated and funded by Japan, between 1968 and 1997.

The influence of the Kyoto School on Japanese thought and feeling suddenly flared into notorious apogee at the precise hour when European centrality, as a geopolitical force, was fatally eclipsed in 1941. That was the year when the Soviet Union, Imperial Japan and the United States entered the Second World War. This not only transformed that conflict from a European into a global struggle, it also marked the beginning of the end of Europe's mastery of its own affairs as America began to expand the reach of its empire by preparing to crush its German and Japanese rivals.

At the time, the events of 1941–42 heralded the conclusive overthrow of the Eurocentric universe that had increasingly dominated Japan's intellectual horizon since the late eighteenth century. At first, this liberating prospect mesmerised the Japanese intelligentsia. It appeared to blunt the provocation of European rationality while offering Japan a previously undreamt of opportunity to achieve intellectual parity with Europe on Japanese terms. But if Europe was ceasing to be the power centre of the globe, it remained the indispensable arsenal of intellectual freedom, creativity and autonomy. The rejection of 'Europe as domination' never precluded, certainly not for the Kyoto School, Europe's value as a vast storehouse of intellectual means to resist the emerging threat of American cultural hegemony.

In Japan, the most famous response to the shattering of Eurocentrism came almost at once in two major published debates staged in 1941–42: 'Overcoming Modernity' ('Kindai no Chōkoku') and 'The Standpoint of World History and Japan' ('Sekai-shi-teki Tachiba to Nippon').[6] The first was attended by an influential group of patriotic writers and scholars, including two Kyoto philosophers. The second was, as noted in Chapter 1, entirely the work of Kyoto thinkers.

There are ample grounds to conclude that the most history-minded members of the Kyoto School were well prepared for this moment. The key figure in setting this train of 'post-White' thought in motion was not Nishida but Tanabe.[7] Whatever their disagreements, Tanabe and the 'gang of four' from the second generation – Kōyama, Kōsaka, Suzuki and Nishitani – collectively generated a remarkable discourse, grounded in Hegelian metaphysics, on the nature of Euro-American centrism. Only by achieving genuine subjectivity had Europe become the master of the globe. Anticipating a time after Europe, Kōyama called for a plurality of worlds. But this newly won autonomy for non-Whites was to be measured against the only standard of achievement that counts before the court of world-historical significance: European subjectivity or mature self-mastery.

Other schools of non-Western reflection may have been equally anxious for European colonial hegemony to pass, but none was more mindful than the Kyoto School of the fact that European centrality was earned and that overcoming modernity would test the political skills, the economic discipline, the intellectual verve and the moral resources of modern Asians to the limit. After the hopes of 1940–42, Japan's defeat in 1945 demonstrated the difficulty of the immense task of overcoming the White West.

Such realism was reinforced during the 1990s. The fading of the Japanese miracle and the crises that shook the economies of Southeast Asia offer stark reminders that victory still eludes East Asians in their long struggle to match American subjectivity. Nevertheless, whenever the anti-White thinker has refused to surrender to the temptations of anger or despair, self-hate or complacency, in favour of hard truths and genuine national achievement, he will find that the Kyoto philosopher has been there before him.

The new attack on the Kyoto School

The work of the wartime Kyoto School of philosophy stands as one of the earliest and most sophisticated Asian efforts to criticise the sources of Euro-American power and to propose an East Asian remedy for it. This is where the greatness of the Kyoto School as a branch of political philosophy will be found. But this greatness will never be exposed without the death of Pacific War orthodoxy and its ruling assumption that the Allied crusade in the Pacific was, in essence, a struggle of democratic morality against the aggressive brutality of Japanese expansionism.

The Pacific War was a war of military expansion by both Imperial Japan and the United States. Japanese aggression was never the whole truth about the Pacific War, but the ideology of American exceptionalism has blinded us to any other truth. This blindness persists to this day, as the US response to the events of 11 September 2001 painfully shows. Why else are we so keen to endorse the curiously self-serving notion that any violent resistance to American hegemony is 'fascistic', as the expression 'Axis of Evil' would appear to imply. Putting the blinkers of exceptionalism to one side allows us to see that the Pacific War was a decisive chapter in the construction of America's global hegemony.

Such sceptical probing has been indispensable since the al-Qaeda terrorist attack on Manhattan and Washington DC. Despite the natural desire to respond with patriotic indignation against Islamic fundamentalist terrorism, the professional student of Asia knows that many of the assertions being made by politicians and media pundits about Asia, be they about the character of Islam or the relevance of the post-war occupation of Japan to the military conquest of Iraq, are nonsense, and dangerous nonsense at that. But any Orientalist worthy of the name also knows that truth-telling on such occasions may put the scholar's reputation, even one's career, at risk.

The fact that the Asian specialist may, from time to time, get into serious trouble at home provides a measure of reassurance that we are more than foot soldiers serving the cause of Western global hegemony. Nevertheless, Edward Said's sweeping indictment of the contemporary heirs of European Orientalism still stands:

> Orientalism [is] the corporate institution for dealing with the Orient – dealing with it by making statements about it, authorizing views of it, describing it, by teaching it, by settling it, ruling over it; in short, Orientalism is a Western style for dominating, restructuring, and having authority over the Orient.[8]

The scholarly servicing of America's global hegemony does not exhaust the labours of the Asian specialist, but there is neither a phrase nor a comma in Said's critique that does not apply to the Asian specialist when we render such service. More than sixty years after Hiroshima and Nagasaki, no serious Japanese thinker argues that the Japanese Navy should be based in San Diego or that the colonisation of New South Wales should be a goal of Japanese foreign policy, but Western writings on Japan continue to treat that nation with moral disdain while observing a strict silence on the provocation of America's empire. To the degree that Pacific War orthodoxy focuses its energies on the single-minded critique of the conduct of the Imperial Japanese Army between 1931 and 1945, it opts out of the present. It is *passé* in the strongest sense of the word.

This risk is most evident among the so-called neo-Marxists of Japan studies. Graham Parkes has exposed the theoretical incoherence, ethical muddles and factual dishonesty of this school of interpretation.[9] In accord with Parkes's criticism, Chapter 4 probes the factual foundations of Harry Harootunian's *Overcome by Modernity*, a major recent statement of the neo-Marxist case.[10] Outside the neo-Marxist camp, more sober approaches prevail. But it is equally true that during the past decade, Japan studies has had its sails scorched by the orthodox mindset that still dominates the mass media. The debacle over the Hiroshima atomic bomb exhibition organised by the Smithsonian in Washington DC in 1995 offered a stern warning about the dangers of our failure to combat what is most obscurant in the orthodox stance.[11]

Rude awakenings

These dangers are painfully evident in the recent controversies among Western scholars, particularly but not exclusively in the United States, over the ethical and philosophical status of the wartime Kyoto School. Looking back now, one can only conclude that a new round of 'Japan critique' (from the German, '*Japanokritik*') appeared to make sense at the time. This new attack on the Kyoto School was a delayed aftershock to the exposure of Paul de Man's anti-Semitic editorials in 1987 and the deepening controversies over

Heidegger's tenure as rector of the University of Freiburg during the early days of the Third Reich that erupted at roughly the same time as the De Man affair.[12] In the early 1990s, non-Japanese philosophers of religion began to scrutinise the wartime stance of the Kyoto School with the kind of hostility that it had long been subjected to by political and intellectual historians in Japan and the West.

Having for decades presented Nishida, Tanabe and Nishitani as essentially apolitical religious thinkers, some of the most influential Western students of modern Japanese religious thought turned against their Japanese heroes in an apparent crisis of liberal conscience provoked by the Heidegger and De Man scandals. Unlike their neo-Marxist colleagues, these Western scholars did not abandon proper standards of research or their hard-won understanding of Kyoto thought. But there was an implicit endorsement of the reasoning behind the victor's justice meted out by the Tokyo War Crimes Tribunal. The implied moral simplicities – Allied virtue versus Japanese evil – are so morally satisfying precisely because they exploit the least fair and most self-flattering comparison possible: *our* high ideals against *their* low conduct. The impact of such self-serving comparisons has been overwhelming. In a stunning intellectual reversal, half a century of cultural relativism, the legacy of Franz Boas and Bronislaw Malinowski, the fathers of modern anthropology, and the theoretical lynchpin of all multiculturalism, was suddenly displaced by the confident armoury of Western values, bristling with moral judgments *à la* Voltaire. All of Nietzsche's warnings about the dangers *to the moralist* of seizing the moral high ground have been ignored.

Many of the strands of this Western crisis of conscience may be sampled in *Rude Awakenings: Zen, the Kyoto School and the Question of Nationalism*.[13] Instead of the generous and adventurous portrait of the Kyoto School as 'a wide-eyed approach to religious philosophy that seemed to answer the need for a serious encounter between East and West as few contemporary systems of thought have', a new clash of civilisations appeared to erupt within Japan studies in which Western scholars denounced Japanese Zen's 'vociferous support for militaristic nationalism', 'the connections between the wartime complicity of Zen leaders and the Zen-inspired philosophy of Nishida', and 'the intrinsic nationalism' of Kyoto thought.[14]

Here, for example, is Heisig's pre-revisionist assessment of Tanabe's wartime stance:

> No fair account of Tanabe's logic of species can fail to see, however, that its goal was a 'theory of national existence' that would serve as a direct critique of the blind nationalism he saw inspiring Japan's engagements in Asia and fascism in Europe … It is therefore altogether wrongheaded to suppose, as some Japanese historians were to do from post-war bandwagons, that Tanabe had composed his *Philosophy as*

Metanoetics in order to dissociate himself from nationalist views he had once espoused. Not only did he never hold such views, but also the lectures on which the work was based were delivered during the war.[15]

In subtle contrast, this is the critique he produced in 1994 at the academic conference that resulted in *Rude Awakenings*:

> At the time, Japan's army was launching the first stages of its fifteen-year campaign in Asia, Tanabe Hajime ... laid the groundwork of his 'logic of the specific' in a series of lectures devoted to social philosophy. By 1934 Tanabe had published the first draft of the idea, and by April of 1937, just three months before the incident at Marco Polo Bridge that triggered all-out war between China and Japan, he published his theory of the racially-unified society as a specific substratum that mediates the relationship between particular individuals and the universal ideals of the human community. Two years later, in 1939, when Japan's writers and intellectuals were still reeling from the loss of freedom of expression, Tanabe applied his new logic to argue that the Japanese nation, with the emperor at its head, has the status of a divine, salvific presence in the world.[16]

The editors of *Rude Awakenings* summarise Heisig's article in this way:

> James Heisig looks at the figure of Tanabe Hajime, whose critics – and indeed whose own philosophy of repentance – have raised questions about his complicity in the war effort. An analysis of the elusive notion of the 'logic of the specific' reveals how Tanabe had within his grasp a philosophical idea leading in the opposite direction from the spirit of nationalism with which he flirted during the war.[17]

In his 1999 essay on Tanabe's *The Logic of the Species*, as well as in his book-length dialogue with Osamu Nishitani, Sakai took issue with both the earlier religious approach as well as the new politically minded revisionism.[18] He accused the old Western proponents of the Kyoto School of being the instruments, witting or otherwise, of what he sees as Washington's reactionary foreign policy in East Asia,[19] a crime exacerbated by what Sakai regards as ignorance of European philosophy among Western students of Japan and a bewildering obtusity to the nationalist thrust of some Kyoto School thinkers not only during the Asia-Pacific War (1931–45) but afterwards as well.[20] Sakai is on the right path here, but it should also be clear now that America's Pacific hegemony effectively precludes any form of Japanese military adventurism, and therefore the sixty-year-old left-wing obsession with Japan's potential for territorial expansion ignores the realities of power today. American empire and its new doctrine of pre-emptive strikes are the geopolitical facts of life that matter most in Pacific affairs, not symbolic visits by Japanese prime ministers to Yasukuni Shrine.

During these 1990s controversies over the Kyoto School, some Western religious scholars began to criticise what they regarded as the political duplicity of their Japanese colleagues. Had the Japanese academic establishment exploited the religious dimension of Kyoto School thought in order to cover up the wartime misdeeds of these thinkers? Heisig, for example, concluded that

> The bearers of the tradition in Japan and their disciples watch bewildered as the moral agenda of the Western intellectual grows to a measure of confidence that is no longer as intimidated by claims about the 'uniqueness' of Eastern culture and wisdom as it might have been a decade or more ago.[21]

The mutual irritation in this dispute was obvious, but the precise targets of such animus were left tactfully unclear. Sakai named no names; neither did Heisig and his allies. None of this should obscure, however, the curious results of this ideological round of musical chairs. Just as Japanese students of the Kyoto School began to assert the importance of philosophy over politics, their Western colleagues demanded that politics ('the moral agenda of the Western intellectual') once again serve as the principal criterion for assessing the philosophic stature of the thinker. In such a climate, Heisig won few converts when he insisted that we distinguish between what he had come to view as the irresponsibility of Tanabe's political views and the soundness of his philosophic insights.

Was, therefore, the era of good feeling that had governed post-war relations between Japanese religious thought and the Western intellectual merely a sham? Tamotsu Aoki, the influential Japanese anthropologist, once contended that the eclipse of pro-Japanese relativism in Western social science during the 1980s was a painful consequence of European decolonisation and America's defeat in Vietnam.[22] Teaching in the United States, Sakai himself located a parallel return to Western values in the rise of religious fundamentalism and White supremacists in the American heartland. At least Sakai is talking about forces and movements at work in the contemporary world, not indulging in nostalgia for the American 'high' of 1945. Nevertheless, Western critics of the Kyoto School tended to argue during the 1990s that Japanese duplicity, not Western sourness, posed the core difficulty.

Targeting Manhattan

A chance remark by Arthur C. Danto illustrates the vulnerabilities at issue. When Giovanna Borradori, the Italian philosopher, interviewed him for her study of contemporary American philosophers, she asked about the motivations that inspired his *Mysticism and Morality: Oriental Thought and Moral Philosophy* (1972).[23] He evoked memories of D.T. Suzuki, the most influential exponent of Zen in the modern West and a fellow traveller of the Kyoto School:

> The East had already been in the air since the fifties. Dr. Suzuki, who after all was a great Zen master, used to teach right down the hall, here at Columbia. I thought that Suzuki's seminars were a little like Kojève's seminars on the 'existentialist' Hegel in Paris. Everybody came to hear Dr. Suzuki, and I think Zen ideas penetrated very deeply into New York consciousness at the time. I got very involved in thinking about the East.[24]

In their different ways, both Sakai and the Western critics of modern Zen philosophy have sought to shatter this idyllic picture of high cultural exchange between East and West. Once again, the key move was to enforce a political reading of the Suzuki era at Columbia in place of the philosophic reading offered by Danto. The political motive that counted in this context was Japan's urgent diplomatic need to re-establish its cultural and political legitimacy during the 1950s, particularly with the end of the American occupation in 1952.

Suzuki found himself in a position not only to influence scholarly opinion at Columbia, one of the most prestigious American universities at the time as well as a major centre of Japan studies, but also to cast his spell over what George Steiner has rightly called the global 'nerve-centre of mid-century we call Manhattan'.[25] The target was well chosen. During the 1950s, New York City emerged as one of the forcing houses of the Western assimilation of Japanese aesthetics and the promotion of the middlebrow taste for Zen spirituality.

To this must be added the crucial fact that New York City was also the home of the new United Nations. If we assume that Suzuki had a political as well as a cultural mission, the two tasks would have reinforced each other because the New York intellectual and arts scene exerted a subtle but sustained influence on this cockpit of international diplomacy. Sakai's sinister gloss on the unholy alliance between American occupation policy in Japan and the Kyoto School tempts one to see Suzuki's seminars as a cynical act of cultural propaganda.

Anti-Zen revisionism suggests that Suzuki sought to exploit the richness of Japanese cultural tradition, or, more precisely, the American vulnerability to the aura of this tradition, to aid Japan's anxious drive to gain readmission into the international community, an effort which also helped, willy-nilly, to rehabilitate the former and still unrepentant ally of the Third Reich. Viewed as a conspiracy, the true intention behind Suzuki's seminars at Columbia was to propagandise the main taste-masters and trendsetters of American intellectual life. If Danto's confession is anything to go by, Suzuki succeeded brilliantly.

The crucial stroke was to persuade Manhattan's cultural elite, including thinkers such as Danto, to accept Suzuki as 'a great Zen master'. Robert S. Sharf warns that

> in the popular imagination a [Zen] master typically manifests his libera-
> tion in spontaneous and often antinomian behaviour, accompanied by
> sudden shouts and inscrutable utterances. Nevertheless, we must be
> careful not to confuse pious mythology with institutional reality.[26]

Sharf has sought to demolish this pious American myth by demon-
strating that Suzuki's mystical image of Zen was an invented tradition,
indeed a largely twentieth-century fabrication, with only tenuous intellectual
relations with Zen religious orthodoxy and no institutional ties of any
significance with the apparently moribund centres of traditional Zen
monastic practice, in Kyoto or elsewhere. In short, 'the world-transcending
tradition of Japanese Zen ... is not the historical fact that Suzuki and others
have claimed, but a distinctively contemporary construct read back into
history' to lend a fake patina of legitimacy to Suzuki's teachings.[27]

Was Suzuki engaged in a kind of cultural conspiracy on the New York
intellectual scene, or merely making an early attempt to influence the mind
of an emerging global hegemon? Suzuki's success in 're-branding' Zen in the
face of the growing American dominance of global culture might be one of
those rare victories of cultural resistance by the non-American world. How
does one suppose the ancient Greeks persuaded the Romans to feel that they
should learn Greek? Perhaps Suzuki's Manhattan offensive should be understood as a more or less desperate effort by a marginalised power to influence
perceptions of Japan in the post-war world's new cultural capital. The
suggestion would be that the fact of American empire has the potential to
alter the entire horizon of our interpretation of the cultural life of the planet
since 1945.

After Auschwitz, philosophy

The progressive-liberal bias that animates the political stance of many
Western students of Japan is not only understandable but also commendable.
But to the degree that left-of-centre intellectuals turn a blind eye to the fact
and threat of American empire, this bias not only distorts our understanding
of the past but also conspires against resisting the impulses that drive the US
crusade to dominate all aspects of global life today. After '9/11', it should be
obvious that the liberal urge to dismiss the ethical importance of Japanese
modernisation is to ignore one extraordinary double truth. First, Japan has
offered more effective resistance to American hegemonic globalisation than
any other non-White society. Secondly, the frequently derided 'Japanese
miracle' has generated the indispensable empirical grounds for challenging
the theoretical foundation upon which American economic dominance rests.
Ever acute in such matters, Marx would have been scathing about such intellectual obtuseness by his would-be left-wing heirs.

The new un-obscured character of American empire will accelerate the
revisionist forces that are rewriting the history of the Pacific War. The

growing problems with the empirical portrayal of the events of the Asia-Pacific War will now deepen into a paradigm crisis. The uncritical portrait of wartime China fostered by Hollywood and the official propagandist machine of both the Republic and the Communist forces in China will be gradually exposed to sceptical probing. Period books such as Malcolm Kennedy's *The Estrangement of Great Britain and Japan* raise questions about Chinese diplomatic and military responsibility for the outbreak and persistence of fighting, for example, in Manchuria in 1931.[28] Like the Albanians in Kosovo, it was in the interest of the Chinese government to provoke Japan into further aggression. How else were the Japanese to be ousted from the Asian mainland if China was too disunited to do the job itself? It was a desperate game, and the Republican regime had to play every card it had.

The imperatives of the wartime alliance between China and the United States have left their stamp on the Allied understanding of the Pacific War. This stamp reflects the myths and propaganda of the Allies' energetic and very successful struggle to win hearts and minds. But the facts eventually dissolve the myths, however comforting. Today, it is not the Japanese right-wing reactionary historian who is wreaking revisionist havoc, but the Western liberal scholar who has begun to examine hitherto neglected wartime archives. Examples of such revisionist empiricism include Frederic Wakeman's 'A Revisionist View of the Nanjing Decade: Confucian Fascism', Marjorie Dryburgh's *North China and Japanese Expansion, 1933–1937* and Rana Ritter's *The Manchurian Myth*. All three historians quietly call into doubt the moral simplicities of Chinese wartime propaganda.[29]

A parallel revisionist offensive has also been unfolding in connection with the character of the government of wartime Japan. Thus, if Peter Wetzler and Herbert Bix have played devil's advocate concerning the late Emperor Hirohito's wartime conduct, Lesley Connors and J.W. Dower have located liberals at the very heart of the Showa regime.[30] In this connection, the revisionary research of Ben-Ami Shillony on Japanese society during the Asia-Pacific War is significant.[31] He offers an important warning against ideological simplifications in his resolute refusal to label Hideki Tojo as a 'dictator' or to employ the term 'fascist' in describing his government.[32] This reflects a broad paradigm shift in the Western understanding of the Pacific War. It is now all but unstoppable.

Such paradigmatic revolution poses a serious challenge to our understanding of modern Japanese philosophy. The research presented by Japanese scholars in *Rude Awakenings* fuels the suspicion that the orthodox interpretation of the Second World War by Western historians, on the left as well as the right, is also highly vulnerable on factual as well as ideological grounds. After more than half a century of liberal orthodoxy, perhaps it is time to learn to see the Second World War not as a single global struggle but as two wars fought at the same time. The battle against Nazism may have to be distinguished from the war between America and Japan for control of the

Pacific and the spoils of Europe's colonial imperium in Southeast Asia. How else is one to explain the fact that America's post-war hegemony in the Pacific was built (as was intended) on the ruins of not one empire but two: the European and the Japanese.

Back to the facts

Japanese war revisionism has long pursued a strategy of defensive micro-empirical revisionism (hereafter termed 'micro-revisionism'). Thus, Allied orthodoxy is not confronted (indeed, it is sometimes even endorsed) but rather the particular facts concerning individual Japanese thinkers are examined in close detail in order to demonstrate that, for example, Nishida or Suzuki or Tanabe were not fascists or chauvinists but apolitical thinkers with disinterested religious agendas. Sakai, for example, has written a micro-revisionist defence of Tanabe.[33]

Efforts to undermine the moral credibility of the Allied interpretation of the Asia-Pacific War are so common in Japan that they provoke no fury, but rendered into English, such research acquires an explosive charge because it challenges the sacred assumption that the Second World War was a wholly right-minded crusade against fascism. The new Western attack on Japanese philosophy will certainly crumble to the degree that it can be shown that the hostile portrait of the Kyoto School painted by intellectual historians since 1945 is empirically false.

The Japanese micro-revisionist undermines Allied orthodoxy not by arguing that Japan should have won the Asia-Pacific War, but rather by chipping away at anti-Kyoto School prejudice by showing that a liberal dimension of Tanabe's philosophical ideas has been, deliberately or otherwise, buried or denied. Such probing is extremely useful, but a much more rigorous critique is in fact necessary.

Nowhere are the failings of Pacific War orthodoxy more evident than in the neo-Marxist criticism of the wartime Kyoto School. The classic summary of the neo-Marxist perspective was set out by Harootunian and Tetsuo Najita in *The Cambridge History of Japan*, where the authors declare: 'In pre-war Japan, no group helped to defend the state more consistently and enthusiastically than did the philosophers of the Kyoto faction, and none came closer than they to defining the philosophic contours of Japanese fascism.'[34] This sweeping judgment is indefensible. It lacks serious grounding in the facts, in knowledge of the relevant texts and in the ethical issues of the case. Indeed, the broad-brush treatment of Kyoto School thought by the neo-Marxist tends to be fatally flawed. In Chapter 4, the reasons are set out for this uncompromising conclusion.

What empiricism is to the researcher, close reading is to the textualist. Nothing has bedevilled the Western reception of Japanese philosophy more than the refusal to read the Kyoto political philosophy *closely*. Peter Dale struck this iceberg when he concluded in *The Myth of Japanese Uniqueness* that Tanabe's philosophy was 'ultranationalistic' because of its supposed links with Kinji Imanishi's notion of a Lamarckian 'species society'.[35] For Imanishi, 'species' is about biology, but for Tanabe, the term 'species' refers to logic and has nothing to do with biology. Tanabe's 'theory of the species' is premised on a brusque and closely argued rejection of all biological genus-and-species theories of human nature and society. In fact, as will be shown in Chapter 7, Dale's ideological approach to Kyoto School philosophy is difficult to defend, on either factual or linguistic grounds.

The close reader of Kyoto School texts discovers that Tanabe's rejection of biological determinism – Lamarckian, Linnaean or Darwinian – is grounded in a rational Hegelian defence of human freedom and communal autonomy. Whatever pressures the nationalist *Zeitgeist* exerted on his social ontology, Tanabe was a philosopher caught in the web of reason. It was his answerability to the claims of reason, in the Graeco-European sense, that exposed him to attack from the thought police and extreme nationalists during what some Japanese call the Asia-Pacific War.

The example of Tanabe provides a sharp warning against the careless application of orthodox dogma to our understanding of the Kyoto School of philosophy *as philosophy*. In other words, to exploit the potential of the Kyoto School in order to do philosophy in the classic Graeco-European mode may require that we cease reading not only Tanabe but all the Kyoto School thinkers solely in the light of the orthodox view of the Second World War.

All this highlights the timely character of Pacific War revisionism. To see the Pacific War as a race war, for example, as John Dower has in *War without Mercy*, does not require that we bury our commitment to our hard-won liberal values but only that we bracket them temporarily.[36] At the same time, to 'internationalise' the concerns and reach of the Kyoto School is to give some margin of manoeuvre for Japanese thinkers seeking to devise a proper metaphysical framework for Japanese national identity in the face of the pressures of ultra-nationalism. This leads us naturally to what may be the most contentious issue of all: the politics of the Kyoto School.

Centre versus periphery

There are ample grounds for insisting that the contest of political ideas in twentieth-century Japan is better understood as a struggle not between left and right but between the political centre and its periphery, that is between practical realism and utopian idealism. In Japan, the ideological extremist, be he an anarchist or an ultra-nationalist, finds himself on the periphery, while pragmatic moderates fight with realpolitikers for control of the levels of power in the centre.

In this configuration, the radical periphery (including the ultra-nationalist) is, by definition, anti-bureaucratic and never 'pro-state' because the state and the central bureaucracy cannot be run on idealist principles. The conflicted relationship between centre and periphery mocks any facile attempt to understand Japanese 'fascism' using only the French Revolutionary categories of 'left' and 'right'. Thus, the centre-versus-periphery dynamic that animates so much of Japanese political reality should force us to ask ourselves exactly what we mean when we describe the Kyoto School as 'pro-state'. From the late *bakufu* until the present, the ultra-nationalist has repeatedly been an uncompromising opponent of the rational imperatives of state power. This is why oppositional politics in Japan so often sets the nationalist extremist against the nationalist bureaucrat. In the end, it set Takamori Saigō against the centralising programme of the Meiji state.

So where did Tanabe and Nishida stand in this contest of power and ideas? Were they pragmatists or idealists? Pro-state or anti-state? Emancipatory rationalists or instrumental rationalists? Moderate nationalists or utopian dreamers? Were they thinkers of the centre or did they stand on the periphery? Furthermore, what do our answers to these questions tell us about whether the Kyoto School is an expression of the *zaiya seishin* (oppositional spirit) that is supposed to inspire Kyoto's resistance to Tokyo's pretensions to intellectual hegemony? A review of the relevant evidence suggests that Tanabe and Nishida were both independent-minded intellectuals but also members of the Japanese establishment. They were moderate nationalists, critical of army policy, but still patriotic supporters of their nation at its moment of greatest danger. If the second generation of the Kyoto School tended to fall under Habermas's rubric of 'instrumental rationalists', Tanabe probably qualified as an 'emancipatory rationalist'. As for the tension between Tokyo and Kyoto intellectuals, Tanabe combined both outlooks: a forceful critic in his public statements and a political manoeuvrer behind the scenes.

Without a proper understanding of the politics of the Kyoto School, we will never understand its philosophy. Ryōsuke Ōhashi, the philosopher and Nishida expert, is correct to insist that the political context for interpreting the Kyoto School must not be allowed to occlude the privileges and imperatives of the philosophic context.[37] Heidegger may have shared Hitler's hatred of Soviet communism and American capitalism, but a genuine harvest of *Being and Time* is impossible if the brutal spectre of Nazism is evoked at every twist and turn of our engagement with what many of us regard as the boldest text in twentieth-century philosophy. These strictures apply as forcibly to Tanabe as they do to Heidegger (see Chapters 8 and 9).

After Auschwitz, the philosophic glories of Russell and Wittgenstein, Husserl and Derrida, Heidegger and Sartre dignify us as a species. *Pace* Adorno ('No poetry after Auschwitz'), they offer us a measure of recompense for the barbarism of our times. In ways that reach beyond the horrors of Belsen, Nanking and Hiroshima, these thinkers demonstrate the human capacity for disinterested greatness. In philosophy, the mind of humanity tenses itself to full strength in pursuit of the claims of the spirit, or what

Hegel called '*Geist*'. Here is to be found a kind of redemption for the thoughtful man and woman in the new millennium.

Post-Whiteness and the Kyoto School

The goal of this book is to make the case for adding philosophy to that list of vital and compelling disciplines that nourish and stimulate the larger project of Japan studies in Britain and beyond. To achieve this ambition, we must accept, without hesitation or apology, the challenge of taking the Kyoto School seriously as philosophy. This challenge includes testing the strength of Japanese thought against the formidable standards at work in German idealism and phenomenology or French existentialism and Marxism (the Anglo-American language and analytic schools are marginal to this enterprise).

Rigour – empirical, textual and ethical – must be our watchword. Any attempt to confine the labours of the Kyoto School to the ghetto of 'world philosophy' should be treated suspiciously until an uncompromising commitment to philosophic excellence is demonstrated by this all-too-politically correct endeavour. No quarter should be extended to any branch of world philosophy that assumes that non-Whites should be congratulated for their apparent incapacity to do real philosophy.

If Hegel were with us now, he would be the first to observe that all notions of post-modernity pivot on a definition of the modern. Tanabe and the second generation of the Kyoto School subscribed to the view that the modern world was the creation of post-Renaissance Europe: the agency of modernity. At the beginning of the Pacific War, it was a commonplace of Japanese intellectual discourse that the fall of France and the unification of continental Europe under Hitler's legions marked a reversal in the course of human affairs so radical, so ripe with significance, that only the Hegelian rubric of the 'end of history' could do it justice.

The defeat of France in 1940 and the eclipse of Europe in 1941 were first and foremost White calamities. This truth was more confidently grasped in Kyoto than in any rival centre of non-Western thought (although, strictly speaking, the Kyoto thinker did not put the argument in racial terms). For the first time since the Russo-Japanese War, an Asian opportunity for the racially subservient to win freedom and take their revenge sprang to life, thus confirming the worst racial fears of European thinkers terrified by the prospect of the decline of the West. Here one must begin if one is to make sense of the Kyoto School's defence of the attack on Pearl Harbour. These philosophers did not praise the military tactics. Their allies in the Japanese Imperial Navy quickly disabused the scholars of any notion that the strike against Hawaii was anything but a folly. It brought disaster on Japan. But the larger issue was East Asian autonomy and how this could be fostered in the face of Western domination and effectiveness. It was the significance of Pearl Harbour that focused the thinking of the Kyoto philosophers. Their sustained meditation on the Pacific War as a phase of *world history* made these Japanese thinkers among the earliest to dwell on the triumphs and perils of American empire.

At stake in this struggle between Japan and the English-speaking peoples was nothing less than the fate of White global hegemony. In this contest between White and non-White, the Kyoto philosopher would have been mindful of the defeat of the Native American and the Black struggles against White ascendancy in North America, of the failure of the Indian nation to modernise and of Negroes to build their own Black nation. But the Kyoto philosopher would have enthusiastically concurred with Du Bois that the future of the globe would be what non-Whites would make it and that Whiteness could only be shattered on the battlefield.

By the spring of 1942, Kyoto philosophers provocatively argued that it was to be in Asia, not Europe, where the next phase of history set in motion by the French Revolution, as Hegel elaborated in the *Phenomenology of Spirit*, was set to unfold. Anticipating the world-historical consequences of the fall of Singapore and the Dutch East Indies to Japanese arms, Kōyama was already warning in 1940 that 'the history of world history *was* European history'.[38]

The abrupt and total collapse of American, British, French and Dutch imperial power in Southeast Asia during the six months after Pearl Harbour gave instant credibility to Kōyama's notion of a new metaphysical paradigm that he called 'world history'. In Kōyama's pluralistic vision, a world history that recognised many histories could not be achieved without overcoming Whiteness. If Sartre argued that 'the native cures himself of colonial neurosis by thrusting out the settler by force of arms', Kōyama's premise was that only war could give birth to a multicultural world.[39]

Multiculturalism as we know it today may be inconceivable without the Japanese military victories over Europe and America in 1904–05 and 1941–42, as well as the Algerian Revolution and the Vietnam War. But Kōyama would have rejected the defeatism that multiculturalism has imbibed from Michel Foucault and other post-structuralists. Sceptical of anti-historical systems of thought, Kōyama celebrated history because he regarded it as the indispensable testing ground for the achievement of non-White subjectivity, the only remedy for White modernity. Sakai is one with Kōyama when he concludes that 'For the non-West, modernity means, above all, the state of being deprived of one's own subjectivity.'[40]

Yoshimi Takeuchi, one of Japan's most tireless thinkers on the nature, cause and cure of Asian inferiority to Europe, once painfully observed that 'history is not an empty form of time. It consists of an eternal instance at which one struggles to overcome difficulties in order thereby to be one's own self. Without this, the self would be lost; history would be lost.'[41] With such insights, we are almost there, at the hitherto hidden shore of what Sartre would have meant if he, rather than Heidegger, had coined the pregnant phrase 'planetary thinking'.

On the subject of overcoming Whiteness, the affinities and tensions between Tanabe and Kōyama are, at many points, as arresting as the prickly but always stimulating dialogue between Sartre and Frantz Fanon. Indeed, the Kyoto School's embrace of the philosophy of history under the influence of Tanabe during the 1930s and 1940s offers the most arresting non-White analogy to the interwar Hegelianism of Jean Hyppolite, Alexandre Kojève and Eric Weil. But the Japanese philosopher benefited from an even more powerful historical compulsion than French Hegelianism because Japanese modernisation has been a drive to achieve world-historical significance in two spheres that the White West could not ignore: high-tech total warfare and the competitive global marketplace.

For the wartime Kyoto philosopher, the principal questions were how should Japan modernise itself and what price would Japanese society have to pay to achieve this goal? The thematic comparisons between Gramsci's prison notebooks and the wartime writings of the Kyoto School are as suggestive as they are numerous. Indeed, if the nation were judged to be as good a candidate for history's prime agency as the proletariat, even Lukács' *History and Class Consciousness* could be fruitfully read against the writings of the Kyoto School between 1940 and 1945. What the Russian and Hungarian Revolutions were to Lukács, the Japanese victories in the Russo-Japanese War, the First World War and the initial phase of the Pacific War were to the Kyoto thinker: evidence that history could be made by men and women determined to do so.

In the end, however, modernisation has proven to be very difficult to achieve. East Asia's recent economic difficulties demonstrate the formidable staying power of the Euro-American-centred universe that we still live in. But the struggle is not over. Furthermore, philosophy has unique powers to illuminate the contours of what today appears to be an immense racial transition in human affairs: the arrival of a post-White world. If Japan studies are to play a full and fruitful role in this extraordinary global drama, we must find a place within our ranks for philosophy as philosophy.

4 Scholarship or propaganda
Neo-Marxism and the decay of Pacific War orthodoxy

God is in the details.

Mies van der Rohe[1]

Prejudices come as a natural food of tendencies which can get no sustenance out of that complex, fragmentary, doubt-provoking knowledge which we call truth.

George Eliot[2]

All orthodoxies decay. This is as true of scholarship as it is of politics and religion. No branch of knowledge – no theory, no body of fact – is immune to the almost organic eventualities of decline and fall. In the natural and social sciences, decaying orthodoxies give birth to paradigm revolutions. In painting and the humanities, the shock of the new delivers the creative deathblow.

Decay is now at work, like an acid, on the bone and marrow of the orthodox interpretation of the Pacific War. The fading of this attractive fable, this all-too-satisfying mixture of fact and myth, is rooted neither in a historical amnesia nor in a lapse in democratic conviction. Rather, this ageing orthodoxy is increasingly paralysed *scientifically* in the face of what Max Weber called 'inconvenient facts'.[3] A growing reluctance among historians to spend sufficient time among the primary sources has resulted in political posturing which has gradually replaced proper scholarly labour. Why sweat in an archive for months, even years, when all one has to do to be taken seriously as a scholar is to assume the correct political stance?

Decay has brought corruption. In Japan studies, the price of this corruption has been high: the will to innovate – and there can be no forward motion in history without innovation – seems to have given way to an irascible sterility. True, Pacific War orthodoxy is still served by a branch of the scholarly establishment. The wheels of this academic industry still turn: well-applauded lectures are delivered *urbi et orbi* while new books and articles flood off the presses. But, examining it more closely, one begins to suspect that the output of this academic machine increasingly consists of provocatively wrapped empty boxes.

Nowhere is the lack of substance more evident than in the assessment of the Kyoto School by the so-called progressive intellectual historians who serve under the 'neo-Marxist' banner.[4] On the reception of Kyoto philosophy in the West, the neo-Marxist has exerted a wide and deeply corrupting influence. The theoretical justification for the abandonment of conventional standards of empirical research and reasoned interpretations by the neo-Marxist is supposedly provided by French theorists such as Barthes, Foucault and Deleuze, but this is nothing but a complicated excuse for a certain obscurity of literary style.

Paris cannot be blamed because neo-Marxists are not intellectually at home in Paris. They lack the requisite command of the philosophical idiom and theoretical complexities of French thought after Sartre. They understand neither the decisive figures in the German pre-history of French structuralism – Friedrich Nietzsche, Wilhelm Dilthey, Edmund Husserl and Martin Heidegger – nor the successive waves of classic French innovation (including post-structuralism and deconstruction) that one associates with Claude Lévi-Strauss, Roland Barthes, Michel Foucault and Jacques Derrida.

If not Paris, perhaps the neo-Marxist is at home in Frankfurt. Unfortunately, there is little evidence that the neo-Marxist has mastered the basic theoretical tools of the Frankfurt School, let alone made peace with the Hegelian–Marxist *grund* that was as indispensable to Walter Benjamin as it was to the young Georg Lukács before him or Jürgen Habermas after him. Rigorously considered, neo-Marxism seems to be Marxism with the Marxism removed. Not at home in Paris, these people are not intellectually at home in Frankfurt either. Neo-Marxism confronts us with a disturbing example of intellectual failure, not in 'old Europe' but in the New World.

If the most influential statement of the neo-Marxist position among historians, as noted in Chapter 3, is 'Japanese Revolt Against the West: Political and Cultural Criticism in the Twentieth Century', the essay that Harry Harootunian wrote with Tetsuo Najita for *The Cambridge History of Japan*,[5] the most recent major statement of the neo-Marxist is contained in Harootunian's *Overcome by Modernity*.[6] This huge monograph, some 200,000 words in length, now stands as an obstacle to the factually persuasive and philosophically sound understanding of the wartime Kyoto School. This chapter offers a close examination of the textual methods and empirical sources of the neo-Marxist approach to the intellectual history of Imperial Japan.

The American armada

In Japan studies, the large monograph is our ruling genre. It constitutes what Henry James called our 'executive means'. When our field changes its mind on an issue of importance, more often than not it is under the pressure of a substantial volume on a single theme by a single author. The witty essay, the best-selling textbook and the provocative collection of scholarly articles are all valued in Japan studies, but if a scholar seeks to be an academic star, then a string of substantial monographs offers the royal road to stardom. Even this professional truth is somewhat misleading because each and every monograph in one's string faces the test of quality. This particular senior common room ambush is formulated thus: 'Yes, I know Professor Bloggs has published seven books. Pity that none of them is any good.' So the issue of quality cannot be avoided, but it remains equally true that, unless one produces a series of substantial monographs, one is not even in the running.

Judgments of quality demand standards of excellence. By what standards should the quality of a large academic monograph be judged? The short answer is impact. No big book has better embodied – as I have repeated often in print – the explosive potential of the long monograph during the past twenty years than Chalmers Johnson's *MITI and the Japanese Miracle*. Here, for once, is a monograph to which the word 'seminal' may be accurately applied. It set off the most fruitful 'war of the monographs' in the history of modern Japan studies.

This very rich hour of monographic greatness did not unfold in a vacuum. The Western scholarly assessment of the political-economic achievements of the Japanese nation after 1945 has been the most exciting collective intellectual adventure in Japan studies during the past sixty years. As a result, it is impossible to write about Japanese modernisation without addressing the facts and insights generated by this major discourse. Harootunian's failure to exploit this monographic literature is one of his most drastic mistakes. On this subject, hiding behind the skirts of the humanities will not do. It is not sensible to ask what modernity is and how it might be overcome without brooding on the monographs of Robert Angel, Robert Bellah, Kent Calder, Ronald Dore, James Fallows, David Friedman, Sheldon Garon, Andrew Gordon, Chalmers Johnson, William Lockwood, R.T. Murphy, Daniel Okimoto, William Ouchi, Hugh Patrick, T. Pempel, Frances Rosenbluth, Henry Rosovsky, Richard Samuels, Laura Tyson, Ezra Vogel and Robert Wade, to cite only some of the best-known participants in the great Japanese Miracle Debate, our very own *Methodenstreit*, that unfolded between the late 1950s and early 1990s.

As one who was actively involved in these controversies, I must confess that it was wonderful to unsettle the complacent proponents of Harvard Business School orthodoxy. Indeed, the *Wall Street Journal* still rails at those of us who proudly formed the Japanese Miracle School. Dick Samuels was riding this monographic wave when he visited Sheffield University during the mid-1990s. On that occasion, the electricity of genuine scholarly prestige was unmistakable.

Equally unmistakable is the fact that American-based scholars have made the monograph into an instrument of academic hegemony. Outside the sheltered glades of Orientalist textualism, Europe has, since Hitler, been comprehensively outgunned in almost every branch of social scientific and post-classical humanistic reflection on East Asia. At least, this is the

American conceit that is assumed by many of my countrymen but out of politeness voiced by few. The suggestion is that the flowering of American research since 1945 has resulted in an academic ascendancy over the field that has put paid, certainly in Japan studies, to the wounding impertinence of the nineteenth-century English wit who asked, 'Who reads an American book?' Thus, in scale, theme and reputation, Harootunian's tome would appear to have a natural and conspicuous place among the armada of US monographs that ensured that 'when a European reads a book on Japan today, it is more likely than not to be by an American'.[7]

Confronted by such claims, the ageing European mandarin comforts himself with the conviction that an intellectual culture incapable of producing a Marx, a Weber or a Keynes will never supplant Europe's centrality. The mandarin drily observes over his sherry that even now, many of the summits remain European. There is, for example, still no American masterwork to set against Joseph Needham's *Science and Civilisation in China*, perhaps the greatest achievement in Asian studies by anyone anywhere in the past century. It is not even obvious that any American scholar outside the humanities (the name Donald Keene comes to mind) has produced an *oeuvre* that matches the sustained pace and focus demonstrated over an entire career by Ron Dore. My Japanese cello teacher once conceded that Japan produced few musicians to match the best European players, but he did insist that in the middle range, Japan could boast a depth of talent that not even Germany or America could equal. Might this also be true of Japanology in the United States? Might the most ambitious projects in American scholarship on Japan demonstrate 'a characteristic near-greatness, a strength just below best'?[8] This suggestion returns us to the armada of large American monographs. Here, and here alone, the question of the hegemony of the United States over East Asian studies will be settled.

The issue is timely because some of the most recent additions to this American fleet have set sail only to be critically bombarded from this side of the Atlantic. Thus, Marius Jansen's *The Making of Modern Japan* has been mauled by R.T. Murphy in the pages of the *London Review of Books*.[9] Herbert Bix was grilled in 2002 at the annual meeting of the British Association of Japanese Studies (BAJS) over his rampant use of sources in *Hirohito and the Making of Modern Japan*.[10] In this battle of the monographs, one edited volume also deserves mention: *Tokugawa Political Writings*, edited by Tetsuo Najita.[11] In an extended review essay of this book in the pages of *Japan Forum*, the official organ of the BAJS, James McMullen all but destroyed Najita's reputation as a serious translator and interpreter of early modern Japanese political texts (and the classical Chinese canon that serves as their foundation).[12] Reading McMullen's assault should make Najita feel like the commander of the Spanish Armada when Drake attacked him in the English Channel. Najita's flawed labours demonstrate an unsettling truth about monographic reputations: once achieved, academic stardom may also be lost.

A close reading of *Overcome by Modernity*

It is through the smoke and debris of the Najita debacle that we row towards Harootunian's huge galleon of a text. The structure is daunting. It consists of an ample preface and six chapters, some of them more than 30,000 words long. The preface, titled 'All the Names of History' (the Nietzschean note is a manifesto and warning), is a forceful exposition of the neo-Marxist methods and ambitions that inform this work. The careful reader will need to peruse it. The main body consists of six chapters:

1   The Fantasy of Modern Life
2   Overcoming Modernity
3   Perceiving the Present
4   The Persistence of Cultural Memory
5   The Communal Body
6   History's Actuality

The summary of *Overcome by Modernity*, which appears at the end of his preface, is a fair example of Harootunian's style, and I make no apology for quoting it at length (my editing queries appear in italics in square brackets, [ ]):

> In chapter 1 I supply an account of the political-economic conditions accompanying Japan's accelerated modernisation during the interwar period. The purpose is to show the circumstances under which [*the*] Japanese began to figure and fantasize [*about*] modern life in the 1920s and 1930s, to talk and write about it more ubiquitously [*vicariously?*] than actually live it. Chapter 2 considers the future of the past, which is the subject of discourse and discussion, that is, it constitutes a form of future anteriority, inasmuch as I concentrate on analysing the famous (or infamous) Conference on Overcoming Modernity, held in July 1942, six months after the war with the United States began. The conference as we shall see was concerned with the experience of the last two decades and beyond and tried to assess the meaning of Japan's modernity in light of a war that many believed was an assault on the West. In chapter 3 I return to the site of modern life in the 1920s and early 1930s – the past of the future represented by the Conference on Modernity – and examine a number of thinkers who began to respond to the challenge of modern life by seeking to understand it and its promise for the future [*see below*]. While many of these writers and thinkers were progressives, they all shared a commitment to the primacy of the performative present. In chapters 4 and 5 I examine what I have called the discourse of the social, a kind of secondary discussion that responded to the challenges posed by modern life and those who promoted its promise for the future. [*Phrase copied and pasted from above?*] This discourse invariably turned toward an indefinite past to envisage a cultural and communitarian endowment that anchored Japanese iden-

tity [*verb or phrase missing?*] to constitute the sign of genuine authenticity and fixity in an environment of ceaseless temporal change. In chapter 6, which must, in part, be seen as a conclusion, I consider some of the texts of Miki Kiyoshi, who, as a consummate modernist thinker, sought often to bring together the various claims of modernity and its critics, to unify folk [*sic*] with a modernist culture devoted to making [*sic*] and technology, politics and culture. Miki often skirted [*flirted?*] with forms of fascist totalizing, even though he also sought to distance himself and Japan from an identity with it. Nevertheless, there is a good deal of folkic [*folkish? popular? nationalist?*] totalism in Miki's thinking, which in lesser hands or more determined thinkers like Takada Yasuma easily slipped into fascism.[13]

This excerpt is but a part of a still longer single, but apparently unedited, paragraph. This stylistic failure stems less from the idiom of Continental theory and post-structuralism than from an inability to control unwieldy masses of English prose. Far more damaging is criticism of the quality of Harootunian's research.

A senior academic, Harootunian is widely respected and influential. Nothing less than the most meticulous examination of his arguments and the manner in which they are presented will do justice to his reputation. He has often been criticised for his impenetrable prose style and his weakness for Franco-German jargon, but his students and admirers have been prepared to struggle with it in order to benefit from his scholarship. The effort has seemed worthwhile only so long as that scholarship has remained unchallenged.

This is a demanding book that appears to draw on a vast range of reading, from texts of the Continental tradition, from Marx to Althusser, as well as the outpourings of the Japanese intelligentsia during the twentieth century. *Overcome by Modernity* must be assessed as a piece of prose, as an exercise in historical research and as an example of theoretical reflection. The close reading developed below focuses on Harootunian's definition of modernity; his interpretation of Nietzsche (in connection with the writer Chogyū Takayama); his analysis of the two most important wartime symposia, 'Overcoming Modernity' and the previously mentioned *Chūō Kōron* symposia, or round-table discussions, of 1941–42 known as 'The Standpoint of World History and Japan'; and, finally, his use of the notion of 'Japanese fascism' as an interpretative conceit.

Beginnings in madness

The opening sentence of *Overcome by Modernity* demonstrates a sad disregard for the rules for treating texts as historical documents. The first line of the preface reads as follows: 'Whatever else Friedrich Nietzsche might have meant when he declared, eponymously, "I am all the names of history"

(Letter to Jacob Burckhardt, Turin 1889), it is conceivable that despite the different historical routes taken, all, invariably, have arrived at modernity' [ix].[14] For anyone familiar with Nietzsche's life and work, Harootunian's citation of this quotation is perplexing. Even more surprising is how he interprets it. But before the issue of interpretation can be addressed, there is the problem of where the author found the quotation. Harootunian's notes tell us that it comes from the English translation of Gianni Vattimo's *La fine della modernità*.[15] It takes nothing away from Vattimo's status as one of Italy's leading contemporary philosophers to point out that in this context, his text counts as a secondary source; Nietzsche's letter to Burckhardt is the primary reference. But Harootunian is offering us the English translation of an Italian translation of a nineteenth-century German text.

The problem is that the author uses secondary literature as a quarry for quotations from what should be primary sources. The only way one can know whether Harootunian's quotation from Nietzsche is accurate is to go back to the original German for which no proper reference is supplied. This is what I call Harootunian's 'Burckhardt problem', and it occurs all too frequently in *Overcome by Modernity*.

This brings us back to the question of how Harootunian interprets Nietzsche's remark. When one of the finest and deepest German thinkers after Hegel declared himself to be 'all the names of history', he was mad. In other words, this mystical declaration may literally mean nothing at all because it was the product of a brilliant mind all but destroyed, probably by syphilis or an inherited schizo-affective disorder. It was written in January 1889, the month of the famous incident in Turino, 'on 3 January or thereabouts', when a weeping, semi-conscious Nietzsche threw his arms around 'a mistreated nag in the street'.[16] Vattimo acknowledges the fact of Nietzsche's insanity; *Overcome by Modernity* contains no information about the German philosopher's medical condition.

Now, there is a school of interpretation that is willing to suggest tentatively that 'Although this statement [Nietzsche's remark about 'all the names'] is made in the context of his mental collapse, from which he would never recover, it may be considered a coherent expression of the position in regard to history that he had been developing since *Human All Too Human*' (Vattimo).[17] Coming in 1878, this text marks, for Vattimo, a key chapter in the break of European consciousness with historicism, thus preparing the ground for the structuralist revolution (particularly its post-structuralist and deconstructive variants). The fundamental flaw in Harootunian's approach to the study of intellectual history as a whole can be traced to his refusal to accept the theoretical consequences of the rupture in Nietzschean thought that unfolded between 1874 and 1882, that is between the second of his *Unzeitgemässe Betrachtungen* ('On the Uses and Disadvantages of History for Life') and *Die Fröhliche Wissenschaft* (*The Gay Science*).

Harootunian claims that Chogyū Takayama, in his essay 'Biteki no Seikatsu Ronzu' (August 1901), exploited Nietzsche's criticism of historicism in order to attack the modernising impulses of Meiji Japan [37–38]. This sounds suggestive, but it is wrong, about both Nietzsche and Chogyū (Takayama is known in Japanese as Chogyū). Indeed, Nietzsche is not mentioned in Chogyū's 'Biteki no Seikatsu Ronzu'. His discussion of 'a few texts by Nietzsche' is found in his January 1901 essay titled 'Bunmei Hihyōka toshite no Bungakusha'.[18] As for 'Biteki no Seikatsu Ronzu', it may occasionally sound Nietzschean, but the line of argument developed there has more in common with D.H. Lawrence, or Bertrand Russell when he was being a journalist. Nothing is less Nietzschean than Chogyū's enthusiasm for recreational sex or his 'implicit denigration of self-control' (Graham Parkes). Both Chogyū and Nietzsche talk about instinct (*honnō*), but there is something much darker and more powerful at work in Nietzsche's meditation on this subject than mere sexual appetite.

Harootunian seems to believe that Chogyū exemplifies the Japanese embrace of the Nietzschean call for overcoming the past, as in the expression 'overcoming modernity'. Although he does not provide proper footnotes in this section for any texts by Nietzsche or Chogyū, Harootunian does have Chogyū speaking about '*chōjin*' (the over- or superman) and '*gendai no chōkoku*' (overcoming the present), which, according to Harootunian, 'undoubtedly carried with it these Nietzschean meanings' [38]. But on the same page, Harootunian quotes Vattimo's observation that 'Nietzsche never used the term for "overcoming" (*Verwindung*)'. This comment and the context Harootunian puts it in suggest that he has not grasped Vattimo's point and therefore misunderstands what Nietzsche is about as a thinker. Nietzsche did speak of overcoming, but he used the word '*Überwindung*' instead of '*Verwindung*', as in the famous passage in *Also sprach Zarathustra* (1883):

> *Ich lehre euch den Übermenschen. Der Mensch ist Etwas, das überwunden werden soll.*

> I teach you the overman. Man is something that shall be overcome.
> (trans. W. Kaufman)

The distinction between '*Überwindung*' and '*Verwindung*' is pivotal. Vattimo explains why:

> *Verwindung* indicates something analogous to *Überwindung*, or overcoming, but is distinctly different from the latter both because it has none of the characteristics of a dialectical *Aufhebung* and because it contains no sense of a 'leaving behind' of the past that no longer has anything to say to us.[19]

Vattimo, one of Italy's most influential interpreters of Nietzsche, is insisting that the German philosopher meant '*Verwindung*' rather than '*Überwindung*' because he was neither a modernist nor a historicist. *Pace* Harootunian, Nietzsche did not believe in historicist 'overcomings'. If this is what Chogyū imagines Nietzsche means, he is mistaken. Therefore, Nietzsche's famous remark about 'all the names of history' does not reinforce Harootunian's gloss; it subverts it. Nietzsche is debunking modernity as a historicist myth, not affirming its singular character.

But even if Nietzsche did mean what Harootunian says he did, the singular character (*ichigenteki rekishi*) of modernity is so contested in contemporary theory that one cannot just declare this to be true as if by fiat and remain a credible participant in this discourse. Indeed, one of the most important questions in every branch of area studies is captured in the phrase 'divergent modernities', as in the title of Julio Ramos's classic *Desencuentros de la modernidad en América Latina*.[20] This has, for example, been the decisive rubric not only in Latin American studies but arguably in every branch of area studies during the past century.

The Japanese argument over the plural nature of modernity, or history, or progress fitfully divides the Japan Romantic School from the second generation of the Kyoto School. The former conventionally assumed the monistic character of progress, and therefore rebelled against history itself; Kyoto School thinkers such as Iwao Kōyama insisted that history had a plural nature *because Japan's modernising success had demonstrated the plural character of history* (the intellectual leap was to imagine, as in the translation of '*gendai*' by Naoki Sakai, 'a time after the modern').[21] This is the central intellectual insight of the Kyoto School on this subject. Here is where Japanese philosophy comes within shouting distance of the Western discourse on the Japanese Miracle set in motion by Lockwood, Vogel and Johnson.

A controversial but tantalising concurrence of opinion and insight links *MITI and the Japanese Miracle* with the writings of the Kyoto School historian Shigetaka Suzuki, notably *The Rise of Europe* (1947) and *The Industrial Revolution* (1950), while calling attention to the comparison between Suzuki and Hisao Ōtsuka's influential research on the foundations of economic modernity and *kokumin keizai* (national economics).[22] The sheer power and potential of this 'horizon event' could have formidably enriched the 'metanarrative apparatus' (Lyotard) that is *Overcome by Modernity* if the author had been less hostile towards social science, Western and Japanese.

Harootunian assumes that modernity is an irresistible force that roars down a single path to which all societies must, willy-nilly, conform. In making this assumption, he is an uncompromising Marxist, that is an unreconstructed Eurocentrist. He thinks that Westerners invented the modern world and that is the end of the matter. It was inevitable, therefore, that Japan would be overwhelmed by Western modernity. Harootunian has closed his mind to any other possibility.

Hardly any of the Japanese thinkers discussed in *Overcome by Modernity* agree with this assumption. Some believe that modernity can be deflected or outwitted or perhaps even stopped. Others hold that alternative modernities are possible. The wartime Kyoto School, for example, was convinced that a Japanese form of modernity – one consistent with many Japanese values and most of its ambitions – was achievable. Guided by this conviction, the Kyoto School metaphysically anticipated the post-war triumph of the Japanese economic miracle. Between 1952 and 1992, a specifically Japanese form of modernity was achieved in defiance of Anglo-American economic logic and business practice. Japan did modernise, but it was not overcome by Western modernity. In this sense, the aspirations embodied in the wartime slogans of 'Overcoming Modernity' and 'The Standpoint of World History and Japan' were fulfilled after 1945.

Fascism is the Achilles heel of the neo-Marxist ideologue. Harootunian and his followers see fascists under every futon. This is their intellectual fetish and theoretical blind spot. They seek to attach the fascist label to as many Japanese thinkers as possible. Although Harootunian cites the important and growing literature on why the concept of fascism is all but meaningless in Japan studies, he skates around these contrary arguments without addressing them.

The student of Japanese history deserves a proper explanation of whom Harootunian regards as a fascist and why. Take, for example, the case of Vattimo, who uncompromisingly defended Heidegger, despite the latter's brief involvement with the Nazi regime in 1933–34. If Vattimo were Japanese, Harootunian would denounce him as a fascist. Victor Farías, whose *Heidegger et le nazisme* helped to spark the global controversy over Heidegger in the late 1980s, has gone so far as to condemn Vattimo as an Italian reactionary.[23] Harootunian's ideological inconsistency on the subject of Vattimo's politics is confusing.

Failures of research

Given the title of Harootunian's book, it was perhaps inevitable that the famous 1942 symposium 'Kindai no Chōkoku' ('Overcoming Modernity') would figure prominently in his analysis. Furthermore, any serious assessment of the 'Overcoming Modernity' symposium tends to invite parallel concerns with the three almost equally famous Kyoto School round-table discussions or symposia, the proceedings of which were published in *Chūō Kōron*, the monthly *sōgō-zassi*, under the titles 'The Standpoint of World History and Japan' (January 1942 issue), 'The Ethical and Historical Character of the East Asian Co-prosperity Sphere' (April 1942 issue) and 'The Philosophy of Total War/Resistance' (January 1943 issue).[24] An edited version of all three symposia was then published in book form, as noted in Chapter 3, by Chūō Kōron-sha under the collective title *The Standpoint of World History and Japan* in April 1943.

These four *zadankai* (round-table discussions) are, by general consent, the most important public debates of the significance for Japan of the transformation of a European war into a global conflict in 1941. To help the reader understand the chronological and thematic questions at issue here, a schema of dates may be of use:

Chūō Kōron symposia (Kyoto)	Overcoming Modernity Symposium (Tokyo)
First Symposium 26 November 1941	
Theme: The Standpoint of World History and Japan	
Second Symposium 4 March 1942	
Theme: The Ethical and Historical Character of the East Asian Co-prosperity Sphere	
	23–24 July 1942
Third Symposium 24 November 1942	
Theme: The Philosophy of Total War/Resistance	

Some of Harootunian's criticism of these symposia is interesting, but he undermines his speculations about the 'Overcoming Modernity' symposium and the *Chūō Kōron* symposia by a mixture of imprecision and inaccuracy. As long as one understands that not all students are *deshi* and that Nishida retired from his chair at Kyoto University in 1927/28, one might say that the ideas behind the *Chūō Kōron* symposia were 'proposed by Nishida Kitarō's students Kōsaka Masaaki, Kōyama Iwao, Nishitani Keiji and Miki Kiyoshi' [42], but the sentence is ambiguous because Miki was not among the participants in the *Chūō Kōron* symposia. There were four speakers. They all belonged to the Kyoto School. But the fourth man was the historian Suzuki Shigetaka, not Miki.

Harootunian goes on to claim that 'This group organized its own symposium early in the war (July 1942) called "The World Historical Position and Japan" which was devoted to discussing the world historical meaning of the war and Japan's unique role in it' [42–43]. This summary statement is a tissue of confusion. First, as our chronological table shows, there were three symposia, not one, and the first symposium took place in November 1941. Second, there was only one symposium that took as its specific theme 'The Standpoint of World History and Japan', but this symposium was held just *before* the beginning of the Pacific War.[25] This means that Harootunian's assertion that the symposium addressed 'the historical meaning of the war' [43] is inaccurate because the war had not started yet. Third, it is obvious that Harootunian has confused the *Chūō Kōron* symposia with the

'Overcoming Modernity' symposium, the only one of the four symposia that was held in July 1942. Fourth, his translation of 'Sekai-shi-teki Tachiba to Nippon' as 'The World Historical Position and Japan' is a literal rendering but misses the precise nuance of the Japanese. The Kyoto School thinkers involved in the *Chūō Kōron* symposia were deeply influenced by Hegel. They were judging Japan's place in history from what they regarded as the most stringent standard of practical, real-world success: the standpoint of world history. The overall title of the *Chūō Kōron* symposia might be better translated as 'Japan from the Standpoint of World History', but either way, '*tachiba*' means 'standpoint', not 'position'.

These confusions lead to further errors. Harootunian goes on to assert that 'The discourse of "The World Historical Position and Japan" departed from the earlier symposium'; but there was no 'earlier symposium'. 'The Standpoint of World History and Japan' was the first. He cannot be referring to the 'Overcoming Modernity' symposium held in Tokyo because this did not take place until July 1942. These are not isolated mistakes. They reflect a pattern of error that can be traced to Harootunian's failure to do the necessary depth of research in the primary sources. One is left with the suspicion that he makes sweeping judgments about the character of the *Chūō Kōron* symposia without having read the texts in question, either the versions as they appeared in the pages of *Chūō Kōron* or the later book.

This neglect of the primary texts is troubling enough, but Harootunian is not careful with his citations of primary texts quoted from the secondary literature. Nor does he seem to know that there are three versions of the *Chūō Kōron* symposia: (1) the original dictation taken at the symposia; (2) the edited version that appeared in the monthly *Chūō Kōron*; and (3) the final version that appeared in book form from Chūō Kōron-sha in the spring of 1943. Thus, in the middle of his treatment of the *Chūō Kōron* symposia, Harootunian quotes Kōyama from the year 1943. But he fails to inform us that his quotation from Kōyama comes from the 1943 publication in book form of the 'edited' (read 'censored') transcript of the symposia.[26]

The reader needs to be alerted to the reality of wartime censorship (self-censorship as well as official). Furthermore, a comprehensive analysis of how the three versions of the *Chūō Kōron* symposia differ has yet to be carried out in any language. The censorship issue aside, the authors and editors had opportunities to alter the texts at each stage of the publication process. There were pressures from all directions. The 1943 book *The Standpoint of World History and Japan* was a wartime best-seller in Japan. The Army censors were so irritated by its success that they had further printings of the book banned. The incident contributed to the eventual closing down of Chūō Kōron-sha as a publisher. Harootunian mentions none of this.

If one turns to the notes, the quotation from Kōyama noted above is said to appear on page 86 of 'Hiromatsu, *Kindai no Chōkoku*' [421]. But the correct title of Hiromatsu's book is *Kindai no Chōkoku-ron*.[27] To drop the '*ron*' is to invite confusing the text of the symposium, the primary source in question, known in Japanese as *Kindai no Chōkoku*, with a book *about* the symposium. The single character '*ron*' allows the Japanese writer to distinguish, for example, between 'The Bible' and a commentary on the Bible.

Even when Harootunian relies on the solid research of other scholars into the primary sources, avoidable complications arise, as with his choice of Hiromatsu. This late and very distinguished Marxist scholar was a careful textualist. His two-volume translation of key chapters from the original manuscript of *Die Deutsche Ideologie* by Marx and Engels is one of the triumphs of post-war Japanese Marxist scholarship.[28] I have had no occasion to doubt the accuracy of Hiromatsu's quotations from the *Chūō Kōron* and the 'Overcoming Modernity' symposia despite his rooted hostility to the ideological stance often on display in these *zadankai*.

The problem is that Hiromatsu's quotations from the 'Kindai no Chōkoku' symposium, to take the example at issue, are selective and brief. One loses any sense of the broader context or the way these Japanese thinkers and intellectuals developed their arguments, as it were, in their heads or on the page. Moreover, as noted above, Hiromatsu is very hostile to the position advocated in the 'Overcoming Modernity' and *Chūō Kōron* symposia. Accurate in themselves, Hiromatsu's quotations are removed from their original context only to reappear on one of his pages where he surrounds them with often fiercely negative commentary. If one comes to Hiromatsu's text in a jaundiced state of mind, as Harootunian clearly does, the temptation is to assume that the purely negative reading is the only sound interpretation.

Dealing with complex texts is difficult. But Harootunian seems prepared to go to extraordinary lengths to avoid the primary sources. Take his treatment of Shigetaka Suzuki, the Kyoto historian and member of the 'gang of four', who participated in both the 'Overcoming Modernity' and the *Chūō Kōron* symposia. Suzuki's observation that the struggle to overcome modernity required the overcoming of democracy in the sphere of politics, liberalism in the sphere of thought, and capitalism in the sphere of economics is probably the most notorious and most frequently cited remark from any of the *zadankai* discussed here. Harootunian quotes Suzuki to set in motion four pages of discursive free association on Suzuki's supposed 'mapping' of the challenge of overcoming modernity [38–41]. But when one examines the textual foundations for Harootunian's meditation on Suzuki, one discovers that he has evidently not read the text he cites.

For example, Harootunian quotes from the '<Kindai no Chōkoku> Oboegaki' that Suzuki presented in connection with his participation in the 'Overcoming Modernity' symposium (the documents that compose *Kindai no Chōkoku* consist of the transcripts of the *zadankai* themselves as well as position papers submitted by the participants). Suzuki's *Oboegaki* was published in the October 1942 edition of *Bungakkai* (*Literary World*) on pages 41–43. But he decided against having his paper published in the book version of *Kindai no Chōkoku* that appeared in 1943. This means that

Suzuki's essay does not appear in the 1979 *fukugenban* of the 1943 *tankōbon* that Harootunian claims to cite.[29] But the 1943 original is the only version that exists in print.[30]

There is no evidence that Harootunian has read Suzuki's original essay in the only version that was published. All he appears to have seen are Hiromatsu's brief quotations from the Suzuki essay in *Kindai no Chōkoku-ron*, and on this slender and incomplete textual evidence, he bases almost four pages of historical 'reflection'. Short of going back to the original text (for which Harootunian does not give the relevant citations), there is no way the reader can verify the soundness of Harootunian's interpretation. The suspicion must be that the reason that Harootunian does not cite this pivotal primary source is because he has never seen it.

Even stranger is the lack of evidence that Harootunian has read the primary sources he claims to have to found. Anyone who is familiar with the text of *Kindai no Chōkoku* knows that Suzuki repeated his remarks on over-coming capitalism etc., albeit in a different form, on the first day of the symposium. In the text, they can be found under the heading 'The Modern Meaning of the Renaissance'.[31] A close reading of this key chapter of *Overcome by Modernity* suggests that Harootunian claims to have read material he evidently has not located, while he has neglected to read the material he claims to have in hand. As for the text of *Kindai no Chōkoku* (*Overcoming Modernity*) itself, the implication is that Harootunian has borrowed the title and argument for his vast book from a Japanese text he has never read.

Finally, in this context, it is important to note that Harootunian is using the old 1980 edition of Hiromatsu's *Kindai no Chōkoku-ron*. This was super-seded by the 1989 edition, published by Kōdansha, which contained important revisions, most significantly the restoration of one chapter that had appeared in the magazine *Ryūdō* (where Hiromatsu's text was first published) but which had been excluded from the 1980 edition. Between the appearance of the 1980 and the 1989 editions of *Kindai no Chōkoku-ron*, Hiromatsu was persuaded by Kōjin Karatani, the literary critic and cultural impresario, to change his mind about the wartime Kyoto School and the 'Overcoming Modernity' symposium. Evidence of this softening of Hiromatsu's line may be found in the *zadankai* 'On Overcoming Modernity' orchestrated by Karatani and Akira Asada in February 1989.[32] This is one of the most stimulating and extended discussions of the Kyoto School and Great East Asian War in recent years, but Harootunian seems to have over-looked it.

In this *zadankai*, Karatani contends that Hiromatsu's own work should be understood as a contribution to Japan's continuing struggle to 'overcome modernity', and Hiromatsu does not disagree.[33] Even this tepid revisionism contradicts Harootunian's stance, which, as we have seen, is highly depen-dent on Hiromatsu's research and criticism. But the revisionist tendency in Hiromatsu's late thought continued to deepen. Indeed, shortly before his

death, he apparently called for an updated version of the Greater East Asian
Co-prosperity Sphere as a step towards regional unity.[34]

An obsession with fascism

Nothing has done more damage to Harootunian's reputation as a serious
historian than his intemperate and ill-judged condemnation of the research
of Horio Tsutomu, the author of an indispensable piece of scholarship titled
'The *Chūōkōron* Discussions, their Background and Meaning', which
appears in *Rude Awakenings* edited by James Heisig and John Maraldo.[35]
Harootunian dismisses Horio's painstaking research and liberating interpretations as 'a thinly disguised whitewash of this symposium, whose major
orientation was philosophic fascism' [421]. Once again, Harootunian's
obsession with fascism gets in the way of a proper examination or understanding of the facts. If he had read Horio's research with the attention it
deserves, he would have at least got the dates of the symposia right. All this
is enough to give fascism a good name.

Fascism is the conceptual fallacy that sinks this great galleon of a monograph. His cherished Marxists aside, Harootunian gives the unmistakable
impression that there is hardly a Japanese thinker who is not contaminated
by the disease of fascism. This is not a credible argument. *Overcome by
Modernity* is a monument to the intellectual disarray of neo-Marxism and
the growing decay of Pacific War orthodoxy as a serious scholarly enterprise.

Neo-Marxism is doomed unless it sets aside its obsession with fascism.
The case for doing just that has been made, implicitly, by a thinker whom
Harootunian both quotes and admires: Slavoj Žižek. In *Did Someone Say
Totalitarianism?*, this celebrated Slovene philosopher concludes:

> the notion of 'totalitarianism', far from being an effective theoretical
> concept, is a kind of *stopgap*; instead of enabling us to think, forcing us
> to acquire a new insight into the historical reality it describes, it relieves
> us of the duty to think, or even actively *prevents* us from thinking.[36]

The accusation that Žižek brings to bear against the concept of totalitarianism may be applied with equal force against the notion of Japanese
fascism. The neo-Marxist needs to free himself from what in German is
called a *Denkverbot*, a prohibition against thinking. Until he does, his work
will continue to be spoiled by one of the field's most reactionary and anti-
empirical shibboleths. More than any other intellectual failing,
Harootunian's idea of fascism – ill defined, misconstrued and misapplied –
has undermined and defaced what should have been another American
monographic triumph. Prejudice is no substitute for research.

5   Wartime Japan as it really was

The Kyoto School's struggle against Tojo (1941–44)

Indicative of the military government's attitude towards the Kyoto School is an incident that took place in 1945 and was reported in the newspapers. A certain Army officer named Kimura urged during a speech that, in preparation for the coming invasion of Japan by America, all American and British prisoners of war, all Koreans, and all Kyoto School philosophers should be put to the spear.

Tsutomu Horio[1]

On the evening of 7 December 1941, very shortly after the news of the Japanese attack on Pearl Harbour had reached the audience which had assembled to hear him speak in New York City's Cooper Union auditorium, the American philosopher John Dewey declared, 'I have nothing, had nothing, and have nothing now, to say directly about the war'.[2] Although the topic he proposed to address that winter evening was 'Lessons from the War in Philosophy', Dewey intended to speak about the 1914–18 conflict. On the global contest of arms that had now engulfed his own country, Dewey had, in his own estimation, nothing to say.

In Japan, the philosophic reaction to the possibility of war in the Pacific was very different. On 26 November 1941, two weeks before the air strike against Pearl Harbour, a small but influential group of Japanese thinkers met in Kyoto to elaborate a rational but patriotic understanding of the crisis in Imperial Japan's relations with the United States and the British Empire.[3] After the war began, 'the gang of four' of the second generation of the Kyoto School – Kōyama, Kōsaka, Nishitani and Suzuki – grappled with what they saw as the metaphysical significance of this epic struggle. Their ideas were informed by the hope that this new world conflict would prove to be the war which finally did end war, and thus succeed where Woodrow Wilson's 'War to end war' had failed. This dream of a world liberated from strife had not been achieved by the flawed post-Versailles debris of open covenants and the ineffectual debates of the League of Nations. Perhaps only a decisive global battle, a new titanic struggle, might finally abolish divisions between nations and empires, races and cultures, thus ushering in a new world order, a new age: what Hegel would have called 'the end of history', a turning point so momentous that it marked the death of one age and the beginning of another.

Pearl Harbour as the end of history

In the three *Chūō Kōron* symposia, these Japanese thinkers brooded on contemporary affairs as philosophers. They cast their arguments in metaphysical language, and their analysis of current events is constrained by the insights and disciplines of Western philosophical tradition. This Japanese debate was, on one level, a subtle commentary on German historicism and its governing assumption that many of the problems, both philosophical and political, most worth thinking about are deeply embedded in the matrix of time and therefore can be solved only in the temporal realm. The body of fact that mattered most in these deliberations was historical fact, and the branch of philosophy most alive in these Kyoto symposia was the philosophy of history. This explains why Suzuki's contribution to these discussions was so fruitful. He may have been a professional historian, but his deliberations on the defining trends of twentieth-century planetary life were so responsive to the powers of philosophy, so ripe with metaphysical need, that he too will be treated here as a serious philosopher.

As Hegelians, these philosophers were realists in their approach to the past. It was Hegel who had famously declared that history is 'the slaughter bench on which the happiness of peoples, the wisdom of states, and the virtues of individuals have been sacrificed'.[4] Given the horrors of history, these Kyoto thinkers tried to elaborate an enlightened vision to give humanity some meaning and moral recompense for the carnage of Imperial Japan's oceanic struggle. The result was a remarkable synthesis, a philosophy of history in shorthand, grounded in one of Hegel's most powerful and provocative ideas: all turning points in the drama of the human race must be judged before the court of world-historical significance.[5]

Guided by Hegel's philosophy of history, the wartime Kyoto School posed one incisive question: had the post-Meiji programme of modernisation transformed the Japanese nation into a world-historical people or not? Rejecting the reigning assumption of all Japanese ultra-nationalists and most moderate nationalists alike, these Kyoto philosophers insisted that the standard for assessing Japan's success as a political, economic and social system was to be found not in the history of the nation but in the history of the world. Remarkably free of ethnocentric bias, they accepted that Hegel's philosophy mattered more to this rigorous process of judgment than that of any Japanese thinker, including Nishida.[6]

The court of world history is unforgiving. It permits no comforting ambiguities, and the Kyoto philosopher sought none. Thus, if the Greater East Asian Co-prosperity Sphere was judged a failure, this was because its ethical character was flawed. To examine the ethical character of the Co-prosperity Sphere – one of the principal themes of the second *Chūō Kōron* symposium

– was to pose this potentially explosive question in an explicit manner, one almost guaranteed to embarrass the authorities. If Imperial Japan proved unable to sustain a campaign of total resistance (that is 'total war') to American power, it would be because Japan lacked sufficient national self-discipline and rational self-mastery, that is subjectivity. The implication is, once again, potentially damning.

Such unsparing questions, and the provocative manner in which they were answered, explain why these three symposia were regarded by the ultra-nationalists, in the government and without, as the stuff of treason. These writings were Imperial Japan's equivalent to the *samizdat* fables and the subversive philosophical probings with which dissident writers and thinkers discomfited the authorities in the Soviet Union and Eastern Europe before the fall of the Berlin Wall. But this was *samizdat* with a difference. The participants were establishment figures who supported the national ambition to replace Western domination over Southeast Asia and the Western Pacific with Japanese hegemony. They concurred with the broad strategy aims of the Greater East Asian Co-prosperity Sphere but they dissented forcefully from the military strategy and, even more sharply, from the brutal means by which this strategy was pursued by the Tojo government. Indeed, they disagreed so sharply with government policy that they conspired to bring Tojo down.

These *zadankai* simultaneously elaborated one of the most cogent defences of Japan's world-historical ambitions to regional hegemony while providing perhaps the most testing examples of criticism from within the Japanese academic establishment of the military policies of the Tojo regime. They advocated 'a third way': neither Anglo-American capitalism nor totalitarianism (be it fascism or a proletarian dictatorship). Having begun their dialogue before the outbreak of war with the theme 'The Standpoint of World History and Japan', the participants in these round-table discussions would meet to assess the meaning of this conflict twice more during the first twelve months of the Pacific War. On 4 March 1942, just after the Allied defeat in the Java Sea and five days before the unconditional surrender of the Dutch East Indies, these thinkers again plunged into controversy with another Hegelian provocation: 'The Ethical and Historical Character of the Greater East Asia Co-prosperity Sphere' ('Tōa Kyōeiken no Rinrisei to Rekishisei'). Then on 24 November 1942, when the war had turned decisively against Japan, they debated 'The Philosophy of Total Resistance' ('Sōryoku Sen no Tetsugaku'). At this critical hour in the twentieth century, no philosophic agenda mattered more to the destiny of the Pacific. The topics were momentous, the participants unignorable.

The Standpoint of World History and Japan

A verbatim record of these discussions was made at the time of the meetings. The transcripts of their debates were then edited and published, as noted in Chapter 4, first as magazine articles and then, after being re-edited, as a book. The texts of these three discussions are the central concern here. Indeed, no twentieth-century philosophic text, with the possible exception of Tanabe's *The Logic of the Species*, remains the object of more intense rumour and speculation than *The Standpoint of World History and Japan*.

In the West, *The Standpoint of World History and Japan* has been discussed by some of the best-known figures in Japanese studies: Kevin Doak, John Dower, Andrew Feenberg, James Heisig, Victor Koschmann, John Maraldo, Masao Miyoshi, Richard Mitchell, Naoki Sakai and Ben-Ami Shillony.[7] But, in the context of recent Western scholarship on wartime Japan, *The Standpoint of World History and Japan* qualifies as one of the most important *untranslated* documents generated by the Pacific War.

What is the text about?

The transcripts of the book version of the three symposia form a considerable mass, some 442 pages in total. Admittedly, this wartime text was printed in easy-to-read format – the book layout is about the size of the old Everyman Classic Library – with about a third of the number of words per page of a standard paperback text published today in Japanese. Nevertheless, it is obvious that the four participants had a great deal to say.

The editors divided the transcripts into sixty-one sections, and the authors added a preface. The table of contents of the three symposia published as a book in 1943 under the umbrella title *The Standpoint of World History and Japan* is as follows:

Preface

Part 1 – The Standpoint of World History and Japan

1 The Reason Why World History has Become a Problem (Today)
2 The Philosophy of World History and the Historiography of World History
3 The European Sense of Crisis and the Japanese Consciousness of World History
4 European Reflections on the Unity of Europe
5 The European Sense of Superiority
6 The Defining Features of European Civilisation
7 The Notion that Two Kinds of Modernity are at Work in Japan
8 The Idea of History in the East (*Tōyō*)
9 Criticising the Theory of Stages of Development
10 The Problem of Machine Civilisation
11 The Problem of Historicism
12 The Problem of our Awareness as Individuals
13 The European Renaissance and Modern (*kinsei*) History

14 Historicism and the Problems of Teaching Japanese History
15 Viewing National History from the Standpoint of World History
16 World History as a Method
17 Philosophy and Reality
18 World History and Mores/Morality (*moraru*)
19 Race, People, Nation (*shuzoku, minzoku, kokumin*)
20 The Problem of Urbanisation
21 Thoughts on America
22 Contemporary Japan and the World

Part 2 – The Ethical and Historical Character of the East Asian Co-prosperity Sphere

1 History and Ethics
2 The Philosophy of World History and the Study of World History
3 World History and its Method(s)
4 The Ethics of (Historical) Turning Points and the Self-awakening (*jikaku*) to World History
5 World-historical Peoples (*minzoku*) and Ethics
6 Japan and China
7 World History and Continental Regions
8 National (*minzoku*) Ethics and World Ethics
9 East Asia as a Region of Peoples (*minzoku*)
10 Western Ethics and Eastern Ethics
11 The Ethics of War and Ethical Wars
12 The Politics of Philosopher-kings
13 The Ethics of the Family (*ie*)
14 Politics and the Spirit of the 'Family'
15 Ethics as the Fundamental Problem of Co-prosperity Spheres
16 Reinventing Japan (*atarashii Nipponjin no keisei*)

Part 3 – The Philosophy of Total Resistance

1 Total Resistance (*sōryoku-sen*) in Historical Context
2 The Concept of 'Total Resistance' (*sōryoku-sen*)
3 Total Resistance (*sōryoku-sen*) and Absolute/Total War (*zettai sen*)
4 Total Resistance in Times of Peace and War
5 The Significance of Wars of Ideas (*shisō sen*)
6 Leadership and Persuasion in Wars of Ideas
7 America and Systems of Total Resistance
8 The Problem of Originality (*sōi*)
9 The Ideal Structure/Organisation for Total Resistance
10 Total Resistance and Creativity/Innovation
11 Co-prosperity Sphere(s) and Total Resistance
12 Co-prosperity Spheres and National (*minzoku*) Schools of Philosophy

13 The Ideas of the East in Historical Perspective
14 The Contradictions of Anglo-American Liberty
15 Co-prosperity Spheres and Justice as Concepts
16 The World-historical Foundations of the National Defence State
17 The Historical Necessity for Co-prosperity Spheres
18 Japan's Subjectivity and its Capacity for Leadership
19 The Historical Character of Subjectivity
20 The Problem of Military Power (*senryoku*)
21 Scholarship and Military Power
22 The Arts and Military Power
23 The Mobilisation (*shūchū*) of Military Power

In some Western assessments of *The Standpoint of World History and Japan*, the temptation has been to ignore the length, complexity and variety of subjects addressed in favour of all-too-brief, indeed blanket, summary. This approach has by and large failed because it has encouraged sweeping generalisations about the text by commentators who have not read it. The reverse strategy is now called for. Only the closest of readings can provide a confident understanding of what Kōyama, Kōsaka, Nishitani and Suzuki thought and said. My original plan for this chapter was to provide a précis of each of the sixty-one sections, but constraints on space conspire against taking this approach; only a proper translation of the entire text will do. But by reproducing the entire table of contents, the hope is that some idea of the scope and seriousness of these debates can be conveyed. It should be noted in passing that this is the first time to my knowledge that the complete table of contents has appeared in English.

Wartime Kyoto philosophy in context

The intellectual credentials of Kōsaka, Kōyama, Nishitani and Suzuki make it unwise to dismiss them as ultra-nationalist ideologues or wartime propagandists. On the contrary, these young philosophers were by the early 1940s assuming the status of the backbone of the rising second generation of the Kyoto School of philosophy. All four participants in the *Chūō Kōron* conferences taught at Kyoto Imperial University. Kōsaka was a professor of philosophy and the director of his university's Institute for the Humanities; Kōyama, an assistant professor in the philosophy department, where he lectured on the philosophy of history; Nishitani was an assistant professor in the department of philosophy specialising in religious thought; while Suzuki taught history at Kyoto University as an assistant professor of European medieval history, a post he took up in September 1942.

Today, Kōsaka and Kōyama, after decades of relative neglect, are being resurrected as key figures in what has been described above as 'the crucial middle phase of the classical Kyoto School philosophy'. Suzuki's stimulating and metaphysically acute approach to world history, so frequently on display in the pages of *The Standpoint of World History and Japan*, also merits a fresh appraisal. In the case of Nishitani, the challenge is different because he is regarded not only as the pre-eminent figure in the third or late phase of Kyoto School classicism but also, by some Western commentators, as one of the world's greatest philosophers of the last half of the twentieth century. However, the moralising fog of Pacific War orthodoxy has obscured the true meaning and intent of Nishitani's political phase as a philosophical thinker. His vast *Kongen-teki Shutaisei no Tetsugaku* (*The Philosophy of Fundamental Subjectivity*), together with his contribution to the symposium 'Overcoming Modernity' as well as his often incisive interventions in 'The Standpoint of World History and Japan', and, finally, the various wartime essays gathered in his collected works, read properly, all cry out for bold and revisionary interpretation.[8]

Behind the textual outpourings of these four thinkers between 1939 and 1944 stand the formidable labours of Tanabe. He was the prime mover in the decisive shift from metaphysical personalism to the philosophy of history that distinguishes the early and middle phases of classical Kyoto philosophy. The late work of Nishida himself should be understood as an almost inevitable response to the impact of Tanabe's momentous abandonment of Kant in favour of Hegel from the late 1920s onwards. As alluded to in Chapter 2, this broad Japanese turn to Hegel needs to be read against the parallel turn to Hegel in French thought that flowered in the aftermath of the Russian Revolution of 1917 and the First World War. The key figures on the French side include Jean Hyppolite, who later taught Hegelian philosophy to Foucault, Jean Wahl, author of the *Le malheur de la conscience*, one of the founding texts of the interwar Hegelian revival in France, and finally two exiles, Eric Weil and Alexandre Kojève. The latter's extraordinarily influential *Introduction à la Lecture de Hegel* transformed the French philosophical scene from the 1930s onwards.

What Kojève achieved as a left-wing Hegelian in recasting Hegel's *Phenomenology of Spirit* and its pivotal notion of '*post-histoire*', Tanabe accomplished as a right-wing Hegelian with his idea of 'the logic of the species' (*shu no ronri*). The role that Bergson and the Surrealists would play in this French turn to Hegel would be matched in Japan by what Tanabe made of Hegel. But it is the post-war dialogue between Jean-Paul Sartre and Frantz Fanon over the nature of Third World or post-White subjectivity that offers the most arresting comparison with the ambitious assessment of Imperial Japan's and East Asia's potential for transforming the history of the world proposed in the pages of *The Standpoint of World History and Japan*. While the Japanese discussion came first, it not only anticipates Algeria's success in overthrowing French rule but sets out a rubric for explaining the post-revolutionary failures of Algerian society. In essence, the Kyoto philosopher was less naïve about the trials facing non-White societies trying to modernise. On this issue, the Kyoto thinkers thought harder and deeper than Fanon or Sartre. *The Standpoint of World History and Japan* may be read as a realistic appraisal of the tragic breakdown of the post-colonial Third World, from North Korea to Pakistan, from Argentina to Zaire. It anticipates at numerous points the harsh assessment of the failures of the developing world elaborated so powerfully in the works of V.S. Naipaul.

Subjectivity (*shutaisei*) – what it is, how it is achieved and how it can be sustained by non-Westerners – forms *the central theme* of these symposia. The close reading of these texts permits no other conclusion: *The Standpoint of World History and Japan* was an exercise in subjectivist philosophy. But it was an act of political intervention, a veiled but still bold expression of public criticism of Tojo's risky and brutally irrational military policies. It was an attempt to call into question the fundamental assumptions of the Great East Asian War (the overarching Japanese term for the Sino-Japanese conflict and the Pacific War) as the Imperial Army was determined to wage it. This subjectivist critique was argued from a thinking nationalist position. The reaction of ultra-nationalist ideologues was ferocious. But, ironically, these extremists read the Kyoto School's metaphysical interpretation of modern Japanese history with more attention than most post-war critics of Kyoto philosophy, either Japanese or Western. As Ryōen Minamoto noted:

> Tadashi Saitō, Shō Saitō, Tsūji Satō, and other right-wing nationalist philosophers who advocated a 'philosophy of the imperial way' criticized the Kyoto School's view of history for its lack of historical will, for not having sacrificed itself to the historical process, for being content to do an analysis from the sidelines, and being a speculative philosophy that runs the danger of classifying the Empire as a particular historical archetype.[9]

The Kyoto philosopher was alarming precisely to the degree that he made the universal speak Japanese. Ultra-nationalists were appalled by any suggestion that Imperial Japanese society should be judged by universal (non-Japanese) standards. Like the American exceptionalist, the Japanese chauvinist believed that his country was in the world but not of it. The Kyoto philosopher rejected this distinction: Japan was both in and of the world. He rejected the self-serving myths of national history in favour of the rigour of world history as Hegel conceived it. This controversy repeated the main contours of the war of words fought out until the mid-1930s over the constitutional interpretations of Tatsukichi Minobe, author of the famous organ-theory of the emperor's place and role in the Meiji Constitution. The ultra-nationalist loathed Minobe and Tanabe because they demanded that all the institutions of Japanese society (and this included, up to a point, even the imperial throne) be subjected to rational analysis.

As one of the most influential critiques of the Tojo regime to appear during the Pacific War, *The Standpoint of World History and Japan* merits careful reading. It, together with the appearance of the hitherto unknown

Ōshima Memos (see below), provides documentary evidence of resistance, public and clandestine, to Tojo's policies from within the Japanese establishment. The severity of the ultra-nationalist reaction to Kyoto School opinion and the forceful steps taken by the Army censors to curb the impact of these writings permit no other conclusion. If we seek to grasp the realities of wartime Japan '*wie es eigentlich gewesen*', or 'as they really were' (Ranke), we might well begin our revisionism with the Kyoto School because these historic documents have the potential, as Ōhashi rightly insists, to transform our understanding of the Pacific War.[10]

The Kyoto School's battle with Tojo

Between 1939 and 1944, the second generation of the Kyoto School, standing on the shoulders of Hegel and Tanabe, buttressed Japan's claims to philosophic greatness.[11] In formulating what today may be understood as a philosophy of anti-White resistance, Tanabe and his fellow philosophers laid the foundations for a powerful Japanese critique of Western hegemony. For the wartime Kyoto School, politics involved not only reflection on the world but action in the world. These philosophers sought not only to understand the world but to change it.

This commitment to political *engagement* brought these thinkers into direct collision with the supporters of the Tojo regime over tactics and strategy. For the Kyoto philosopher, the struggle against Tojo to bring this conflict to a peaceful conclusion was unavoidable. In this battle on the home front, Yasumasa Ōshima – scholar, philosopher and establishment 'networker' – may qualify as one of the unsung heroes of the Japanese wartime resistance. His role in the story of the wartime activities of the Kyoto School was quietly reasserted in a relatively short essay he produced for the twentieth anniversary of the ending of the Pacific War which appeared in *Chūō Kōron* in August 1965. The essay was titled 'The Greater East Asian War and the Kyoto School: The Political Participation of the Intellectuals', and Ryōen Minamoto has described it as 'an extremely valuable resource on the activities of the Kyoto School during the war, written by someone on the inside'.[12]

Until the discovery of *The Ōshima Memos* by Ōhashi in 2000, Ōshima's place in the history of the Pacific War was judged to be confined wholly to the world of scholarship. A trusted intimate of the major figures in the wartime Kyoto School, he was later responsible for writing the *Kaisetsu*, or concluding commentary essay, for both volumes of the text of Tanabe's *The Logic of the Species* in the collected works. These authoritative *Kaisetsu*, which appeared in 1963, reflect Ōshima's detailed knowledge of the manuscripts of the thirteen essays that the editors of *The Complete Works of Hajime Tanabe* (*THZ*) judged to form *The Logic of the Species*. Two years later, in 1965, Ōshima published his essay in which he suggested that the Kyoto School had been actively involved in the politics of wartime resistance to Tojo. The issue came to the fore in his discussion of the impact of wartime censorship on the various versions of *The Standpoint of World History and Japan*. Quoting Ōshima's remark on the editorial necessity for veiling criticism of Tojo policies in 'two or three layers of cloth', Tsutomu Horio observes:

> What was actually published in the pages of *Chūō-Kōron* was not the full or accurate transcripts. Political conditions at the time left the publishers with the choice of either 'veiling statements in two or three layers of cloth' or facing suppression by the authorities (in particular, elements associated with the Army).[13]

Equipped only with this insight into the realities of the Kyoto School's fight with the Army censors, one reads the various versions of *The Standpoint of World History and Japan* with sharper eyes. The gap between the magazine version and the final book tends to be subtle. For example, when it observes that the Jews are being crushed as a people, the earlier text compares their fate to that of the Ainu, while the book drops this reference to a Japanese example of genocide and replaces it with a reference to the fate of the American Indian at the hands of White Americans. But read as the imposition of universal and rational, that is European, assumptions on the definition of Japanese national identity, the text bubbles over with controversy. The sections on Japan's intervention in China offer, and not merely between the lines, a damning critique of the strategy (and, implicitly, the tactics) of the Imperial Japanese Army and how such conduct betrayed the ideals of pan-Asianism.

The investigative labours of Ōhashi have now confirmed Ōshima's political role in the intellectual struggle against Tojo. *The Ōshima Memos* is a substantial collection of notes, lectures and official documents from a series of meetings between key figures of the Kyoto School and anti-Tojo Navy policy intellectuals between February 1942 and July 1945.[14] Ōhashi has produced a complete version of the available texts that compose *The Ōshima Memos*, as well as a substantial commentary on the texts and their political and philosophical context, in *Kyōtō-gakuha to Nippon Kaigun* (*The Kyoto School and the Japanese Navy*).[15]

These secret discussions lasted through most of the Pacific War. Officers of the Yonai 'peace' faction represented the Imperial Navy. The main spokesmen, including Captain Sōkichi Takagi of the Kaigun Chōsa-ka (Navy Research Section), worked in the Navy Ministry. They were joined by a varied group of intellectuals centred on Tanabe and the four participants in the three *Chūō Kōron* symposia. Motomori Kimura, Ichisada Miyazaki and Daijirō Hidaka also attended regularly. Invited guest speakers included Hideki Yukawa, who won the Nobel Prize for physics in 1949.

This is how Michiko Yusa describes the pre-Pacific War origins of these secret sessions:

Nishida had already been concerned about the escalation of the war in China when Navy Captain Sōkichi Takagi, who was in charge of a 'think tank' made up of able-minded men, approached him for a philosophical perspective that he might use to give direction to the Navy. For some time already the Army and Navy had been at loggerheads for control of Japanese military policy. Nishida complied, hoping that in some way his ideas might influence the course of events. The association between the Kyoto School and the Navy may be said to have begun with that meeting that Kumao Harada arranged on 18 February 1939 ... Nishida recommended Iwao Kōyama, a former student teaching at Kyoto University, as someone who might take part in the initiative of the Navy.[16]

The man assigned to arranging the meetings and inviting the participants as well as taking the notes of the meetings was Yasumasa Ōshima. This is how Ōhashi summarises the content of *The Ōshima Memos*:

The main themes discussed included the intellectual situation at home and abroad and the historical background to the war. The outlook for the future, the ideology of war and recommendations for changes in national policy were put forward. Among the latter, the most important was how the war could be brought to an end and eventually including discussion of how the Tojo Cabinet might be overthrown. As the end of the war approached, the debate shifted to how defeat would affect national consciousness.[17]

Ōhashi goes on to insist that *The Ōshima Memos* represents what he calls 'only the tip of an iceberg' of the documents that may yet come to light on elite opposition to the Tojo line.[18] In analysing the data available as well as speculating about what yet may be found, it is vital to understand the risk that opponents of the Tojo regime, such as the Kyoto School, took in criticising government policy. Takagi's diaries note the official warning issued as early as 1937 that 'the life of anyone who attempted to engage in peace negotiations [with the enemy] could not be guaranteed' by the authorities.[19] For the peace faction within the Navy to move to bring down the Tojo regime was, to use another phrase from the time, 'to stamp on the tail of a tiger'.[20]

The campaign of the ultra-right against the authors and publishers of *The Standpoint of World History and Japan* was relentless. Denunciations of Kōyama's *Philosophy of World History* as offensive to the *Kokutai* (national polity) by the rightist press set the tone for this vitriolic assault. Furthermore, police conduct suggested that the unquestioned eminence and elite connections of Tanabe and Nishida offered no shield from investigation or potential arrest for sedition. Chūō Kōron-sha, the publishers of *The Standpoint of World History and Japan*, were eventually shut down by the military authorities even after further publication of the symposia text was banned.[21] These threats were not imaginary, as the jail deaths of Kiyoshi Miki and Jun Tosaka demonstrated. Both of these most promising members of the pre-war Kyoto School second generation had been arrested for their involvement in left-wing causes. Ōhashi argues convincingly that if the contents of *The Ōshima Memos* had come to the attention of the authorities, Tanabe, Kōsaka, Kōyama, Nishitani and Suzuki might have suffered the fate of Miki and Tosaka.[22]

Such pressures must be kept in mind when reading *The Standpoint of World History and Japan* as well as *The Ōshima Memos* because examination of the texts discloses no overt criticism of Tojo by name, let alone any proposals for removing him and his allies from power. In the case of the *Chūō Kōron* symposia, Ōshima acknowledged in 1965 that 'All the rather extensive criticism of the Hideki Tojo was expurgated as well as all censure of the Army'.[23] Similarly, there is no explicit discussion of how to bring down Tojo in *The Ōshima Memos*, probably because of the way Ōshima himself edited the texts. Given the dangers of arrest, this was prudent. But how do we know that the Kyoto School philosophers and their naval allies advocated overthrowing Tojo?

Ōhashi insists that one has to read *The Ōshima Memos* alongside the diaries and other private writings (published after the war) of the participants in these secret conferences to understand the true intent behind these meetings. He is in no doubt that plans to bring down the Tojo Cabinet were discussed in detail by the participants in the secret Navy–Kyoto School talks.[24] In fact, Ōshima himself claims that the first *Chūō Kōron* symposium held on 24 November 1941, the one published as 'The Standpoint of World History and Japan' in January 1942, was intended as a direct appeal to the Japanese public over the heads of the Tojo regime, but that this initiative was overtaken by events, as by the time the first symposia appeared in print, the war had already come to the Pacific.[25]

Careful reading of the published texts as we have them provides proof of the radical nature of Kyoto School criticism of Army policies. At many points in *The Standpoint of World History and Japan*, the opinions set forth approach those voiced by other government critics such as Tadao Yanaihara, the colonial policy intellectual.[26] Excellent as his research is, Horio is overstating the case when he concludes that the elimination of direct attacks on Tojo from the texts of *The Standpoint of World History and Japan* leaves the impression of 'total support for the war effort among the Kyoto School thinkers'.[27] There is support for the war as an idea. The Kyoto School is prepared to support the use of force to resist globalisation and to break the West's colonial hegemony over Southeast Asia and the Western Pacific. They viewed Pearl Harbour as an inevitable event because one day Western hegemony of the Pacific had to be forced back. But their treatment of Tojo's policies in the Pacific and China is almost always sceptical if not hostile.

Tanabe and co-prosperity spheres

Given the gross misunderstandings and wilful misinterpretations that have been inflicted on the wartime Kyoto School, *The Standpoint of World History and Japan* and *The Ōshima Memos* offer reasonable and plausible grounds for rethinking our understanding of the Pacific War. At worst, the stance of Tanabe and his fellow philosophers can be characterised as '*hanteisei-teki na sensō kyōryoku*', or 'anti-establishment war cooperation' (Ōhashi). At the very best, the Kyoto School produced one of most important examples of public dissent from the policies of the Tojo regime to appear in print during the Pacific War. For the revisionist historian, this is the stuff of revolution.

The Kyoto School thinkers were philosophers, and it should surprise no one that *The Ōshima Memos* should have also contained a text of fundamental philosophical interest. The text in question is the lecture Tanabe gave to the ninth of these secret Navy–Kyoto School gatherings on 29 September 1942. Titled 'On the Logic of Co-prosperity Spheres' ('Kyōei-ken no Ronri ni Tsuite'), Tanabe's presentation is important on two counts.[28] First, this text undermines all of the unsubstantiated accusations of ultra-nationalism and fascism disseminated by the reactionary supporters of Pacific War orthodoxy. Secondly, and of more lasting interest, this lecture marks a significant break in the apparent silence of Tanabe *as a philosopher* between the appearance of *The Development of the Concept of Existence*, published between October and December 1941, and *The Logic of the Species as Dialectic*, which appeared in August 1946. Having come to light only in 2000, the text of this lecture does not appear in *THZ*, but this hitherto lost text is of intrinsic philosophic importance to appreciating the trajectory of Tanabe's thought. A translation of 'On the Logic of Co-prosperity Spheres', the first into English, appears in the Appendix of this book.

The lecture of 1942 is cast in abstract language and is metaphysical in its reasoning, but its message is clear. Freed from the shadow of official censorship, Tanabe has unleashed his sceptical powers, and the result is a bold but also dangerous expression of political candour. Like Caesar's Gaul, Tanabe's lecture is divided into three parts: the family, the state and co-prosperity spheres. A dialectical logic drives Tanabe's argument, and he exploits ideas he had previously developed elsewhere in a more detailed and academic manner. Tanabe spoke his mind, confident that the intellectuals and Navy officers in attendance were united in the conviction that Japan's wartime course had to be radically altered, and that this process of putting the nation back on course had to begin with hard, clear thinking about global realities.

Tanabe begins by challenging one of the shibboleths of traditional Japanese conservatism: the patriarchal family as a model for the organisation of the rest of society, be it corporate paternalism or emperor-centred politics. Rejecting this notion as fundamentally flawed because unempirical – families do not function this way in reality – Tanabe proposes a Hegelian definition of the family in which this basic unit of human existence is always viewed as a fragile unity beset with structural tensions arising from the fact that mothers and wives come from outside the male-centred family, while daughters join other families as wives to become mothers, thus perpetuating the dynamic tensions of the family structure.

Given Tanabe's notion of the conflicted family that must strive perpetually to maintain its cohesiveness, the conservative notion of the family, imperial or otherwise, cannot serve, by definition, as a model for the state organised in imitation of the 'simple' family because no family is 'simple'. Quite the contrary, the state not only reproduces all the tensions of the family but furthermore must work tirelessly to secure absolute sovereignty over a fixed piece of territory. To this conflicted concept of the state, Tanabe adds the insistence that the state can never achieve lasting stability. The moment the state acquires unity, the forces of disintegration set to work on its structure. Thus, the state is less an object of secure identity than a perpetual exercise in creative destruction.

Tanabe's anti-essentialism anticipates the later structuralist rejection of binary logic and its assumed stabilities. Tanabe and Derrida have no time for essentialism. As for recent Western criticism of his wartime philosophy, Tanabe goes on to assert in uncompromising terms that 'the state as a state cannot be defined simply as a species'. This statement confounds Tanabe's critics because almost all of them have assumed that the term 'species' in the expression 'the logic of the species' refers uniquely to the state, and to a fascist definition of the state at that.

In several digressions, Tanabe dips into the metaphysical horizon that underwrites his speculations on the family, state and the co-prosperity spheres. He focuses particularly on the classical metaphysical ideas of Plato and Aristotle, Kant and Hegel. Here also, in this 1942 lecture, the student of *The Logic of the Species* can locate the crucial 'missing link' between Tanabe's idea of the state as 'absolute incarnation' (*zettai no Ō-genteki sonzai*) and his apparent post-war downgrading of the state to the status of mere 'expedient means' (*hōben sonzai*).[29]

The word 'apparent' is important here because 'On the Logic of Co-prosperity Spheres' calls into doubt the suggestion that *zange*, or 'repentance' – 'metanoetics' is the technical term – governs Tanabe's thinking between 1942 and 1947. Rather, there seems to have been a see-saw struggle during this crucial five-year period between the reigning subjectivist thrust of *The Logic of the Species* and the temporary lapse into objectivism (*tariki*, or 'other power', is not a political scientific idea) that seems to dominate many important parts but not all of the monumental *Zangedō toshite Tetsugaku*, or *Philosophy as Metanoetics*.

Finally, it is Tanabe's understanding of co-prosperity spheres that qualifies as this lecture's most arresting dimension. From the outset, Tanabe insists that he is addressing general ideas, not factual singularities. He is brooding on how the idea of a co-prosperity sphere might work in any comparable historical conditions, not just the particular circumstances of the autumn of 1942. Because he takes as axiomatic the state's need for unchallenged sovereignty over its territory, he attempts to understand how this principle may be squared with the need for regional integration. From the standpoint of the contemporary politics of the European Union, Tanabe is attempting to struggle with what might be called the challenge of 'pooling sovereignty'.

Without such effective pooling, no politico-economic bloc can be fostered. The challenge is how to orchestrate a bloc among nations that vary in their relative powers and resources as well as their degrees of subjectivity. In response, Tanabe argues for limitations not only on national sovereignty in the name of East Asian regional integration but also on the exercise of Japanese power. This places 'On the Logic of Co-prosperity Spheres' firmly in the multicultural debate on the future of the Japanese empire which was one of the most important neglected discourses of the 1930s and early 1940s.[30]

In this lecture, Tanabe anticipates Benedict Anderson's recent argument that regionalism begins with hegemony.[31] Anderson insists that hegemonic powers are indispensable to a region's geographic coherence: only a hegemon can create a region. Tanabe would accept this point but would also contend that all hegemonic powers must take their responsibilities to non-hegemonic powers seriously. Blocs often have one pre-eminent power. Germany's place within the European Union is close to what Tanabe had in mind in the economic sphere. The realities of Japanese military superiority in East Asia suggest an analogy with that of the role of the United States in NATO.

In *The Standpoint of World History and Japan*, America's dominance within the Americas figures prominently in the minds of the participants. During most of the twentieth century, the United States may not have wanted to be responsible for governing Latin America but it did insist on the right to intervene at will to reorganise the region in ways consistent with Washington's calculation of the national self-interest. In policy terms, the Monroe Doctrine stands somewhere between the approach of Tojo and that of the Kyoto School.

In the case of the United States and Imperial Japan, neither hegemon was prepared to accept interference in regional affairs by outside powers. Both refused to tolerate military rivalry within the region and reserved the right to intervene at will in the affairs of any and all the lesser powers in the region. Taking these realities as a given, Tanabe pushes the argument towards the NATO or NAFTA model while recognising the need for more cooperative and egalitarian impulses as we see at work today in the European Union and the British Commonwealth.

Nevertheless, Tanabe insists on calling a spade a spade when deliberating on the inevitable imbalance of power between the hegemon and the other members of the co-prosperity sphere. Nations vary in their subjectivity; this is an objective truth. Tanabe has no time for what we would call today 'polit-ically correct' pretensions about equality between nations. Nevertheless, in the context of Japanese domestic politics in the autumn of 1942, Tanabe's speculations would have caused uproar if he had gone public with them because they boldly call into question the follies of the Tojo government's aggressive approach towards Japan's East Asian neighbours.

Tanabe insists that Japanese imperial policy, as it was being implemented in 1942, departs from the ideals of co-prosperity spheres. He also argues that any attempt to foster regional integration and unity will falter unless the ideals of genuine co-prosperity are scrupulously adhered to. Bludgeoning other nations and peoples into joining a bogus Greater East Asian Co-prosperity Sphere will never work. Unlike Tojo, Tanabe believes in Pan-Asianism. He has confidence in Japan's historic role as hegemon. But he insists that this world-historical moment will only flower if the Japanese state pursues this vision with reason and realism, intelligence and humanity.

In defence of the Kyoto School

6 Taking Kyoto philosophy
seriously

How to philosophise with a hammer.

Nietzsche

The Kyoto School has been defined as 'the philosophical movement centred at Kyoto University that assimilated Western philosophic and religious ideas and used them to reformulate religious and moral insights unique to the East Asian cultural tradition'.[1] What is missing from this definition is any recognition that the Kyoto School also produced a profound meditation on the nature of politics, history and society in a world dominated by the West. The previous five chapters have demonstrated that there is more to the project of the Kyoto School than the modernisation of Zen tradition. During the 1930s and 1940s, Kyoto thinkers created a philosophy of history worth comparing with the historicist ideas developed by any of Hegel's successors in Europe after 1831. This Japanese meditation on the provocation of post-Whiteness was driven by what Nietzsche called 'the will to render the world thinkable'.

The Kyoto School as political philosophy

Nishida set Japanese philosophy on the path to modern greatness. Brooding, imperious and brilliant, he moved from the University of Tokyo (Tōdai), where he had been marginalised as an undergraduate for his high-school involvement in anti-government protest, to Kyoto University in 1910. In what proved to be a decisive step, Nishida discovered another Tōdai-educated philosopher who exhibited a talent, at many points, equal to his own: Hajime Tanabe. Responding to a deep intellectual affinity, Nishida eventually invited Tanabe to join him in Kyoto, and secured a post for him in the philosophy department in 1919.

While one of the most influential alliances in modern Asian thought was taking shape in Kyoto, the seeds for the second generation of the Kyoto School were already being planted. Not long after Tanabe made his momentous move to Kyoto, a high-school student came, quite by chance, across a copy of Nishida's *Thinking and Experience* in a Tokyo bookstore. The student was Keiji Nishitani. Inspired to read everything Nishida had published, Nishitani would make his way to Kyoto to study under the master. Today, most students of Japanese religious philosophy regard Nishida, Tanabe and Nishitani as the three greatest Japanese philosophers of the twentieth century.

In addition to this talented trinity, D.T. Suzuki, the most famous exponent of twentieth-century Zen, played a crucial role in the genesis of the Kyoto School. Rightly regarded as the most influential Japanese thinker outside Japan during the past hundred years, Suzuki stimulated Nishida's effort to recast the insights of a fossilising Zen tradition into a contemporary, semi-secularised idiom. A prolific writer and mesmerizing lecturer, Suzuki, perhaps more than any other thinker, helped to internationalise Zen. This prepared the way for the popularisation of Kyoto School philosophy as an apolitical fashion and spiritual cult.

However, as was shown in Chapter 2, Zen in general and the Kyoto School in particular have, since the late 1980s, come under severe attack among the very scholars who had previously promoted a sympathetic and essentially religious portrait of the Kyoto School. The nature of this assault, and the reasons behind it, are explored in some detail in Chapters 1 and 5, but this burst of political fire, however misdirected, has opened the way towards a sounder and less naïve appreciation of Kyoto School philosophy, both as philosophy proper and as a system of historical and political reflection in its own right.

One of the most important consequences of such political revisionism is that long-neglected philosophers – the thinkers who played a vital role in the formation and consolidation of the Kyoto School as a philosophy of history and politics – may now be reassessed in a fresh and constructive light. This is particularly true of the four authors of *The Standpoint of World History and Japan* who figured so prominently in Chapters 4 and 5. Between 1939 and 1942, Kōyama, Kōsaka, Suzuki and Nishitani taught the non-Western world how to philosophise with a hammer. Their insights should demolish any notion that the Kyoto School is solely a movement in the philosophy of Asian religion. It is in this context that one should understand Tanabe's uncompromising insistence that, *pace* Nishida, Japan had to create an intellectual space or clearing within the national culture where philosophy can be pursued free of religious compulsions.[2]

Ever since Imperial Japan attacked Pearl Harbour and inflicted the greatest naval defeat ever suffered by White America – the day, in the words of one Afro-American activist, that 'one billion coloured people struck back' – the rediscovery of the political and historical dimension of Kyoto philosophy has only been a matter of time. Certainly, no convincing portrait of the totality of the Kyoto School is possible as long as the crucial political phase that unfolded between 1931 and 1945 continues to be wilfully misunderstood or neglected. The implied choice between religion and politics is false. We must complement our sophisticated understanding of the Kyoto School as a philosophy of religion with a critical but constructive assessment of the Kyoto achievement in the sphere of politics, history and society.

The German connection

Nothing was more crucial to the ambition, language and philosophical horizon of Kyoto School metaphysicians than their embrace of German philosophy.[3] Tanabe and Nishida spurred each other on during successive phases of this complex act of trans-cultural appropriation and exploitation. The power of German thought would inspire Tanabe to travel to Germany in 1922. Later, Miki and other members of his generation of Japanese philosophers would follow in his footsteps to study under the masters of the Southwest German School who taught at Heidelberg, Marburg and Freiburg.[4]

The Japanese philosophic pilgrims arrived in Germany at a crucial stage in the contemporary evolution of European thought. In the wake of Germany's calamitous defeat in 1918, the long reign of neo-Kantianism was beginning to be challenged by Nietzschean restlessness and a Hegelian revival. These Kyoto students rapidly entered into the new mood. They tended to shun or merely linger at some centres of German philosophic excellence (Tanabe studied briefly under Alois Riehl at Berlin, for example) in favour of the historical orientation of Heidelberg or, more crucially, the blossoming of phenomenology and ontology at Marburg and Freiburg.

The ambitions of Tanabe, Miki or Nishitani (he studied in Germany in the 1930s) mock any attempt to classify them as mere 'exchange students'. Their mental powers were formidable, indeed, and their unsettling precocity was at work in their early discovery of Heidegger's genius. Tanabe, for example, was on Heidegger's trail well before *Sein und Zeit* rocked the German intelligentsia when it appeared in 1927. This Japanese adventure of the mind stands as one of the most remarkable chapters in the entire history of cross-cultural exchange between literate civilisations.

Since the appearance of *Sein und Zeit*, Heidegger has relentlessly consolidated his claim to be one of the greatest thinkers of our time. Japanese philosophers have played a crucial if long-ignored role in fostering Heidegger's reputation. Thus, if George Steiner could write, at the time of Heidegger's death in 1976, that the secondary literature on the German thinker already totalled more than 4,000 entries, this explosion of scholarly interest began with Nishida's students after their return from Germany.[5] Indeed, it has been suggested that the young Jean-Paul Sartre first heard about Heidegger from Kuki Shūzō. This peripatetic Japanese philosopher criss-crossed Europe on a series of extraordinarily successful talent-spotting missions between 1921 and 1929.

These Japanese students did not seek only to discover the latest and most fashionable examples of European philosophic excellence but also to exploit them philosophically. In 1924, the year Tanabe had returned home from Germany, he published 'A New Turn in Phenomenology: Heidegger's Philosophy of Life'.[6] Graham Parkes believes this essay to be 'the first substantial commentary' published on Heidegger in any language.[7] Japanese leadership in Heidegger studies was affirmed in 1933 when Kuki produced

Heidegga no Tetsugaku, often credited as being the first book-length study of the magus of Freiburg

A torn manuscript page in Heidegger's hand occasioned what may be the supreme monument to the labours of these young Japanese thinkers. The manuscript in question is the text of the lecture on 'Ontology: Hermeneutics of Facticity' given in the summer term of 1923. The last page or two of Heidegger's first attempt to grapple with death and nothingness are missing. In the *Gesamtausgabe*, the editor notes that the text 'breaks off suddenly in the middle of the train of thought'.[8]

Tanabe was in the audience on this historic occasion. Furthermore, his lecture notes were 'for sixty-five years the sole source for Heidegger's first words on the topic of death'.[9] The idea that a Japanese student's notebook might provide essential knowledge of one of the key moments in the evolution of Heidegger's thought by allowing us to paper over a gap in the *Gesamtausgabe* suggests that, even at the earlier stages of this ontological revolution, East Asians were indispensable auditors to the essential music of Heidegger's ontology.

Heidegger's conversations with Tanabe may have had a significant impact on the genesis and design of *Sein und Zeit*. True, the subsequent reappearance in 1989 of the text of Heidegger's lecture titled 'Aristotle Introduction' (October 1922) does anticipate some of the points made in the 1923 'Ontology' lecture, but East Asian philosophy appears to have helped not only to precipitate but also to sustain Heidegger's endeavour to 'twist free' of the Kantian legacy in metaphysics. Certainly, the neglected story of the influence of specifically East Asian ideas, Japanese and Chinese alike, on Heidegger's ontology allows us to dismiss out of hand any suggestion of a one-sided German tyranny over the Japanese mind during the twentieth century.

Midwives to the Heideggerian resurrection of European metaphysics, Tanabe and his generation ensured that Japanese students of philosophy have, ever since, extended inexhaustible attention to Heidegger's vast *oeuvre*. During the past seventy years, more secondary literature may have appeared on this German thinker in the forbidding cocoon of the Japanese language than in any Western tongue, including German and French. This huge effort has been crowned by six different translations, between 1939 and 1970, of *Sein und Zeit* into Japanese. One consequence of this great enterprise of the Japanese spirit is that it is no longer credible to trace the trajectory of Heidegger's thought only by reference to Greek, Latin, German and French sources. At decisive moments in Heidegger's meditation on death and nothingness, the 'way' and the 'saying', Chinese and Japanese texts were crucial. The European student of Heidegger can no longer credibly ignore this light from the East.[10]

Is Kyoto philosophy, *philosophy*?

If the 'singular Japanese focus on European excellence has helped to generate a depth and breadth of response to the philosophic tradition, from

Kant to Heidegger, as alert and informed as can be found anywhere outside Europe', why does 'the mind of the European philosopher remain closed to the great flowering of thought in Japan under the aegis' of the Kyoto School of philosophy?[11] Is there more to such scepticism than Eurocentric hubris and philosophic authority? Perhaps the Japanese achievement in philosophy is thinner than the first part of this argument has assumed. To overcome such doubts, four objections must be met:

1   Japanese philosophy does not qualify as philosophy.
2   The Japanese philosophic achievement is too meagre to merit serious Western attention.
3   To *study* Japanese philosophy is not to *do* philosophy.
4   The Kyoto School, the greatest school of Japanese philosophy, is nothing more than a nationalist ideology.

While the second, third and fourth objections are attacked from a variety of angles throughout this book, this chapter seeks to meet the fundamental criticism that Japanese philosophy is not philosophy. Certainly, one does not have to be an analytic philosopher to be sceptical about many of the values and strategies of argument that prevail in modern Japanese thought. Plato, Aristotle, Leibnitz and Descartes share with Russell, Wittgenstein, Frege and Husserl the conviction that philosophy is about reason. Philosophy, where it is rigorous, must be more than an elegant chat about poetry. No amount of rhetorical puffery or nationalist egotism can transform the methods and standards of cultural criticism or the history of ideas into what these worthy disciplines are not: *philosophia*.

Many Western defenders of Japanese philosophy and their Japanese allies have greeted such scepticism with an evasive silence. Few have matched Parkes's courage in attempting to confront European demands for philosophic rigour:

> A major source of resistance to both Heidegger's and Asian thought stems from a complex of prejudices to the effect that: the proper medium for philosophic writing is the treatise rather than any more literary form; philosophy must work in intellectual concepts rather than play with poetic images; in such work reason is primary and imagination secondary, if not downright counter-productive; and rational and logical argumentation is the only appropriate method. If these are taken as criteria for philosophy, then most of Heidegger's writings and the majority of the major texts in Asian thought fail to qualify.[12]

If the major texts of the Kyoto School 'fail to qualify' as philosophy, the entire rhetorical armoury that I have employed above to make the case for the philosophic merits of the Kyoto School is vulnerable. Such scepticism calls into question not only all talk of Nishida's 'brilliance' or Tanabe's 'precociousness' but also the confident use of the expressions such as 'religious philosophy' or 'the philosophy of history' in connection with the Kyoto School. The analytic philosopher may push this criticism further. If prepositional logic alone counts as philosophy, no amount of secondary literature on Heidegger, nor any number of renderings of *Sein und Zeit* into Japanese, can work the required alchemy of transforming Japanese word magic, however brilliant, into the discourse of reason. What must be done, therefore, to ensure the reputation of Japanese philosophy as philosophy?

First, we must make a compelling defence of methodological pluralism *within* the walls of philosophy itself. It is one thing to acknowledge the power of the analytic tradition and quite another to insist, in a dogmatic spirit, that only analytical philosophy merits the proud title of 'philosophy'. The advocacy of methodological pluralism should begin with the abundant evidence that philosophic positivism often muddles what empiricism makes clear. The anti-empirical bias in philosophic positivism, a vice that it shares with rational choice theory and economic positivism, is its greatest failing. This flaw explains why analytical philosophy, more often than not, may cause havoc when misapplied to the soft underbelly of philosophy: metaphysics, political philosophy, pure and applied ethics, the philosophy of the social sciences, and the philosophy of history.[13] But any effective defence of the Kyoto School must be able to demonstrate how and why the application of inappropriate and procrustean methods and approaches derived from symbolic logic and the natural sciences can have a debilitating impact on other branches of philosophy. In such matters, there is no substitute for methodological self-awareness. One cannot claim to be a philosopher, Japanese or otherwise, without it.

To insist that there is more to philosophy than prepositional logic does not mean, however, that anything and everything counts as Asian philosophy. Quite the contrary, it is long past time for attacks on reason and the claims of logical discourse to cease among the proponents of the Kyoto School. Japanese philosophy cannot be philosophy if it opts out of reason. So, to repeat, the education of the student of Asian philosophy must include the cultivation of a clear and profound understanding of philosophic method if the authority and progress of the subject is to be secure.

To this first imperative must be added a second: the avoidance of bogus or inflated claims on behalf of Japanese philosophers. Defenders of the Kyoto School frequently display a weakness for such rhetorical excesses. Thus, to assert, for example, that Miki or Tetsurō Watsuji went 'beyond' Heidegger's philosophy, or that Kuki anticipated and therefore surpassed Sartrean existentialism, is idle posturing unless it can be shown, line by line, chapter by chapter, book by book, that the Japanese texts in question should replace *Sein und Zeit* or *L'Etre et le Néant* in the canon of philosophy.

Parkes meets this challenge. When he asserts, for example, that 'Heidegger's influence on Nishitani has been greater than on any other prominent Japanese philosopher, and that the latter's understanding and assimilation of Heidegger's thought is deeper ... than that of his predecessor and contemporaries', he offers up specific texts by Nishitani for dissection.[14] Such acts of constructive criticism have an indispensable role to play in the Western reception and evaluation of Japanese philosophy. The translations and close readings of Kyoto School texts included in this book are an attempt to address this imperative.

Japanese and European philosophy compared

If the depth of the Japanese response to twentieth-century European philosophy is peerless outside Europe, the standard for judging what the Japanese have accomplished from Nishida onwards must come from within Europe itself. Germany has influenced the philosophic cosmos that the Kyoto thinker takes seriously because German-speaking thinkers occupy the summits of this cosmos. The French recognition of this achievement has been clear-sighted and fruitful.

Indeed, the French response to the tradition of German philosophic excellence, from Kant and Hegel to Husserl and Heidegger, is unrivalled. All the virtues that the French brought to painting, from Ingres to Matisse – 'the vaulting ambition, the total seriousness, the readiness to dare anything'[15] – have been mobilised to ensure the extraordinary triumph of intellectual talent and philosophic verve that is French philosophy after Bergson. The strategy of the major French thinker has been as simple as it has been bold. When Sartre meditated on *Sein und Zeit*, when Foucault translated Nietzsche's *Unzeitgemässe Betrachtungen* while sitting on an Italian beach, or when the young Derrida proceeded fitfully to 'deconstruct' Husserl's *Der Ursprung der Geometrie als intentional-historisches Problem*, the ambition was to produce a rival text, in French, that could be set confidently on the canonic shelf next to the original German provocation. The result has been a unique triumph of French *esprit*.

Both American and Japanese philosophy appears to stand in the shadow of the Franco-German summits within the Continental tradition. Commenting on the American philosophic scene, Steiner has identified the crucial lapse: 'American philosophers edit, translate, comment upon and teach Heidegger, Wittgenstein or Sartre but do not put forward a major metaphysics'.[16] In the philosophic tradition at issue, producing a major metaphysics is the supreme test of philosophic greatness. For a national school to fail to produce a philosopher capable of creating that major metaphysics is to stand defeated. Hence, the burden of expectations falls, in the American tradition, on an exemplar thinker such as Charles Sanders Pierce or, to take a more recent example, Richard Rorty. In Japan, the same burden weighs, of necessity, on Nishida, Tanabe and Nishitani, for if Japan can claim a major metaphysician, he will almost certainly be found among the ranks of the Kyoto School.

The Italian comparison

Philosophic genius rarely flourishes in a cultural desert. The chief obligation of an intellectual community must be, therefore, to enhance the opportunities for 'the quantum leap which is genius'.[17] To this end, a serious culture 'will try to keep its educational-performative-social institutions open-ended, vulnerable to the anarchic shock of excellence'.[18] As no other, this need underscores the importance of national schools of philosophy.

For a late-developing philosophic power, such as Japan, the sober assessment of native capabilities and external standards of achievement is indispensable. In its themes and compulsions, the Italian tradition provides a suggestive measure to gauge the strengths of twentieth-century Japanese philosophy. Like the Japanese philosopher, the Italian thinker has pursued a 'line of reflection which, starting with Heidegger and Nietzsche', has permeated 'an entire sector of twentieth-century *mitteleuropean* philosophy'.[19] This concentration on German thought has stimulated also a hearty appetite among Italian and Japanese thinkers for things French.

Italian and Japanese philosophers have also been profoundly influenced by the trials and tribulations of state-building and modernisation. One consequence has been a sustained engagement, in Italy and Japan, with the complex developments of Marxist thought, both the Western Marxist camp (Bloch to Habermas) and the orthodox East. The ideological gap between East and West has been bridged, for both traditions, by Georg Lukács, perhaps the most influential twentieth-century European philosopher in Japan before Sartre.

Like Heidegger, Tanabe and Gentile have been accused of being philosophers of fascism. This accusation against Tanabe cannot be sustained by the close reading of key texts. Indeed, Gentile is a more difficult target than some of the critics acknowledge. Furthermore, these representative figures of the Japanese and Italian schools of philosophy engaged seriously with Marxism. The touchstone of this more generous, and I believe more truthful, approach to interwar philosophy is to be found in Heidegger's famous salute to Lukács's *History and Class Consciousness* at the conclusion of *Sein und Zeit*. Gentile's works were praised by Lenin; Marx left his mark on Gentile's philosophy of Actualism.[20]

If Tanabe's great opus, *Philosophy as Metanoetics* (1946), repeatedly engages Marxist thought, Japanese Marxists such as Katsumi Umemoto were among the first to respond seriously but critically to this neglected classic.[21] Indeed, it is possible to argue that the radical nationalism of such post-war Marxists as Shō Ishimoda and Seita Tōma make them the principal (if not the most philosophically sophisticated) heirs of the wartime Kyoto School and its focus on the imperative of a national awakening to reason and genuine subjectivity.[22] In contrast, the condemnation of the Kyoto School by American neo-Marxists tends to be philosophically unpersuasive because their grasp of the Marxist canon is so poor.[23]

Liberal revisionism highlights the curious truth that while Italy's encounter with fascism, strictly defined, was more serious than that of any other Axis power, nationalism, in both war and peace, has left a deeper mark on Japanese thought. One caveat must therefore inform any attempt to compare and contrast Italian philosophy from the time of Antonio Labriola (1843–1904) with Japanese philosophy, in its modern Westernised mode, after Amane Nishi (1829–97). Many Italian philosophers are uncomfortable with the very idea of subjecting Italian philosophy to the parochialism of a national school because of the rooted Italian commitment to universal values and a pan-European vision of humanistic culture. St Thomas may have been born near Aquino, but any attempt to confine this European giant to a narrow nativist niche carries little conviction in Italy, and rightly so. In short, Italians tend to be better Europeans than Japanese are good East Asians. But it should also be noted that the Kyoto School's response to continental Asian thought, especially Buddhism and Taoism, has at many points been profound.

Italian philosophy has exerted profounder influence than Japanese philosophy. But within the ambit of contemporary political philosophy – particularly the themes of modernisation, Marxism and the cultural politics of late development – arresting parallels between Japan and Italy invite intelligent perusal. Whatever their differences, Croce and Nishida dominated their respective national schools with the kind of unrivalled influence that has been almost unthinkable in Britain, France and Germany (the rather pale example of John Dewey in the United States may be instructive here). The comparisons between Miki and Gramsci, Tanabe and Gentile have already been noted. Such examples should encourage us to speculate on who the Japanese equivalents of Galvano Della Volpe (an Italian Althusser?) or the phenomenologist Enzo Paci or the post-modernist Giannni Vattimo might be. Or, to reverse the perspective, what is the Italian equivalent of *Basho no Roki-gaku*, the extraordinary wartime study of Nishida by Risaku Mutai, or Kōsaka's unexpectedly moving exercise in hagiography, *Nishida Kitarō to Watsuji Tetsurō*?[24]

Karl Löwith's critique

Such author-by-author, text-for-text comparisons are the very stuff of philosophic judgment and discrimination. The invidious comparison allows one to put the powers of modern Japanese philosophy to the necessary test. Yet even to pose such comparisons is to violate one of the most enduring conceits of Japanese high culture: the unwillingness to subject native texts to rigorous comparison with the literary achievements of other civilisations. This Japanese taboo on unflattering trans-cultural comparisons has been nearly 1,500 years in the making. The taboo has its roots in ancient Japan's unequal encounter with Chinese and Korean high culture.

The domination of Japan's cultural horizon by China and Europe has provoked a subtle and complex Japanese response. At one level, according to

Masao Maruyama, the Japanese intellectual relentlessly pursues foreign cultural novelties because he dreads being regarded as out of date (*jidai okure*).[25] One can easily imagine Maruyama's dismissive assessment of the energetic, sometimes frenzied, Japanese appropriation of the latest developments of German thought after the First World War. On another level, the faddish nature of such 'borrowings' (*tsukai sute*) must be weighed against the intensity of the modern Japanese hunger for German and French ideas. Only the best will satisfy this Japanese appetite for things foreign. The contrast with the American stance vis-à-vis European high culture is not necessarily to Japan's disadvantage.

The psychological pressures that result when a complex literate culture willingly opens itself to foreign excellence are disturbing. Strategies have to be devised to maintain native equilibrium in the face of this external challenge. In his essay 'European Nihilism', Karl Löwith, one of Heidegger's most brilliant German students, offers his interpretation of how Japanese students of Western philosophy cope with the pressures of foreign texts.[26] His insights are based on his period in Italian and Japanese exile, between 1933 and 1941, after he was forced to flee Nazi persecution.

First, this is Löwith on Asian resistance to criticism:

> The Orient does not endure the kind of inconsiderate critique, either of itself or others, in which all European progress is grounded. The very critique of what exists, of the state and nature, of God and human beings, of principles of faith and prejudices – this power of making distinctions, which embraces everything, calls it into question, doubts it, and investigates it, is a basic element of European life, without which that life is unthinkable.[27]

On how the Japanese student approaches a European text:

> This character of free [European] appropriation appears to me to be lacking for the most part in Japan. The students do indeed study our European books with dedication, and they understand them thanks to their intelligence; but they do not draw from their studies any consequences for themselves as Japanese. They do not make distinctions and comparisons between such European concepts as will, freedom, and spirit and what corresponds to these in their own lives, thinking, and speaking; or to put it more precisely, they avoid doing this.[28]

On what the Japanese make of European philosophy:

> They proceed into the text of a European philosopher as if doing so were a straightforward matter, without seeing the primordial foreignness of the philosopher's concepts in comparison with their own concepts ... They live as it were on two levels: a lower, more fundamental one, on

which they feel and think in a Japanese way; and a higher one, on which
the European sciences from Plato to Heidegger are lined up. And the
European teacher asks himself: where is the step on which they pass
from one level to the other?[29]

Löwith raises testing questions about how Japan has absorbed European
philosophy, and not only during the 1920s and 1930s. This German philosopher asks us to look more closely not only at what Japanese students are
taught about the European philosophic tradition but also at how professional Japanese philosophers have been trained, and therefore at how they
deploy the language and intellectual tools of the West when they do philosophy. Löwith's analysis offers a battery of tests that need to be applied when
assessing the general character of the Kyoto School's encounter with
European ideas.

It may be that Japanese students live, even now, on two levels intellectually, but what about Japanese philosophers? If foreign ideas unsettle by their
very foreignness and uncontested superiority, how does the professional
philosopher cope with a lifetime of living, in trained intimacy, with such
pressure on his identity as a thinking Japanese? Does the distressed
psychology of the nationalist thinker explain why a conspicuous number of
otherwise cosmopolitan Japanese thinkers succumbed to intellectual conversion – a kind of mental retreat into the womb of native values (*Nippon e no
kaiki*) – that the Japanese call '*tenkō*'?

The pressures of nationalist identity exerted considerable impact on
Nishida and Tanabe as thinkers, particularly during the period of the
wartime Kyoto School, between 1931 and 1945, but they did *not* live on two
levels in the way Kuki and Watsuji appear to have. Rather, Tanabe and
Nishida illustrate the truth of Löwith's contrasting argument:

> European civilisation is not a garment one can don when the need arises
> and then take off again; on the contrary, it has the uncanny power to
> shape the body and even the soul of the one who wears it, in conformity
> with itself.[30]

Over a lifetime of intense reflection on European philosophy, Nishida and
Tanabe displayed a rare degree of personal and intellectual integration. One
suspects that the extraordinary command of European ideas that Nishida
and Tanabe display (and much the same may be said of Nishitani) could not
have been achieved without an effective personal synthesis, both metaphysical and psychological.

The importance of Buddhism, particularly the Zen tradition, does loom
large in the early Nishida, but it is not obvious that Zen functioned as a
nativist palliative or metaphysical 'security blanket' during his most creative
phase as a philosopher. For Tanabe and Nishida, the danger was that of
falling between the two levels, the nativist and the European, thus running

the risk of becoming incomprehensible both to one's countrymen and to European tradition. The severe criticism of the prose styles of Tanabe and Nishida by native speakers of Japanese offers one measure of this risk.

The demands of (European) philosophy at its most technical provide an opportunity to separate the sheep from the goats among philosophical proponents of national identity. Take, for example, the unignorable discipline that Aristotle imposes on Nishida and Tanabe when these Japanese thinkers brood on the idea of 'intuition'. All the Western philosophers that matter to Nishida and Tanabe, from Descartes, Leibnitz and Spinoza to Wolff, Kant and Hegel, worked out their systems of thought within the strict constraints of Aristotle's distinction between 'intuition' and mediated knowledge, a distinction that forms the core of his complex, indeed ambiguous, treatment of the ideas of *nōésis* and *aísthēsis*.

To the degree that Nishida insists on the 'primordial' unity of object and subject, this problem cannot be sidestepped. A comparable difficulty is involved in Tanabe's attempt to move, in a metaphysically responsible way, from the category of the 'temporal' to that of the 'world' at the beginning of his meditation on the logic of the species in the early 1930s.[31] This kind of technical pressure dramatically shrinks the gap between Löwith's two levels, and this narrowing means that reason counts decisively in the philosophy of Nishida and Tanabe in ways that leave them suspended uncomfortably between the rigours of Western metaphysics and the romantic defence of native identity. And this, as much as any other factor, may explain why the Kyoto School was so in tune with the feelings of solidarity that united wartime Japan but still remained a target of ultra-nationalist ire.

Kyoto philosophy: dead or alive?

In 1907, Croce published his famous essay 'Ciò che è vivo e ciò che è morto nella filosofia di Hegel' ('What is Living and What is Dead in the Philosophy of Hegel?'). A century on, the same question needs to be asked of the Kyoto School. Have these Japanese thinkers met the four objections posed above? It is my conviction that the principal monuments of the Kyoto School, religious, political and mathematical (the last being another neglected dimension), offer proof that Japanese philosophy does qualify as philosophy. This achievement can withstand serious Western scrutiny. The Kyoto School is no mere metaphysical outcropping of a nationalist ideology. Its incomplete nature provides the contemporary thinker, Japanese or otherwise, with an opportunity to *do* philosophy.

Reviewing the genealogy of the Kyoto School over the past century, Nishida's shift from British to German philosophy early in his career was decisive. The German philosophic tradition from Kant to Heidegger became the foreign tradition that has counted in Japan. In the long Japanese struggle to redefine themselves metaphysically, that is rationally, as a people, the *Zeitgeist* has spoken German. But Bergson and William James were important to the Kyoto School. So was Whitehead, who continues to attract serious attention in Japan.[32] Nevertheless, in the political and historical sphere, Kyoto School reflection on Japan's imperial destiny was informed as much by native sources and domestic imperatives as by European ones.

The historical revolution in Japanese philosophy initiated by Tanabe in the late 1920s calls into question the orthodox assumption that the overarching philosophic goal of the Kyoto School, and therefore its sole achievement, lies in the reinvention of Zen Buddhism. The apolitical reading of the Kyoto texts is ethically suspect and philosophically jejune. More disheartening still are recent polemics which insist that the nationalist thrust of Kyoto School thought during the Asia-Pacific War did not represent a temporary break with this religious enterprise but rather its poisonous fulfilment.[33]

As an adventure in post-White thinking, Tanabe and the second generation of the Kyoto School created a philosophical horizon that allowed Japanese philosophy to grasp what was at stake metaphysically in Imperial Japan's gory contest with the White West. For the Kyoto School, anti-Western resistance defined the future of Asian resurgence. They were right but fatally ahead of their times, and thus prophets without honour, at home or abroad.

During the twenty-first century, White West hegemony, the racial imbalance that has defined our global society for half a millennium, seems almost certain to pass away. Tanabe, Kōyama, Suzuki, Nishitani and Kōsaka were among the earliest thinkers to sense the enormous opportunity but also the great test facing those who would seek to realise this change. American hegemony now stands in the way of this renaissance. For any society that would take up this challenge, the Kyoto thinker's gift for metaphysical vision and historical realism has provided future generations with the philosophical tools to dream forward.

7 Racism and the black legend of the Kyoto School

Translating Tanabe's *The Logic of the Species*

The Jew is a man who has always read; the Protestant has read for three hundred years; the Catholic for only two generations.

Charles Péguy[1]

The scheme of origins, authority and continuum in force in the Marxist world derives its sense of identity and its daily practices of validation from a canon of texts. It is the reading of these texts – exegetic, Talmudic, disputative in an almost pathological degree of semantic scruple and interpretative nicety – which constitutes the presiding dynamic in Marxist education.

George Steiner[2]

Philosophy cannot be evaded. To study philosophy, Japanese or otherwise, is to hold firm to the Socratic legacy. Such a commitment demands adherence to certain principles. It is axiomatic to this enterprise, now more than 2,500 years old, that neither politics or ethics, nor religion or science has any *essentialist* superiority over philosophy as a form of human understanding. The confident grasp of human reality is so elusive, so resistant to ready comprehension, that one approach may exhibit profounder insights than another, on this subject or another, in this age or another.

Philosophers cease to be philosophers if they offer any quarter to those who insist that philosophy is inferior in essence to other kinds of knowledge. On the subject of the Kyoto School, the defence of this proposition requires philosophers to take their stand on the textual facts of the case. Close reading is our *métier*. In the light of the recent crises that have engulfed the Western appreciation of modern Japanese philosophy, it is time for rapiers.

A question of race

In 1986, *The Myth of Japanese Uniqueness* was published in London.[3] It was one of the first books in a new series of research monographs to appear under the imprimatur of the Nissan Institute for Japanese Studies, founded earlier in the decade at Oxford University. This controversial book was seen by some as the Nissan Institute's declaration of independence. The Institute may have been the grateful beneficiary of generous funding from one of Japan's leading corporations, but this book made it clear that those monies had in no way impaired the academic freedom or dulled the critical edge of the scholars associated with the Institute.

The author was Peter Dale, the Australian controversialist and student of comparative mythologies. Drawing on the dissective techniques of Freudianism, neo-Marxism and the structuralist analysis of myth, Dale mercilessly deconstructed the discourse of Japanese national identity, or *Nihonjin-ron*. Dismissing this discourse as pseudo-scientific and politically malicious, Dale conducted an unsparing examination of the European textual sources, often German, exploited by some of the most influential Japanese ideologues in their attempt to give their populist discourse a veneer of academic respectability. *The Myth of Japanese Uniqueness* stirred fierce controversy in Japan, but such a dissection was overdue. To that degree, the field of Japan studies remains in debt to Dale. The reputations of Kinji Imanishi, the anti-Darwinian evolutionist, and Tetsurō Watsuji, the influential philosopher, may never recover, certainly in the minds of many Westerners, from Dale's assault.

Can one be equally sanguine about Dale's battering of the leading lights of Kyoto School philosophy? Nishida's ideas are assessed discursively in *The Myth of Uniqueness*, most notably in connection with Dale's criticism of Imanishi, and the writings of modern Japan's greatest philosopher are judged harshly. On the other hand, Tanabe has a slight place in Dale's analysis, serving only to illustrate aspects of the climate of ideas which fostered Imanishi's flawed theories. Here I propose to question how fairly and accurately Tanabe is treated in *The Myth of Japanese Uniqueness*.

Dale may have touched on Tanabe's work only briefly but, because his book attracted a wide readership, his broad-brush treatment has had an influence not only in Britain, Australia and North America but also, to a surprising degree, in Continental Europe. Thus, Dale's curt dismissal of Tanabe as an 'ultranationalist' may have encouraged a generation of Western scholars to neglect this Japanese thinker. Given this impact, the record needs to be put straight about what Tanabe actually thought and wrote rather than what has been hitherto surmised or supposed.

The index of *The Myth of Japanese Uniqueness* contains only two references to Tanabe. These occur on pages 194 and 196. The second of these citations refers to a third footnote on pages 199–200. Although unmentioned in the index, this is the most important comment on Tanabe's thought because it identifies Dale's sources of information about the Japanese philosopher: G. Piovesana's *Recent Japanese Philosophical Thought* and a translation of a single, comparatively short section from *The Logic of the Species*, rendered into English by David Dilworth and Taira Satō, that appeared in *Monumenta Nipponica* in 1966.[4]

Dale mentions Tanabe in his reprise of Imanishi's quarrel with Darwin (the chapter viciously titled 'Monkey Business'). In this slashing attack, Dale declares his intention to 'concentrate only on those aspects [of Imanishi's theories] which highlight his nationalism and his relationship to *Nihonjin-ron*'. Dale then goes on to observe:

> As I have already hinted, his [Imanishi's] formulations owe a great debt to certain social and theoretical ideas which were anti-individualist, linked in part to the rise of fascism in Japan, and explicitly aimed at 'overcoming the modern'. A deeper analysis would quickly show how his theory melds Watsuji's notion of *aidagara*, Nishida's subject-object epistemology and Tanabe Hajime's 'logic of the species' in a biological idiom.[5]

The accusations made against Tanabe in this passage are partly direct, partly associative (as in the expression 'guilt by association'). Imanishi is linked with anti-individualism, fascism and the Japanese struggle to 'overcome the modern'. The last of these probably refers to the war of words that most famously, or notoriously, erupted at the wartime symposium 'Overcoming Modernity', which has been selectively assessed, above, in Chapter 4.

Dale's accusations against Imanishi for his anti-individualism and fascistic tendencies extend to Tanabe as well. Before we examine this charge against Tanabe, we must address this business of Imanishi's melding of Tanabe's logic of the species 'into a biological idiom'. In the quotation cited above, it is obvious that Imanishi is doing the melding, but the reader is left wondering whether Tanabe's idea of species logic lent itself, in Dale's mind, to being easily melded.

This question is answered decisively in Dale's second paragraph dealing with Tanabe:

> His [Imanishi's] development of the theory of a 'species society' (*shushakai*) as the fundamental unit of evolutionary change draws on Lamarck but betrays a certain conceptual affiliation to the 'logic of the species' (*shu no ronri*) of Tanabe Hajime's ultranationalistic philosophy. 'Species' here is the mediating ground of the nation, midway between the genus of mankind and the individual, which coerces or negates the individual, or as Tanabe quaintly put it, may 'force the individual's spontaneous obedience' but is, in turn, negated by the totality, thus being the 'expedient means' (*hōben*) through which the individual apparently realises himself in 'Absolute Nothingness'.[6]

This is a mistaken summary of Tanabe's position. It does not reflect what *The Logic of the Species* actually says. To be fair to Dale, the more testing question at issue here is whether he was led astray by the sources he cites on Tanabe, particularly the translation of Tanabe's 1946 essay 'Benshō-hō toshite Shu no Ronri' ('The Logic of the Species as Dialectic').

Translating *The Logic of the Species*

'The Logic of the Species as Dialectic' is a demanding text. It resists translation because no confident command of Tanabe's essay is possible without a precise understanding of what he means by 'species' (*shu*), 'expedient means' (*hōben*) or 'absolute nothingness' (*zettai mu*). Dale ignores the Buddhist and metaphysical contexts in which these ideas have their natural home. Instead, he exploits the 'common-sense' surface meaning of these mysterious and unsettling expressions to brilliant rhetorical effect. The problem is that the surface common-sense meaning is not correct.

There is also the problem of the misleading quotation. Take, for example, Tanabe's reference to the power of the collective to 'force the individual's spontaneous obedience'. This is how Dilworth and Satō render the relevant passage:

> Consequently, not only is it [the species] a specialization and limitation of the absolute spirit as the universal, it also contains the power of binding and controlling the subjective spirit of the individual. In the case of the individual resisting and opposing it, it has the power and authority to coerce the individual's submission. In the instance of the individual affirming and developing it through the mediation of the absolute spirit, it has the power and authority to force the individual's spontaneous obedience.[7]

Confronted with this dense piece of Hegelian–Tanabean reasoning, the reader unfamiliar with this tradition of dialectical philosophy may be tempted, as Dale is, to conclude that something suspect, if not actually dangerous, is lurking in the metaphysical undergrowth, but this is not so. One would have to footnote almost every other word in the above passage to explain conclusively why this is not so, but Tanabe is not attempting to justify totalitarianism, fascism, authoritarianism or racial chauvinism because he is not totalitarian, fascist, authoritarian or racist.

Since the decline of Marxism in the 1970s, European intellectuals have lost their once native feel for dialectical reasoning because the recent revival of Hegelianism has not focused on this aspect of German idealism. In contrast, Tanabe was utterly at home in dialectical logic *as a form of logic*. This philosophic system contains a built-in countervailing mechanism, as is true of the laws of supply and demand in economics. Press hard on any dynamic aspect of reality and another aspect will come into play that matches it, thus allowing one to progress to a higher level of resolution. If civil authority must act to curb the excesses of aggressive individualism and selfishness, individuals must restrain the excesses of state power. Thus, in his supposedly 'fascist' speech of 1943 titled 'Life or Death', Tanabe endorses an almost Lockean insistence on the right of ordinary people to rebel against misrule.[8] In this dialectical analysis of wartime politics, Tanabe develops a sophisticated Germano-Japanese reworking of the Latin tag '*Contraria, contrariis, curantur*' ('Opposites are cured by opposites').

So, a fatal absence of the essential *Bildung* can trap the incautious student of Tanabe's *The Logic of the Species*. The translation that Dale uses to attack Tanabe's language in 'The Logic of the Species as Dialectic' poses numerous difficulties for the unwary. To start, one must appreciate where the relatively brief section in English stands within the overall design of Tanabe's vast work.

This translated essay is the first of the six that form Tanabe's *Shu no Ronri no Benshō-hō* (*The Dialectic of the Logic of the Species*). This set of six essays concludes the second of the two volumes (6 and 7) of *The Complete Works of Hajime Tanabe* in Japanese (*Tanabe Hajime Zenshū – THZ*) devoted to his magnum opus. The English translation is therefore just a single section of one of the thirteen essays published between 1934 and 1946 that make up *Shu no Ronri*. A chronology of the texts in question makes clear why one should be sceptical about an assumption that 'The Logic of the Species as Dialectic', this translated essay, provides a representative statement of Tanabe's principal arguments:

The Logic of the Species

Table of Contents

1 From the Schema of 'Time' to the Schema of the 'World' (published in Nov. 1932)
2 The Logic of Social Ontology (Nov., Dec. 1934 and Jan. 1935)
3 The Logic of the Species and the World Schema (Oct., Nov., Dec. 1935)
4 Ontology: Three Stages (Nov. 1935)
5 The Social Ontological Structure of Logic (Oct., Nov., Dec. 1936)
6 Responding to Criticism of *The Logic of the Species* (Oct. 1937)
7 Clarifying the Meaning of *The Logic of the Species* (Oct., Nov., Dec. 1937)
8 The Limits of Existential Philosophy (Oct. 1938)
9 The Logic of National Ontology (Oct., Nov., Dec. 1939)
10 Eternity, History, Action (Oct., Nov., Dec. 1940)
11 Ethics and Logic (Nov. 1941)
12 The Development of the Concept of Existence (Oct., Dec. 1941)
13 The Dialectic of the Logic of the Species (Aug. 1946)

'The Logic of the Species as Dialectic' appears in section 13. Dilworth and Satō are correct to observe that 'The following section is a good example of Tanabe's blending of Pure Land Buddhist and Christian religious categories with Western philosophical concepts, such as those of Hegel and Kiekegaard.'[9] But 'The Logic of the Species as Dialectic' is also burdened by the grave weaknesses of the religious-philosophical paradigm discussed below in Chapters 10 and 11.

Tanabe's *The Logic of the Species* is best understood as a classic experiment in metaphysical reasoning about the political-historical realm. To exaggerate the Buddhist-Christian dimension of Tanabe's thought detracts from the fundamental importance of *The Logic of the Species* as 'subjectivist' political philosophy. Students working within the religious-philosophical paradigm that has dominated the Western reception of Kyoto School thought since 1945 deal only casually with questions of political philosophy; they have concentrated their talents and energies on explaining the precise nuance of Buddhist religious thought at the expense of historical context. So while there is great merit in any attempt to ground the Western understanding of *Shu no Ronri* in a proper translation of the original, it is somewhat problematic to begin with 'The Logic of the Species as Dialectic'. But, to be fair, the translator has to start somewhere. So does this translation succeed?

Textual complexities abound. While 'The Logic of the Species as Dialectic' is the first section of *Shu no Ronri no Benshō-hō*, Tanabe added a three and a half page-long 'Preface' to the text. Dilworth and Satō translate two and a half sentences (including an incomplete rendering of one of those long Germanic sentences that Tanabe resorted to so frequently) from this 'Preface' as a footnote to their translation of 'The Logic of the Species as Dialectic'.

Relying on this translation, Dale might have easily gained a false impression of Tanabean political philosophy, and it appears that he did. Here is my translation of the entire section in question followed by the Dilworth–Satō rendering:

Between 1934 and 1935, I [Tanabe – translator] was engaged in the study of the logic of dialectical reasoning, what I came to call 'the logic of the species'. Using this logical approach, I proposed to investigate the actual structure of society as a state [*kokka shakai*] *understood as a system of dialectical relationships*. My motive for proceeding in this way was as follows: First, I wanted to address the [the kind of] nationalism that was coming to the fore in those years as a philosophical problem (*tetsugaku no mondai toshite*). This meant I had to criticise two currents of thinking at the same time: the theory of liberalism (*jiyūshugi no shisō*) that dominated Japanese (*watakushi-tomo no*) thinking [from the 1920s] as well as the totalitarianism that emerged in the mid 1930s [at the time of my writing, i.e. 1934–35] and which was based on a simple-minded nationalism. I thought about this problem in the following way. My goal was to uncover a rational foundation for the Japanese state. This vision of the state required that realism and idealism be united in a practical way. How could this be achieved if liberalism took the individual as its prime agency (*shutai*) while totalitarianism took the ethnic nation (*minzoku*) as its prime agency (*kitai*)?

My answer was that this conflict had to be looked at from the standpoint of absolute mediation. Consistent with this standpoint, these two contrasting agencies could be understood as being dialectically related, and thus mutually mediating and mutually negating, in such a way that the conflict between these contrasting agencies could be overcome in the dialectical formula: the abstract nation as abstract individual/the abstract individual as abstract collective (*kitai soku shutai, shutai soku kitai*). As it is my conviction that the state has to be grounded in morality, I wanted to guarantee the rational foundations of the state while at the same time to curb [literally: to rectify], to the degree that my limited ability to influence events permitted, the irrational policies being put forward at the time in the name of so-called [political] realism.

This is the Dilworth–Satō condensed version, which is less a translation than a free paraphrase:

The motive of my investigation was to make a philosophical analysis of the nationalism, which was coming to the fore at the time [in the 1930s]. In so doing, I criticized the individualism, which had dominated us in the past. At the same time, I denied the totalitarianism, which was being erected in place of a simple nationalism. By their mutual negation I mediated the former's concept of the subjective individual and the latter's fundamental concept of race … I wished to guarantee, on the one hand, the logical foundation of the concept of nation by thoroughly placing it on a moral basis, and to correct, on the other, at least as far as possible, the irrational policy of actualism which was then prominent in Japan.[10]

The section from Tanabe's 'Preface' that I have translated above describes the essence of Tanabe's approach to the crisis of the Japanese state in the 1930s. In the main, Tanabe's argument is with Hegel and not with Pure Land Buddhism, Christianity or Kierkegaard. However, there is a Buddhist dimension to this approach, and knowledge of basic Christian belief provides the Westerner with an invaluable tool to appreciate Tanabe's emphasis on what might be called sublimation of the individual in faith. Taken out of context, Tanabe's remark about 'expedient means' (*hōben*) sounds like Orwellian doubletalk (as Dale intends), but read in a Christian or Buddhism context, it takes on a less threatening meaning. Here is the Dilworth–Satō rendering of the sentence in question:

In contrast to this, the species as particular, as the existential mediation of the totality as Nothingness, becomes the expedient means (*hōben*) in which individuals transform themselves into Nothingness, and thereby edify and save each other.[11]

This is not the language of John Stuart Mill, but if one compares the attitude of the faithful towards the Church as the Body of Christ or the unchosen destiny of the 'Chosen People' in the Old Testament or the collective demands of the *Ulmah* in Islam or even the Western cult of patriotic self-sacrifice ('*Dulce et decorum est pro patria mori*'), Tanabe's stress on the imperative for individual sacrifice for the collective good as redemptive has an ancient and honourable lineage. What is more, Tanabe brings to his reflections on the political collective a highly developed sense of the moral. This contrarian, almost anarchistic, impulse is very Japanese. Nevertheless, such *zange*-inspired speculation is not pivotal to the principal architecture of *The Logic of the Species*. Repentance, or *zange*, becomes the focus, and even then not entirely, only towards the end of the Pacific War when Tanabe swerved from his commitment to secular political change into a relatively brief but intensely felt absorption in the idea of metanoetics. This means that *zange* as a motif comes into its own only in the last of the thirteen sections that form *The Logic of the Species*.

Race wars

Tanabe's political philosophy does not consist of a dangerous brew of fascism, racial biology and Buddhist muddle. Dale appears to think that '*hōben*' (expedient means) refers to the individual, but in fact, as the Dilworth translation makes clear, it refers to the state itself. Tanabe is arguing that if the state has failed to observe the highest moral ends of East Asian subjectivity, the state itself may be deconstructed as part of an act of general national atonement.[12] Nevertheless, how Dilworth and Satō render one word at the beginning of 'The Logic of the Species as Dialectic' may have contributed decisively to Dale's impulse to blacken the reputation of Tanabe in particular and the Kyoto School in general. That word is 'race'.

In the second paragraph of their translation of 'The Logic of the Species as Dialectic', Dilworth and Satō have Tanabe talking about 'racial society', 'the specificity of the races', and individual geniuses belonging to a 'historical period and race'.[13] In all three cases, Tanabe does not use the Japanese word for race ('*jinshu*' or '*shuzoku*') but the word '*minzoku*', which in this context clearly refers to 'nation' or 'a people', as in the expression 'We, the peoples of Asia' ('*Warera Ajia sho-minzoku*' or '*kokumin*'). In Japanese, one speaks of the 'Mongoloid race' (*mongoru jinshu*) or the 'White race' (*hakujin jinshu*), not '*mongoru minzoku*' or '*hakujin minzoku*' (except in the plural, and then the usage is anachronistic).

Arguments about race raise two fundamental issues. One has been posed by Kevin Doak concerning the idea of the Pacific War as a 'race war', as proposed in, for example, John Dower's *War without Mercy: Race and Power in the Pacific War*.[14] Dower's case for regarding the Pacific War as a war between the races assumes that the term '*minzoku*' almost always meant 'race' in wartime Japanese writing. If '*minzoku*' normally referred to 'ethnic nationalism' rather than to 'race', Dower's argument about *the Japanese half* of this would-be race war may have to be reconsidered.

Doak rejects the idea that '*minzoku*' always means race. One consequence is that, in his *Dreams of Difference*, his translation/paraphrase of one key sentence from the 'Preface' of Tanabe's essay being discussed here departs significantly from that of Dilworth and Satō because it highlights how arbitrary translators can be about whether '*minzoku*' refers to 'nationalism', 'ethnic nationalism' or 'race':

> My [Tanabe] motive was to take up as a philosophical issue the problem of ethnic nationalism (*minzoku-shugi*), which was emerging at the time and, while criticizing the liberal thought that had dominated us for so long, to negate the so-called totalitarianism that is based merely on ethnic nationalism.[15]

In the same spirit and for the same reason, Doak took *War without Mercy* to task in his remarks at the 2003 Leiden University conference on 'Historical Consciousness and the Future of Modern China and Japan: Conservatism, Revisionism and National Identity', organised by Rikki Kersten and Axel Schneider. In his remarks, Doak blamed Dower for introducing the contentious issue of race into an already overheated debate on the nature of the Pacific War. The suggestion would be that as a discourse, the Japanese approached their struggle with the Anglo-Saxons with a less racist vocabulary than that employed by the Allies. For the translator of wartime Kyoto School texts who is uncertain about what the word '*minzoku*' means, the supreme test must be Masaaki Kōsaka's *Minzoku no Tetsugaku* (*The Philosophy of the Nation*) of 1942.[16]

Linguistically, I am with Doak on this issue. '*Minzoku*' may sometimes refer (ambiguously) to race, but the English word 'race' cannot be casually and uniformly translated as '*minzoku*'. The terms '*minzoku*' and 'race' are not equivalent. When an English native speaker uses the word 'race', the scope for misunderstanding is small (race may not be a scientific concept, but we all know, or think we do, what we mean when we use the term). This is not the case when a Japanese employs the word '*minzoku*'. This is why to put the word 'race' into Tanabe's mouth is deeply suspect. Hence, also, the suspicion that for American soldiers who fought the Pacific War, like those who fought in Korea and Vietnam later, their struggle was a race war in a way it may or may not have been for the Japanese.[17] But I have welcomed Dower's *War without Mercy* because it helps to shatter Allied illusions about why we fought the Pacific War. If our 'good war' was a race war, it was not a 'good war'. In contrast, Pacific War orthodoxy insists that only the Japanese side was racist. This position is indefensible. Whatever the Japanese struggle was, the American struggle was racist. In such insights are the beginning of wisdom and the end of (White) American exceptionalism.

The only sense in which '*minzoku*' refers to race in English is in old-fashioned expressions such as 'the British race' or 'the Welsh race' where the term clearly refers to a specific ethnic identity. Any claims for biological precision in such expressions are confounded by the fact that one used to be able to qualify simultaneously as a member of the Welsh, British and White races. These definitional boundaries are not always observed in informal discourse in Japan, and indeed there can be definitional slippage even among educated authors. The expression '*Yamato minzoku*' suffers from the same ambiguities that attached themselves to expressions such as 'the British race', so there is a potential 'biological' conundrum for the careless writer of Japanese. But Tanabe was not a careless writer.

There is one further twist to this linguistic trap. The ways by which words such as 'nation', 'ethnic food', 'people' and 'race' are mapped not only differ between languages but also change within the same language over time. This means that Japanese usage has to be handled with sensitivity. There is no point for the translator to take infinite care with Buddhist terminology only to use political concepts with reckless abandon. If the pernicious temptations of the politics of translation are to be curbed, fairness and accuracy require that every time the words 'nation', 'state', '*ethnos*', 'race' and 'people' are used in an English translation of a wartime Kyoto School text, the original Japanese term should be cited.

After Auschwitz, decolonisation and the post-war struggles in Western societies for racial equality, there is no more effective way of slamming the door on liberal discussion of a thinker and his ideas than to label him as a 'racist'. So, was the mistranslation of '*minzoku*' as 'race' in the English version of 'Benshō-hō toshite Shu no Ronri' accidental? Do we find here yet another example of the malign influence of Pacific War orthodoxy? To put the word 'race' repeatedly into Tanabe's mouth is to make him sound as if he were a racist. Such mistranslations may have made it all too easy for Dale to leap to the false conclusion that Tanabe was an 'ultranationalist'. Trapped in this politically incorrect language, the unwary can mistakenly assign a biological meaning and therefore a morally suspect colour to the word 'species'.

Tanabe borrows the word 'species' from Aristotelian logic. Species, in this context, has nothing whatever to do with biology. Therefore, to use the word 'race' in the translation of *The Logic of the Species* is to risk committing a tendentious slander against one of Japan's greatest modern thinkers. In their different ways, the translations or interpretations of such key words as 'expedient means', 'species' and '*minzoku*' (translated as 'race') appear to vilify Tanabe, but in unpersuasive ways. What, therefore, is to be made of Tanabe's use of the expression 'spontaneous obedience'?

The Talmudic eye

In one of the classic English parodies of the serious quiz show, a benighted contestant is asked, 'What swims in the sea and is caught in nets?', and the contestant immediately (and correctly) replies, 'Henri Bergson'. Perhaps this French philosopher can come swimming to our rescue over the moral conundrum supposedly at work in Tanabe's use of the expression 'spontaneous obedience'.

This is how Dilworth and Satō render the offending passage in which Tanabe summarises, with the concept of 'species' in mind, how he understands what Hegel means by 'objective spirit':

> It has both cultural and political content. Consequently, not only is it a specialisation and limitation of the absolute spirit as the universal, it also contains the power of binding and controlling the subjective spirit of the individual. In the case of the individual resisting or opposing it, it has the power and authority to coerce the individual's submission. In the instance of the individual affirming and developing it through the mediation of absolute spirit, it has the power and authority to force the individual's spontaneous obedience.[18]

In interpreting this passage, the first challenge is logical. Why does one need to 'force' spontaneous obedience if that is the one form of obedience that logically requires no enforcement? Furthermore, there has been a sudden reversal of argument in Tanabe's summary because he has turned *from* the notion of 'forcing' obedience on a resisting subject *to* the opposite idea: compelling the spontaneous obedience of an individual who 'affirms' the role of species. On the face of it, none of this makes sense.

Confronted with this overt softness of logic, one begins to probe for more weaknesses in the offending sentence. For example, the translators have chosen to render '*ken'i*' as 'power and authority'. In Japanese, '*ken'i*' refers to authority far more often than it does to power, but if one translates '*ken'i*' as authority (as Tanabe intends), the thrust of the sentence alters. Authority is a much more subtle notion than power; authority requires legitimacy, it is something lawful or quasi-lawful to which we give adherence freely and with conviction. By testing the translation in this way, the idea that Tanabe is wholly dependent on Hegel in developing this argument begins to crumble. More telling, the assumption that the Japanese philosopher defines the metaphysical relationship between the state and the individual in authoritarian terms disintegrates with it.

Radical doubts are now in order. 'Spontaneous obedience' does not sound Hegelian. Furthermore, the Japanese translation of 'spontaneous obedience' (*jihatsu-teki ni fukujū sashimuru ken'i o yūsuru*) is manifestly a borrowing from Western language and sounds odd even in Tanabe's rather abstractly Westernised style of writing Japanese.[19] But 'spontaneous obedience' does sound Bergsonian, and we know that after Hegel, Bergson is the other great Western influence on *The Logic of the Species*. The contrasting notions of 'open societies' and 'closed societies' that figure so prominently in *The Logic of the Species* come from Bergson. For any translator of Tanabe, the Bergson text that matters decisively here is *Les deux Sources de la Morale et de la Religion* of 1932.[20]

It may be no accident, therefore, that the expression '*obéissance spontanée*' has a prominent if somewhat intriguing place in *Two Sources of Morality and Religion*.[21] It is prominent because the term 'spontaneous obedience' appears early in the table of contents. It is the third item in the summary of themes contained in Chapter 1 ('Moral Obligation'). But it is intriguing because the expression does not appear in the text proper, in either the Japanese or the English translation. This is because it does not appear in the anticipated place in the French original itself. To understand what Bergson means by '*obéissance spontanée*', one has to read the whole of Chapter 1 because the argument is subtle and has little or nothing to do with political coercion.

From the standpoint of the translator of Tanabe, one question is compelling: how is the expression '*obéissance spontanée*' rendered into Japanese? Tanabe himself uses the phrase '*jihatsu-teki ni fukujū*' noted above. In the 1936 translation of *Les deux Sources de la Morale et de la Religion*, Kōji Hirayawa translates the expression as '*jihatsu-teki fukujū*'.[22] Hirayama's usage is so close to Tanabe's to justify exploring the possibility that Bergson is an unacknowledged but potent influence on Tanabe's language.

In Chapter 1 of *The Two Sources of Morality and Religion*, Bergson attempts to explain why humanity tends to obey, quite spontaneously, rules and commands, either intentionally or out of habit, hundreds of times every day. Bergson goes on to argue that without such obedience, the social order may crumble and humanity perish. Indeed, in some ways, this submerged continent of our almost instinctual responsiveness to authority provides the indispensable foundation for all the acts of independence and rebellion that we call 'freedom'.

Where does this theory place the late Bergson in the larger picture of European thinking during the early twentieth century? His idea that natural or habitual obedience produces a healthy spontaneous order suggests a comparison with the individualist convictions of Herbert Spencer (1820–1903), the English thinker who was so influential in Japan during Tanabe's youth. Spencer argued that left to themselves, human beings are naturally orderly and therefore in no need of external regulation, by either state or church.

Positivism is the contrasting faith. The rise of social determinism from the late nineteenth century onwards – Darwin, Marx and Freud – called attention to the vast areas of human conduct that are immune to rational choice and free decision. Bergson predictably carved out a unique position between these conflicting outlooks in *The Two Sources of Morality and Religion*. Furthermore, he did so in a way that reflects the powerful concern with the social morality one finds, for example, in Emile Durkheim, the great French sociologist. Both Durkheim and Bergson were alert to the need to secure a decent order in the face of society's weakness for spontaneous violence. Here the long shadow cast on French thought by the slaughter of the Paris Commune of 1871 is obvious.

What does all this mean for Tanabe in general and for the passage from *The Logic of the Species* under scrutiny? The Bergsonian analysis of man's neither-one-thing-nor-the-other relationship with Nature appears to have subtly transformed how the Japanese thinker exploits what Hegel meant by 'objective spirit'. In the passage under consideration, Tanabe declares that he is describing Hegel's position (as distinct from his own). But Tanabe had formed his position on this issue a decade before in the 1930s. Tanabe's standpoint, as opposed to Hegel's, inevitably reflects the Japanese philosopher's deep interest in the anthropology of Lucien Lévy-Bruhl, that is with the nature of totem societies, as well as with pre-rationality, or what Claude Levi-Strauss later called '*la pensée sauvage*' (the savage mind). Myth-ruled communities dominate Tanabe's deliberations in a way that is not true of Hegel. This intellectual horizon is as vital to Tanabe as it is to Bergson in their long and fruitful meditation on the nature of 'closed' societies.

What is at work in the passage from *The Logic of the Species* being examined is a kind of Hegel–Bergson–Tanabe synthesis in which the objective spirit is brought into shouting distance of Nature. Dialectical logic orders this synthesis, but this is no authoritarian tract, no Hobbesian denunciation of anarchy, and no fascist call for political surrender to primordial instinct. The language is metaphorical. Bergson and Tanabe accept the fact that human beings are also animals. Thus, both philosophers are concerned with the twilight zone between the rule of reason and the compulsions of instinct. Tanabe roams this twilight world to map more accurately the boundary that links open and closed societies. Here Tanabe does not advocate anything; he is offering an objective perusal of our nature as thinking animals. Understand Tanabe in this way, and the neo-Marxist critique of the passage under analysis begins to buckle and crack.

What, then, are we to make of the words 'force', 'coerce' and 'enforce' in this passage, the words that leave the liberal most uneasy with Tanabe's line of argument? We have already identified a logical problem housed in the contradictory idea of having 'to enforce spontaneous obedience'. Furthermore, the translation of '*ken'i*' as 'power and authority', in the light of a Hegel–Bergson–Tanabe synthesis, may mislead. '*Ken'i*' here refers to some notion of authority, but not to power or compulsion in the legal or military sense. The contested expressions 'force', 'coerce' and 'enforce' are all translations of the same Japanese term: '*kyō-sei*'. What does this word mean?

The conventional dictionary definitions of '*kyō-sei*' include 'compulsion' and 'coercion' as nouns, and 'compel', 'force' and 'coerce' as verb roots. But when we say 'instinct made the dog do that', we are talking about the promptings of nature, not the prod of a policeman's baton. Similarly, when a hero proclaims, 'I was forced to go into the fire to rescue the child; there

was no time to wait', the compulsion implied has nothing to do with political coercion. So when we use the word 'force' in this context, we must not
yield to the temptation to emphasise physical coercion at the expense of
other meanings of the word. So, what do Tanabe and Bergson really mean
by '*kyō-sei*'?

The Japanese translator of *Le Deux Sources de la Morale et la Religion*
provides the essential gloss. In his translation, Hirayama takes particular
care in rendering one crucial sentence early in Chapter 1:

> The laws which it [society] promulgates and which maintain the social
> order resemble, moreover, in certain respects, the laws of nature. I admit
> that the difference is a radical one in the eyes of the philosopher. To him
> the law which enunciates facts is one thing, the law that commands,
> another. It is possible to evade the latter; here we have obligation, not
> necessity.[23]

In French, the last sentence is '*A celle-ci l'on peut se soustraire: elle oblige,
mais ne nécessite pas.*'[24] In a rare gesture towards linguistic precision,
Hirayama actually cites '*obliger*', *in French*, in his Japanese text. He translates '*obliger*' as '*kyō-sei*'.[25]

With this rendering of '*kyō-sei*', the key to unlocking the true meaning of
Tanabe's summary of Hegel (with Bergson lurking between the lines) at last
falls into our grasp. The text begins to make sense. In French, the nuance of
'*obliger*' reaches from the realm of compulsion to the English meaning of
'oblige' – 'to bind or constrain (someone to do something) by legal, moral,
or physical means' (*Collins English Dictionary*) – and even to the idea of
'cause'. Substitute 'oblige' for 'coerce', 'force' and 'enforce' in the English
translation of 'The Logic of the Species as Dialectic' and the text is transformed. At last, we are in a position to read Tanabe as this great Japanese
philosopher intended us to read him. And this discovery drives home one
lesson above all: the only organ that will do justice to Tanabe's *oeuvre*, in all
its splendid complexities, is the relentless, tireless Talmudic eye such as we
find at work in the textual labours of Marx, Walter Benjamin and Derrida.

8 When is a philosopher a moral monster?

Tanabe versus Heidegger versus Marcuse

> No state can long survive, let alone flourish, if it turns its back on reason.
>
> Tanabe[1]

> The law of reason has of itself the force of law based on human rationality independently of the determinations of the legislator or of custom.
>
> Minobe[2]

To think is to gamble. In *The Myth of Japanese Uniqueness*, Dale complains that Nishida's 'subject-object ontology' not only helped to pave the way for the scientific absurdities of *Nihonjin-ron* but also contributed intellectually to Japan's plunge into fascism and world war.[3] This argument wraps the Kyoto School in political controversy but at a philosophic price. To the degree that Nishida was a *philosopher* of his time, Dale's criticism implies the rejection of an entire generation or phase in modern philosophy, Western and Japanese. The attempt to think beyond the subject-versus-object conundrum involved thinkers as diverse and important as Bergson, Croce, Husserl and William James. Nishida was in very good company.

By criticising Nishida for his philosophy, one may lend one's voice to the denigration of philosophy itself. This willingness to demean philosophy has wide support across Japan studies in the West, particularly among the former Allied powers. Indeed, American scholars have often led the attack. The goal of this chapter and the three chapters that follow is to ask whether the most recent phase of this attack on modern Japanese philosophy can withstand serious scrutiny.

Fascist philosophy?

Is fascist philosophy possible? Gianni Gentile (1875–1945) offers the test case. This Italian thinker was a self-confessed Fascist philosopher and one of the intellectual mainstays of Mussolini's regime from its inception in 1922 until its humiliating end in 1943. Gentile was a Fascist with a capital 'F'. If he was not a fascist in the way his critics mean when they attack 'fascist philosophy', no one was. Yet, even in the case of Gentile, the canvas of historical realities of

Italian Fascism cannot be painted entirely in black and white.[4] In contrast to what Second World War orthodoxy has led one to expect, there is a radical divide between much that Gentile advocated (Italian modernisation and national self-reliance, for example) and what most opponents of fascism find objectionable about the collection of prejudices, ideas, policies and values that is fascist ideology. The man was not all bad. This is an empirical statement first, and a moral one second. Note, once again, how orthodoxy has allowed itself to be caught up in moral essentialism. If the man did one thing bad, or even many things, he is evil in essence. This is a metaphysical conclusion, not an empirical one. This judgment is not a judgment of fact.

If a closer reading of Gentile – the easiest of targets – exposes Second World War orthodoxy to convincing accusations of myth and propaganda, of neglect of the facts and self-serving moralising, the conventional Allied interpretation of the war as a whole may be more brittle than many suspect or fear. If our portrait of Italy under Fascism might benefit from some judiciously grey touches – a modicum of moral objectivity, more care in handling matters of philosophical language, more politically balanced interpretations and greater attention to inconvenient facts – might this also be true of our understanding of wartime Japan?

Six decades after 1945, philosophy – Italian, Japanese and German – has come to stand near the emotional heart of the contemporary battle to interpret the greatest conflict in human history. Since the late 1980s, Second World War orthodoxy has added an unexpected twist to the accusations of fascism routinely made against Tanabe and Heidegger. Now Kyoto School philosophy is being condemned *because* of Heidegger's apparent lapses. Advocates of this new line of attack do not overtly blame Tanabe or Nishida for Auschwitz, but rather they insist that because the knives have come out for Heidegger, the wartime Kyoto School must also be made to feel the blade. The supposed 'revelations' in Victor Farías's *Heidegger et le nazisme* (1987), for example, have contributed directly and powerfully to the explosion of anti-Kyoto School criticism that has recently shaken Japanese studies in America and elsewhere.

How the scandal provoked by Farías among French intellectuals in the late 1980s led to a fresh assault on the Kyoto School during the 1990s is a long and complex story which will be examined in detail in Chapters 9, 10 and 11, but here the focus is on the 'German problem' of the Kyoto School. Implausible on many counts, this problem may be defined in a single question: were Heidegger and Tanabe moral monsters? This question will be answered in three ways. First, the Japanese–German foundations of the accusation of philosophic fascism are scrutinised. Secondly, Tanabe's reflections on Heidegger's philosophical reaction to the German Uprising of 1933 are examined more closely than they have been previously in English. Thirdly, the post-war letters exchanged between Heidegger and Herbert Marcuse are subjected to a revisionist reading. The goal of this analysis is to solve philosophy's 'Japanese problem' by resolving its 'German problem'.

The case against Tanabe

The *Japanese* critique of Tanabe's politics between 1931 and 1945 is regularly grounded in pacifism. Because he was a wartime patriot who supported his country in its struggle with the Allied enemy, Tanabe was not a pacifist. But in post-war Japan, not to be a pacifist is to be ethically beyond the pale for a large section, perhaps the majority, of the Japanese intelligentsia. This stance may explain why many of Tanabe's left-wing critics find his 1943 lecture, titled 'Life or Death', delivered to newly drafted students preparing to depart for the front, far more objectionable than anything he wrote about political collectivism in *The Logic of the Species*. How could a great philosopher send students off to war? The very idea is morally revolting. That Tanabe might have criticised the wartime government of Japan or even conspired with a faction of the Imperial Navy to bring down the Tojo Cabinet is irrelevant to the unreconstructed pacifist.

The *Allied* critic of Tanabe tends not to be a pacifist. The Allied objection to Tanabe is that he was a nationalist thinker who believed in the Japanese Empire and condoned Japanese resistance to White hegemony over the Western Pacific and Southeast Asia. Implicit in Allied criticism is the complaint that Tanabe was complicit in Japanese violence against the Allies. Thus, for Western orthodoxy, war itself is not wrong, but wars of expansion prosecuted in an aggressive and barbaric manner are. The Allied case focuses more on the concrete example of the Pacific War than on matters of principle such as pacifism.

The Allied moral case is built on the essentialist assumption of the Tokyo War Crimes Tribunal that only the Japanese (and some of its colonial subjects) violated international law, and therefore any Japanese who supported the Pacific War is vulnerable to moral condemnation. Perhaps the real objection against Tanabe is that he did not rally to the defence of parliamentary privileges that even Japanese parliamentarians were abandoning at the time. Edwin O. Reischauer argued in his famous essay 'What Went Wrong?' that the pre-war Japanese elite failed to sustain the dream of 'Taishō Democracy'.[5] Tanabe was part of that flawed elite.

There are nationalist and self-serving elements in the Western critique of Tanabe, but the focus of its ire is the supposedly 'illiberal' character of the wartime Kyoto School. The Kyoto philosopher was not only opposed to 'us' but he (supposedly) failed to demonstrate sufficient loyalty to liberal civilisation. Objections to Heidegger's conduct in 1933 reflect similar moral concerns. However, a close reading of Tanabe's writings during the Great East Asian War – *The Logic of the Species* as well as his wartime lectures and occasional writings, including the controversial lecture on 'Life or Death', to say nothing of the anti-Tojo *Ōshima Memos* – does not, in my view, sustain the Allied critique.[6] To read the relevant Heideggerian philosophical texts for the same period – from 'The Self-assertion of the German University' to *The Letter on Humanism* – in a similarly untendentious way is to reach the same conclusion. The Allied critique is not grounded in the facts of the matter.

Tanabe, Hobbes and Schmitt

Tanabe as a thinker addressed problems of modernity, authority and solidarity that bore a family resemblance to the problems of late feudal and early modern Europe. Hobbes and his problems were implicitly important to Tanabe as they were explicitly vital to Carl Schmitt, perhaps the most brilliant legal mind of Weimar Germany. Tanabe was as alert as Tatsukichi Minobe, the most influential constitutional theorist of interwar Japan, to the country's liberal democratic potential. But Tanabe was more aware of the many obstacles that stood between Japan and the realisation of this potential.

If Tanabe as a political philosopher was not a liberal, in the Anglo-American-French sense of the word, what was he and what might he have of value to teach us today? Tanabe, like Heidegger, sought a third way between communism and capitalism. This was partly a cultural concern and partly a practical objection. It was not obvious that liberal capitalism secured the values of high culture, including philosophy, nor that the Japanese state could make liberal capitalism work without tearing Japanese society apart. Like many Japanese and Western intellectuals at the time, Tanabe doubted the efficiency of liberal democracy and the effectiveness of Wall Street capitalism.

Contemplating the decline of the constitutional order of Weimar Germany, Schmitt developed a penetrating critique of liberal democracy that has, at numerous points, yet to be refuted. In a similar vein, it may be asked whether contemporary East Asia has solved the problems that Tanabe addressed with such elaborate metaphysical care between 1934 and 1946. His reflections on pre-democratic subjectivity may make him relevant to a world in which the crisis of post-democratic subjectivity appears to be deepening.

Tanabe's claim to contemporary and future relevance begins with doubts about the staying power of the inner forms (rather than the institutions) of liberal democracy. The democratic wave that triumphed over fascism and communism during the twentieth century was not inevitable. Nor does democracy have a claim on eternity. The decline of political literacy in the Anglo-Saxon homeland of democracy (can democracy survive without 'high' literacy?), the cynicism that grips electorates in Japan and the democratic West, the powerful appeal of populist decadence, the dismissal of democratic civic education as boring, and the success of technocratic manipulation of the economy, by autonomous central bankers, for example – all suggest that classic parliamentary democracy – government by, for and of the people – may not define the future of the advanced post-industrial world. The 'world wide web' has spawned a new form of elitism sometimes called the 'netocracy' (Alexander Bard). Most web innovations are either indifferent to traditional democratic institutions and values or erode them. But, then, why should liberal democracy, this creation of the nineteenth century, necessarily define our future if so obviously it has not defined anything but our recent past?

Post-industrialism and post-modernism may be followed by post-democracy. The erosion of the democratic faith and the broad contemporary surrender to the realm of pleasure and instinct, including electronic stimulation, may thrust us into a world about which Tanabe has more to say than John Dewey or Harold Laski. What we are as a group, what we may need as a species, may reach beyond contemporary definitions of civic duty and parliamentary procedures. These developments should not be welcomed by any thinking democrat, but, if they form a secular trend, the liberal world may have to struggle to survive.

This highlights the importance of species and subjectivity. What we are as a group may increasingly turn on what we can achieve as a group. The new century may need to dwell less on freedom because the discourse of liberty has always assumed the existence of an effective agency. Anglo-Saxon modernity takes agency for granted, from Robinson Crusoe on his lonely island to the idea of the yeoman archer as 'a free Englishman' down to the Industrial Revolution's concept of 'the economic rationalising individual'. The New World has always bathed in the luxury of matured subjectivity, from its ideal of the rugged pioneer to Franklin D. Roosevelt's celebration of 'common man' and the achievements of today's liberated woman. This has been the unacknowledged European secret of American national success. What divides the English-speaking democracies from the so-called Third World even now is that we can assume the existence of subjectivity, and therefore we speak endlessly of liberty, while the Third World lacks the miracle of subjectivity, and therefore dismisses the discourse of liberty as so much cant.

In a post-White era, the challenge will be the nurturing, *ex nihilo*, of agency itself. To the degree that humanity's fundamental ability to set and achieve goals, to manage the planet rationally, is in doubt, subjectivity, the central concern of the wartime Kyoto School, may come to define the intellectual agenda of the future in a way that Heidegger's intuition of 'deep ecology' resonates so powerfully in global consciousness today.

Tanabe versus Heidegger

Imperial Japan was a rational state. In legal terms, it was a kind of *Rechtstaat*, a nation of laws where judicial reason exercised substantial sovereignty. In economic terms, it was a market-driven society, modernising and rationalising in a way that Max Weber would have respected. Imperial Japan may have better reflected the collectivist ambitions espoused in Friedrich List's *System of National Economy* than the individualist principles set out in Adam Smith's *The Wealth of Nations*, but it was a dynamic, competitive and growing economy. Politically, it was a mixed constitution, legitimated by a monarchy and administered by a powerful bureaucracy; but pre-war Japan was also a nation where liberal (and potentially democratic) forms had a prominent and growing place.

At every point that Imperial Japan was a successful society, it was a rational society. Either strictly rational ends were pursued by rational means (modern transport and mass production in heavy industry, for example) or traditional values and energies were mobilised for rational ends. In this context, it should surprise no one that some of the most important thinkers of Imperial Japan, men such as Tanabe and Minobe, were rationalists.

No idea that the Japanese imported from the West influenced or disconcerted them more than reason, in all its wonderful ramifications, from logical analysis to industrial rationalisation. The guardian deity for the post-war Japanese understanding of this historical transformation is Weber, the German sociologist who not only classically grasped the religious origins of Western capitalism in the Protestant work ethic but also predicted our current discontents at being trapped in the 'iron cage' of globalisation. The impact of reason on the Japanese *Geist* after the Meiji Restoration of 1868 may explain why philosophy, a distinctive European obsession, mattered so much to the educated elite of Imperial Japan. It is the power of reason, as Kant, Hegel and Weber understood it, that explains why some of the finest minds of Imperial Japan sought to understand modernity philosophically rather than merely scientifically or empirically.

In political-philosophical terms, the deepening crisis of Japanese society after the Wall Street Crash of 1929 registered in the declining prestige and apparent efficacy of rational argument within the public sphere. This affected both the way the *Kokutai* (the national polity) could be discussed and the way that policymaking was debated and determined (as opposed to the rational way policymakers normally attempted to implement it). The relative eclipse of reason (this eclipse was relative and, strictly speaking, rather limited) was largely a matter of language: restrictions on certain kinds of modes of argument. But as language and public argument were indispensable to the labours of intellectuals of all ideological stripes, any closing of national ranks in the face of domestic and international crisis inevitably had a demoralising effect on many Japanese intellectuals.

Minobe and Tanabe represent two 'ideal typical' (Weber) responses to the narrowing of the scope of national discourse during the 1930s. The story of Minobe's fall from public grace – and disgrace and censorship were all that he suffered (note that left-wing artists and intellectuals often had to endure worse during the grim era of McCarthyism in post-war America) – is famous and well documented.[7] At almost the same time as Minobe was losing his commanding place in the legal establishment, Tanabe asserted his role as the defender of reason in the Imperial Japanese state with his essay 'The Logic of Social Existence'. This would become the core of his monumental *Shu no Ronri* (*The Logic of the Species*), his 'crowning achievement'

(Heisig) as a philosopher. The torch of Japanese reason had passed from Minobe to Tanabe.

In 'The Logic of Social Existence', Tanabe developed his first formulation of the '*ronri* [logic] of the *shu* [species]'. The classical Greek ontological schema of universal, species (the specific or particular) and the individual (in Japanese, *fuhen*, *shu*, *ko*) provided the indispensable framework and point of departure for Tanabe's metaphysical project. His central contention remains beyond dispute: Western philosophers had traditionally concentrated on the 'universal' and 'the individual', thus leaving the concept of the species under-theorised. In this vast edifice of reflection, Tanabe sought to fill this gap in classical ontological reasoning. Only in this way could the 'social' as a logical category be embedded in reason. If the social could be rationalised in a way that transcended (in the Hegelian sense) the mythical imperatives of the Japanese *Kokutai*, the subversive potential of myth could be deflected in a way that Minobe's comparative constitutionalism had proven unable to do. The rational foundations of the Meiji state could, once again, be made intellectually secure.

Minobe as a legal thinker sought to make the law speak Japanese, that is to make two distinct modes of being, thinking and feeling, work in tandem: the *Rechtstaat* and the *Kokutai*, or 'Japanese way of life' (Miller). In a parallel project, Tanabe sought to make the Graeco-German philosophy of the rational state speak Japanese, thus to overcome the dynamic tension between state and nation/people in order to realise an effective Japanese amalgam of the *nation-state* (*minzoku-kokka*), or 'national-popular state'.[8]

This ambitious goal is what transformed *The Logic of the Species* into a meditation on the problematic nature of the Japanese concept of '*minzoku*' (nation or people or ethnie). Some have concluded that, given the times, this was a dangerous undertaking, but there was nothing that Imperial Japan needed more during the 1930s than a clear, rational understanding of itself as a nation (*minzoku soku kokumin*). This is what Tanabe attempted to provide in *The Logic of the Species*.

How could such an endeavour be described as 'fascist'? Tanabe *does* concentrate on the collective at the expense of the universal and the individual. To attempt to theorise about the state, nation or ethnie during an era of mounting nationalist sentiment *did* risk pandering to populist feeling rather than attempting to tame it. But none of this makes Tanabe into a moral monster. Why? For a conclusive answer, one must turn to another of the great metaphysical texts of this turbulent era: Martin Heidegger's Rectoral Address.

Tanabe on Heidegger

Indifferent to our future, the orthodox critique of Heidegger and Tanabe has also failed to map our moral past with sufficient care. This Allied consensus certainly conspires against a sound understanding of modern Japanese and

German philosophy. Increasingly *passé*, Allied criticism of the Kyoto School in general and of Tanabe in particular is transforming philosophical analysis into political carping. On the subject of Heidegger, it already has.

This German philosopher has long been the victim of shotgun criticism, and although the fire has been much more intense during the past two decades, close reading of the texts in question undermines rather than strengthens criticism of Heidegger. Such attacks are rarely philosophical in nature because these would-be Nazi-hunters search for ethical lapses and political misstatements rather than logical errors or metaphysical inconsistencies. In *Heidegger et le nazisme*, Farías's laboured indictment of the conservative intellectual climate of Heidegger's Catholic childhood, for example, is strained to the point of hysteria because the Chilean journalist seems desperate to blame Heidegger for the *Shoah*.[9]

Heidegger welcomed the German Uprising because he believed that it endorsed his metaphysical vision. His enthusiasm for the Nazi government expressed in his speeches and addresses reflected his hope for a comprehensive national renewal in the face of desperate crisis. He responded to this tumultuous period with his Rectoral Address of May 1933. Löwith called *Die Selbstbehauptung der deutschen Universität* 'a stylistic masterpiece', but it was much more. 'The Self-assertion of the German University' has become one of the most widely read and fiercely debated public addresses by any major philosopher since Socrates.[10]

Tanabe was one of the first great philosophers to examine the core arguments of the Rectoral Address.[11] Only four months after Heidegger delivered his *Rektoratsrede*, Tanabe responded in a three-part essay dated 5 September 1933 and published between 4 and 6 October 1933 in the prestigious mass-circulation Japanese newspaper *Asahi Shinbun*.[12] The content, tone and sceptical engagement of Tanabe's 'The Philosophy of Crisis or a Crisis in Philosophy?' makes the work of contemporary critics of Heidegger seem thin, philistine and morally unserious.

Reading Tanabe's criticism of Heidegger, one is left wondering if the principal Allied objection to Heidegger as a German thinker is anchored elsewhere, less in his political statements of the early 1930s and more in his post-war 'silence' on the subject of the *Shoah*. This matters even more, one suspects, than that single provocative remark praising the 'inner greatness' of national socialism, made in the context of a discussion of Nietzsche's call for the revaluation of all values, at the end of his *Introduction to Metaphysics*, published in 1953. Certainly, Heidegger's 'silence' has been the source of more unease than almost anything he wrote before he resigned as Rector of Freiburg University in 1934, a decision that signalled the beginning of Heidegger's abandonment of his illusionary hope that the German Uprising would open the way to the philosophic rediscovery of Being by Western civilisation.[13]

Tanabe's intellectually honest engagement with Heidegger's ideas contrasts sharply with the tendentiousness that has reigned in the former

Allied nations since the Farías thunderclap broke over Paris. True, Heidegger's political writings of 1933–34 demonstrate that he was caught up in the nationalist excitement and ethnic assertion that swept Germany when Hitler formed the final government under the Weimar Constitution. We know now that this uprising opened the door to the destruction of one of the last powerhouses of world-class European thought, of which this German philosopher was one of the great figures. But, to paraphrase Georg Lukács' famous remark about his expulsion from the Communist Party after the 1956 Hungarian Revolution, Heidegger thought that the Nazis were joining him in 1933, not the other way round. Heidegger was far too egotistical, far too confident of his mental powers (and he had every reason to be confident) than to 'follow' anyone else's movement. To conclude that 'Heidegger was a lifetime Nazi' (Rockmore) is not persuasive. Such observations suggest that one has not understood the man. If one is blinded by the Allied Gaze, one never will.

But, to the degree that criticism of Heidegger's politics (if he can be said to have such a thing) is grounded in a convincing understanding of his philosophy, it is his Rectoral Address of 1933 that has served as the lightning rod of liberal censure. Unfortunately, almost all attempts to move this controversy away from the realm of political cliché and prejudice to the seminar room and the demanding labour of carefully analysing a Heideggerian text has been bedevilled by the hypocrisy of the Allied Gaze. Heidegger's reputation has been stained by the same politics of misreading as we have seen in the case of wilful Western misunderstandings of Tanabe's writings during the same period under consideration: 1931–45.

As a result, we have tendentious translations of 'The Self-assertion of the German University' to set alongside our tendentious renderings of *The Logic of the Species*. Given the pernicious impact of the Allied Gaze, this was all too predictable. The resulting failure of the orthodox to sustain a metaphysically coherent critique of so-called 'Axis philosophy' only highlights the supreme irony of all criticism of so-called fascist philosophy: the fact that one of the earliest and most incisive attacks on Heidegger's Rectoral Address was made by Tanabe himself.

Criticising Heidegger

On 27 May 1933, Martin Heidegger, the newly appointed head of Freiburg University, delivered his famous inaugural address, 'The Self-assertion of the German University', as rector.[14] Coming five months after Hitler had assumed the chancellorship of the doomed Weimar Republic in January 1933, the *Rektoratsrede* achieved immediate notoriety, and not only in philosophic circles. More than half a century later, the bitter chorus of criticism of the Rectoral Address continues unabated. Richard Wolin, for example, has concluded that 'at the beginning, Heidegger tried to reconcile a philosophical "discourse on spirit" with the demands of the German Revolution, but the result was a miscarriage, a monstrosity, about whose failure neither side had many illusions'.[15]

This judgment is too severe. The 'Final Solution' was a monstrous horror. The anti-Jewish Nürnberg Laws were a gross miscarriage of German justice. But to give a chapter on Heidegger's philosophy the title 'Arbeit Macht Frei', as Wolin does, is morally beyond the pale.[16] It resurrects all of Julien Benda's grim warnings about 'the intellectual organisation of political hatreds'.[17] Heidegger's 'politics of Being' may have been a failure, but the terms 'miscarriage' and 'monstrosity' do not apply. Heidegger was not responsible for Auschwitz.

His brief involvement in German politics was entirely against the grain of his anti-subjectivist metaphysics, much as Nishida's wartime activities did not derive from his philosophical position. Outside his overtly political tracts of 1934–35 – and the Rectoral Address does not qualify for a place among these very contentious writings – there is nothing in Heidegger that is as dark, as uncannily unsettling, as we find in Wagner or Nietzsche. Heidegger's Rectoral Address was not an act of political cynicism, nor was it a 'philosophical somersault into primitivity'.[18] But to understand why it was none of these things, we must listen, delaying any rush to judgment, in the name of philosophic truth and political fairness. In any pursuit of objective criticism, Tanabe is a judicious guide.

He titled his essay on Heidegger 'The Philosophy of Crisis or a Crisis in Philosophy?' The first translation into English of this key text appears in the Appendix to this book. That a great Japanese newspaper should have chosen to publish this demanding and indeed historic piece in its pages offers yet another impressive demonstration of the intelligence and generosity of the Japanese spirit in that turbulent hour. With typical scrupulousness, Tanabe identifies the precise circumstances, his textual sources and his own motives for responding to Heidegger's Rectoral Address.

In Part I, Tanabe offers a summary of the German text, placing the ideas of Heidegger in a classical Greek context. Having attempted to give a balanced and accurate version of Heidegger's position, Tanabe goes on, in Part II, to pose the central question: 'Armed only with the awareness of the powerlessness of knowledge is it possible to establish, with this principle alone, the foundations for a positive metaphysics of the nation-state?' Tanabe traces the weaknesses that hamper Heidegger's call for Germans to embrace a politics of Being to the German thinker's dependence on Aristotle. In particular, Tanabe argues against Aristotle's notion of *theoria*, or the active contemplation of reality.

In a conceit that Burke would have approved of, Tanabe argues that Aristotle's ideas did not work because the Greek philosopher lacked practical experience of the rough and tumble of political life. Aristotle's deficiency contrasts sharply with Plato's profound involvement in the great political dramas of his time. In philosophic terms, Tanabe is declaring his preference for an active, that is subjectivist (*shutai-teki*), philosophy, one that takes man as the centre of creation, over an objectivist metaphysics that insists that man must conform to a transcendent force, be it the cosmos or nature for the ancient Greeks or God or Heidegger's Being. This is the ruling motif of *The Logic of the Species*, and so powerful is the subjectivist thrust of Tanabe's thought that it reduces *Zange toshite no Tetsugaku*, his would-be apology of 1946 for his wartime stance, to a temporary aberration within the overall architecture of his thought.[19]

The human world over the cosmos; action rather than contemplation; Plato rather than Aristotle. Tanabe's position is clear and coherent; Heidegger's stance suffers by comparison. And there Tanabe might have left it, but in Part III he boldly shakes the groundwork of his own thinking. He proceeds to rehearse the often-told tale of Plato's failures in the sphere of practical politics, from the death of Socrates to the Syracuse debacle. Tanabe evokes Hegel's tragic conception of the struggle between the state and philosophic truth, 'of the tragic readings of man and of man's relations to the state which has its dual source in Greek tragedy and in the emblematic episode of the death of Socrates'.[20]

Throughout his critique of Heidegger, Tanabe's commitment to reason is unflinching, even though he acknowledges the limits of reason. He was determined to demythify Japanese thought by bringing rationality and nationalist faith into explosive proximity, as it were, on the same page. Few Japanese philosophers have taken the duty to act responsibly in the political sphere that the modern metaphysician inherits from the civic culture of the ancient Greek polis more seriously than Tanabe. Furthermore, he embraced this strenuous vocation not during the flowering of Taishō-era tolerance (or was it indifference?), nor during the comparative security of the post-war American occupation of his country, but rather during the most testing days of Japanese civilisation between 1931 and 1945.

Anxious to deflect criticism of Tanabe's wartime writings, some of his defenders have been keen to describe this Japanese thinker as a great philosophic mind who happened also to be a political naïf.[21] This is not persuasive. Tanabe knew what he was doing. He was determined to shore up the rational foundations of Imperial Japan because he believed that Japan was moving towards its own 'tryst with destiny' (Nehru).

Because tragedy has an inevitable place in the human condition, the potential for tragedy as the world historical moment drew near had to be faced. Even after the Minobe affair reached its dramatic conclusion in October 1935, Tanabe pressed on with his *The Logic of the Species*. Historical necessity demanded it. Tanabe's supreme concern was that the Japanese people, sustained by the ark of reason, successfully navigate the most dangerous crisis in their national history. This concern manifests itself throughout his wartime writings, from his 1933 essay on Heidegger to his 1942 lecture titled 'The Logic of Co-prosperity Spheres', his secret memorandum for the naval opposition to Tojo.[22] The one thing the man was not was naïve.

Moral monsters: Heidegger versus Marcuse

Is a balanced, accurate and objective portrait of the philosophy of the Kyoto School or Martin Heidegger possible? Allied orthodoxy would have us believe that such balance, accuracy and objectivity is possible but not desirable because it is immoral to argue the case for either Heidegger or the wartime Kyoto School. Tanabe and Heidegger are fascist philosophers, and no amount of condemnation is too much.

There are dangers in making so relentless and one-sided a case for so long because the critics, no less than the criticised, live in metaphysical glasshouses. The orthodox mind does not perceive its vulnerability because it has yet to be exposed to full-blooded criticism. Orthodoxy is highly vulnerable, and the post-war correspondence between Heidegger and his student, Herbert Marcuse, provides an opportunity to expose its factual and ethical weaknesses.

The indictment

Heidegger's greatness is reflected in his students. Talent sought him out. He attracted some of twentieth-century Europe's most promising young philosophers, including Karl Löwith, Hannah Arendt, Hans Jonas and Herbert Marcuse. His German students of Jewish descent were forced to flee the Third Reich, but Heidegger refused to follow in the footsteps of such famous self-exiles as Thomas Mann. Even after he resigned from the Freiburg rectorship in despair over the metaphysical failure of the German Uprising, he chose to remain in Germany. This decision inflicted severe strain on his relationship with his students. In the case of Marcuse, profound ties of intellectual friendship were eventually shattered by the events of the Second World War, or, more precisely, because of Marcuse's reaction to those events.

The bitter and unnecessary rupture between Heidegger and Marcuse unfolded in three letters exchanged after the war. Early in 1947, Marcuse visited his former teacher in Todtnauberg, Heidegger's rural retreat in the Black Forest. Having 'thought for a long time about what you told me during my visit', Marcuse wrote to Heidegger from Washington DC in late August 1947.[23] In response to this letter and a package of food, Heidegger replied from Germany, after an extended delay, with a letter dated 20 January 1948. Marcuse answered, many months later, in another letter from Washington dated 12 May. In a handful of pages, two of the most creative minds of the past century, hitherto bound by the complex psychology of the teacher–student relationship, parted company. The long silences between the letters matter as much as their content. Read carefully, certainly more carefully than it has been read, this brief correspondence offers a touchstone for radical revisionism in twentieth-century philosophy, both German and Japanese.

Wolin has set forth the orthodox view in his gloss of the three letters which he translated for his edited volume *The Heidegger Controversy*.[24] He takes Marcuse's side, refusing to subject him to any critical scrutiny aside from hinting at his *naïveté* about Heidegger's politics.[25] Given the Third Reich's aggressive ideology, its brutal expansion and its harsh, often savage, administration of occupied Europe, this is hardly surprising. Nazism's genocidal conduct towards Slavs and Jews has stoked the flames of orthodox criticism as nothing else. One can debate the pros and cons of the Pacific War (with difficulty), but morally the European war is closer to the Sino-Japanese struggle of 1937–45. The difficulty with Second World War orthodoxy is that the absolute moral convictions that the Allied scholar has brought to his research have encouraged an unsound interpretation of both the historical facts and the philosophical ideas at issue.

Orthodox criticism of Heidegger employs strategies of reading that offer a close analogy to those applied by Allied critics of the wartime Kyoto School. One result is that the often-sophisticated philosophical analysis of a major text is undermined by the unsettling simplifications of less careful political scrutiny. By giving ethical politics its head, the student of wartime thought subverts his philosophical analysis. The more the commentator identifies with his moral certainties, the more likely that the inconvenient facts at issue, that is facts which undermine his own party position, will be ignored or evaded.

Faced with the controversial subject of Heidegger's politics during the only overtly political chapters in the philosopher's life, Wolin does something very revealing: he traduces not only Heidegger but also Marcuse. Thus, on the collapse of Marcuse's 'existential Marxist' project, Wolin strains on the lead of his philosophic training to get closer to the pulpit of moral judgment. The rooted American preference for politics over philosophy feeds something little short of moral rage. The seriousness of Marcuse as a thinker is neglected in Wolin's surrender to raw emotion and intense resentment:

> But whatever the inner, conceptual grounds may have been for the breakdown of Marcuse's project of 'existential Marxism', the immediate cause for its dissolution seemed to owe more to the force of objective historical circumstances: Hitler's accession to power on January 30, 1933, followed by Heidegger's enthusiastic proclamation of support for the regime four months later.[26]

'Objective historical circumstances'? What is objective or historical in this summary? First, on no textual grounds whatever, Marcuse's principal project as a thinker at the time is judged to be of inferior importance, *for Marcuse*, than the headlines of the extremely confused political circumstances – and they were confusing to everyone involved, even the Nazi hierarchy – that prevailed during the final months of the Weimar Republic.

It may be obvious to us now what was happening then, but it was not clear then, to Marcuse or Hitler or Heidegger. The words 'objective' and 'historical' have no meaning in this context applied to Marcuse, the thinking German of the spring of 1933. Wolin's view is suspect precisely because it judges the case with the one advantage that Marcuse did not enjoy: the perfect vision of hindsight.

More unsettling still is Wolin's final phrase: 'Heidegger's enthusiastic proclamation of support for the regime four months later'. The political reader without philosophical training may read this to mean that Heidegger rallied to the new regime as an uncomplicated political act. This kind of phrasing unwittingly confirms the bias that the Allied reader may bring to his understanding of Heidegger. Unmentioned in the text but noted in a footnote is the fact that this supposedly 'political proclamation' is in fact the dense and anything but straightforward Rectoral Address itself. As with Marcuse, Wolin encourages the philosophically ignorant to ignore the fact that Heidegger was a philosopher before he was any kind of political actor.

Confronted by the failure of Marcuse's 'existential Marxism' or Heidegger's brief surrender to 'the politics of Being', we must slow down. We must parse every phrase, we must scrutinise every word if we are to do justice to these men as thinkers. The orthodox approach risks confirming our own ethical and ahistorical prejudices. In short, the only 'objective' fact in Wolin's summary is the date of Hitler's seizure of power.

In his next paragraph, the problem deepens. Wolin observes:

> In retrospect, Marcuse insists that during his stay in Freiburg, he never remotely suspected Heidegger of harbouring even covert pro-Nazi sentiments. Thus, the philosopher's 'conversion' to the Nazi Socialist cause in the spring of 1933 took him – and many others – by complete surprise.[27]

Marcuse was right to be surprised because Heidegger did not harbour pro-Nazi sentiments. His wife may have been another matter, but Heidegger welcomed 'the German Uprising' *on his own terms*. There was no 'conversion' because Heidegger was not a Nazi in the way that *is being implied*. Nuance is all here. Marcuse is the confused and confusing one here, not Heidegger. And furthermore, Marcuse, as the next passage that Wolin cites makes clear, is aware of the limitations of judgments after the fact:

> Now, from personal experience I can tell you that neither in his lectures, nor in his seminars, nor personally, was there ever any hint of [Heidegger's] sympathies for Nazism … So his openly declared Nazism came as a complete surprise to us.[28]

Marcuse then plunges into a *post-factum* search for the sources of Heidegger's sudden support for Hitler in texts such as *Being and Time*.

Fearful of charges of *naiveté*, Marcuse is keen to deflect criticism of his own enthusiastic endorsements of Heideggerian philosophy. Equally telling, Marcuse stresses how 'easy' it is to make '*ex-post*' observations after the events in question, a point that Heidegger's many critics are keen to ignore. Clearly under pressure, Marcuse is trying to fend off a variety of doubts. But the suspect ploy here is to sidestep Marcuse's principal point: '*there was no hint of Nazi sympathies in Heidegger's lectures or seminars during the final years of the Weimar republic*' because there was no sympathy of the kind that is assumed by Heidegger's later critics.

Marcuse seeks to avoid the one error that almost all of Heidegger's more recent critics commit: *petitio principii*, begging the question. One concludes that Heidegger was a Nazi because one has already assumed he was a Nazi, thus logically spoiling one's entire analysis. The presumption of guilt dictates the verdict. What is a Nazi? Where, in the entire literature of critical assessment of Heidegger's experience as a thinker living under the Third Reich, is there evidence of an answer to this question that withstands strict scrutiny?

Historians have struggled with this question over half a century, just as the Allied powers grappled with it when they tried to 'de-Nazify' Germany after the war. Empirical mantraps are everywhere in this debate. Does one have to be a party member to be a Nazi? Does it matter to one's definition if the person in question joined the party in 1927, 1930 or 1942? Or left the party in any of those years? If one can become a Nazi by signing a piece of paper, can one cease to be one by signing another? Heidegger effectively withdrew from active involvement in the cultural politics of the Third Reich in 1934. Can one's definition of a Nazi cope with such shifts in position?

Is the old codger who gossiped to the authorities about his neighbours in Dresden in 1936 a Nazi because he was a party member, and the thug who murdered Jewish children in Lithuania during the German occupation not a Nazi because he did not belong to the party? Confronted with such factual and moral conundrums, the historian becomes cautious in his judgments (if all Germans were Nazis, none were). Thus, when Beistegui presses the argument that 'Heidegger was a Nazi, a Nazi from the start, a Nazi till the end', this philosopher strikes the bold note while the historian is dumbfounded at so audacious a claim.[29] To define what a Nazi was in rigorous fashion is a demanding and frustrating task, both ethically and empirically. For the critic in search of easier answers, the trick is to make the accusation without the definition.

Letter from Marcuse to Heidegger (28 August 1947)

This is the longest of the three letters. Marcuse focuses on two distinct subjects: Heidegger's *political position* before his resignation as rector of Freiburg University and his political-philosophical *status* after his 1934 resignation. The first is about Heidegger as a political actor. The second centres on how others regarded Heidegger.

The first subject takes up two sentences. Marcuse writes:

> You [Heidegger] told me that you fully dissociated yourself from the
> Nazi regime as of 1934, and that you were observed by the Gestapo. I
> will not doubt your word.[30]

On the subject of the facts of Heidegger's period as rector of Freiburg
University, Marcuse offers no challenge: 'I will not doubt your word.' If we
accept Heidegger's word on the facts of 1933–34, as Marcuse does, the entire
anti-Heidegger critique, certainly since 1987, collapses. If the facts are otherwise, Marcuse is wrong, and his argument falls to pieces. Wolin is silent on
this factual dilemma.

Marcuse's concern in the bulk of the letter is how others have come to
regard Heidegger since the overthrow of the Third Reich. Marcuse wants
Heidegger to do what Tanabe did, or appeared to do, in *The Philosophy of
Metanoetics*, that is recant. Marcuse writes accusingly, 'You never publicly
denounced any of the actions or ideologies of the regime. Because of these
circumstances you are still today identified with the Nazi regime.'[31] Note
that it is not Heidegger who is identifying with a now dead regime; it is
others who are identifying him with it.

Marcuse reveals more about his psychology than Heidegger's politics.
Marcuse stands in dread of other people's opinions; Heidegger does not care
a fig. He knows that his philosophic legacy will withstand any kind of political debunking. His confidence in the tradition, and the staying power of
this tradition, is absolute. Less well grounded, Marcuse nervously flits from
position to position.

In a display of *petit bourgeois* timidity, Marcuse struggles to keep up
appearances lest the neighbours say hurtful things. Like someone who spots
a beggar after he has just dined expensively, Marcuse pathetically debates
the ethical fine points of whether he should send a food package to a
famine-ridden and war-shattered Germany. Heidegger would have rather
gone hungry than engage in such ethical pettifogging. Marcuse's blend of
moral posturing and self-abasement is embarrassing:

> I excuse myself in the eyes of my own conscience, by saying that I am
> sending a package to a man from whom I learned philosophy from
> 1928–34.[32]

The heart of Marcuse's complaint is at once *post-factum* and chronologically
confused:

> A philosopher can be deceived regarding political matters; in which case
> he will openly acknowledge his error. But he cannot be deceived about a
> regime that has killed millions of Jews – merely because they were Jews
> – that made terror into an everyday phenomenon, and that turned

everything that pertains to the ideas of the spirit, freedom, and the truth into its bloody opposite.[33]

As shall be shown, the key moral lacuna here is Marcuse's singular focus on the *Shoah* at the expense of the suffering of the war's many other victims. This is the source of Marcuse's moral monstrousness.

Letter from Heidegger to Marcuse (20 January 1948)

Almost certainly embarrassed for his former student, Heidegger responds with dignity and scrupulousness:

> I received the package mentioned in your letter of August 28. I believe that I am acting in accordance with your wishes and in a way that will reassure your friends if I allow its entire contents to be distributed among former students who were neither in the Party nor had any association whatsoever with National Socialism. I thank you for your help also on their behalf.[34]

In the bulk of his letter, Heidegger addresses six points:

1   'Concerning 1933: I expected from National Socialism a spiritual renewal of life in its entirety, a reconciliation of social antagonisms and a deliverance of Western *Dasein* from the dangers of communism. These convictions are expressed in my Rectoral Address (have you read it *in its entirety?*).'

Heidegger goes on to concede, however, that some of his remarks, both in the Rectoral Address and in his public statements at the time, were 'misleading' (*Entgleisung*).[35]

2   'In 1934 I recognised my political error and resigned my rectorship in protest against the state and party.'

On this point, Marcuse is in accord with Heidegger ('I will not doubt your word').[36]

3   'You are entirely correct that I failed to provide a public, readily comprehensible counter-declaration; it would have been the end of both me and my family. On this point, Jaspers said: that we remain alive is our guilt.'

Marcuse does not dissent from this point; how could he, or we?[37]

4   'In my lectures and courses from 1933–44, I incorporated a standpoint that was so unequivocal that among those who were my students, none fell victim to Nazi ideology. My works from the period, if they ever appear, will testify to this fact.'[38]

If factually correct, Heidegger's claim may stand as the most compelling of all his rebuttals to his many critics. *None fell victim; none.* What kind of Nazi is this?

5   'An avowal after 1945 was for me impossible; the Nazi supporters announced their change of allegiance in the most loathsome way: I, however, had nothing in common with them.'[39]
6   'To the serious legitimate charges that you express "about a regime that murdered millions of Jews, that made terror into an everyday phenomenon, and that turned everything that pertains to the ideas of spirit, freedom, and the truth into its bloody opposite," I can merely add that if instead of "Jews" you had written "East Germans" [i.e. Germans living in eastern Germany], then the same holds true for one of the Allies, with the difference that everything that has occurred since 1945 has become public knowledge, while the bloody terror of the Nazis in point of fact had been kept a secret from the German people.'[40]

Letter from Marcuse to Heidegger (12 May 1948)

In a self-righteous and patronising letter, Marcuse brings his correspondence with Heidegger to a close. Marcuse responds only to two of Heidegger's six points: the first and the sixth, and those only in part. The larger part of Heidegger's defence is either implicitly accepted or ignored.

In response to Heidegger's argument that 'I expected from National Socialism a spiritual renewal of life in its entirety', Marcuse abandons his previous argument, setting aside the historical record and closing his mind to the evolving nature of the Nazi dictatorship in favour of an essentialist condemnation of the German people for their blindness to the threat National Socialism posed from its inception in the 1920s ('We knew, and I myself saw it too, that the beginning already contained the end').[41] In short, the German people had no reason to rise up in the 1930s, and certainly had no reason to invest their hopes in a revolution of any kind, let alone one orchestrated by the radical right.

On the sixth point, Marcuse is vicious ('I would like to treat only one portion of your letter; otherwise my silence could be treated as complicity').[42] The point of contention is Heidegger's comparison of the fate of the hundreds of thousands, perhaps even millions, of East German civilians at the end of the Second World War with the Jews in the *Shoah*. Marcuse insists that

With this sentence [the one in which Heidegger notes 'I can merely add that if instead of "Jews" you had written "East Germans" [i.e. Germans murdered in or driven from eastern Germany], then the same holds true for one of the Allies' [the Soviet Union]] don't you stand outside the dimension in which a conversation between men is even possible – outside of the *Logos*?

To show moral regard, the barest of human sympathy, for the catastrophe that overtook whole communities in East Prussia and Pomerania is not to stand outside of the *Logos* (humane reason). At this point, Marcuse is teetering on the brink of ethical bankruptcy. But his blood is up and he proceeds to attack ethical relativism: 'For only outside of the dimension of logic is it possible to explain, to relativize [*auszugleichen*], to "comprehend" a crime by saying that others would have done the same thing.'[43]

This is a classic position. What follows, however, is at best puzzling and at worst dishonourable. Marcuse can barely control his anger (which may explain the specious reasoning and neglect of the evidence that weakens his attack on Heidegger). After denouncing as absurd and immoral any comparison between the fate of the East Germans and the Jews (a comparison carefully examined below), Marcuse goes on to make a hypothetical point:

> On the basis of your argument, if the Allies had reserved Auschwitz and Buchenwald – and everything that transpired there – for the 'East Germans' and the Nazis, then the account would be in order.[44]

This comment is rhetorically powerful but irrelevant. Heidegger is not drawing a hypothetical comparison (if the Allies had done this or that). He is talking about the facts concerning the calamity which the Red Army inflicted on hundreds of thousands of East Germans. Heidegger is not talking about the United States and Britain; he is talking about the Soviet Union. Nor is Heidegger asking us to compare humanity with inhumanity. Marcuse desperately raises false arguments, about Britain and America, and for that matter the *Shoah* itself. Why? Because with a single phrase ('one of the Allies'), apparently oblique but in fact damningly exact, Heidegger squeezes his student at a most sensitive point: the complicity of the Soviet Union in the mass slaughter of civilians.

Careful reading of Marcuse's final letter shows it to be an unseemly and dishonest attempt to deflect criticism from the murderous political system that was the Soviet Union under Stalin. Perhaps it reflects the nostalgia for the Bolshevik Revolution that even now afflicts left-wing European intellectuals. Maybe Marcuse has communism's often-heroic resistance to fascism in mind. But Heidegger points the accusing finger at the Soviet Union, and Marcuse refuses to answer the accusation. How could he? It was true.

On the subject of the conduct of the Red Army in East Prussia, Gdynia-Danzig and Pomerania, Marcuse is either ignorant or lying. The actions of the Red Army were murderous and barbaric, little short of genocidal. Here is Antony Beevor, the British historian, in *Berlin: The Downfall 1945*, on conditions at the beginning of the Soviet assault on East Prussia:

> Property was being looted and destroyed and civilians needed for forced labour were killed for little reason. Chaos was also caused by the number of civilian 'citizens of the USSR who came to East Prussia to collect captured property'.[45]

Beevor reports that between February and April of 1945, at least 130,000 German civilians were sent as forced labourers to the Soviet Union. Most of them were women, who were compelled to leave children behind in the most dreadful of circumstances.[46] As for the fate of the German civilians who remained, Beevor remarks that the NKVD rifle regiments were supposed, according to Stalin, to be a police force, but 'it is still striking how little they intervened to stop looting, rape and the random murder of civilians':[47]

> On 12 March, two months after Chernykhovsky's offensive began, the NKVD chief in northern Prussia reported to Beria that 'suicides of Germans, particularly women, are becoming more and more widespread'. For those who did not have a pistol or poison, most of the suicides consisted of people hanging themselves in attics with the rope tied to the rafters. A number of women, unable to bring themselves to hang a child, cut their children's wrists first and then their own.[48]

> It is interesting that Russian historians today still produce evasive circumlocutions. 'Negative phenomena in the army of liberation,' writes one on the subject of mass rape, 'caused significant damage to the prestige of the Soviet Union and the armed forces ...'. This sentence also indirectly acknowledges that there were many cases of rape in Poland. But far more shocking ... is the fact that Red Army officers and soldiers also raped Ukrainian, Russian and Belorussian women and girls released from slave labour in Germany.[49]

Beevor concludes that the mass rape of women, from Axis and Allied countries alike, 'completely undermines any attempts at justifying Red Army behaviour on the grounds of revenge for German brutality in the Soviet Union'.[50] As for the Red Army's conduct of the war itself, here is Beevor on the Red Army's assault on Danzig and Gdynia:

> Fighter-bombers strafed the towns and port areas. Soviet Shturmoviks treated civilian and military targets alike. A church was as good as a bunker ... Wounded waiting on the quays to be embarked were riddled on their stretchers. Tens of thousands of women and children, terrified

of losing their places in the queues to escape, provided unmissable targets.[51]

The evidence from hitherto secret Soviet archives goes on and on. The rape of East Prussia was a descent into barbarism on a horrific scale. During the first week of the Soviet offensive, thousands of German families were dragged from their homes and shot to death. But Marcuse insists on denying the morally indefensible:

> How is it possible to equate the torture, the maiming, and the annihilation of millions of men with the forcible relocation of population groups who suffered none of these outrages (apart from several exceptional circumstances).[52]

'Several exceptional circumstances'? This phrase will stand as one of the most callous and disgraceful remarks by a great philosopher during the past century. In this exchange of letters, there may be a moral monster at work but it is not Heidegger.

Nazism and the crises of the Kyoto School

9 Heidegger, Nazism and the Farías Affair

The European origins of the Kyoto School crises

Death is a master from Germany.

Paul Celan

Martin Heidegger is the greatest philosopher of our time. His only rival for this accolade is Ludwig Wittgenstein. Both philosophers exhibited the rare power to shake the foundations of how we understand ourselves as human beings. Heidegger's impact outside philosophy, for example, on the rest of the humanities and the social sciences has been profound. He was *ein Meister aus Deutschland* – a master-thinker from Germany – who has at many points mastered us and our moral-metaphysical world. This truth reaches beyond the powers of even a great poet to deny. On the subject of Heidegger, Paul Celan's famous dictum will not stand.

Metaphysical balls

Like Rousseau, John Stuart Mill and Nietzsche, Heidegger commands universal influence. His life and work have helped to ensure European domination of the summits of human thought despite the challenge of American 'soft power'. The fact that this European titan has provided the cause and occasion for a contemporary revolution in the philosophic study of the Kyoto School by Westerners should surprise no one. Here, once again, the vulnerability of Japan studies to the force and weight of European tradition has been dramatically exposed. Whether the student of modern Japan has made the most of this Heideggerian moment is the question at issue here.

The global debate that had erupted in the late 1980s over Heidegger's politics – the so-called 'Farías Affair' – dealt a severe blow to the reputation of Kyoto School philosophy in the West. Indeed, in the wake of the Farías Affair, Kyoto School studies suffered one paradigm crisis only to be beset by another. In the first, political moralists battered the dominant post-war religious paradigm. In the second, an unwieldy synthesis of religious philosophy and Pacific War orthodoxy was attempted but, under the impact of historical revisionism, this alternative paradigm is itself now in danger of collapse.

This second crisis, which has deepened since the turn of the millennium, raises two fundamental questions. First, can one do Kyoto philosophy under the baleful eye of Pacific War orthodoxy? Does Kyoto School philosophy qualify as a rigorous school of political thinking? Careful weighing of the historical evidence and the close reading of the principal texts of the wartime Kyoto School force one to conclude that the grip of Pacific War orthodoxy must be broken if our understanding of the Kyoto School is to be grounded in historical fact rather than Allied myth and propaganda. At the same time, the field of Kyoto School studies should embrace a historic compromise that recognises the validity of Kyoto philosophy as an ethically respectable and intellectually compelling branch of political philosophy while at the same time acknowledging the soundness of the original religious approach *within its sphere*. Only by banishing Pacific War orthodoxy and negotiating an academic ceasefire will this cycle of paradigm crises be broken, allowing the student of Japanese philosophy to return to the productive order of 'normal science' (Thomas Kuhn)

If a German problem (Heidegger's politics) has provoked this Japanese problem (the rediscovery of the true politics of the wartime Kyoto School), the reverse may also be true: a Japanese solution may offer a cure for our German problem. The controversy over Heidegger's reputation has, as has been noted, played a decisive role in the crisis that has engulfed the Western understanding of Kyoto philosophy since the early 1990s. Having borrowed so much from Europe, maybe it is time for Japan to repay the favour philosophically. This trans-cultural quest can best be pursued by turning not to the politicised groves of Japan studies in the West but to the Japanese philosophers and intellectuals who have made themselves at home in the philosophy of Heidegger.

When the scandal erupted in the late 1980s over Heidegger's relatively brief tenure as rector of Freiburg University after the demise of the Weimar Republic, the Japanese intelligentsia instantly responded. Things could hardly have been otherwise, as Japan is home to the world's oldest and most productive Heidegger industry. But precisely because the Japanese have studied the works of this German titan for so long and with such care, the controversies provoked by the appearance of Farías's *Heidegger et le nazisme* in 1987 only grazed Heidegger's status in Japan as the most influential German philosopher since Nietzsche.[1]

Among Western students of the Kyoto School, particularly in North America, *l'Affaire Farías* ignited an intellectual panic of the first order. We lost our philosophic nerve. The resulting crisis inflicted severe damage on the reputation of the Kyoto School in the United States and even parts of Western Europe. By contrast, the Japanese never took their eye off the metaphysical ball despite the political turbulence generated by the Farías Affair. In the West, we allowed this ball to drop. Today, if students of modern Japanese philosophy, Western and Japanese alike, are to move forward *together*, the causes and consequences of the contrasting national reactions to the Farías Affair must be meticulously examined. Here the evidence at issue in this *scandale d'estime* will be set out so that what was truly at stake in the Farías scandal for the student of the Kyoto School may be judged by all. Here, also, a Japanese solution to our German problem may be found.

The Farías Affair

The explosion set off by the publication of *Heidegger et le nazisme* was astonishing. Indeed, the aftershocks of this great controversy are still being felt everywhere that genuine thought is taken seriously. Translated into French from the manuscript written in Spanish (and German), Farías's polemic attempted to probe the tenuous and often wilfully misunderstood relationship between Heidegger and Hitler. But there is no doubt that the author, a Chilean journalist of Jewish descent, managed to provoke one of the bitterest intellectual quarrels to grip France since the May Events of 1968. Partly, it was a matter of timing. Claude Lanzmann's epic-length film *Shoah* had appeared in 1985 while the drama of the arrest, deportation, trial and conviction of Klaus Barbie ('the butcher of Lyon') unfolded between 1983 and 1987. Reality conspired with culture to set the scene for another chapter in the world's long war of words about Heidegger's 'politics of Being'.

The global debate over '*le cas Heidegger*' initiated by Tanabe is well into its first century. As so many of the facts aired in the controversy were already known – and Hugo Ott's *Martin Heidegger: Unterwegs zu seiner Biographie*[2] that appeared in 1988 added more – it was Farías's dismissive tone, muckraking methods and almost smug moral superiority that caused the greatest offence and elicited the sharpest rebuff. His critics pounced mercilessly on his lapses and excesses. His mistake about the location of the Sachsenhausen concentration camp – it was near Berlin rather than Frankfurt – invited particular scorn in Germany.

In France, the response was equally frosty. Jacques Derrida spoke for many when he bitingly observed that it appeared that Farías had not spent 'more than an hour' reading Heidegger. If one reads with the intensity of Derrida, the charge probably sticks. The accusation that Heidegger's critics have not done their philosophic homework cuts deep. The profoundest text on Heidegger's encounter with National Socialism to appear in 1987 was not *Heidegger et le nazisme* but Derrida's *De l'esprit*.[3]

Paris was well prepared for this polemic because intellectuals in France had been quarrelling about the magus of Freiburg long before Farías appeared on the scene. In other words, Farías's book was very far from being the first text in French to examine Heidegger's attempt to co-opt National Socialism and transform it into a programme of metaphysical reconstruction. There were two major French debates before the Farías Affair. The first was fought out in the pages of Sartre's journal, *Les Temps modernes*, between 1945 and 1948.[4] The second was sparked by the appearance of a translation of Heideggerian writings by Jean Pierre Faye.[5] The principal exchanges of critical fire between Faye and François Fédier appeared in the journal *Critique* between 1965 and 1967.

Defenders of Farías such as Luc Ferry and Alain Renaut have been keen to minimise the importance of these earlier fracas because they did not address doubts about Heidegger's personal involvement in the politics of the Weimar collapse, a fact exacerbated both by the failure of the Heidegger family to permit access to some potentially sensitive documents and by the 'withholding' of information in France by influential Heideggerians such as Jean Beaufret and his allies.[6] Such criticism is only to be welcomed, and the obscurantism of Heidegger's supposed defenders is only to be censured.

Sartre, Löwith and Hannah Arendt had a much better appreciation of Heidegger's faults than Farías's supporters acknowledge. Secondly, Sartre, Löwith and Arendt were fundamentally unmoved by the negative facts that were already in the public domain. Even Marcuse had great difficulty in bringing himself to break with Heidegger, and only then in morally suspect circumstances. These philosophers of an earlier, more enlightened, age brought to *le cas Heidegger* a deep respect for his philosophy as a project of thought. This may explain why the more one knows of Heidegger's work, the less one is impressed by Farías's criticism.

France's first Heidegger controversy erupted with Löwith's essay 'Les implications politiques de la philosophie de l'existence chez Heidegger' which appeared in *Les Temps modernes* 14 (1946–47).[7] This in turn provoked rebuttals from Eric Weil and Alphonse de Waehlens, who set out the conventional pro-Heidegger position: 'Nazism had nothing to do with his philosophy.'[8] But, *pace* Ferry and Renaut, the depth of Löwith's insights into the relationship between Heidegger's 'anti-metaphysical metaphysics' and his endorsement of the German Uprising remain salient. There is an understandable blindness in Löwith, his judgment is often impaired (he had much to be angry about), but wherever the battle over Heidegger's *philosophic* legacy has been waged fruitfully, it has been and remains a struggle to capture, line by line, trench by trench, the positions developed in his essay.

Heidegger's critics, on both sides of the Atlantic, have often wilfully ignored the intellectual context of these two French debates. This context is defined by the classical philosophic quarrel fought out among Heidegger, Sartre and George Lukács – the three most influential European philosophers in twentieth-century Japan – between the completion of Lukács' *History and Class Consciousness* (1923) and the publication of Sartre's *Critique of Dialectical Reason: Theory of Practical Ensembles* (1960). Here, for example, is Georg Lukács' observation in 1967 on the impact of *History and Class Consciousness*:

> To assess the impact of the book at that time [1923], and also its relevance today, we must consider one problem that surpasses in its importance all questions of detail. This is the question of alienation,

which, for the first time since Marx, is treated as central to the revolutionary critique of capitalism and which has its theoretical and methodological roots in the Hegelian dialectic. Of course the problem was in the air at the time. Some years later, following the publication of Heidegger's *Being and Time* (1927), it moved to the centre of philosophical debate.[9]

After the First World War and the Russian Revolution of 1917, one question above all defined the intellectual horizon of the European thinker: how should European civilisation morally rebuild itself in the chaotic wake of the violent collapse of the nineteenth-century bourgeois order? In their different ways, Lukács, Heidegger and Sartre all attempted a philosophic answer to this challenge. The political urgency and intellectual excitement of this endeavour did not abate until Europe's 'social question' was solved by the massive extension of the welfare state and the gradual dissolution of the working class as an agent of political reform from the late 1960s onwards. In the wake of the 1914–18 war and the Russian Revolution, the European philosophic tradition transformed this social question into a forcing house of ideas. Thus, Lukács' anticipation of the discovery of Marx's early writings, so crucial as founding texts of the Frankfurt School, echo in Heidegger's labours, from the oblique references to *History and Class Consciousness* at the conclusion of *Being and Time* to the overt engagement with Marxist humanism in the *Letter on Humanism*. The Marxism of the late Sartre is a monumental if quixotic recoil against this intellectual quarrel.

The Lukács–Heidegger–Sartre debate provides the indispensable study in contrast with the intellectual horizon of the crucial middle phase of the classical Kyoto School, the one that unfolded between c. 1927 and c. 1945. Dominated by Tanabe, this broad turn to history and political philosophy broke with the first phase of the classical Kyoto School in which Nishida's focus on pure intuition and anti-metaphysical personalism prevailed. What Green, William James and, at one remove, the early Bergson were to Nishida in the first phase, the late Bergson, Hegel and, to a degree, Fichte and Schelling were to Tanabe in this middle phase. (In his middle and final phases, Nishitani's engagement with nihilism and existentialism prevailed: his first German master was Hegel, who was later replaced by Nietzsche and Heidegger.)

Hegel was so important to the wartime Kyoto School that one is tempted to argue that these Japanese thinkers anticipated the French interwar and post-war obsession with Hegel. Certainly, this German philosopher is a defining presence in *The Logic of the Species*, *The Standpoint of World History and Japan* and the Kyoto School contribution to *Overcoming Modernity* (Suzuki and Nishitani). These texts suggest that Hegel was, at every crucial juncture, decisive to the Kyoto School's long and intense meditation on subjectivity and the nation-state as historical agency that was sustained by Tanabe and the second generation of the Kyoto School.

The challenge was to find a way to conceptualise a modernity that was neither bourgeois nor white. What the proletariat was to Lukács, the Hegelian rational state was to Tanabe – an agency of revolutionary change. The conventional critic, Japanese or otherwise, of Cartesian subjectivity who has recently stressed the somatic or bodily aspect of the Chinese character for '*tai*', or body, in '*shutai*' must be warned that Hegel's idea of the subject, whatever its roots in the meditations of Descartes, is halfway to Weber's concept of rational, goal-orientated activity and Adam Smith's notion of 'economic man'. The intellectual bridge in the momentous passage in European thought is, of course, Karl Marx.

All this, including the Heidegger debate of the late 1980s and early 1990s, demonstrates the price students of the politics of Kyoto School philosophy pay for their failure to make themselves *chez-nous* in Continental thought after the Russian Revolution. If one seeks a cure for the malign impact of a decaying orthodoxy in our reception of modern Japanese philosophy, the quality and seriousness of the philosophic interventions in the earlier French debates point the way forward. To the degree that this is true, the Farías Affair (including its impact on Japan studies) represents a drastic Western defeat of mind.

Lukács–Heidegger–Sartre

Nothing undermines the political case against Heidegger more conclusively than what Sartre, Derrida and Levinas have made of the work of the most original and penetrating German thinker of the twentieth century. Sartre may have observed, at the beginning of his *Critique of Dialectical Reason*, that 'The case of Heidegger is too complex for me to set forth here', but the global impact of *L'Etre et le Néant*, still the most consequential of all the re-readings of *Being and Time*, belies the notion that *any* moral or political lapse could utterly negate the greatness of Heidegger's *oeuvre*. The student of Heidegger or the Kyoto School who privileges ethics parading as politics over philosophy breaks faith with philosophy.

As heir to the ancient Greeks, the European thinker must link his political stance to the examined philosophical life. Philosophise, and then live. This is Socrates' credo. In this tradition, philosophy is not kept in some dusty academic corner removed from the practical demands of politics and ethics. The privileging of politics and ethics above philosophy is, *finally*, intellectually incoherent. It is to opt out of Graeco-European reason, but this is exactly what the severest critics of Heidegger and the Kyoto School ask us to do.

Philosophy has its rights. To philosophise, one is compelled to submit to the discipline of philosophic knowledge itself. Such submissions are acts of caring (*Sorge*), of yielding to the compulsion of ontological astonishment. The imperative to mobilise one's mental resources to the limit in response to what the Greeks called '*thaumazein*' and Paul Valéry hailed in *Le Cimetière*

Marin as 'true thought' (*une pensée* that allows us to partake in the *le calme des dieux*) defines the fundamental stance of the Graeco-European tradition when confronted with the demands of intellectual creation of the first order.

The urge to monumental achievement begins with the flash of insight such as Poincaré (a key figure in Tanabe's early mathematical studies) famously suffered when he once alighted from a bus, or as Sartre experienced in that celebrated encounter with Raymond Aron in a pre-war Paris café. Just back from Berlin, Aron declared that the outcome of a serious philosophical discussion could hang on the nature of a cocktail glass, that is on the phenomenology of the immediately visible as developed by Husserl. Thunderstruck, Sartre rushed down the Rue St Michel to buy a copy of Levinas's pioneering study of Husserl's phenomenology. Shortly thereafter, Sartre made his own way to Berlin. Primed by his encounter with Husserl's thought, Sartre was ready to discover Heidegger. Captured by the Germans in 1940, Sartre spent his internment meditating on *Sein und Zeit*. The principal fruits of this sustained meditation would be harvested in *L'Etre et le Néant*.

Sartre's canonic response to Heidegger set the scene for one of those philosophic acts that illustrate the fundamental flaw in the reasoning of Heidegger's critics in the Farías Affair. After 1945, the recriminations against Heidegger at Freiburg University for his conduct in 1933–34 turned Sartre into a potential saviour for the German thinker. Initially, therefore, Heidegger was desperate to solicit Sartre's support. But almost immediately afterwards, the inherently objectivist character of Heidegger's fundamental ontology reasserted itself when he denounced the subjectivist foundations of Sartrean existentialism in his *Letter on Humanism*. At the moment of considerable threat to his reputation, perhaps even to his personal liberty, Heidegger stood his ground in the name of philosophical integrity. There he stood; he could do no other. No peasant cunning was at work here. Nor was any at work in 1933 when the political opportunist might have triumphed over the philosopher. Heidegger's *Letter on Humanism* is a statement of uncompromising metaphysical conviction. There is a similar ambush waiting for the naïve critic of the wartime Kyoto School.

At the two moments of greatest public pressure in his career as philosopher, Heidegger remained fundamentally objectivist in his approach. This is the hallmark of the committed religious or quasi-religious thinker. The hydraulics of the soul unites private feelings and the universe. Our essence, our true nature as human beings, lies outside ourselves; salvation, inner peace, reincarnation and enlightenment can be achieved only by conformity to God, the cosmos, nature or karma. By contrast, subjectivism is man-centred. It is Sartre who sounds the anti-religious Voltairean note within existentialism. *Engagement* is subjectivist. Amid all the political-ethical fog of 1987–95, the fact that Sartre was an atheistic subjectivist and Heidegger a meta-religious objectivist has been neglected to the peril of our appreciation not only of twentieth-century European thought but also of the Western understanding of modern Japanese philosophy.

How can Heidegger, who was so fierce a critic of Cartesian object/subject dualism, be regarded as an objectivist? Several streams of thought fed Heidegger's dissatisfaction with neo-Kantian dualism, but none was more important than his uncompromising rejection of the supposed *centrality* of positivist science in the definition of human existence. Only by deflating the exaggerated prestige of the natural sciences by reducing them to mere 'ontic' endeavours could Heidegger clear a place for the restoration of metaphysics to its former pre-eminence. He attacked positivism and its model of human understanding in which we intellectually yield to the laws of nature in order to exploit nature because this attitude towards nature stood in the way of his fundamental ontology.

Nevertheless, the attack on dualism does not define Heidegger's ontology. It is not man who speaks language but language who speaks man. The Shepherd of Being is not an agent. Being and language, in Heidegger's usage, are not scientifically objectivist concepts but metaphysical totalities to which the German thinker urges us to surrender in the name of 'caring' (*Sorge*). In this sense, Heidegger is fundamentally objectivist, and, to the degree that he was an objectivist in this sense (and only in this sense), any attempt to blame his philosophy for his political shortcomings is fundamentally misconceived.

An example from recent French thought may make the point clearer. The battle between Sartre and his deconstructionist critics was, in part, a struggle over the powers (and dangers) of the subject as human agent. Philippe Lacoue-Labarthe tightens the resulting metaphysical double bind when he ominously concludes that 'Nazism is a humanism', that is National Socialism as a set of ideas is a subjectivist man-centred philosophy.[10] The same charge may be levelled with equal force against democratic liberalism and the political philosophy of the wartime Kyoto School, not because fascism is bad or democracy is good, but because both are philosophies of political action that require political actors, that is subjects. But *Heidegger* allowed none of these things. He never privileged subjectivity, not in 1933, nor in 1946, nor at any other time.[11]

Marxism is a revolutionary political doctrine, and therefore it also, in post-Heideggerian terms, should be condemned as a humanism. The subject-versus-object conflict was a crucial metaphysical issue in Lukács' relentless criticism of the anti-subjectivist thrust of Heidegger's thought. Two texts are pivotal to Lukács' war against Heidegger. First, there is his 1949 essay titled 'Heidegger Redivivus' (written in response to Heidegger's *Platons Lehre von der Wahrheit, mit einem Brief über den Humanismus*), and secondly, there is the massive *The Destruction of Reason*. But Lukács also made war on the objectivist thrust of late Marxism, particularly the impact of Engel's weakness for scientism. It is no accident that dialectical materialism bears the main brunt of Lukács' assault in *History and Class Consciousness*.

This stance condemned Lukács to a two-front war. Thus, as dissatisfied as Lukács was with Heidegger's philosophy of Being because it was at once reactionary and anti-agent (which has been judged as over-determined but I see as contradictory), he was also a fierce opponent of what he regarded as Sartre's bourgeois personalism. Lukács' assault on Sartre was famously delivered in *Existentialisme ou Marxisme?* This circle of repulsion and attraction was completed when Sartre produced his textual monument to Western Marxism, co-founded by Lukács and Karl Korsch, with the publication of the first volume of *Critique of Dialectical Reason* in 1960.

In this sense, the war of words and ideas went round and round, but all the major participants were clearer (most of the time) about what their opponents were arguing than tends to be true today of Heidegger's critics. What these classic twentieth-century thinkers shared was greater than the sum of their very real differences. Their battles dominated much of the thinking of the progressive European thinker from 1923 until 1968 and beyond. One of this struggle's most striking features is the repeated attempt by some of the original minds of the interwar period – Adorno, Marcuse and, later, Lucien Goldman – to align Heidegger and Lukács. The philosophical horizon generated by Lukács and Sartre but also by Heidegger has proven to be of world-historical significance in the realm of thought. And this philosophic achievement brings us back to the Farías affair.

Where is the subject?

The defenders of Heidegger assume the existence of this horizon and show their respect for it by relentless critical engagement. By contrast, recent ethical-political critics of Heidegger often seem to have lost sight of the metaphysical horizon. This appears to be equally true of the political critics of the wartime Kyoto School. In this, they are victims of the liberal politics of forgetting. No other lapse has more seriously bedevilled the labours of the North American student of Heidegger or the Western critic of the Kyoto School.

Many of the denunciations contained in *The Heidegger Controversy: A Critical Reader* and *The Heidegger Case: On Philosophy and Politics* insist on raising partisan politics and wartime propaganda to the stature of the moral absolute.[12] As in the case of the Western critic of the wartime Kyoto School, the assault on Heidegger since Farías has sought to punish the philosopher in the name of a morally dubious and psychological self-serving 'truth' that claims to be all that is liberal and decent. This posture often departs from the political facts of the case. When the apolitical humanist 'discovers' politics, he wanders unsuspectingly onto the grounds of the political scientist who tends to treat ethical arguments pretending to proper politics with profound suspicion.

In discussions of the Second World War, accusations of ethical relativism are frequently nothing more than a moral smokescreen designed to delay the acceptance of new facts about the war. Nevertheless, this revisionist tide will eventually sweep all before it. Granted, because of the *Shoah*, revisionism about the war in Europe must demonstrate its ethical credentials when it defends the cause of empirical truth, but in the Pacific theatre, the revisionist is already on the march. Philosophically, the implications of this revisionist crusade are clear. To the degree that students of Heideggerian or Kyoto School philosophy have erected their understanding on the sandy foundations of Allied orthodoxy (the *Shoah* apart), their arguments are vulnerable. This is truer today than at any time since 1945. With each passing day, the vice of new facts will tighten.

The historical problem is only half the difficulty. Once the historian of ideas finishes his political essay, he has no need to make peace with philosophy. The same cannot be said for the philosopher. This is why the Farías bandwagon poses such a threat to the student of philosophy. Goldman's famous question – 'Where is the subject?' – underscores the kind of intellectual coherence and clarity that any philosopher working in this tradition must display. Within this constellation of thought, Goldman's question was not just inevitable: it was over-determined. If one does not understand the almost banal obviousness of Goldman's query, one has not begun to master the basic language and logic of the Lukács–Heidegger–Sartre paradigm. Goldman harassed Michel Foucault and Derrida with his question when these two thinkers were consolidating what outside France is called the 'post-structuralist' revolution in the late 1960s. It formed a tradition against which one could fruitfully think.

Goldman's question will not go away. It may have appeared to some to be a final roll of the dice of a proud intellectual enterprise: revolutionary European Marxism. But the problem of agency conceived as a subject is unignorable. To be a subject is to be an agent or actor. To act, or, more precisely, to have mastered the skills which enable one to act in the world, is to be almost inevitably tempted to show one's power over those who lack a matching degree of subjectivity. The key word is 'inevitable'. Neither Imperial Japan between 1931 and 1945 nor the American empire since proved able to resist opening the Pandora's box of subjectivity, as the tragic trajectories of both imperial enterprises have shown. If a nation has the power, it tends to use it.

Derrida's determination to deconstruct the subject was rooted in bitter political experience: the abuse of French subjective power during the Algerian Revolution. In the case of Foucault, the rejection of the subject was also grounded in political experience, that of the grim years of Vichy and the German occupation of France. In those circumstances, those who possessed subjectivity acted, but to act then was to err. But fascism does not exhaust the problem, nor has democracy found a cure. The same anti-subjectivist critique may be applied to the final phase of the Pacific War, from the fall of Saipan in July 1944 to the atomic incineration of Hiroshima and Nagasaki – 'the Japanese Holocaust' – when the United States descended into democratic barbarism by sustaining a one-sided racial massacre on a huge scale. The temptations of subjectivity were too great. At the crucial moment, the moral test was not met. The American people could not resist the temptation to exercise their genocidal powers over the prostrate Japanese people.

Subjectivity is Janus-faced. Without subjectivity, we cannot make the world work. But to achieve the self-mastery at the heart of subjectivity is to acquire the skills to lay waste to the achievements of any other society that lacks a similar degree of subjectivity. This is the tragedy of subjectivity that Heidegger, and Derrida after him, believed united the Third Reich and its foes in a mortal embrace. This is the one opposition between Nazism and non-Nazism that they believed needed to be relativised. The implications of this insight for the moral interpretation of the Pacific War are profound and irresistible. Tanabe was the first to sound this warning.

This subjectivist conundrum explains why Goldman's question about the subject proved to be fatal to his claims to contemporary relevance within the Lukács–Heidegger–Sartre paradigm. If Goldman revered Heidegger, he worshiped Lukács. To deny subjectivity in the 1960s was to reject the possibility of revolutionary action in the Marxist mode. For Goldman, this was to close the door on the future. Luc Ferry and Alain Renaut, in *Heidegger et les Modernes*, should have known better than to resurrect Goldman's question to defend not communist revolution but the democratic way, that is 'public decisions based on public discussion and argumentation by subjects', in the wake of the Farías Affair. This was a predictable if finally unpersuasive move within the Lukács–Heidegger–Sartre discourse because such arguments fatally seek to evade the paradox of subjectivity and its inherent weakness for evil as well as good. This evasion forms the fatal flaw in Richard Rorty's critique of Derrida and Habermas.[13]

The philosophy of subjectivity, as shaped by Heidegger and Derrida, may be the most powerful way of dissecting the moral dilemmas of American and Japanese imperial expansion. Is there a better philosophic or social scientific explanation for why history's 'greatest' experiment in democracy kept millions in slavery and butchered its way across an entire continent in an orgy of ethnic cleansing?

The same paradox is at work in the defining dynamic of the Great East Asian War: the struggle to liberate the East from White domination and to make Imperial Japan the masters of continental Asia. Goldman's ethically loaded question has a Japanese implication. The central theme of the wartime Kyoto School – Tanabe, Miki, Kōyama, Kōsaka, Suzuki and Nishitani – was Japanese *subjectivity* and its inevitable temptations. In the 1930s, Imperial Japan was on the verge of genuine Western-style self-mastery, and it proved even less able than the United States to resist the urge to show its power. This is why subjectivity, as Tanabe argued in his 1933 critique of Heidegger's Rectoral Address, almost always spells tragedy. Goethe's insights about this danger were incisive. To focus so singularly on human subjectivity at the expense of all else is to sign a Faustian pact with the Devil. Make man the centre of the world, and hell draws near. This is why 'Nazism is a humanism'.

Heidegger was an uncompromising opponent of subjectivism. The 'politics of Being' are objectivist through and through. Heidegger was drawn to the German Uprising because he thought it would open the way to the recovery of Being in the world. *As soon as* he discovered that the Nazi movement would not serve his ontological revolution, Heidegger the philosopher abandoned National Socialism. But he still suffered from a predictable nostalgia for what might have been – how the German Uprising might have taken a Heideggerian turn and become a genuine opening to Being for all humanity, and that includes, by definition, European Jewry.

10 Heidegger and the wartime Kyoto School

After Farías – the first paradigm crisis (1987–96)

Is there anything in the philosophy of Heidegger that would have made his involvement in Nazism impossible?

Joseph Grange[1]

Is there anything in Nishida's thought that kept him from becoming an ultra-nationalist?

Jan Van Bragt[2]

The ricochet of the Farías Affair damaged the Western commitment – moral, aesthetic, religious and metaphysical – to Kyoto thought. Surveying the scarred landscape of Kyoto School studies today, no other conclusion seems possible. This assault on Martin Heidegger stroked and satisfied the philistine complacencies of the Anglo-American mind. It has opened us neither to Being nor to *satori* (the liberation from the compulsion to mean). Rather, this debacle fed our moral resentments by confirming our most self-flattering prejudices. In Nietzsche's drastic phrase, the Farías Affair unstrung the bow of our mental and moral powers. It made us, as thinkers, less than we are.

Only a Hegelian, philosophy's perennial optimist, could discover something positive amid this metaphysical rout. Viewed dialectically, one might argue that this crisis may yet prove to have been an essential detour on the march towards a more profound and richer understanding of modern Japanese ideas. If Japan studies is to renew its commitment to the totality of Kyoto thought, a dialectical reading must be brought to bear on two of our most influential responses to the Farías scandal: *Rude Awakenings* and *Philosophers of Nothingness*.[3] Here *Rude Awakenings*, which appeared in 1994, will occupy stage centre, while the impact of *Philosophers of Nothingness*, translated from the Spanish in 2001, will be assessed in Chapter 11.

A paradigm disintegrates

Zen scholarship has been one of the glories of Asian studies. If the Japan specialist has enriched high culture, this religious-philosophical project has been at the very heart of this contribution. During the past half-century, the philosophic labours of the Kyoto School have often been understood as a form of Zen religious thought. This is only a partial truth but one that appealed to the ambitions and generosities of those Orientalists who regarded themselves as the proud heirs of European Romanticism.

Like the great poets, travellers, translators and scholars of Orientalist tradition, many Western students of modern Zen have sought to find their kingdoms of moral and aesthetic redemption beyond the pale of European civilisation. This stance has encouraged a profound empathy and receptiveness towards Asian modes of thought. As a late flowering of the Romantic spirit, the religious appropriation of the Kyoto School by Western students since 1945 has been impressively productive.[4] Those who dismiss Japanese studies as a scholarly backwater have only to peruse the pages of Fr Dumoulin's *Zen Buddhism: A History* or Jan Van Bragt's translation of Nishitani's *Religion and Nothingness* to be disabused of this dubious notion.[5]

Romantic empathy is not, however, the stuff of radical criticism. Whatever the powers of its poetry, its formidable contribution to the arts of Japan, and its tantalising ability to mock the Western weakness for aggressive argument and metaphysical dogmatism, Zen thought has always been vulnerable to three of the strongest critical impulses in European philosophy: the compulsion to subject any and all arguments to the discipline of strict logic; the imperative to submit all social and cultural phenomena to ethical critique; and, finally, the urge to discipline politics with the government of reason. Zen scholarship in the European Romantic mode has exhibited a steadfast refusal to bring these sharp Western swords to bear on Japanese religious thought. This generosity of spirit has been vital to the formidable success of the Western appropriation of Zen, both as a counter-cultural cult and as serious scholarship. In other words, this appropriation has been premised on a broad suspension, a bracketing *à la Husserl*, of logical, moral and political discriminations.

Given the inherent restlessness of the Graeco-European mind and its rooted determination to spare nothing, Zen was one day going to be put to the question. In the wake of the Farías Affair, the question was put. The result was a *tatami*-room full of broken metaphysical crockery. The damage was severe because the Western offensive did not confine itself to *haiku* and *kōans* but rather proceeded to scrutinise the wartime words and conduct of Kyoto School thinkers with an eye to criminal proceedings. This prosecution was grounded in the Allied mythology of the Pacific War. The resulting unholy alliance between moral criticism and Pacific War orthodoxy wreaked havoc on the academic reputation of Zen and the Kyoto School. In the name of the morality of the Allied powers, the Orientalist was suddenly being urged to turn his back on more than fifty years of scholarly achievement because of a belated discovery of 'politics' by Western students of the humanities. But these Western critics assumed that the Graeco-European mind which spares no one would spare them.

Whatever its virtues as a school of religious discipline and artistic practice, Zen was judged unforgivably flawed, ethically and politically, in the new post-Farías climate. The Asia-Pacific War (1931–45) supposedly exposed these flaws. Religious philosophers and theologians who argued otherwise were accused of closing their eyes to a set of shocking moral lapses. This new combative posture among Western scholars was worlds away from the Orientalist generosities one finds, for example, in Dumoulin's *Zen Buddhism in the Twentieth Century*.[6]

When *Rude Awakenings* appeared in the mid-1990s, it signalled a general revolt among an influential group of American and European scholars against the religious approach that had broadly governed the Western understanding of Kyoto philosophy since 1945. In this sense, *Rude Awakenings* marked a revival of the old controversies about the political posture of Japan's leading non-Marxist philosophers between 1931 and 1945. Many Zen thinkers and religious writers during the Asia-Pacific war did appear to unite the traditional indifference to ethical imperatives one associates with Zen in particular and Buddhism in general, with aggressive support for Japan's military challenge to the regional hegemony of America and Imperial Britain.

Romantic-minded Western scholars had also taught themselves to overlook displays of the endemic cultural hubris and nationalist sentiment in post-war writing on the Kyoto School by Japanese scholars. Furthermore, the post-war splendours of Zen scholarship would have never been achieved if the Western weakness for political and ethical criticism had not been strictly bracketed from the outset. But Kyoto philosophy is more than religious thought. It is also a serious school of political and historical philosophy, and until the religious grip on Zen research had been loosened, the potential of the Kyoto School as political and historical philosophy might never have been appreciated.

To the degree that the fallout of the Farías Affair on Japan studies helped to bring these truths to the fore, this destructive episode in the reception of Japanese thought in the West was a heavily disguised blessing. But the sword of ethical criticism, once unsheathed, can cut in more than one way. By raising the moral stakes so high, the Western turn against Kyoto thought has helped to expose, quite inadvertently, Pacific War orthodoxy to the full force of factual revisionism. The breaking of metaphysical crockery is no longer confined to the *tatami-beya*. Quite the contrary, it is now becoming increasingly obvious, almost by the day, that Allied wartime propaganda, and the academic school of history that arose from it, could never have provided a sound approach to modern Japanese political philosophy.

Returning the Allied Gaze

Among the ranks of the contributors from the former Allied powers to *Rude Awakenings: Zen, the Kyoto School and the Question of Nationalism*,[7] the

Farías Affair appears to have played a decisive role. On this issue, James W. Heisig and John C. Maraldo, the American editors, are emphatic:

> If there is one factor we can point to as having brought the political aspect to the fore, it is the case of Martin Heidegger. In the light of new revelations of Heidegger's associations with the German Nazi Party, affections for Heideggerian thought underwent a sea change, and in the process, the consciousness of a generation was awakened as never before to the political consequences of supposedly apolitical philosophers and scholars. It was only a matter of time before this rude awakening was transmitted to those attracted to the philosophy of the Kyoto school, not to mention Zen Buddhism.[8]

Since the 1990s, the Allied critics of the wartime Kyoto School have swept aside ethical, empirical and philosophical cautions. Seven years after the Heidegger and De Man scandals erupted, Heisig and Maraldo announced an ethical revolution in Western attitudes towards Japan's leading modern philosophers. In the 'Editors' Introduction' to *Rude Awakenings*, they concluded:

> Among intellectual historians of Japan, particularly those working in the United States, the enthusiastic reception of the Kyoto school philosophy in Europe and North America came as something of a surprise. For, by and large, the comparative philosophers who were giving these Japanese thinkers their warm welcome had simply overlooked the political implications of their thought, especially during World War II. Today, the situation has clearly changed.[9]

This change demanded a leap of logic. It was one thing to subject classical texts previously understood almost entirely in philosophic-religious terms to uncompromising moral critique, but it was quite another to give a blanket endorsement to Pacific War orthodoxy. There is no obvious logical link between critique and orthodoxy here, but the 'Allied' writers in *Rude Awakenings* have assumed there is one. Granted, none of these scholars from the former Allied powers explicitly endorses the morally indefensible victors' justice at work in the Tokyo War Crimes Tribunal. But neither do these Western scholars subject these orthodox assumptions to critical scrutiny; rather, these assumptions are judged to be beyond moral or empirical challenge.

The Allied Gaze explains why the metaphysical fallout from the Heidegger scandal has been heaviest not in the West but among *the Allied powers that fought and won the Second World War*. Confident of yet another victory, the 'Allied' contributors to *Rude Awakenings* tried to restage the old struggle between the Allied and Axis powers of the Second World War. The fifteen contributions divide broadly along Axis-versus-Allied lines.

Methodologically, this divide is revealing. The students from the former Allied powers bring a fierce morality to their research. Facts and interpretations that enhance the force of their ethical judgments are prominent, while contrary evidence and arguments are ignored. The Japanese scholars by and large seek to demonstrate in a detailed empirical manner that these Kyoto thinkers were either apolitical religious scholars or establishment opponents of the Tojo regime.

Viewed philosophically, this contest of interpretations is more complex. The Allied critics of Japanese philosophy have to fight a two-front struggle because the wartime Kyoto School was itself divided metaphysically. To put the matter concisely, Nishidan philosophy was not a humanism. He was anti-subjectivist in his approach to philosophy, that is anti-agency. It is not easy to blame a philosophy for political mistakes if it does not allow for political action. One could conceivably be a logical positivist and a fascist, but one would not be a fascist because one was a logical positivist. In the case of Nishida, all one can argue is that the objectivist/personalist character of Nishida's ideas failed to discourage what the Allied critic sees as unethical conduct. In this context, Nishida's failures are those of omission rather than commission. His actions (including his speeches and occasional essays) during the Pacific War can be judged in the conventional way, but his activities as an establishment figure do not proceed from his metaphysics. The analogy with Heidegger is close.

Tanabe and the Kyoto School 'gang of four' are all subjectivists. They propose a philosophy of action in the world. They are, therefore, in principle much easier targets for those determined to make ethical judgments. But the liberal critic must proceed carefully because there can be no democracy without subjectivism. The subjectivist strain in wartime Kyoto thought is, by definition, closer in values and potential to the Allied position itself. Nishida's philosophy is worlds away from political action.

In confident possession of what they believe to be the moral high ground, the Western contributors to *Rude Awakenings* poured scorn on the leading figures of the Kyoto School. Thus, Robert H. Sharf declares that [if] 'Hannah Arendt has commented on the "exasperation" we sometimes feel when confronted with the fact that Plato and Heidegger were drawn to "tyrants" and "Führers"', then 'the apostles of pure Zen' may have fallen victim to the same '*déformation professionelle*'.[10] Although he acknowledges Nishida's opposition to Army adventurism, Andrew Feenberg holds that Nishida also 'supported Japanese hegemony in Asia and he was an enthusiastic advocate of the emperor system. Indeed, for Nishida the imperial household lay at the centre of both the political and cultural systems'.[11]

This looks clear, but in fact such judgments muddy the philosophic waters. The implied journey from *An Inquiry into the Good* to Nishida's feelings about the emperor as a thinking and feeling Japanese in the early 1940s is very long, perhaps impossibly so. Feenberg notes, for example, that 'On reading Nishida's war writings, the comparison with Heidegger immediately springs to mind', but he goes on to argue that this comparison breaks down because Heidegger's 'private National Socialism' was expressed in 'the official language of the Nazi state', while Nishida's nationalist rhetoric was softened by his 'culturalist standpoint'.[12] This line of reasoning does not persuade.

The Belgian scholar Jan Van Bragt moves the ground of his attack from philosophy to moral psychology. His article in *Rude Awakenings* tackles what he calls Farías's 'single overwhelming question': 'Is there anything in Heidegger's philosophy that would have made his involvement with the Nazi's impossible?' Objectivist philosophies are not about politics, and therefore looking for barriers in such schools of thought to this or that ideology or policy agenda is inevitably frustrating. Daoism is not Confucianism. Despite various qualifications and protestations of loyalty to Japanese philosophy, Van Bragt concludes that these Japanese thinkers lacked the kind of moral fibre that might have prevented them 'from being swept up into the prevailing whirlwind of nationalism'.[13] But metaphysics is not about moral backbone.

In his criticism, Andrew Feenberg's contribution was, on many counts, pivotal. He is Professor of Philosophy at San Diego State University and an expert on Western Marxism. His reputation as a scholar was established with two important books: *Lukács, Marx and the Sources of Critical Theory* (1981) and *Marcuse: Critical Theory and the Promise of Utopia* (1986).[14] His field of specialisation made him alert to the way that the Kyoto School has been shaped by the discourse of twentieth-century European philosophy. Whatever else it may be, the crucial middle phase of classical Kyoto School philosophy is a response to the creative weight and metaphysical tensions that shaped the Lukács–Heidegger–Sartre paradigm understood as a reaction to the decay of neo-Kantianism.

The intellectual labours of Tanabe, Kōyama, Kōsaka, Nishitani, Suzuki and Miki were caught in the web of Graeco-European philosophy. Whitehead and James aside, Anglo-American philosophy, certainly in the analytic tradition, might be another planet. These thinkers are at home in the principal schools of Continental philosophy after Herman Lotze (1817–81): neo-Kantianism, Heidelberg historicism, Dilthean hermeneutics, Bergsonian vitalism, French Hegelianism, phenomenology, existentialism, Heideggerian ontology and, at one remove, Lukácsian Marxism.

If the formidable challenge of illuminating the complex weave of mutual influences that link Continental and Japanese philosophy between 1923 and 1968 is to be met, the approach at work in Feenberg's *Lukács, Marx and the Sources of Critical Theory* suggests the way forward. Although Marxist thinkers occupy stage centre in this study, Heidegger has an honourable place as a study in contrast. Neither Heidegger's philosophy nor his politics is criticised in any significant way in the more important references to his work in *Lukács, Marx and the Sources of Critical Theory*. This is in contrast to the bitter complaints about Heidegger in Feenberg's contribution to *Rude Awakenings*.

Axis deconstruction

No fact about the articles collected in *Rude Awakenings* is more disturbing than the divide between writers from the former Allied powers and Japan itself. The Farías Affair, *as an event in Japanese studies*, set West against East. The Western savaging of the Kyoto School set the losers of the Second World War against the winners. The Japanese scholarly reaction to the other great intellectual scandal of the *annus horribilis* that was 1987 casts an unsettling light on this Allied-versus-Axis struggle among students of philosophy.

At the end of 1987, as the controversy over Heidegger gripped Paris, another war of words erupted on the opposite side of the Atlantic. On 1 December, the *New York Times* published a front-page story titled 'Yale Scholar's Articles Found in Pro-Nazi Newspaper'. The scholar in question was Paul de Man. The scandal revealed that De Man was the author not only of the seminal *Blindness and Insight* but also of a number of anti-Semitic editorials written during the German occupation of Belgium. In the words of Richard Wolin, the De Man affair would all but destroy the international reputation of 'the most articulate North American advocate of deconstruction'.[15]

In the United States, the exposure of De Man provoked rejoicing among hard-pressed cultural conservatives and affronted, homespun 1960s radicals such as the cultural critic Camille Paglia who had been thrown on the defensive by the new French tyranny over American intellectual life. In Japan, where deconstruction had been readily absorbed as yet another stimulating intellectual fashion from Europe, the impact of De Man's fall from grace was minimal. Even the purely scholarly repercussions from the De Man controversy were far less destructive there than in the United States. Nevertheless, when Kōjin Karatani, the Japanese intellectual and cultural impresario, organised a round-table discussion in February 1989 to assess the wartime Kyoto School and the contemporary relevance of the idea of 'Overcoming Modernity', he opened his table talk, or *zadankai*, with a reprise of the De Man affair.

Karatani spoke for many Japanese intellectuals when he declared that he was undisturbed by the revelations about what the 20-year-old De Man had written during the war. After all, Karatani argued, Japan and Continental Europe both experienced the moral trials of the last war: many Japanese intellectuals had been attacked for their 'collaboration' with the military authorities during the Asia-Pacific War. This was a matter of not only ethical blacks and whites but also moral greys.

In making this argument, Karatani harked back to Yoshimi Takeuchi, the China literary specialist and radical leftist supporter of Mao's Great Cultural Revolution, who once controversially observed, in his influential essay on 'Overcoming Modernity', that the distance between regime criticism and regime support in wartime Japan was 'no thicker than a single sheet of paper'.[16] Takeuchi was no defender of Tojo's government. His point is subtler: many Japanese intellectuals have sought to wrap themselves in pacifist moral certainties but at the price of empirical self-delusion about the grey realities of wartime Japanese society. The Allied critics of the Kyoto School suffer similar kinds of self-delusion about the moral ambiguities of Allied wartime conduct.

Karatani takes a nuanced approach to the facts of the Second World War. As someone who knew De Man, Karatani claims that his suspicions were first aroused by the Belgian literary critic's abandonment of his native country for the United States after the war:

> De Man was constantly mindful of his wartime experience. This was my unmistakable impression. There was something darker about his work, something unreflected in his efforts to give a formal American cast to deconstruction.[17]

Karatani's round-table discussion on the wartime Kyoto School brought together Akira Asada, his formidable sidekick, Wataru Hiromatsu, the author of *On 'Overcoming Modernity'* (a work that figured prominently in Chapter 4), and Hiroshi Ichikawa, the son of Hakugen Ichikawa, perhaps Japan's leading critic of the wartime lapses of Japan's Zen establishment. Hiroshi Ichikawa's participation in the discussions is of particular interest because, five years later, Christopher Ives would make Hakugen Ichikawa's criticism into a battering ram in an uncompromising attack on the war responsibility of Japanese Buddhism in his contribution to *Rude Awakenings*.

Ives's determination to recruit Ichikawa to the Allied camp in his quarrel with the supposedly 'Axis' defence of the Kyoto School may be the defining thematic gesture of the entire book. Because not a single Japanese contributor to *Rude Awakenings* was willing to endorse the 'Allied' indictment presented at the New Mexico conference that occasioned the book, the Westerners were reduced to recruiting dead Japanese, such as Ichikawa, to their cause.

Throughout Karatani's symposium, which takes the work of Kitarō Nishida and the Kyoto School as its *Leitmotif*, there are striking parallels and disturbing contrasts with the *Rude Awakenings* conference. But Karatani's instincts were sound in making De Man his point of departure. This is because of the decisive role played by deconstruction theorists in the Western humanist's 'rediscovery' of politics. In his preface to *White Mythologies: Writing History and the West*, Robert Young spoke for his generation of left-wing scholars when he concluded that 'In recent years the field of literary and cultural theory has, broadly speaking, been determined by a preoccupation with the 'political'.'

The De Man scandal marks a turning point in the development of deconstruction away from the radically anti-subjectivist posture that it had assumed until 1987 and towards a new but rather conventional engagement with the discourse of human rights that followed 1987. Abandonment of the most radical form of anti-subjectivist critique was the price that had to be paid to secure the beachhead of deconstruction in American academe after the Farías–De Man scandals. But it encouraged Heidegger's critics to assume falsely that the trials of subjectivity do not apply to democratic states as well.[18] No philosophic truth is more subversive of the moral assumptions of Pacific War orthodoxy.

The stance of Japanese thinkers such as Karatani highlights the importance of the one contribution to *Rude Awakenings* from the Third World: the article by Agustin Jacinto Zavala, from Mexico, titled 'The Return to the Past: Tradition and the Political Microcosm in the Later Nishida'.[19] This piece may prove to be prophetic. When revisionism has finally triumphed over Pacific War orthodoxy, when the rights of philosophy are no longer compromised by suspect forms of ethical blackmail, when we can finally grasp the wartime Kyoto School as it really was, Jacinto's approach may come into its own. He surveys the morally demanding terrain of Kyoto philosophy with generous authority:

> As synthesis, then, the present is the self-identity of everything given in the past and the manifold negations that move the past into the future. When Nishida refers to the synthesis as an 'identity', he does not have in mind a mere harmonizing of opposite energies, but the creation of something new, a 'new world'. In this sense, identity neither eliminates nor alleviates opposition, but integrates the opposing elements in the service of something greater.[20]

The tolerance and philosophic sympathy at work in Jacinto's intervention contrast sharply with the accusatory stance adopted by the Kyoto School critics from the principal Allied powers. Such Japanese sanguinity in the face of the fierce row elsewhere over Heidegger offers a quiet warning to the Western student of Japanese philosophy against overreacting to the accusations of Farías and his allies. As for the treatment of Japanese philosophy in Japan, the steady drummers of philosophic scholarship have ensured that the current revival of Kyoto thought continues to deepen and broaden. The recent but varied contributions of Masakatsu Fujita, Toshiaki Kobayashi, Kunitsugu Kosaka and Ryōsuke Ōhashi all need to be mentioned in this context.

Back to Foucault

The disintegration of the old religious-philosophical paradigm has opened the door to *Victory at Sea/Band of Brothers* nostalgia, thus threatening to thrust the obscurantism of Allied wartime propaganda into the seminar room, the library and the private reflections of the Western scholar of Kyoto thought. One rhetorical question captures the new threat: if Tanabe and Nishitani were fascists, how can they also be eminent philosophers?

Allied orthodoxy offers no answer to this question with which the philosopher can live.

When Farías posed this question about Heidegger, he assumed that no effective defence of the author of *Being and Time* was possible. When the proponent of Pacific War orthodoxy presses an analogous indictment against Tanabe or Nishitani, he plunges the field into crisis. The moral absolute at work in this critique subverts the very coherence of philosophy as a credible field of metaphysical reflection and academic research within Japan studies. Only Pacific War revisionism offers the necessary defence. The suggestion is that no Westerner can be an effective student of the Kyoto School without being a revisionist. There is no middle ground.

The moral-minded myth-making of Pacific War orthodoxy has all but guaranteed a wretched outcome. Thus, the philosopher is now urged to mimic the posture of the neo-Marxist historian of Japanese ideas and assume the Allied Gaze when studying Japan: this is the equivalent in modern Japan studies of the one-sided power/moral relationship that Michel Foucault so forcefully debunked in *Surveiller et Punir, Naissance de la prison* (1975). It is at work in the male gaze in Western painting and the Orientalist gaze in colonialist ideology and scholarship. The ruling assumption of the neo-Marxist intellectual historian is that the Japanese is his moral inferior. This is why the Allied Gaze cannot be returned.

The strategy of metaphysically holding one's nose, of distinguishing the man from the ideas, the politics from the philosophy, does not work *as philosophy*. What point is there in lecturing undergraduates about *An Inquiry into the Good* or *The Logic of the Species* as philosophic models to be avoided? One cannot do philosophy if one surrenders to the despairing conclusion that 'Heidegger was a Nazi, Nazi from the start, Nazi to the end.' Nor can one teach Kyoto philosophy if one begins with Van Bragt's bleak question: 'Is there anything in Nishida's thought that kept him from becoming a ultra-nationalist?' These counsels of despond are *philosophic* dead ends. They come with signs reading '*Huis Clos*'.

Is there no way out of this moral maze? The revisionist challenges the ethics and the psychology of Pacific War orthodoxy with a moral catechism beginning with Jesus' question: 'Who is without sin here?' Who fought the Pacific War without committing crimes against humanity? Who stands in unambiguous and unquestioned command of the moral high ground? Who wears the white gloves? The answers to these questions are straightforward and require no philosophic erudition for a proper response. Pacific War orthodoxy is helpless before such probings. The Tokyo War Crimes Tribunal evaded such questions and today there are still no answers. As a result, Pacific War orthodoxy is morally suspect and intellectually bankrupt. It therefore must not be allowed to undermine sound scholarship. If we are to find another way forward, one in keeping with the highest European ideals of truth and decency, we must learn to return the Allied Gaze.

11 Nazism is no excuse

After Farías – the Allied Gaze and the second crisis (1997–2002)

> Our age is the age of the intellectual organisation of political hatreds. It will be one of its chief claims to notice in the moral history of humanity.
>
> Julien Benda[1]

The insertion of the Allied Gaze into the study of modern Japanese philosophy and religion has been the most damning consequence of the paradigm crisis set off by *Rude Awakenings*.[2] A curious schizophrenia has resulted: when the Allied scholar broods on a purely religious and metaphysical aspect of Kyoto School thought, all is well; but as soon as a wartime issue appears on the horizon, out pops the Allied Gaze, and with it the full panoply of Allied moral condescension towards the Japanese. The resulting 'politics' is as often morally hypocritical as it is philosophically incoherent. Of all the rude awakenings suffered by Japan studies since the Farías Affair, this may be the rudest.

Back to the facts

How is the Western student of Japanese philosophy to think his way out of this cul-de-sac? Certainly, no way will be found as long as this dilemma is understood as a double bind which compels the philosopher to make impossible choices: Morality or philosophy? Conscience or empirical truth? This is an intellectual dead end. Having allowed the neo-Marxist to paint us into this corner, we must now learn to paint ourselves out of the specious logic and flawed scholarship of '*Japanokritik*'.[3] Only when the empirical confusions of the neo-Marxist are exposed can the philosophers begin to learn how to square their commitments to philosophy with the common-sense imperatives of morality. The empirical test is at once simple and unforgiving. The student of the wartime Kyoto School needs only to peruse the arguments and conclusions of the neo-Marxist to learn how *not* to understand the Kyoto School of philosophy.[4] The factual foundation of *Japanokritik* is so sandy, its textual reliability so suspect and its arguments so tendentious that the philosopher may safely conclude that the researcher who echoes neo-Marxism on the Kyoto School is going to get many of the most important facts of the matter wrong.

This depressing truth can be illustrated. Take, for example, Andrew Feenberg's article 'The Problem of Modernity in the Philosophy of Nishida' in *Rude Awakenings*.[5] In the empirical section which begins this stimulating piece of analysis, Feenberg the philosopher has placed his trust in neo-Marxist historical scholarship, a mistake we have all made. Influenced by the neo-Marxist's propagandistic approach to the wartime Kyoto School, Feenberg's opening sentence reads:

> In the 1930s and early 1940s, Japanese philosophy reflected the political climate by becoming more nationalistic and authoritarian. With a few honourable exceptions, the major thinkers, such as Kuki Shūzō, Tanabe Hajime, and Watsuji Tetsurō, defended Japanese imperialism.[6]

What is wrong with this summary statement can be laid squarely at the door of the neo-Marxist who has uncovered no evidence for concluding that Tanabe, for example, was 'authoritarian'. On the politics of the wartime Kyoto School, Feenberg would have been more ably served by Naoki Sakai's research on Tanabe, Graham Parkes's analysis of Kuki and Christopher Jones's work on Watsuji.[7] Agreed, the Kyoto School *tends* to be nationalistic, but no more so than its responsible conservative contemporaries were in Germany, France or the United States, all of whom also defended the right of national overseas expansion. The Kyoto School was not ultra-nationalist. The nineteenth-century expression 'liberal nationalist' offers a much more accurate description of where the wartime Kyoto School stood on the ideological spectrum of Imperial Japanese society.

The facts of the matter are unambiguous. Tanabe was not a defender of the Tojo regime, nor a supporter of the Japanese Army's brutal policies on the Chinese mainland. *The Ōshima Memos* leaves no room for doubt.[8] Perusal of the comments made by four of the leading lights of the second generation of the Kyoto School in *The Standpoint of World History and Japan* confirms this conclusion about the liberal nationalist character of this group of Japanese philosophers. Feenberg cites Peter Dales's *The Myth of Japanese Uniqueness* as his source on the 'imperialist background to Japanese thought before the War', but, as has been shown, Dale is not reliable on Tanabe, the key Kyoto School figure at issue.[9]

In his second paragraph on page 151, Feenberg observes that 'philosophers' enthusiasm for government policy varied widely and Nishida was by no means the worst'. This conclusion is not persuasive. Nishida and Tanabe opposed Tojo's policies. Their views made them the object of investigation by the authorities. Nishida and Tanabe supported the criticism made in *The Standpoint of World History and Japan* by Kōyama, Kōsaka, Nishitani and Suzuki, views that were attacked by the ultra-nationalist press and censured by the Army. Tanabe was the prime mover in the secret discussions with anti-Army intellectuals in the Imperial Navy.

True, these philosophers were patriotic thinkers. They supported their country at its moment of supreme danger. They objected to the West's global hegemony. They wanted their country to expand overseas and exercise a prudent and progressive leadership role in East Asia. They were loyal critics of imperial Japan, but they were critics. On the subject of imperialism, their recommendations on colonial government, for example, were closer to the enlightened views of Tadao Yanaihara than those of the Tojo clique.[10]

Citing the rather anodyne opinions expressed by Nishida in *The Problem of Japanese Culture*, Feenberg once again trustingly draws on neo-Marxist 'research' in his assessment of 'the recent revival of interest' in the four most famous wartime symposia ('Overcoming Modernity' and the three *Chūō Kōron zadankai* collectively known as 'The Standpoint of World History and Japan').[11] Here the sorry impact of neo-Marxist propaganda is evident.[12] Take, for example, Feenberg's dating of the four famous wartime round-table discussions. The first of the *Chūō Kōron* discussions was held in 1941, not in 1942. Similarly, the transcript of the third *Chūō Kōron* symposium was published in 1943, not in 1942.

It matters that the first symposium was held *before* the outbreak of war because of the argument that the participants sought to warn against precipitate military action, but these hopes were overtaken by events. It is essential to know that the third symposium was published more than half a year *after* the Battle of Midway, when the war had turned against Japan. These imprecisions of dating can almost certainly be traced to faulty neo-Marxist scholarship. Such fundamental errors of fact invite errors of analysis and interpretation.

Back to philosophy

Stripped of its empirical defences, the moral critique of the wartime Kyoto School begins to disintegrate. Contrary to our first impression, we are not confronted with a double bind, some intolerable choice between morality and philosophical truth, but the rather less testing question of whether we prefer empirical truth over speculative fantasy. It is the facts of the case that call into doubt the brave effort of some Western scholars to glue together a new paradigm from the broken pieces of the old. James W. Heisig's *Philosophers of Nothingness* stands as the principal statement of this search for a compromise between political criticism and apolitical religious philosophy.[13]

The price for this compromise is high. It demands the uncritical embrace of Pacific War orthodoxy. It asserts the essential inferiority of philosophy to a suspect 'politics'. And it closes the door on the chief achievement and glory of Kyoto School thought between 1931 and 1944: political and historical philosophical reflection. Instead of solving the first crisis, books such as *Philosophers of Nothingness* have plunged Kyoto School studies into a new paradigmatic crisis.

To be fair to Heisig, the old religious-philosophical paradigm was all but incapable of dealing with political reality, Japanese or otherwise. The examination of Kyoto thought by the philosopher of religion during the past half-century has assiduously avoided any form of substantive dialogue with the realm of the political scientist and political historian. That was its strength and its weakness. In the wake of this first crisis, Kyoto School studies might have fruitfully mimicked the post-war development of Asian studies as a whole: the shift from the high textualism of European classicism to the Weberian rigours of American-style social science.

Political science and rigorous historical research offer a sensible way forward. But unfortunately this is not what the critics of the religious paradigm have meant by 'politics'. For such critics, 'politics' means neither research on political institutions nor the study of political philosophy but something much narrower and less scientific: the ethical criticism of wartime Japan from an Allied perspective. Ignoring the unsettling potential of Pacific War revisionism, these apostate religious scholars have opted for the ethical 'certainties' of 'good war' orthodoxy. This neglect of the political facts of the case unites the traditional Orientalist approach with the more anti-Japanese thrust of recent Kyoto School research in the West. Edward Said famously admonished the guild about such moral and intellectual dangers in *Orientalism*, arguably the most important book ever written about the perils of area studies, but his warnings have been resolutely ignored.[14]

'Good war' nostalgia set the stage for a second crisis, in which Allied wartime propaganda has poisoned Western attitudes towards modern Japanese philosophy. The coherence of philosophy as a respectable field of metaphysical reflection and academic research within Japan studies has been seriously undermined. Given the factually flawed nature of much orthodox scholarship, a wretched outcome was guaranteed. Essentialism has been the principal flaw. The defenders of Pacific War orthodoxy uncritically assume that the United States, as a society and political system, is incapable of committing an offence against the moral order that would in any way compromise the worthiness of America's national essence – our *Kokutai*. But the proponent of Pacific War orthodoxy also implicitly denies the worthiness of the Japanese essence. The orthodox view is that the crimes committed in the name of the Japanese state during the Pacific War have irrevocably defiled Japan's national essence. This Allied metaphysical bias explains why the wrangle between Pacific War orthodoxy and revisionism has gone on so long, and why it could go on forever. This is not, at root, a battle over facts; it is a struggle over *amor patriae*, or national self-regard.

Whatever the defects of Pacific War orthodoxy, *Philosophers of Nothingness* remains an impressive achievement.[15] The author is the director of the Nanzan Institute for Religion and Culture at Nagoya's Nanzan University, and he has devoted the bulk of his working life as a scholar, editor and translator to winning a place of honour for religious scholarship in general and Kyoto School philosophy in particular within Japan studies.

Heisig's role as editor of *Rude Awakenings* and author of *Philosophers of Nothingness* has transformed him into one of the most influential contemporary thinkers about Japan because of the decisive role he has played in orchestrating the rebellion against the old religious-philosophy paradigm. Farías's assault on Heidegger may have sparked this rebellion, but Heisig has led the new Western attack on the Kyoto School among Western experts on Japanese philosophy.

In *Rude Awakenings* and *Philosophers of Nothingness*, Heisig comes across as an angry critic of the Japanese philosophic establishment: 'When Nishida's (Japanese) commentators – even the best of them – cite him in support of their own ethnocentrism, or at least their own privileged position to read him, they are no longer talking about Nishida but about themselves.'[16] Heisig has no time for such Japanese insularity. He finds the national cult of uniqueness at once offensive and ridiculous.

Rejecting one of the laws of Japanese intellectual life, Heisig insists that the reputation of the Kyoto School as philosophy rises and falls entirely with its international reputation. Japan, by itself, does not provide the standard that counts in these matters:

> I have no hesitation in claiming that ... our reading of Aristotle and Descartes, Kant and Hegel, Heidegger and Nietzsche, should be different after reading Nishida, Tanabe and Nishitani. To the extent that this is not the case ... the Kyoto philosophers have failed to live up to their goals. It is as simple as that.[17]

Heisig is determined to wound the Japanese philosophic establishment. He concludes that the greatness of Nishida, Tanabe and Nishitani 'completely eclipses the scholarly contribution that professional Japanese philosophers specializing in Western thinkers have made in the twentieth century'.[18] Indeed, it is around this triangular structure of Nishida–Tanabe–Nishitani that *Philosophers of Nothingness* is organised.

Heisig is at his best in analysing apolitical philosophical and religious concepts. Here is Heisig at full strength on what Nishida meant by 'transcendence':

> As with everything in Nishida's philosophy, so here, too, all questions of logic and metaphysics had to answer to the fundamental question of illuminating the self. It is not a matter of finding a standpoint from which to 'transcend' opposition but rather of bringing it down to the problem of consciousness, a standpoint of 'transcendence' as he called it. In this sense, the final paradigm for the union of opposites in reality lay not in the cosmos but in the self-awareness of the individual.[19]

When Heisig focuses his energy and powers of analysis on philosophic matters, his strengths are obvious. But when he turns to the political philosophy of the wartime Kyoto School, his powers desert him. Confronted with accusations of fascism against Tanabe and Nishida, he falls back on the hoariest cliché in the entire controversy over Heidegger: that his philosophy had nothing to do with his politics. This is Heisig's central conclusion on the relationship of politics and philosophy in the wartime Kyoto School:

> *One has, deliberately or otherwise, to ignore the greatest bulk of the writings of these thinkers to arrive at the conclusion that anything approaching or supporting the imperialistic ideology of wartime Japan belongs to the fundamental inspiration of their thought.*[20]

The prose is tortured because the commitment to philosophy is not deep enough. The Allied critic of the Kyoto School lacks metaphysical stamina. It would appear that, unless one is a complete Hellene and European, the slightest ethical turbulence may cause one to falter in one's vocation as a philosopher. Faced with bogus and hypocritical charges of 'philosophic fascism' or 'philotyranny', the true heirs of Socrates concentrate their critical powers on the factual and logical foundations of such accusations. They pursue the philistine and Euro-hater to his lair. They spare no one and nothing in the defence of the truth that is philosophy.

This lack of stamina undermines the fundamental structure of his argument by short-circuiting the strict *philosophic* analysis of the late Nishida, the middle Tanabe and the early Nishitani. Of the seventy-one sections that compose *Philosophers of Nothingness*, nineteen (Sections 28–46) are devoted to Tanabe, the co-founder, with Nishida, of the Kyoto School. Heisig begins with two sections (28 and 29) in which he reviews Tanabe's life and work as a whole (including his style of philosophical thought). In Sections 30–32, the intellectual core of Heisig's assessment, the early Tanabe is generously analysed. The focus here is what Tanabe brought to his philosophical partnership with Nishida at Kyoto University, what he learned from Nishida and why Tanabe eventually broke with him.

In Section 33, where the genesis of *The Logic of the Species* is traced, Heisig's assessment of Tanabe takes a suspect turn from which it never recovers. Over the next seven sections, Tanabe ceases to be primarily an object of philosophic interpretation. A kind of political/ethical criticism comes to the fore. Tanabe is consistently judged from the standpoint of Pacific War orthodoxy. Heisig subjects Allied battlefield and diplomatic conduct to no criticism whatever, but the Japanese people and state are judged to be essentially evil. Therefore, Tanabe's merits as a philosopher are determined by the test of Allied virtue. Any hint of love for his country or loyalty to his emperor or support for the Japanese empire is condemned as 'nationalistic'.

Only a close reading of the relevant sections of *Philosophers of Nothingness* allows one to grasp just how pernicious the impact of this essentialist critique of Tanabe is. True, in Section 32, Heisig muses on the *philosophic* reasons why Tanabe turned to the themes of history, politics and society (themes crucial to the late Nishida and the early Nishitani): for Tanabe, 'absolute nothingness is a kind of dynamic, almost a kind of *élan vital*, that keeps the dialectic of interrelatedness going'. The Bergsonian note, *élan vital*, is just one of a number of crucial concepts that Tanabe borrowed from the French philosopher's repertoire of ideas in developing his logic of the species.

By contrast, in Section 33, Heisig delivers his first bombshell when he observes that one of Tanabe's motivations for devising a new logic (thus breaking with Nishida's 'logic of locus', or *basho no ronri*) was a practical concern with, in Tanabe's words,

> seeking out the rational grounds to the controls imposed by the society as a nation on its individual members.[21]

The syntax of this translation leaves the precise meaning obscure. But if the suggestion is that Tanabe wanted to make oppression rational, this is false. Furthermore, this ominous, almost Orwellian-sounding remark is not put into context. Heisig does not cite the rest of the whole sentence, let alone the paragraph, from which it is drawn. Yet the quotation cries out for a plausible explanation. What does Tanabe actually mean here? What has brought Tanabe to this conclusion? Why does Tanabe think in this way? Heisig offers no convincing answers to any of these questions, but they form the heart of the matter.

Heisig's rendering harks back to the contentious politics of translating Tanabe's *The Logic of the Species* encountered in Chapter 7. Heisig demonstrates an impressive command of the Western philosophic background to Tanabe's system of thought. This is not in doubt; we are not dealing with the pretensions of a neo-Marxist here. Rather, the difficulty is, as has been shown, that one must have a sound understanding of key terms such as '*obéissance spontanée*', as Bergson used the expression in *Les Deux Sources de la Morale et la Religion*, before one can begin to understand what Tanabe means precisely by '*jihatsu-teki ni fukujū*'.

In Heisig's translation, the interrelationship of the objective and subjective spirit in Hegelian dialectical logic is pivotal. When the translator tackles Tanabe's philosophy of *l'obligation morale*, to take the point at issue, infinite care must be exercised. This is particularly true, as Heisig would be the first to acknowledge, when treating how Tanabe uses concepts from such complex Western thinkers as Bergson and Hegel. But having allowed a damning ambiguity, Heisig decides that, in the name of Pacific War orthodoxy, he must stick the knife in. Thus, he observes:

> Allusions to the first concern with the role of the state as a limit on the individual were already present in his earlier writings, but had not figured in his idea of absolute mediation or in his grounding of history

in absolute nothingness. Already in 1922, for example, years before Japan's military buildup and at the height of Taishō liberalism and its positive mood of democracy, Tanabe had published such remarks in an essay on 'The Notion of Culture'.[22]

It is one of Heisig's (post-Farías) rhetorical strategies to attach an aura of blame to Tanabe's wartime writings by juxtaposing the dates of his publications with developments in Japanese military or foreign policy during the 1930s and early 1940s. Heisig does not assert that Tanabe was somehow responsible for the Manchurian Incident or the Nanking Massacre, but an implied guilt by association is manifest. Note that Japan's 'military buildup' is mentioned even though it is chronologically irrelevant to what Tanabe is writing about. But the seeds of suspicion, however vague, are effectively planted here in order to be harvested later to devastating rhetorical effect.

From the late nineteenth century onwards, but particularly between 1931 and 1945, Imperial Japan was an expansionist military power which sought to create the kind of hegemonic relationship over East Asia that the United States had long exerted over Latin America. Furthermore, the American urge to assert its power over the Western Pacific was strong and growing. Discussion of America's hegemony over the rest of the Americas figures prominently in some of the most important wartime Kyoto School texts, but Heisig ignores these global realities and the provocation of US power, thus encouraging the *American* reader to seize the moral high ground and play judge and jury over any Japanese philosopher who supported Japanese resistance to globalisation and the rise of American empire. Japanese imperialism was an aggressive provocation, but there is an element of legitimate anti-Western resistance in the Japanese stance.

Pacific War revisionism has left no mark on *Philosophers of Nothingness*. No attention has been paid to the mountains of facts, facts damaging to the Allied mythology of the war, that have been discovered since the destruction of Hiroshima and Nagasaki. The moral certainties of our 'good war' have been steadily undermined during the intervening decades. Finally, the world has changed. The principal geopolitical trends of our age are the consolidation of America's global hegemony and the arrival of a post-White world. Both trends fatally undermine the contemporary relevance of Pacific War orthodoxy. This triple failure suggests that the compromise paradigm that underwrites Heisig's principal arguments about the wartime Kyoto School does not offer a lasting solution.

When dealing with the Kyoto School as religious philosophy, Heisig displays all the traditional strengths of the Orientalist approach to Japanese thought. But Pacific War orthodoxy has distorted crucial sections of *Philosophers of Nothingness*, particularly the treatment of the political philosophy and political activities of the middle Tanabe, the late Nishida and the early Nishitani. Such distortions are the price the student of the Kyoto School pays for orthodoxy. This price should confirm the contrary truth: only the liberal revisionist historian of the Pacific War offers a humane escape route from Heisig's central dilemma: if Tanabe and Nishitani were fascists, how can they also be great philosophers?

Heisig attempts to remove the nationalist bones from the metaphysical flesh of the wartime writings of Nishida, Tanabe and Nishitani in ways that, finally, do not convince because it is precisely their powers as political philosophers that make the wartime Kyoto School so important. It is like blaming Hobbes for his brilliant, world-shaping reflections on monarchical absolutism or censuring Carl Schmitt for his penetrating analysis of the nature of sovereignty. Tanabe, Hobbes and Carl Schmitt are all thinkers of the first rank.[23] They live to rethink the world. Our world.

Regarded as notorious by those who have not read it properly, *The Logic of the Species* is not fascist, but it is nationalist in the thinking, rational Hegelian mode. It is my suspicion that no persuasive interpretation of Tanabe's supreme achievement is possible unless we read it as a powerful Japanese contribution to the philosophy of subjectivity, of 'post-White' reasoning. If we set aside the blinkers of Pacific War orthodoxy, we may begin to see how the wartime Kyoto School not only anticipates but also transcends the argument over colonialism and the nature and destiny of a post-White world proposed by Sartre and Fanon. Tanabe and the Kyoto School gave new political meaning, at once rich and profound, to the classic call for 'the plurality of worlds'.

Racism: Locke and Kant versus the Kyoto School

To repeat: to understand the wartime Kyoto School properly, one must be a Pacific War revisionist; there is no third way. The force of this claim can be demonstrated by perusing Heisig's interpretation of Tanabe's 'The Notion of Culture'. His summary of this early essay only partially confirms Heisig's suggestion that Tanabe believed that individual rights should be sacrificed on the altar of state power. But such fine distinctions become almost irrelevant when Heisig concludes the paragraph in question with this remark:

> The root of the problem, as he [Tanabe] saw it, lay in a rush from a stress on the individual to humanity as a whole organized in the form of western democracy but 'ignoring respect for the race and forgetting the important significance of the nation'. What was needed was a new philosophical ideal distinct from that of Western states.[24]

Race? In the Japanese original, Tanabe does not use the word '*shuzoku*' (race) but '*minzoku*' (people or nation or ethnie). Heisig's rendering here puts a word in Tanabe's mouth that he did not utter. Furthermore, Heisig concedes the point. Buried deep into Heisig's 'Notes' for Section 33, after three rather dense paragraphs, the author admits:

> Not too much should be made of the term *race*, which did not have all
> the connotations it has today. The Japanese term Tanabe used, *minzoku*,
> could as well mean *ethnos* or *Volk*. On this, see Doak 1995.[25]

Given what Heisig has stated in the text of *Philosophers of Nothingness*
(the only bit most readers read), the content and place of this astonishing
admission is inexplicable. But having softened the meaning of the word
'race' in a footnote, he suggests that '*Volk*' is an acceptable translation of
'*minzoku*'. In careful *German* usage, '*Volk*' offers a suggestive rendering of
'*minzoku*', but the word '*Volk*' is used *in English-language* Allied scholarship
in order to browbeat the Germans about the war. The word '*Volk*' means
'people' or 'nation' in German, as in the expression '*die Völker Afrikas*' ('the
peoples of Africa'). It is not the German equivalent of the English word
'race'.

So why exploit the Nazi nuance of the word '*Volk*' *in English* when the
words 'nation', 'people' or 'ethnic group' provide a sound rendering of the
Japanese term in question? The answer is morally reprehensible. To translate
'*minzoku*' as '*Volk*' in English allows one to link Tanabe and Nishida,
vaguely but damningly, to the horrors of the Third Reich. This is why 'race'
is the preferred translation of '*minzoku*' among the orthodox. But what we
know about Nazism now offers no excuse for making tendentious assertions
about Japanese philosophers writing in the 1930s.

Heisig cites the research of Kevin Doak, but the arguments of this
American historian undermine Heisig's case.[26] Doak insists on rendering
'*minzoku*' as 'nation' and '*minzoku-shugi*' as 'nationalism'. The distinction
between *kokka-shugi* (literally, 'statism', which Doak translates as 'official'
or state nationalism) and *minzoku-shugi* (ethnic or popular nationalism) is
central to the arguments he developed in *Dreams of Difference: The Japan
Romantic School and the Crisis of Modernity* and elsewhere.[27] Doak rejects
the specious renderings of '*minzoku*' such as 'race' or '*Volk*'.

Note that in strict usage, the expression '*Herrenvolk*' means 'master
nation' or 'master people'. The German equivalent of 'master race' is
'*Herrenrasse*'. The conventional English translation of '*Herrenvolk*' as
'master race' is incorrect. It harks back to the imprecisions of pre-war
discourse in which the word 'race' was indiscriminately applied to many
ethnic groupings (e.g. the Welsh, German or Japanese 'races'). Strictly
speaking, White, Black and Mongoloid are racial designations, not Bulgar,
Jewish or Korean. In the linguistic world born out of the horrors of the
Final Solution, the word 'race' must be used carefully to avoid giving
offence. The resort to the term 'race' in orthodox writings on German and
Japanese intellectual culture before and during the Second World War is
often as linguistically indefensible as it is politically reactionary. In Asian
studies, such usage reeks of the morally dubious failings of Orientalism.

So what place has the word 'race' in philosophy? The debate within
Western philosophy over racist attitudes in the writings of John Locke and

Immanuel Kant reveals how disloyal Western critics of the Kyoto School have been to philosophy itself. This issue has been aired in a series of articles in *Radical Philosophy*, beginning with Robert Bernasconi's 'Will the Real Kant Please Stand Up: The Challenge of Enlightenment Racism to the Study of the History of Philosophy'. Bernasconi's main targets are Locke and Kant as *philosophers*. He acknowledges Locke's active and influential role 'in British colonial activities' and 'his investments in the slave trade', but these facts 'raise no philosophical questions'.[28] Bernasconi's concerns are elsewhere:

> Although the precise role that Locke played in writing *The Fundamental Constitutions of Carolina* is unknown and may never be settled, it seems that, when that document grants to slave-holders 'absolute power and authority' over their Negro slaves, the reference to 'power' was added to the manuscript in his [Locke's] own handwriting to read: 'Every Freeman of Carolina shall have absolute power and Authority over his Negro slaves, of whatever opinion or Religion soever.'[29]

In its caution about language, fact and argument, Bernasconi's critique of Locke is worlds away from the neo-Marxist assault on the Kyoto School. First, note how Bernasconi draws a firm distinction between the philosophic discourse proper and the realm of political opinion and the history of ideas. Such boundaries command little or no respect among the proponents of Pacific War orthodoxy. But where in the writings of Tanabe or Nishitani can be found an equivalent of Locke's moral callousness? Secondly, Bernasconi may be keen to convict Locke of philosophic lapses, but he demonstrates scrupulous care in treating the relevant manuscript sources. The contrast with the biased sloppiness of neo-Marxism is painful. Finally, even Bernasconi, to say nothing of Locke's defenders, reveals a rooted respect for Locke as a great thinker. He acknowledges the force of the careful reading of the relevant passages on slavery in Locke's *Second Treatise on Government* that present a morally more attractive picture of the English thinker.

There are similar lessons to be learned from Bernasconi's struggle with Kant's racism:

> Turning to Kant, it is hard to know whether the fact that Kant scholars waited for non-specialists like Emmanuel Eze and me to raise the issue of Kant's racism was because these scholars did not know the full range of Kant's works very well – which would be somewhat damning if true – or because they persuaded themselves that there was nothing here worth discussing.[30]

Again, the sense of restraint and professional respect is plain. Bernasconi is making a very serious point, but there is no rush to impugn the motives of his professional colleagues, to charge them with fascism or racism or moral duplicity. Again, the contrast with recent controversies sparked by the neo-Marxist *Japanokritik* is embarrassing for Japan Studies. None of this means that Bernasconi pulls his punches:

> It is true that some philosophers ... when writing on the 'Critique of Teleological Judgment', saw that some of the central problems addressed in that work were first formulated by Kant in his essays on race. However, the racism that is apparent in those essays, as in his lectures on anthropology and on physical geography, was almost never brought into relation with his teleology, his moral philosophy, or his essay on universal history, in spite of the obvious question that they raised: how could his racism coexist with his moral universalism?[31]

Among students of Western philosophy, even critics such as Bernasconi insist that three tasks must define the examination of thinkers 'that are prima facie racist': (1) the careful identification of the exact statements in question; (2) the meticulous weighing of contextual questions to avoid applying contemporary moral values to a different age; and (3) establishment of the relevant intellectual sources for the controversial texts at issue. In neo-Marxist writings on modern Japanese philosophy, none of these standards tends to be observed because fascist and racist motives are assumed almost willy-nilly, and once such a motive is assigned, the serious study of philosophy is instantly abandoned.

In the study of European philosophy during the Enlightenment, we find the judicious and cautious examination of thinkers who are prima facie racists; in the study of modern Japanese philosophy, we find vicious accusations against thinkers who are not racists or fascists. It is Bernasconi, not the Allied critique of the wartime Kyoto School, who provides a responsible standard for how questions of race should be treated in philosophy.

The moral critique of the 'good war'

If Tanabe and Nishitani were fascists, how can they also be eminent philosophers? It is over this conundrum that students of Japanese thought have stumbled. There is a parallel failure in the Allied assessment of the philosophical achievement of Heidegger. The misjudgments of *The Politics of Being: The Political Thought of Martin Heidegger* have encouraged the angry excesses of *Heidegger's Children: Hannah Arendt, Karl Löwith, Hans Jonas and Herbert Marcuse*.[32] In both cases, the empirical case against Heidegger is vulnerable to a brutal form of critical deconstruction.

Surveying the shattered spiritual (*geistig*) landscape, littered with damaged reputations and scarred texts, left in the wake of 'Typhoon Farías', De Beistegui renews the call for 'salvaging Heidegger, his texts, that is, a matter of not letting closure of thinking silently take place'.[33] But from what precisely must we be saved?

From that simple equation which, willy-nilly, is slowly being accepted, an equation so simple and so convenient that it has become almost irresistible: Heidegger was a Nazi, Nazi from the start, Nazi till the end. To this equation, it is not a question of opposing a counter-proposition, the revisionist version of the first equation: Heidegger was not a Nazi, he never was. This, too, is impossible: the evidence is too massive, too brutal: devastating. Heidegger's involvement was, at least for a few months, total and unconditional.[34]

There is a flaw in this apparently irresistible equation. Someone else, an outside party, is present. That someone must do the leaping when we leap to the conclusion that 'Heidegger was a Nazi, Nazi from the start, Nazi till the end.' So, who would play God here? Who has the right to judge Heidegger, or, for that matter, to censure Nishida, Tanabe and Nishitani? Who wears the white gloves? With such questions, the moral stature of a handful of Japanese thinkers sets us on course collision with Pacific War orthodoxy.[35] As the total revaluation of the evidence and interpretations of the Second World War gathers pace, it would appear that only liberal revisionism – enlightened, empirical and rational – can deliver us from the self-deluding myths of our so-called 'good war'. Ends never justify means. The Pacific War is no exception to this iron ethical rule. The worthiness of our war goals did not justify the barbarism of our battlefield methods. To argue otherwise is illiberal and uncivilised.

After America, philosophy

12 Nothing shall be spared

A manifesto on the future of Japan studies

> The very critique of what exists, of the state and nature, of God and human beings, of principles of faith and prejudices – this power of making distinctions, which embraces everything, calls it into question, doubts it, and investigates it, is a basic element of European life without which that life is unthinkable.
>
> Karl Löwith[1]

Reason or emotion? Science or poetry? Universalism or uniqueness? Ethics or identity? Markets or networks? The individual or the group? Conscience or nation? Sense or sensibility? Friend or foe? Every Western student of Japan must take a stand on the central divide that defines Japanology not only as a way of thinking but also as a way of being in the world. Viewed against the great sweep of European history, the fundamental choice is between the universal imperatives of the Age of Reason and the species claims of European Romanticism. To take sides in this great debate is to reveal the basic assumptions that govern how one teaches, what one reads and why one writes.[2]

An examination of the state of the field today, in Europe, North America or Australia, suggests that there is no contest. Surely, the high decencies of the Enlightenment have triumphed over the suspect doctrines of the Romantic. After Hitler, we are all universalists. Either we pursue a theory, such as rational choice, that aspires to the universal reach of the natural sciences, or we are ethical universalists, proponents of liberal democratic values that we believe transcend cultural differences. Newton and Locke rule our intellectual world. They are who we are when we are at work.

The problem is that the object (*taishō*) of our studies, the Asian subject (*shutai*), has not made the same set of choices. To an unsettling degree, most Japanese intellectuals have not stood on the same side of the divide between the Enlightenment and Romanticism as we in the West hope we do. Even when Japanese intellectuals do stand with us, their hearts are not entirely in it. The tug of emotion, poetry, identity, religion, group, nation and sensibility are too strong. Even today, to opt into reason, into universalism, into science, into liberal values is frequently to opt out of Asia.

This divide over values may explain why Japan studies displays a rooted hostility to Japan, particularly to the Japanese quest for a satisfactory form of national identity. This disdain is rooted in the history of Japan studies, but the contest between Enlightenment values and Romanticism frames this hostility. This clash of civilisations may explain why, with the exception of Middle East studies, no branch of area research displays more resentment towards its object than does Japanology.

By contrast, the enduring goal of the Latin Americanist during the past century has been to understand and to strengthen Latin American social power, that is the Latin American national-popular state (*minzoku-kokka*), against the incursions of monopoly capital. Thus, according to Alberto Moreiras, one of the most influential voices in contemporary Latin American studies, 'Critical reason for that period was an aesthetic-historicist project that looked to preserve and reinforce the specificity [Tanabe's *shu-teki kokka*] of Latin American social power against an invasive and threatening outside.'[3] In Japan studies, we have reversed this ambition, thus transforming the Japanologist into the agent of an invasive and threatening Other.

Settling accounts

The life and death of E.H. Norman, the Canadian Marxist historian of Japan, has iconic stature. He is a reminder that Asian studies may be a dangerous vocation. Having produced a series of brilliant assessments of the class tensions that clouded Japan's modern development, his career was destroyed during the red purges that engulfed North America after the eruption of the Cold War. It was during this grim era that Owen Lattimore, the great student of modern Mongolia, acquired an FBI file 40,000 pages long and eventually fled to Britain. Among China hands, one did not have to be a communist to fall foul of the authorities. When John Davies, the American scholar-diplomat, argued that Chiang Kai-shek's corrupt republican regime was doomed in its struggle with Mao's communists, this distinguished China hand was sent into Latin American exile.[4]

Once the Cold War erupted, a North American scholar had only to tell the truth about Asia to become the object of official harassment. But Norman may have paid the ultimate price. His tormentors, so Norman's friends insist, drove him to suicide. If this were not enough, some of the most distinguished figures in post-war Japan studies, liberal anti-communists to a man, sought to efface Norman's legacy from Japan studies. They acted out of fear, not vengeance. They concluded that Japanology would not survive as a serious taxpayer-funded field in the university if it bore the radical Marxist stamp. Despite these efforts to bury his memory, Norman has not been forgotten. But the larger lesson was learned, particularly in the United States. Criticism of American foreign policy by the Asian specialist would be tolerated but not radical criticism, not sceptical probing that calls into doubt the 'essence' of the United States, its fundamental legitimacy as a state and a nation.

Nearly a half-century after the anti-communist purges of McCarthyism, R.T. Murphy decided it was time for a settlement of accounts between Norman and his academic opponents, notably Marius Jansen and Edwin O. Reischauer, two of the leading proponents of the application of modernisation theory to the study of Japan. In a longish review essay in the *London Review of Books*, Murphy retells the story of this clash as an intellectual tag team event pitting Jansen and Reischauer against Norman and his chief post-war defender, John W. Dower.[5]

Murphy sees this struggle as a battle between titans. Norman is described as 'the most important pre-war Western scholar of recent Japanese history', while Jansen is celebrated as 'a man who had a good claim to be the pre-eminent historian of Japan in the Western world, particularly of its early modern period'.[6] As for Reischauer, what he may have lacked in intellectual firepower he more than compensated for with his influence in the public realm, as a teacher, as a recruiter of academic talent, as a talent-spotter at Harvard and as John F. Kennedy's ambassador to Tokyo.[7] As for Dower, he is now regarded by many as the dean of American historians of twentieth-century Japan.

Mindful of Dower's reputation, Murphy focuses his attention on an anthology of Norman's works edited by the MIT historian in 1975 where 'Dower reserved some of his most scathing remarks for Jansen – no one, with the exception of Reischauer, came in for more critical treatment.'[8] But, finally, Murphy celebrates Norman not as a critic, nor as a Marxist, nor as transmitter of made-in-Japan theories about how that country works, but rather as a master painter of historical portraits. In his characterisation of Aritomo Yamagata, Meiji Japan's arch centraliser and the current bugbear of preference for ageing Japan bashers, Jansen offers six pages of description in *The Making of Modern Japan*, but he appears to lose the thread of his own argument according to Murphy.[9] By contrast, Norman's thumbnail sketch of Yamagata is almost worthy of Keynes in its psychological penetration and historical insight. Murphy concludes that 'Norman's and Jansen's contrasting treatments of this formidable figure give a sense of how far Jansen falls short of the standard Norman set.'[10]

Standards. Now there is a word to conjure with. Whatever doubts one may have about this attack on Jansen and Reischauer, Murphy correctly links standards of academic excellence, in the writing of political history and political science, to the soundness of our grasp of Japan as a society and as a regime because *the first goal of Japan studies is not to criticise or to praise Japan but to understand it.*

The view from Europe

Today, Japanology must begin all over again. This is Rikki Kersten's conclusion.[11] Her overarching demand suggests that it is not only the Japanese policymaker who has been frustrated by the long recession of the 1990s, the so-called 'lost decade', but also the Western student of Japanese society. Certainly, the experience of post-Bubble Japan has added yet another unanticipated chapter to the ever-surprising chronicle of Japanese modernity since the eighteenth century. It should also be clear that with the ending of the Cold War, the old ideological struggles between left and right have become irrelevant. Cold War liberalism is now as dead as Soviet Marxism, or should be. So, from where should we begin if we are to begin all over again?

If we are to transcend the broken hopes of Norman's Marxism as well as the Eurocentric or US-centric assumptions of the modernisation theorist, we must return to the greatest of all social scientists, the one who more than any other set the whole project of modern area studies in motion: Max Weber. Norman's legacy illustrates why this call for a return to Weber is not an unthinking genuflection before the glories of social scientific tradition. The classics can wound. Weber's 'Wissenschaft als Beruf', or 'Science as a Vocation', is the case in point.[12]

In his famous lecture of 1918, Weber warned against partisanship in the classroom. On this subject, Weber is uncompromising: 'Politics is out of place in the lecture room.'[13] He goes on to insist that

> The primary task of a useful teacher is to teach his students to recognise 'inconvenient' facts – I mean facts that are inconvenient for their party opinions. And for every party opinion there are facts that are extremely inconvenient, for my own opinion no less than for others.[14]

Norman did not take this warning to heart. This failure matters because the most consequential gift that this socialist of the chair gave to Japan studies was not his watered down version of pre-war Japanese Marxism but rather the spirit of anti-capitalist critique. Norman's ghost was active in the savaging of the Modernisation School. It fed the refusal of many Western academics to acknowledge the achievements of the post-war Japanese economic miracle. This was a singular lapse, both intellectual and moral, for which Norman was partly to blame.

The trouble does not end there. A few heirs to the tradition of utopian dissent, and not only in the United States, have been tempted to make ethical criticism into a substitute for rigorous scholarship. This is one of the dire consequences of stripping away the Marxist framework of Norman's analysis. If one dispenses with the positivism that the late Marx shared with Engels, and, at the same time, insists that empiricism serve only would-be progressive causes, whole kingdoms of inconvenient facts will be discarded.

The saddest consequence of all is that the economic, political and social programmes that after 1952 lifted almost the entire population of Japan – now more than 125 million people – out of poverty, despair and national humiliation into work, health and lives of productive, humane pride have been rejected by many Western academics who prefer to belabour the supposed emptiness of post-war Japanese affluence. True, Japan has paid a political price for its miraculous rise, and it is still paying it. But the Japanese Miracle proved that alternative modernities are possible and that one did not have to be a White Christian or Voltaire to be civilised. Post-war Japan has had no need for a Mussolini to get the trains to run on time, and the Western academic, on both the left and the right, should celebrate this fact.

The unhappy left-wing marriage of ideological bias and one-eyed empiricism may explain why opponents of the Modernisation School have produced many fine studies but no monument that can be set with confidence alongside the six volumes of *Studies in the Modernization of Japan*.[15] In that astonishing harvest of talent, and many of the most outstanding students of modern Japan contributed to it, is to be found Jansen's revenge on his many critics.

Nevertheless, Norman has emerged as the victor from his posthumous struggle with the anti-communist establishment of post-war Japan studies. The critical spirit, utopian in its aspirations, left-wing in its politics, has triumphed, particularly here in Europe. If we are to begin all over again, we must take the critical spirit as our point of departure because it holds the field. But the path forward will never be opened if we insist on endlessly re-fighting yesterday's wars. Renewal demands innovation. We must find a fresh paradigm, a new vantage, in Löwith's phrase, to dissolve old orthodoxies and propel us into a new future.[16] The Kyoto School offers such a paradigm.

Frankfurt, Paris and Oxford: old Europe and the future of Japan studies

It is time for us, not the Japanese, 'to come home to Japan' (*Nippon e no kaiki*). We must stop viewing the Japanese nation as an unreconstructed member of the Axis. Rather, we need to recognise its potential as a force for good: a restraint on the arbitrary exercise of American power and a building bloc in the construction of the new post-White order that is the planet's destiny. We must sweep away the dogmas imposed on the field by Norman as well as Reischauer and scrap the Cold War-era ban on radical thinking if we are to confront the moral, intellectual, political and scientific challenges posed by 'the global war on terrorism' and the consolidation of America's military domination of the planet. Whatever the risks, we must become truth-tellers.

Latin American studies offers the crucial rubric: critical regionalism. As Europeans, as heirs of the ancient Greeks, criticism is in our blood. Our lives as civilised beings after Socrates are unthinkable without it. But the vocation of the critic brings with it certain disciplines. The critic must take to heart Nietzsche's warning about the self-serving nature of ethical interpretations of human action in the political sphere.[17] When good confronts evil there is almost always another less savoury motive at work behind the good intentions. This does not mean that evil should not be contested, but it does suggest that the higher the moral temperature, the greater the need for a rigorous examination of conscience.

Three representative thinkers of 'old Europe' may help us to make the case for critical regionalism and to exploit the virtues of the Kyoto School as a new paradigm for Japan studies. First, there is the vantage of the Frankfurt School. Japanese philosophy as an object of Western thought provides us with a uniquely powerful tool for dissecting what Theodor Adorno would have called 'America's unmastered past'. Having spent too many decades picking over the bones of the fallen Japanese imperium, the historian of Japan should now turn to the neglected history of the rise and consolidation of the Pacific's other empire: America's. To redress this history of neglect is to rethink the significance of the Pacific War. So bold an enterprise requires a formidable repertory of ideas, insights and interpretations. The wartime Kyoto School provides such a repertory.

Secondly, there is the view from Paris. Our next proposition takes its point of departure from Lucien Goldmann's classic question: where is the subject? If Whiteness, as a set of values and practices, institutions and capacities, is to be overcome, it can only be overcome by the post-White subject. Nietzsche, Heidegger and Derrida have taught three generations of Europeans to think against the subject, but the future of the planet may require a metaphysical counter-revolution. We must breath new life into the broken subject. We must return to Hegel. The wartime Kyoto School never left him.

Thirdly, one may view our new post-White horizon from Oxford. Whatever the urgencies of planetary politics, Japan studies remains an academic adventure of mind. A scholarly renaissance demands a paradigm revolution, one capable of generating and sustaining the productive order that is normal science. Paradigm revolution requires that we learn to tell the story of the Kyoto School in an entirely fresh way. This is a double labour, one that unites the rigours and disciplines of philosophy with the sparkle and humanity of intellectual history. This is Isaiah Berlin country.

The Kyoto School and America's unmastered past

> Progress is self-assertion, the conquest of an area in which the agent can freely develop and create by eliminating (or absorbing) whatever obstructs it, both animate and inanimate ... this path may lead to terrestrial paradise, but it is strewn with the corpses of the enemy.
>
> (Isaiah Berlin)[18]

If the contemporary American critic longs to declare, with Dostoevsky, that Europe is nothing but a graveyard, then Europeans must resurrect their dead. Only by exploiting the traditions of old Europe can we begin to master the central theme of the new history of the United States, the history of our national future: the rise, consolidation and fall of the White Republic. The Pacific War is one of the decisive chapters in this story, and the political and intellectual role of the Kyoto School in this drama was as inspired as it was brave. This is the lesson of documents such as *The Ōshima Memos*. The Kyoto School waged a secret struggle against Tojo in order to bring him down as prime minister. At the same time, these philosophers sought to make rational sense of the murderous trends of the violent twentieth century.

Japanese texts such as *The Standpoint of World History and Japan* and *Overcoming Modernity*, as well as *The Ōshima Memos*, have the potential to transform the American understanding of the Pacific War. From a Japanese perspective, the Pacific War was a double struggle – a war of imperial expansion and a battle for Asian liberation from Western domination. From a White American perspective, it was at once a war against Japanese imperialism and a struggle to secure US domination of the Pacific.[19] The main conclusions of the Tokyo War Crimes Tribunal stand in the way of an honest assessment of the truths that define our imperial and racial destiny.

Kyoto School reflection on the nature of ethnic struggle should encourage us to risk a still bolder racial interpretation of the Pacific War, one that builds on the findings of John Dower in *War without Mercy*.[20] The Pacific War was a decisive moment in the domestic racial history of the United States. Tojo prepared the way, on more than one front, for the decline and fall of Roosevelt's White Republic. The overcoming of Whiteness, as an accelerating global political and demographic trend, began with Pearl Harbour. The mastering of our unmastered past begins with the revisionist history of the Pacific War.

The Kyoto School and the overcoming of Whiteness

> Yet the dark places are at the centre. Pass them by and there can be no serious discussion of the human potential.
>
> (George Steiner)[21]

Less than fifteen years after the Battle of Wounded Knee in 1890, the last armed resistance by Indians to the ethnic cleansing of North America, the Indian dream of vanquishing White power was realised on the other side of the Pacific when the Japanese Navy destroyed the Russian Baltic fleet in the Straits of Tsushima. The Russo-Japanese War (1904–05) was the first significant defeat of a European war machine in open conventional battle fought with modern technology inflicted by non-Europeans since the high tide of the Turkish invasion of Europe in the seventeenth century. This Japanese triumph was greeted with jubilation by anti-White nationalists across the colonised world. For them, the Russo-Japanese War sounded the tocsin of freedom.

Japan's emergence as a great power provoked a crisis of confidence in Washington. Not since the threat of Anglo-French intervention in the Civil War had American leaders been so alarmed at a threat from abroad. America's White establishment suffered its first panic about a non-White challenge to the military security of the republic. After Japan's victory, a former army officer named Homer Lee began to write a secret War Department study which warned against complacency in the face of the Japanese threat. Based on this research, Lee published *The Valour of Ignorance* in 1909. The book included a preface written by two former senior War Department officials. Lee bleakly predicted that unless the United States rearmed on a significant scale, Japan might rapidly capture the Philippines, Hawaii and perhaps even Alaska should war break out in the Pacific. He even warned that Japanese forces might one day develop the capability to seize San Francisco and, from this strategic position, to occupy the entire Pacific Coast of the United States.

Lee's best-seller would prove prophetic. Just thirty-two years after the appearance of *The Valour of Ignorance*, the Japanese Imperial Navy would all but destroy the pride of the American Pacific battleship line at Pearl Harbour. Within the next few months, attacks were made on Alaska and on shipping off San Francisco and Long Beach. By April 1942, the Japanese had overrun all the East and Southeast Asian colonial empires of America, Britain, France and the Netherlands. A new force had been loosed on the world, and it was not White.

In the end, the United States would crush its Asian rival, but not before it had waged one of the deadliest struggles in its long march to planetary domination. After three centuries of almost unbroken aggression against the non-White world, White Americans had finally met a non-European foe capable of serious resistance. In the Japanese, the American Indian had found their unlikely avengers. Sitting Bull would have saluted Tojo's boldness.

Given their fate at the hands of the White Republic, is it possible that American Indians would have flourished if the Western United States had become part of Japan's Pacific realm? In retrospect, Japanese administration does not seem a more hateful prospect than what the Indians actually did suffer on their reservations in the half-century between Wounded Knee and Pearl Harbour.

Hypothetical questions are the *bête noire* of the professional historian, and rightly so. But Mark Peattie has concluded in *Nan'yō: The Rise and Fall of the Japanese Micronesia, 1885–1945*[22] that some island communities prospered under Japanese colonial administration in ways that have been unmatched by American rule since 1945. This raises a troubling issue for the orthodox interpretation of the Pacific War.

Japanese colonial administration in the South Pacific exhibited an impressive commitment to developing what the philosopher calls the subjectivity of the native population. Pacific War orthodoxy is mute when confronted with such facts because such truths undermine the essentialist assertions of Allied propaganda. For sixty years the orthodox mind has dwelled on the harshness of Japanese rule in Korea, but has given hardly a glance to the relatively successful story that Japanese administration achieved in Taiwan. The Japanese empire was a story of harshness and success. We must find an interpretation of the Pacific War that accounts for both.

From the writings of the wartime Kyoto School, we know how the Japanese mind responded to this titanic contest with America for oceanic mastery. How should we react today to this defence of Japan's Pacific War? If orthodoxy clings to its Allied-versus-Axis interpretation, the revisionist insists on understanding the Pacific War within the rubric of 'trans-war history', that is within the long history of the rise and consolidation of the White Republic.

The expansion of the White Republic was a catastrophe for its many victims, beginning with the crushing of the Native Americans. But in moral terms, the grimmest hour in the history of this expansion was 'the Japanese Holocaust', the almost wholly one-sided racial massacre of Japanese soldiers and civilians during the final phase of the Pacific War: the series of 'turkey shoots' that marked the American advance to the gates of Japan, the firebombing of more or less defenceless Japanese cities after the fall of Saipan, and the atomic incineration of Hiroshima and Nagasaki. This interpretation of these events – and these must be counted among Steiner's 'dark places' – should also be considered in any serious reflection on the totality of the American imperial experience as a nation.

Arnold Toynbee once claimed that 'Nineteenth-century Asia had only these alternatives: to accept the West and to survive after complete surrender to Westernization; or to resist and perish'.[23] Who among all the victims of the aggression of the White Republic would understand the full terror of this claim better than the Native American? We must keep such victims in mind when we recall that the Kyoto School proposed a cure for the Asian dilemma that reaches far beyond the scope of either E.H. Norman or the Modernisation School. If we, as thinkers and philosophers, seek the shock of the new, here we will find it.

The idea of subjectivity is pivotal. In the Kyoto School interpretation of the Pacific War, Tojo's government allowed itself to be trapped by Roosevelt into a military misadventure with disastrous consequences for the Japanese people and their empire. The manner in which the war was begun, waged and lost reinforces the view that however modern the Japanese had become by 1941, they still lacked what the philosopher would call sufficient *shutaisei* (subjectivity) to conduct themselves as a self-possessed nation capable of fighting a war of total resistance.

The disastrous failure of Imperial Japan recalls Fanon's grim warning:

> An underdeveloped people must prove, by its fighting power, its ability to set itself up as a nation, and by the purity of every one of its acts,

that it is, even in the smallest detail, the most lucid, and most self-controlled people. But this is very difficult.[24]

Imperial Japan found this task impossibly difficult. In the end, Tojo's Japan could neither live in peace with its neighbours nor effectively fight a war to establish any form of lasting hegemony. Indeed, the Japanese regime could not even bring the war to a sensible conclusion when it was lost. The Kyoto School of philosophy assessment of the war was at once brilliant, damning and conclusive. No subsequent school of interpretation, neither Western nor Japanese, has matched it.

If the world does face a post-White destiny, non-Whites must learn to manage the planet. The history of Japanese failure, during the Pacific War as well as the current economic troubles, is the supreme parable on post-White modernity because no non-White society has demonstrated a greater degree of subjectivity than modern Japan. It is with this truth in mind that one may fruitfully read the writings of the wartime Kyoto School against a wide variety of post-war texts, from Hisao Ōtsuka's reflections on the nature of economic subjectivity, to the 1980s debate on Japanese industrial policy fought out among Chalmers Johnson, Kent Calder and Dick Samuels, to Kazuo Yoshida's *Heisei Fukyō no Jū-nen-shi* (*The Heisei Recession: A Ten-year History*).[25]

The Kyoto School as a paradigm revolution

The student of the wartime Kyoto School seeks to overturn all previous paradigms. No interpretative history of the Kyoto School will stand unless it recognises the three-stage development of classical Kyoto philosophy, that story of the successive domination of Nishida until 1927, Tanabe between 1928 and 1946, and Nishitani after the war. But narrative success depends on one caveat: we must actually read the texts in question before we decide whether or not to indict the authors. One of the first scholars to read Tanabe, in a fair-minded way, and report the results in English was Naoki Sakai.[26] When he pulled his finger out of the dyke of Western orthodoxy about the Kyoto School, he committed a revolutionary act. The field remains in his debt.

The focal concern of the middle phase of the Kyoto School was political philosophy. We must read the relevant texts not as some absent-minded lapse from Zen Buddhism but as political thought in the classic sense. Tanabe's *Logic of the Species*, Kōsaka's *The Historical World* and Kōyama's *The Philosophy of World History* are worthy Japanese responses to the canonic achievements of Plato, Hobbes and Hegel.[27] Any ambitious scholar of Japan who has a taste for what Thomas Kuhn once famously called 'revolutionary science' should feed greedily on these textual outpourings of the wartime Kyoto School. In other words, these Japanese philosophers fashioned a vessel for Japanology to renew itself, to begin all over again. From Kyoto one may voyage '*au fond de l'Inconnu pour trouver du nouveau*'.[28]

After America, philosophy

American history hangs on a paradox. How is it that Jefferson's 'empire of liberty' began with the ethnic cleansing of North America and has now reached its apogee with 'shock and awe' in the Middle East? There is nothing in American thought, in the work of pragmatists such as John Dewey and Richard Rorty, that can explain the horrors of White America's violent and continuing assault on the non-White world. *Pace* Rorty, the Vietnam War was no aberration.[29] It was part and parcel of the violent trajectory of racial and economic aggression that gave birth to the White Republic and our global empire.

If the pragmatist is loud with moral evasions, philosophers who have wrestled with subjectivity, from Tanabe to Foucault, have understood the problem clearly. Terror is built into the very fabric of democracy because democracy requires subjectivity, and subjectivity includes among its powers the urge and the capacity to destroy its enemies. This is why the formula 'After philosophy, democracy' makes no sense.[30] Philosophy must outlive democracy because philosophy is about truth-telling in a way that democracy is not.

Great democracies survive, flourish and expand by deceiving themselves about their violent impulses. This is not a statement of criticism but of fact. We democrats consistently overstate our virtues not because our virtues are not genuine but because we are not always virtuous. Far from it. But to protect the illusion of democratic virtue, the illusion that we never do anything that defiles our essence, there are certain things we will not say, perhaps not even think. All of our ethical failings are mere epiphenomena. America's essence is not secured with the facts but rather metaphysically in a way that anticipates and circumvents all possible empirical challenges. In this way, we gag philosophia lest she point out that democratic empires frequently go about naked.

This truth returns us to the long tradition of American bad faith about the founder of modern European philosophy. The conventional American criticism of Descartes is that he was obsessed with private metaphysical irrelevances whereas Jefferson, Emerson and Dewey were responsible intellectuals of the public sphere. But when the French philosopher declared in the 'First Meditation' that 'I shall apply myself seriously and freely to the general destruction of all my former opinions', the democrat trembles because he prefers the noble lie of democracy to the truth. He is not confident that his dream can withstand the truth.

The scholar of modern Japan should take such Cartesian urgings to heart. If the events of 11 September 2001 have now all but closed the American mind to the risks and dignities of radical criticism of the national or, if you will, racial essence, Europe must snatch up the torch. In this context, the Kyoto School provides a unique vehicle for those who would brood on the ethical consequences and practical dangers of America's Asian imperium because it allows us to meet the moral challenge posed by Löwith.

European life is unthinkable without the critical spirit, but that critical spirit spares nothing. For almost sixty years, the orthodox Allied interpretation of the Pacific War has been spared the liberating lash of liberal criticism. It should be spared no longer.

Appendix

Translations of two texts
by Hajime Tanabe

The Philosophy of Crisis or a Crisis in Philosophy

Reflections on Heidegger's Rectoral Address[1]

Hajime Tanabe

Part I

Among contemporary German philosophers, no one has recently attracted greater attention in Japan than Martin Heidegger. With this claim there can be no dispute. But last year he joined the National Socialist (Nazi) Party.[2] This year, when the education policies of Hitler's government resulted in the dismissal of Jewish scholars from teaching positions and the transformation of the universities by nationalist (*kokka-shugi*) academics into fortresses of the Reich, Heidegger was elected rector of Freiburg University. Rumours at the time suggested that the appointment was the work of higher powers. In what can only be described as the German equivalent of the Japanese 'descent from heaven', this comparatively young scholar – Heidegger at 44 has just entered his prime – was given a post normally reserved for the most senior of academic veterans. Furthermore, it has been only four years since this German philosopher returned to Freiburg from Marburg. Obviously, in these exceptional times, the man is the object of enormous expectations not only at Freiburg but also throughout the German academic community.

I have now learned that Heidegger took the theme of 'The Self-assertion of the German University' as the subject of his Rectoral Address, a speech that is given before the entire faculty of Freiburg University. I say 'learned' because I have yet had no opportunity to see the text of the address. But, quite by chance, an older colleague kindly brought to my attention an article by Heidegger with the title 'Scholarship (*gakumon*) as Service to the National Defence' which appears to offer a summary of his Rectoral Address that had recently appeared in a German newspaper. Whether this article represents a reliable summary of Heidegger's remarks I am not in a position at the moment to confirm or deny. But then it is not my prime intention to offer a critique of his lecture but rather to respond broadly to the issues Heidegger has raised. To this end, I would like to dwell at length on the content of this published summary. Surely, given the circumstances, a provisional assessment of the remarks of the rector of Freiburg University should be allowed.

According to Heidegger, the German university is the highest academic organ charged with the education of those who would lead and protect

Germany in the pursuit of its national destiny. These organs have their origins in true knowing (*Wissenschaft*) and their goal is achieved through this knowing. As a result, the essence of the German university is revealed in the exercise of the will, the will to knowing. This exercise of the will reflects the fact that the university is the keeper of the historical and spiritual trust of the German people, a nation brought to self-consciousness by the German state. But the essence of knowing, the questioning of the foundations of knowing, can be revealed only through human philosophic self-consciousness. Historically, this foundation manifested itself first with Greek philosophy and nowhere else. Via the *logos*, driven by the insistence that one must attempt to understand the totality of being, European man originated 'true knowing'.

Knowing, however, as Aeschylus famously observed, is a far weaker thing when compared to fate. The incalculability and unpredictability of existence is the true foundation/font of knowing. As a result, it is precisely when knowledge strives to unveil the totality of existence that its powerlessness is revealed. Knowing is a creature born out of powerlessness. This is why the Greeks called it '*theōría*'. But, even *theōría* involves *energeia* [activity]. Indeed, for the Greeks, *theōría* was the supreme realisation of pure action. The Greeks did not regard knowing as a cultural ornament or superstructure, but rather as the innermost determining feature of the totality of human existence in a polis or the political community of the nation (*minzoku kokka*). Knowing is questioning while standing firm in the midst of the uncertainty of the totality of being, a condition that defines our unfathomable fate. The self-awareness of our powerlessness before our fate forms the core motive behind the tireless pursuit of knowing.

After the Greeks, with the rise of the theological worldview of the Christian Middle Ages and the mathematical and technological thought of modern times, this core truth (*kakushin*) has been lost sight of, and the foundations of true knowing forgotten. We do not seek to find this truth in the past; rather, we must seek it in the future. This foundation will exert its greatest strength in the future only when knowing once again becomes the innermost basic necessity of human existence.

This essence, therefore, is to be found in standing firm amidst the anxiety that defines the totality of existence, and seeking to unconceal, totally, the concealment of being. In this way, the people (*minzoku*) may achieve a hard clarity about the true nature of the dangers, both from within and without, posed by the world as it is. This, and this alone, is the true world of the spirit.

Perhaps spirit is the expression of the readiness that results from intuitional knowledge of this essence. After all, the spirit has its origin in the consciousness that results from the intuited knowledge of the essence of existence. The strength of a people rooted in blood and soil may be a bottomless depth conceived in darkness, but the spiritual world of a people is the world of self-consciousness, and it is this fountainhead that generates the greatest tremors and the most powerful of emotions in the innermost depths of its being. It is the greatness of this spiritual world alone that makes a people great. Confronted with the choice between historical great-ness or ruin, the future of the German people will depend on its resolute decisiveness [when confronted with the choice between the world of the spirit and its opposite].

Inevitably, true knowing must reject so-called 'academic freedom'. According to Heidegger, knowing is a kind of intellectual labour compa-rable in status to working for the national defence or service on the battlefield. This is in keeping with the fact that true knowing manifests itself when the coercive threat to existence is most powerfully revealed. By seeking to bring into question the unfathomable nature of being, true knowing calls the people to labour service and to battle, and thereby to be immersed in the state [*polis*]. In the university, teachers and students alike must serve the common struggle. But it must also be said that the essence of the university and true knowing will not be revealed, as it were, overnight. Rather, one must wait for the profundity of truly grounded self-reflection and self-asser-tion. Whether or not this will end in the confusion and ruin of the Western spirit will depend on the determination of the German people to become a historical and spiritual nation. To this end, individuals are to participate in the collective decision of the nation. Heidegger holds that today, young Germans are already showing their vigorous determination to do just that.

Part II

Above I have given a summary introduction of Heidegger's address by drawing on the contents of an article from the German press. Here I will respond to the ideas presented. A number of doubts inevitably arise. Heidegger seeks to move beyond the ontology of self-consciousness that he has hitherto advocated. But is it possible to assign the kind of positive significance that Heidegger does to the state or a people (*minzoku*)? Armed only with the awareness of the powerlessness of knowledge, is it possible to establish, positively, with this principle alone, the foundations for a meta-physics of the nation-state? Has he demonstrated that this essence offers sufficient reason to make intellectual labour into a knowing that serves the state?

Having said as much, I must declare that I have no intention of attempting an exercise in scholarly criticism based on incomplete material. But I do propose to take issue with several points Heidegger makes. Is it possible to establish a credible relationship between knowing and the state by the set of interconnected arguments that Heidegger makes? Is it really the case that the foundations of European knowing, as revealed in Greek philosophy, are necessarily mediated by an essentialist interpretation of this knowing, recog-nising only *theōría* as the self-consciousness of the powerlessness of knowledge in the face of the essence of a fated destiny, and, from this *theōría*, is one to seize on only a single aspect of the necessary movement of service to a people rooted in the depths of the uncertainty of being? Does this cohere as an argument?

First, an obvious fact should be stated. What Heidegger calls 'Greek philosophy' is represented almost entirely by Aristotle and his idea of *theōria*. But Aristotle was not born in a powerful polis (*toshi*), and his understanding of the Athenian polis (*kokka*) and its civic politics was less than secure. Furthermore, according to Barnett, Aristotle was also the man who became tutor to Alexander the Great but had almost no impact on the man who took Greek culture and transformed it into a world empire.

To put the point another way, Aristotle may have been a philosopher, but he was strictly a bystander as Greek politics approached its decisive moment of crisis. But if one turns one's attention to Plato, Aristotle's teacher, one encounters an entirely different mission for philosophy. Recent scholarship on Plato sees him as a practical philosopher whose chief philosophical motivation was the creation of a state conducive to the ideals of beauty and justice, where citizens would be morally formed by the law. For Plato, existence was not an unfathomable fate. Quite the contrary, people chose their destinies. In making these choices, existence should be the cultivation of freedom in accordance with the ideals of beauty.

Perhaps inevitably, given this stance, Plato sought on more than one occasion to realise his philosophic ideas in the political sphere. His passionate devotion to the polis was the fundamental motivation driving his intellectual development. In reaction to the execution of Socrates, his master, by an overripe democracy of Athens at the time, Plato took as his supreme philosophic ambition to lay the foundations for a government by an aristocracy composed of the philosophically educated. The most powerful source of Plato's passion for politics was, of course, the inspired personality of Socrates.

Plato's philosophy was one of the great examples of a 'philosophy of crisis'. Is it here that one should look for a philosophy of crisis? Is it here in Plato's philosophy and its plans for reforming the popular order through education and the law, and thus to overcome a crisis in politics by restructuring the state by the exercise of human reason? Note that Plato assigned a role to non-philosophical knowing in the mediation of the political education of the citizen.

In distinct contrast, guided by the tradition of Aristotle, and the idea of *theōria* as the ultimate mission of philosophy, Heidegger's philosophy can never be a philosophy that, in the end, makes political leadership and the reform of the state its prime concern. It follows, therefore, if philosophy is only the contemplation of the political progress of the state through time understood as nothing more than the unfolding of the fated necessity of being, only the object of contemplation, there will be no effort to involve oneself in politics or attempt to influence the leaders of society. The spiritual superiority of knowledge, if limited only to the idealistic overcomings of *theōria*, an idea grounded in the passive recognition of our awareness of our powerlessness before the forces of fate, will never solicit the kind of practical leadership necessary if one is to shape existence by participating in it. In short, by overemphasising one aspect of the problem, the other is neglected; the circle is never completed.

The problem is finally more profound. Philosophy is that which takes as its life the positive autonomy of the rational spirit, a philosophy that takes as its essence the practical character of absolute consciousness. When limited to a contemplative ontology of self-consciousness, philosophy itself feels threatened in its essence. For being to serve reason, being must participate in reason. To refuse to involve oneself practically in society and to surrender merely to one's fate, this is to reject philosophy however much one insists on the superiority of self-consciousness.

Could it be that Heidegger's philosophy is not a philosophy of crisis but rather a doctrine that may plunge philosophy into a crisis? When one recalls how during the Middle Ages Aristotle's philosophy degenerated into the handmaiden of theology, it may not be unfair to suspect that is where this new crisis in philosophy finds its roots.

Part III

Things are perhaps not quite so straightforward. Thinking back, one has to recall that Plato travelled twice to Syracuse in an effort to realise his conception of the ideal state. He lived in the palace, plunging himself into political activity, and on both occasions he failed. The political processes of the state did not yield to his philosophy. Was not this a case of the destined necessity triumphing over philosophy? Then there is the example of Socrates himself, the patriot who fought bravely on the battlefield for his country only to be condemned to death by his countrymen in the name of the security of the state. Does this not demonstrate that what the state judges to be essential for its survival is informed by the compulsions of political necessity rather than by philosophic principles?

Reflecting on the historical significance of Socrates, Hegel observes that the political decline of Athens, the liberation of the critical spirit vis-à-vis both politics and religion, and the right to freedom of thought, or, to put it another way, inward autonomy, all unfolded together. Indeed, Socrates was the supreme embodiment of intellectual liberation from within. It was the contradiction between the realities of the state and the principle of inward freedom that occasioned Socrates' tragic end. The Athenians themselves put him to death to protect the authority of the nation's laws. But, as they had already become infected with the principle of inward autonomy, Athenians, by judging and condemning him, proclaimed the demise of their own state. It was this outcome, according to Hegel's philosophy of history, that made this episode the embodiment of the highest tragedy.

If Hegel was right, Plato's philosophy, understood as a philosophy of crisis, reveals itself as a philosophy of national reconstruction inspired by

Socrates. The resulting philosophy is not one that mediates the historical realities of the state and demands of political necessity, but rather one that asserts eternal ideals in the name of intellectual principles alone. This philosophy clashes with politics rather than seeks to guide it. In response, the state ignores philosophy, understanding political exigency as the expression of irresistible necessity. Such a state will seek to confine philosophy to the safe activities of intellectual contemplation alone. This plunges philosophy into a crisis of the first magnitude.

The metaphysical consequences are profound. Neither the state nor philosophy will recognise the superiority of the other. Each side seeks absolute authority, but any attempt by one side to force submission on the other necessarily invites rejection. But this means that when one side rejects the claims of the other, its own claims are inevitably rejected. Because only one absolute may be acknowledged (reason does not allow two), the rejection of one side by the other inevitably ends up meaning that neither wins acceptance and therefore both are denied. By rejecting the other, one rejects oneself.

The consequences for the state are grave: to reject philosophy and acknowledge only the rule of political necessity as a standard for state conduct exposes the state to the judgment of history, a judgment that in the end it cannot endure. No state can long survive, let alone flourish, if it turns its back on reason.

When Athens rejected the philosophy of Socrates and Plato, Athenians proceeded down a one-way street to their destruction. In the same way, when philosophy disregards the historical necessities that press on states in a self-satisfied manner, philosophy invites its own ruin. The fate of late Greek philosophy is one of the best-known examples of such a failure.

Abandoning struggle, each side should recognise that the realist moment and idealist moment form an absolute identity. This holds out the promise that a concrete unity of these two moments is achievable. This is what Hegel's expression 'What is rational is actual, and what is actual is rational' means.

However, the unity-in-conflict of the rational and the actual, according to Heidegger's philosophy, confines the activity of reason exclusively to the self-consciousness of our powerlessness in the face of reality. This prevents philosophy from having any effective degree of practical impact. There is a conflict of essence between Hegel's reason and Aristotle's *theōría*. Hegel's reason is more than the passive contemplation of existence one finds in Aristotle; rather, reason seeks, via a mediation with praxis, to achieve the self-conscious (*jishō-jikaku*) unity of reason and reality; but it is precisely here, in the rationality of reality, that one finds also the potential for tragedy.

As a philosophy of freedom, German idealism transcends the reach of the Greek ontology. It is strange that Heidegger does not stress the importance of the inward freedom and autonomy that distinguishes German from Greek philosophy when he hails the significance of true German wisdom (*gakumon*) [*Wissenschaft*]. It is impossible for philosophy merely to contemplate fate and serve the state, in the way Heidegger assumes, and remain philosophy. Rather, true philosophy should grasp the eternal principles that ground the political process, and seek to transform them, practically, into power. While maintaining its autonomy at every point in this process, the self should seek in a self-conscious [that is rational] way to achieve a concrete identity with the state, and thereby secure the inward spirit that must characterise any state that would be rational.

But surely only this kind of unity from within can ensure the precise kind of intellectual service that is required? Yet, even if this is the case, the very action that can unite, in a practical way, these conflicting extremes almost always includes a tragic dimension, with all its attendant dangers. Perhaps it is as Plato claimed: this kind of unity can only be effectively secured by the rule of inspired guardians. I suspect that it is only under these strict conditions that the Platonic philosophy of crisis can fulfil its true mission.

5 September 1933
(Translated from the Japanese by David Williams)

On the Logic of Co-prosperity Spheres

Towards a Philosophy of Regional Blocs[1]

Hajime Tanabe

Today I would like to talk about the structures of co-prosperity spheres, touching, in a very formal way, that is only abstractly, on the logical dimension at issue. I take this approach because I have no concrete knowledge of the problems posed by co-prosperity spheres, and therefore what I have to say will be of a very general character. But then we are not dealing here with a temporary phenomenon, a single specific case, but rather with an organisational arrangement that can be compared with two of the most basic (*tanjun na*)[2] structures of our society: the family and the state.

I The Family

Not long ago an article appeared in the Kyoto University newspaper on the subject of the family. In this article, the contemporary proponents of the Japanese spirit sought a basic model for society in an idea of the family. I, for one, am extremely doubtful about the suggestion that the family provides the basic model for the larger community or social collective (*kyōdōtai*). In fact, such advocacy tends to be rather unempirical in its claims because it ignores the actual structure of the family as we know it. Interestingly, the theoretical assessment of this subject highlights the way such advocacy of the family as a social model departs from factual reality. I would therefore like to make this sceptical view my point of departure in the discussion that follows.

   At first glance, the family appears to have what in German might be called an '*einfach*' [simple] structure. But, from my standpoint, however much any community or society may appear to have an uncomplicated structure, in fact, such institutions necessarily have what I call a species structure (*shu-teki kōzō*). To assert that a social group or organisation has a species structure means that the social body in question is naturally and inevitably vulnerable to disruption and disunity (*bunretsu-sei*) from within. The family as a community emphatically does not possess an *einfach* structure that is immune to such disruption. Quite the contrary, it is characterised by a complex hierarchy or a vertical dynamic as well as a horizontal or egalitarian dynamic. It unites time and space with its need to persist over time in space. All this is contained within the species structure of the family, ensuring its formal complexity

It is important to note, however, that the family unites hierarchical and horizontal dynamics directly, without any mediation (*baikai*), and it is for this reason that the family may superficially appear to possess an *einfach* structure. But, looked at more carefully, the species character of the family, and its vulnerability to disunity, becomes obvious. Take, for example, a totem society or, for that matter, a society united under a transcendent religious principle. In neither case can one conclude that the society displays a seamless *einfach* unity. In the case of the totem society, the totem itself embodies the hierarchic dynamic while the contradictory claims of the horizontal dynamic are manifest in the imperative for tribal members to marry outside the tribe. James George Frazer [1854–1941], the British anthropologist, was one of the first scholars to demonstrate this point conclusively in *Totemism and Exogamy* (1910).

On the subject of the family, one can go further. In the first place, the relationship between parents and children necessitates an *Ordnung* that persists over time (*prior posterior*). But, in addition to this hierarchical relationship, there is also a vertical relationship between husband and wife. In *Phenomenology of the Spirit* [1807], Hegel gives this contradictory dynamic a metaphysical interpretation. In the section on Greek tragedy, Hegel offers his famous interpretation of Antigone's dilemma. In essence, the Greek heroine is caught between the imperatives of her blood relationship with her brother, what Hegel calls *göttliches Gesetz* (φυδις), and the claims of the law, or *menschliches Gesetz* (νόμος). For Hegel, the tension between divine law and man-made law ensures the Greek family's vulnerability to disruption. In a similar way, the family itself is exposed to the contrary demands and stresses of the natural or divine imperatives that arise from the relationship between parents and children as well as between siblings within the same family, *göttliches Gesetz* (φυδις), but also from the man-made *menschliches Gesetz* (νόμος) or the moral imperatives that govern marriage.

In fact, only when faced with destruction will a tribal society cease to seek brides outside its ranks. In this way, the family, supposedly the simplest and most basic unit of society, embodies within it the double structure of the external as internal, the outside as inside. From the child's point of view, the parent as a parent, as mother or father, is inevitably, in some vital sense, from outside the family. The family is thereby a unity of insider and outsider, horizontal and vertical relationships. As such, it qualifies as an example of a species society, one that is emphatically prey to all the potential of disruption that comes with its species character. Certainly, the family does not persist in a perfection of unified harmony and stability. Any unity is the reverse side of the coin of this disruptive capacity. Furthermore, the conflicted nature of the family is eternal. The cycle of internal disunity and external tension persists as long as the institution of the family lasts.

Another example of the family's complex, semi-conflicted structure is the problem posed by the wife's relations in the question of inheritance (*sōzoku*). In this case, the hierarchical dynamic triumphs over the horizontal relationship. But at the same time, these maternal relations themselves are subject to the interplay of external and internal, as well as to the tension between conflicting interests and the need for unity. The common-sense view is that the family brings into potential conflict a mother-in-law from within the family and a daughter-in-law from outside, but in fact both women have come from outside. The mother-in-law brings her distinctive 'foreign' colour to the family no less than her daughter-in-law does. The mother of the mother-in-law is doubly foreign, an outsider twice removed, as it were, but this can result in a strange and complex reversal of roles. The mother of the mother-in-law often takes the sympathetic stance towards the new wife.

Such social phenomena exemplify what I mean by a species group or society. A family by its very nature is a kind of species group. It cannot possibly be described as a simple unified unit immune to the primordial stresses of disruption and disunity that the family contains in its very structure; its stability and unity is always under potential threat. Sincerity and good intentions are not enough. All the members of the family must labour tirelessly to secure domestic tranquillity and harmony. What nature confers on the family is not '*Sein*' (existence) but a dialectical task linking *Sein* and *Sollen* (what is and what ought to be). The 'is' has to be the 'ought', and the 'ought', the 'is'.

Obviously, limits must be placed on this nearly infinite potential for domestic disruption and disunity. Therefore, in the case of the family, whatever disunity may threaten it, however unlimited are the kinds of complexity that may come to characterise it, the weight of the law (*koku hō*), the *Grenze*, cannot permit the destruction of the unity of the family. This serves to disguise the *zweifach* [dual] character of the family, thus encouraging some to see the family as essentially one and unified in its essence. But any attempt to construct an illusionary singularity out of something that is essentially dual by nature is doomed to failure.

II The State

With this approach in mind, I would like to examine the differences between the family and the state. In the case of the state, vertical interests tend to prevail over horizontal ones. Thus, the vertical order that links sovereignty and the rulers with the ruled, that is the subjects, must prevail over the centrifugal tendencies that characterise horizontal interests. In addition, there is the connection with history or persistence over time. Indeed, the priority that time exerts over human society tends to persist as seniority [English in the original]. Nevertheless, the state must also have horizontal relationships otherwise it will not be a state. The same dynamic is at work here as we find with time: the present must be linked to the contradiction of the present that is the past and future if the present is itself to exist. The term 'contradiction' must be stressed because the unity of past, present and future does not translate into a finished harmony.

Just as I argue that the inverse of harmony is perpetual strife, so I hold that the inverse of unity is always tension. From my viewpoint, the obverse of the unity of the past, present and future is the fierce opposition between the present, on the one hand, and the past and future, on the other. Thus, in any state or settled (*ittei*) society there are inevitably conflicts between old and new, conservatives and reformers, and the old and the young.

In addressing such questions, I must note that my position is the complete opposite of that taken by the materialist [that is Marxist] interpretation of history. But, having said as much, I should also note that I am not one of those people one finds so often today who blindly reject, root and branch, the materialist interpretation of history. The arguments contained in the materialist interpretation are powerful; the only question is how far one is convinced by them. Having considered the matter carefully, I find myself taking entirely the opposite view of history. The main reason is that the materialist view of history reduces everything to the productive nexus. Assuming that the productive relationships in society are the decisive ones, the materialist makes such relationships the standard by which to assess all the problems and trends of society. Thus, the politics of every society is judged to be ruled by a single class that divides that society.

Accordingly, from this point of view, class tension and struggle over their conflicting interests is the normal condition of society. Absolute [that is complete and enduring] unity is unachievable as long as this condition persists. Only by total defeat of one class by another can true harmony be achieved. The goal of history, as the materialist historian sees it, is the acquisition of power by the working class. With this power, this class crushes its opponents and imposes unity on society. As productive power is founded in social relations, overt struggle between workers and capitalists is the practical expression of this idea.

By contrast, the species view of society holds that struggle and harmony are sides of the same coin. One may trace the roots of a conflict to harmony because harmony's very existence ensures that conflicts will occur. Such insights are closed to the historical materialist because of his insistence on class struggle as a means to achieve a harmony that precludes further struggle.

While it is beyond my powers to disprove the claims of historical materialism on empirical grounds, it seems to me to be undeniably true that the source of human conflict cannot be traced solely to the productive nexus. Human beings as human beings live a species existence. This existence has its point of departure in the disruptions caused by the tension between horizontal and vertical interests as well as between the internal and the external imperatives of human life. At least that is what I believe. Accordingly, no final triumph of harmony will ever be achieved by workers in a class war in the face of the primordial weakness for conflict that defines the species character of society, a weakness that arises as soon as parents give birth to a child, and as often as a daughter takes a husband.

Social conflict between human beings is unavoidable because they are human beings. *Pace* the historical materialist, the triumph of the labouring classes cannot end human conflicts because human conflicts do not change human nature. The conflicts of history are rooted more deeply in the structure of time itself. This is the source of the tragic fate of humanity. This truth does not mean one can therefore ignore conflicts between the ruling classes and workers or other tensions over economic interests. But the solution to such struggles – and this is equally true of the conflicts between old and young, between men who work with their brains and (who therefore rule over) men who work with their muscles – is not to be found in the ideas of historical materialists. Indeed, the understanding of such conflicts must be found in an entirely different intellectual approach. Social conflicts occur between parties that are linked in ways that precede their conflict. Or, to reverse the proposition, struggle between parties that share absolutely nothing is, strictly speaking, unthinkable. Conflicts arise from the same nexus as our potential for cooperation and harmony.

Hellenism urges us to view the Greeks only in the light of pure *einfach*, but to do so is to depart from historical reality. Beyond the light, there is always darkness. This inverse relationship between light and dark underscores tragedies of history. With time, beauty becomes more concrete and less pure. Nuance begins to colour social relations. Shadows always accompany the light. Yet human intelligence stands with the light. Even the intelligence involved in war finally stands on the foundations of light, that is human harmony. This dependence, this final ground of unity, explains why we can speak of darkness, and indeed struggle itself. The same logic is at work in expressions such as Pascal's description of man as '*roseau pensens*' [thinking reed, *roseau pensant*]. The very notion already includes, indeed must assume, the possibility that something greater than a '*roseau pensens*' exists.

This insight leads us to another issue. This link between harmony and struggle depends on the existence of a 'greater' species, that is the universal genus. Without this genus, the comparison of species with each other, the conflict between them, is impossible. This is the assumption of conventional metaphysical logic. Yet, if this is the case, genus is in fact a form of species. It is from this genus itself that conflict arises. Therefore, the real genus is not a larger species, not the extremity where species find themselves in intense struggle with other species, and this means, idealistically speaking, that what might be called the 'universal' must be unexpressed, but at the same time, this 'genus' must unify the temporality that translates all space into a horizontal relationship and the spatial-ness that translates all time into a vertical relationship. As it is an idea [*kan-nen-teki ni*], it does not represent a generality or a universal.[3] It can be nothing else but nothingness (*mu*). But note that this is a nothingness that manifests itself only in action.

A digression. What does it mean to say that nothingness manifests itself only as action? True, Hegel famously taunted Kant for urging the swimmer to learn how to swim before getting into the water, but one must have learned how to swim before getting into the water. Just to get into the water means that one has not learned to swim. The former avoids death; the latter dies. In short, Hegel is suggesting that one has to die in order to learn how not to die. To die before dying is the contradiction housed in Hegel's example of learning to swim.

In a famous collection of Zen poetry, it is observed that 'the person who is not clear about death tastes death often before he actually dies'. This is in essence a confusion between the idea of death and death itself. To learn to swim is to risk death before one dies. There is no contradiction in the idea that one must taste death before it is necessary in order to understand death. To take a contemporary example, to prepare oneself for flying today is one of the best examples from ordinary experience of anticipating death before dying by risking it. But what stands perpetually in this contradiction is human existence itself.

What this tells us about human behaviour, our actions, is that we act always in the shadow of a contradiction: death before death. This is what is really at issue in the lesson of the lotus in the flame or Luther's *Rosenkranz*, the rose that flowers at the heart of the cross of daily existence. It penetrates our every action. Always, from the standpoint of absolute nothingness, resurrection lies in wait at the bottom of history. The present that is history is to be found in the *Rosenkranz*, in the flame in the lotus, that makes the history that includes history. It also follows, however, that any recognition of the reality of conflict, as we find in historical materialism, that then goes on to see resurrection and unity at the bottom of history can only meet with my total rejection.

Let me make the same point schematically (*schematisch*).[4] Metaphysically, there must be a place where two temporalities can meet and overlap: there is the past (the status quo) and the future (progress) that drags it forward while being retarded by it. This is how time enters society. However, viewed vertically, this point of overlap is unity. This also means, therefore, that tragedy is already interwoven into the fabric of the structure of society by virtue of this temporal and historical dimension. But it is also true that at the bottom of the structure of society is to be found the unity of absolute nothingness that cannot be conceived either ontologically or specifically, i.e. in species terms.

Human action originates from the depths of this nothingness. What I call 'the universal' is the ontological unity of the species that is achieved, without divine intervention, by this absolute nothingness. From the standpoint of the Greek enlightenment (*hikari*), Plato thought of the universal as an infinite complexity of species. The internal content of what I call 'species' is what the late Plato termed 'substance' (*shitsuryō*). What the early Plato thought of as the 'idea', what he called 'εἶδος', represents the unifier of all existence. In this connection, the five examples of the greatest genera elaborated by Plato in *The Sophists* are of particular interest.

Plato's five greatest genera include difference (sameness), motion, rest, activity and passivity. Unlike Plato's conception of ideas during his so-called middle phase, none of these genera have content; they are pure forms. Nevertheless, all of them are linked to society (κοινωνία γενῶν = *Gemeinschaft der Gattungen*). They are necessarily present in all subjective (*shutai-teki*) structures, although from the forms themselves the particular subjective structure cannot be specified nor can it be defined. Consequently, when medieval scholastic philosophers failed to understand transcendental categories (*transcendentaria*), and therefore did not draw on such ideas in Aristotle, they turned to Plato's universals (γένοι = *Gattungen*). And what I call 'universals' (*rui*) are what Plato termed 'γένοι'. Plato thought of the universal as the absolute negation of species. Universals cannot be specified. They are confined entirely to our subjective employment. Mediated by the species, existence takes the form of the individual.

The state has, logically speaking, an exact structure. It cannot exist only in time, that is with only the kind of vertical duration of 'before' and 'after'. In the horizontal [or spatial] sphere there is the individual. As a consequence, the state as a state cannot be defined simply (*tan ni chokusetsu-teki ni*) as species. The individual must have a place in the unity that proceeds from the standpoint of eternal conflict between one species and another. In the state, this individual serves as sovereign and leader. It is from this that public authority (*ōyake*) comes into play.

The representative of the unity and peace of the state, which, from itself, eternally constitutes this public individual, for its members, must be the law. To give priority only to relationships of duration or a political order in which ruled are ruled is not enough. The powers that be must address the needs of the ruled, while, at the same time, the governed should, on their own initiative, take the lead in cooperating with their rulers in a national deliberative forum (*kaigi*). The laws of the nation must not be forcefully imposed from above but must win the consent of the ruled. Here alone it must be stressed that equality must prevail among all the members of a state from the collective standpoint of the historical present. Rule as self-government must have a democratic dimension.

This does not mean that the equality of horizontal relationships that characterises American-style democracy is, in itself, sufficient. Nor are hierarchical or vertical relationships between the ruler and ruled alone to prevail. The state is not a simple association of human beings. To the degree that the state is a state there has to be a clear order, but one in which rule equals self-government and vice-versa. Of course, the vertical relations that allow the state to survive are essential, but true harmony means that equality must complement the imperatives of duration.

III Co-prosperity spheres

Above I have set out how co-prosperity spheres can be compared to social organisations that we already have. I have tried to explain in simple language the abstract logical aspects of the family and the state. As I have already touched on the differences between the family and the state, here I would like to dwell on the differences between the state and a group of states, as might occupy a much larger territory than most conventional states, and the unity that must characterise any co-prosperity sphere.

Conventionally, a state is defined by an essential unity of vertical and horizontal interests. However, in the case of the conventional state, some form of vertical interest (uniting rulers and ruled) must triumph over horizontal interests if the unity and sovereignty of the state is to be secured. The consolidation of the state's sovereignty over its own territory is the absolute imperative of any state. This imperative must outweigh any other; it must come first. In the case of a tribal society in which the tendency towards division along horizontal interests is at once pronounced and natural, the state must artificially impose a degree of order based on the idea of ruler and ruled on these tribal divisions. In short, the interests of the state must be judged of prior importance, and the state must enforce a degree of order if it is to function and survive.

Yet, at the same time, to the degree that such a state is erected over a tribal society – and this will be true even if the state seeks to legitimate itself by embracing an ever higher degree of transcendence, grounded in absolute negation [that is the legitimacy of the state will be grounded absolutely in a universal principle rather than a relative specific one], over the tribal character of that society – one challenge will remain. This state will not be grounded in an ever greater degree of universalisation unless its degree of external integration and harmony matches its degree of internal integration and harmony. It follows that the desired degree of harmony in a state's external relations, and this is true of any and all states, is impossible to achieve unless this harmonious unity applies to humanity as a whole [i.e. a universal state with a single world government].

Nevertheless, owing to circumstances beyond human control, most states begin to disintegrate almost as soon as they achieve a minimum degree of unity. The pattern appears to have almost no exceptions. Similarly, states begin to reconstruct themselves as soon as they disintegrate, and start to disintegrate almost as soon as they have consolidated their power. The tendency of states to disintegrate is driven by the rise and decline in their power, and the problems generated by the imperative of the state to attempt to persist over time. In other words, the reason that states exist at all derives from their ability to consolidate their power and maintain their unity, but, at the same time, and this is certainly true in the case of a tribal society, the state's success in consolidating its power does not put to an end the tendencies towards horizontal disintegration that it inherits from its tribal roots. The only way the state of a tribal society can maintain its unity is to limit the dangers from tribal-inspired disintegration, and this can be done only by imposing some form of control from above.

Let us look at the example of a monarchy. In such cases, sovereignty is handed down to the subjects who share in it equally. Given the structure of such states, this is inevitable as long as the state persists as a state. A state's sovereignty is indivisible; no denial of this principle can be permitted if the state is to survive as a state. It also follows that given this kind of [political] order, the state's sovereignty must be recognised by horizontal peers [i.e. other states] if the state's stability is to be maintained in the face of [domestic] pressures of a horizontal nature. These must be prevented from endangering the state's unity as a whole.

It is from this imperative that the logical necessity for co-prosperity spheres arises. The dynamic of such regional organisations of states mirrors the shared responsibility and unity of individuals living within a state. Indeed, because the individual units that compose a co-prosperity sphere are individual states, the sense of responsibility and equality towards a co-prosperity sphere, the sense of its being *für sich*, should be even stronger than that felt by the individual subjects who compose a state.

Nevertheless, relationships between the states that form a co-prosperity sphere will remain extremely vulnerable to disruption. Indeed, the dangers are so many and varied that relying on the equal sharing of responsibilities between member states is insufficient. As a result, it might be thought that one state should try to impose a desirable degree of sharing of sovereignty on the other states within the co-prosperity sphere. But this would be impossible given the very nature of the state as described above. Indeed, it contradicts the fundamental process by which states are formed.

In such circumstances, how might a genuine sphere of shared prosperity – one that mobilised the full potential of the nation-state – be achieved? One option might be for the individual members of the co-prosperity sphere to resolve to limit or dilute their own individual national sovereignty not by force but voluntarily. In philosophic terms, the individual states would in effect deny their particular essence to create an institutional 'other' by submitting to the absolute [non-relative] claims of the universal [*zettai no tachiba*].

If the members of the co-prosperity sphere pursued this course, what principle of cooperation would have to be embraced by all the members? How would they be bound together by the cooperative absolute [the universal]? It would require a measure of cooperation and authority. Here cooperation refers both to the horizontal sphere, in which nation-states are equals, and to the vertical sphere as well, in which there is a hegemony in which the other members are in effect governed. The dynamic involved is a dialectical circle involving not only a marriage of order and equality but also the marriage of equality with the enforced persistence over time that must characterise all institutional arrangements that last.

Burdens fall on both parties in this equation. The more dominant partner – the leading nation – occupying a position of relatively greater power in our circular schema – does not rest on its laurels but actively takes the lead in helping the more dependent members of the co-prosperity sphere to secure genuine sovereignty and national development. For their part, the junior partners of the sphere do not wait passively to be led but rather seize the initiative, in keeping with national self-awakening, in order to meet their responsibilities as full partners in the co-prosperity sphere. In short, the led should pursue their own development as part of a programme to achieve true national autonomy.

In the more abstract language of philosophy, this means that if the potential for actual equality exists in the variety of historical presents [*reshiki-teki genzai*] that define the contemporary reality of the individual members of the co-prosperity sphere, then the capacity for a self-generating order must also be found there. This dialectical circle provides the defining principle of any co-prosperity sphere. This idea depends necessarily on the theory of cyclical dialectics in which duration becomes equality, equality becomes duration, time becomes space and space, time. The point here is that duration or historical persistence is threatened unless there is equality between states, while states of unequal development can only achieve equality over time. Similarly, space [the state's territory] is a meaningless attribute unless the state as a geographical entity persists and develops historically, while historical reality can achieve nothing without a geographical stage for human action to unfold.[5]

The motivation behind my attempt to conceive of a logic of co-prosperity spheres in this manner may be traced back to a round-table discussion among economists held earlier this year (a record of this discussion appeared in the July issue of the magazine *Nippon Hyōron*). Among the participants, Kōzō Sugimura and Kiyokimi Nagata from Keio University concluded that a new economic theory must be developed because it is impossible to construct a Greater East Asian economy using traditional economic logic. Indeed, this need for a fundamental new logic of the world has already been recognised by philosophers. As it is unreasonable to expect economists to address the philosophic dimension of this challenge, I have tried to think through this new logic.

Nevertheless, this economic discussion raised an important issue: the question of stages of economic development. The German theory of developmental stages, or *Stufentheorie*, proposes three stages: (1) household economy (*Hauswirtschaft*); (2) the city economy; and (3) the national economy (*kokumin keizai*). The point I would like to emphasise here is the contradiction that *Stufentheorie* highlights in the British approach to human equality. On the one hand, British missionaries have tended entirely to ignore relative stages of economic development between peoples in favour of an entirely non-discriminatory definition of equality in which everyone everywhere is fundamentally the same.

In reality, of course, the advanced nations relentlessly exploit the less developed world in the pursuit of their material interest, such exploitation being impossible without the very inequality between nations that the missionaries deny. The key here is the state's ability to exercise its powers over time. Vertical hegemony rather than horizontal equality is what counts for the advanced powers. But Western colonialism attempts to hide the realities of economic exploitation behind this pretended commitment to equality.

One must conclude, therefore, that if Japan is successfully to construct a co-prosperity sphere, then this suspect Anglo-American approach must be rejected in favour of one that encourages the self-sufficiency of the states that belong to this co-prosperity sphere, while at the same time attracting the voluntary and independent cooperation of all the states involved in the economic development of the co-prosperity sphere as a whole. To address this double need, it is essential, as I have noted, that an entirely new logic of cooperation between states serve as the defining principle of any successful co-prosperity sphere.

The following are my thoughts about the structure of such a co-prosperity sphere. The gap between developed and developing nations must not be obscured but faced openly. This means, on the one hand, that all the distinctions that arise from the differences in the stages (*stufen*) of economic development of the members of the co-prosperity sphere – the link between the persistence of power and order as well as the hierarchy of power between states that results from this relationship – need to be acknowledged clearly by both leader and follower states. But it also implies that this imbalance of power must not result in the imperialistic exploitation of one side by the other. The autonomy of the developing states needs to be advanced and their sovereignty recognised. Effective integration between the member states is vital to the success of any great project such as that of building a co-prosperity sphere.

This is what one can see in this match between integration and cooperation, in the persistence of the state in time (history) that mediates space to become duration. Similarly, space (geography) mediates time, action in space thus unfolds in duration, thus simultaneously making visible the concrete nature of history's unfolding. Time as historical duration is at one and the same with action in space. This motion is finally cyclical in nature, returning to its starting point in order to begin at the beginning all over again.

The ancient Greeks thought that nature was governed by the cyclical pattern of time. But in ancient Greece, a limit was assumed to apply to the notion of cyclical time. The limit was contained in the idea that in the process of time returning to its starting point, the historical world destroyed itself, thus allowing nature to free itself of history. In other words, the Greeks did not think that time's conclusion of its cycle implied any new beginnings, that is the Greeks believed in the eternity of the present. For them, the subject (*shutai*) found itself caught in a present. The self was neither mediated by the past nor aware of any movement into the future. The ancient Greeks believed that they were caught in what Nietzsche called 'the eternal return', an endless submission to the suffering of existence or what Nietzsche defined as 'life'. In the concrete reality of history, however, the cyclical nature of time assumes a development into new beginnings. Thus, time's return to the start of the cycle means that history as the persistence of an order has a specific liberating meaning, a *für sich*, for the subject.

In conclusion, a true co-prosperity sphere must not be a mere marriage of convenience between lip service on behalf of equality between nations and a sordid reality of exploitative hegemonies of power as one finds in Western imperialism. To avoid such contradictions, a proper co-prosperity sphere must, as explained above, derive its structure from a specific principle. In philosophic terms, this principle allies the state's duration in time with the imperative of equality between states, just as the imperative of equality between states must translate into the persistence of order that defines the state. A metaphysical cycle uniting leadership and cooperation and resulting in true integration must be aimed for and achieved.

29 September 1942
(Translated from the Japanese by David Williams)

Notes

1 Roman questions: American empire and the Kyoto School

1 All that follows is a footnote to Alexis de Tocqueville's famous remark on the racial destiny of the United States. Race is the key. But race does not exist in the essentialist sense often assumed. Furthermore, the Kyoto School almost never discussed race in the way most Americans, White and non-White, do even now. These philosophers were not racial minded.
2 Bob Woodward, *Bush at War*, New York: Simon & Schuster, 2002.
3 Mathew Parris, *The Times*, 1 February 2003.
4 Roy Jenkins, *Churchill*, London: Macmillan, 2001, p. 659. The pronoun 'I' has been added to the quotation.
5 Anatol Lieven, 'The Push for War', *London Review of Books*, 3 October 2002, pp. 8–11. The success of American action against aggressive Balkan dictatorships has encouraged US Democrats to embrace intervention against troublesome regimes elsewhere (Iraq, for example). It may work, and it may achieve worthy ends. But the very success of such interventions also strengthens American imperial domination. It worsens the imbalance of power.
6 Ernst Jünger's 'Totale Mobilmachung' has been translated by Joel Golb and Richard Wolin as 'Total Mobilisation', and the translation can be found in Richard Wolin (ed.), *The Heidegger Controversy: A Critical Reader*, Cambridge, MA: MIT Press, 1993, pp. 119–139. The quotation may be found on pp. 130–131. Italics added.
7 *Sekai-shi-teki Tachiba to Nippon* (*The Standpoint of World History and Japan*), Tokyo: Chūō Kōron-sha, 1943. To distinguish this book from the round-table discussion of the same title that appeared in the January 1942 issue of *Chūō Kōron*, the title of the round-table discussion or symposium will henceforth be placed in inverted commas (i.e. 'The Standpoint of World History and Japan').

2 Revisionism: the end of White America in Japan studies

1 'Thought for the Day', *Independent* (London), 29 May 2003, p. 18.
2 Sadao Asada, 'Japanese Perceptions of the A-bomb Decision 1945–1980', in Joe C. Dixon (ed.), *The American Military and the Far East*, Washington: GPO, 1980, p. 216. Cited in Ronald H. Spector, *Eagle Against the Sun: The American War with Japan*, London: Cassell & Co., 2000, p. xvi.
3 Interviewed in Nagoya, Japan, by the author on 18 October 1997.

4 *Ibid.* Nolte is a controversial figure in the German debate over the Second World War. In my interview with him, his rejection of Holocaust denial was uncompromising. He would not be quoted here otherwise.

5 Yoshimi Takeuchi's essay is unfortunately titled 'Kindai no Chōkoku' ('Overcoming Modernity'), which is the same title as the famous round-table discussion (*zadankai*) of July 1942. To add to the potential confusion, one of the most widely used reprints of his essay has been published together with the texts of the 1942 symposium: Tetsutarō Kawakami and Yoshimi Takeuchi (eds), *Kindai no Chōkoku*, Tokyo: Tomiyama-sho, 1979, pp. 273–341.

6 The most instructive text on the subject of lying, ideology and myth-making in Japan studies is William R. LaFleur, 'A Half-dressed Emperor: Societal Self-deception and Recent *"Japanokritik"* in America', in Roger T. Ames and Wimal Dissanayake (eds) *Self and Deception: A Cross-cultural Philosophical Enquiry*, Albany, NY: State University of New York Press, 1996, pp. 263–285.

7 For the text of The Ōshima Memos, see Ryōsuke Ōhashi, Kyōtō-gakuha to Nippon Kaigun: Shin Shiryō 'Ōshima Memos' o Megutte (The Kyoto School and the Japanese Navy: On the New Historical Documents, The Oshima Memos), Tokyo: PHP, 2001.

8 Ryōsuke Ōhashi (ed.), *Kyōtō-gakuha no Shisō* (*The Thought of the Kyoto School*), forthcoming.

9 Dale Maharidge, *The Coming White Minority: California, Multiculturalism, and America's Future*, New York: Vintage Books, 1999.

10 John W. Dower, *War without Mercy: Race and Power in the Pacific War*, New York: Pantheon Books, 1986.

11 Roberto Suro, *Strangers Among Us: Latino Lives in a Changing America*, New York: Vintage, 1999, p. 20.

12 Jean-Paul Sartre, 'The Respectable Prostitute' ('La Putain respectueuse'), in *In Camera and Other Plays*, trans. Kitty Black, London: Penguin, 1982, pp. 37–38.

3 Philosophy and the Pacific War: Imperial Japan and the making of a post-White world

1 *The Negro*, 1915.

2 Masaaki Kōsaka, Shigetaka Suzuki, Iwao Kōyama and Keiji Nishitani, 'Sekai-shi-teki Tachiba to Nippon' ('The Standpoint of World History and Japan'), *Chūō Kōron*, January 1942, p. 185. I have recast my rendering from the translation by Naoki Sakai of the key passage from Kōsaka because, although it departs from what Kōsaka literally said, Sakai does capture the essence of what Kōsaka certainly meant. Sakai's own translation may be found in 'Modernity and its Critique: The Problem of Universalism and Particularism', in Masao Miyoshi and H.D. Harootunian (eds), *Postmodernism and Japan*, Durham, NC, and London: Duke University Press, 1989, p. 110.

3 Naoki Sakai, 'Nihon Shakai Kagaku Hōhō Josetsu' ('Methods in Japanese Social Science: An Introduction'), in *Iwami Kōza Shakai Kagaku no Hōhō*, III, *Nihon Shakai Kagaku Shisō* (*Iwanani Course on Methods in Social Science*, Vol. III, *Japanese Social Science as Thought*), Tokyo: Iwanami Shoten, 1993, pp. 12–14. This argument is repeated more recently in Naoki Sakai and Osamu Nishitani, <*Sekai-shi*> no Kaitai: Honyaku, Shutai, Rekishi (*The Dissolution of 'World History': Translation, Subject, History*), Tokyo: Ibun-sha, 1999.

4 'Kaisetsu', in Iwao Kōyama, *Sekai-shi no Tetsugaku* (*The Philosophy of World History*), ed. Hidefumi Hanazawa, Tokyo: Kobushi Shobō, 2001, p. 470. I must confess my envy at the depth of Hanazawa's knowledge of Kōyama's huge *oeuvre* and his passionate commitment to his subject.

5 Cornel West, *The American Evasion of Philosophy: A Genealogy of Pragmatism*, Madison, WI: University of Wisconsin Press, 1989, p. 237.

6 Tetsutarō Kawakami and Yoshimi Takeuchi (eds), *Kindai no Chōkoku* (*Overcoming Modernity*), Tokyo: Tomiyama-sho, 1979. Masaaki Kōsaka, Keiji Nishitani, Iwao Kōyama and Shigetaka Suzuki, *Sekai-shi-teki Tachiba to Nippon* (*The Standpoint of World History and Japan*), Tokyo: Chūō Kōron-sha, 1943.

7 Note, to reiterate a cardinal point, the wartime Kyoto School, certainly in the texts discussed here, excluded almost all mention of race and race war. But if we are to squeeze the maximum contemporary value from the middle phase of the Kyoto School, the rubric of 'post-Whiteness' is invaluable. This is my rubric, not Tanabe's.

8 Edward W. Said, *Orientalism*, Harmonsworth, Middlesex: Penguin Books, 1985, p. 3.

9 On this contentious subject, see Graham Parkes, 'The Putative Fascism of the Kyoto School and the Political Correctness of the Modern Academy', *Philosophy East & West* 47(3) (July 1997): 305–336, and Parkes's review of Leslie Pincus, *Authenticating Culture in Imperial Japan: Kuki Shūzō and the Rise of National Aesthetics* (1996), in *Chanoyu Quarterly* 86 (1997): 63–70.

10 Harry Harootunian, *Overcome by Modernity: History, Culture and Community in Interwar Japan*, Princeton: Princeton University Press, 2000.

11 Nothing is odder about this whole business than the way it has transformed the neo-Marxist into defender of American hegemony in the Pacific.

12 For a brief reprise of the basic facts of the De Man controversy, see Richard Wolin (ed.), *The Heidegger Controversy: A Critical Reader*, Cambridge, MA: MIT Press, 1993, pp. xi–xii, xix n. 2.

13 James W. Heisig and John C. Maraldo (eds), *Rude Awakenings: Zen, the Kyoto School and the Question of Nationalism*, Honolulu: University of Hawaii Press, 1994.

14 *Ibid.*, pp. xvii, vii, viii and x.

15 James W. Heisig, 'Foreword', in Hajime Tanabe, *Philosophy as Metanoetics*, trans. Yoshinori Takeuchi, Berkeley, Los Angeles and London: University of California Press, 1986, p. xvii.

16 James W. Heisig, 'Tanabe's Logic of the Specific and the Spirit of Nationalism', in Heisig and Maraldo, *op. cit.*, p. 255.

17 *Ibid.*, p. ix

18 Naoki Sakai, 'Ethnicity and Species: On the Philosophy of the Multi-ethnic State in Japanese Imperialism', *Radical Philosophy* 95 (May–June 1999): 33–45; Sakai and Nishitani, *op. cit.*

19 *Ibid.*, pp. 239–241.

20 *Ibid.*, pp. 237–238.

21 Heisig, 'Tanabe's Logic of the Specific and the Spirit of Nationalism', *op. cit.*, p. 256.

22 Tamotsu Aoki, 'Bunka no Hiteisei' ('Culture as Negation'), *Chūō Kōron*, 1987.

23 Giovanna Borradori, The American Philosopher: Conversations with Quine, Davidson, Putnam, Nozick, Danto, Rorty, Cavell, MacIntyre, and Kuhn, Chicago and London: University of Chicago, 1994, p. 98.

24 *Ibid.*

25 George Steiner, 'The Archives of Eden', in *No Passion Spent: Essays, 1978–1996*, London and Boston: Faber & Faber, 1996, p. 285.

26 Robert H. Sharf, 'Whose Zen? Zen Nationalism Revisited', in Heisig and Maraldo, *op. cit.*, p. 43.

27 *Ibid.*, p. viii.

28 Malcolm D. Kennedy, *The Estrangement of Great Britain and Japan, 1917–35*, Berkeley and Los Angeles: University of California Press, 1969, pp. 90–92, 158–228.

29 Note that such revisionism among Chinese scholars implies no approval of Japan's brutal onslaught against Republican China. These scholars are, like their colleagues in Japan studies, 'liberal revisionists'. Wakeman's article is contained in Frederic Wakeman Jr and Richard Louis Edmonds (eds), *Reappraising Republican China*, New York: Oxford University Press, 2000, pp. 141–178. The monographs are Marjorie Dryburgh, *North China and Japanese Expansion, 1933–1937: Regional Power and the National Interest*, Richmond, Surrey: Curzon, 2000, and Rana Ritter, *The Manchurian Myth: Nationalism, Resistance, and Collaboration in Modern China*, Berkeley and Los Angeles: University of California Press, 2000.

30 See Peter Wetzler, *Hirohito and War: Imperial Tradition and History Decision Making in Prewar Japan*, Honolulu: University of Hawaii Press, 1998; Herbert Bix, *Hirohito and the Making of Modern Japan*, London: Gerald Duckworth, 2001; Lesley Connors, *The Emperor's Adviser: Saionji Kinmochi and Prewar Japanese Politics*, London: Croom Helm, 1987; and J.W. Dover, *Empire and Aftermath: Yoshida Shigeru and the Japanese Experience, 1878–1954*, Cambridge, MA: Harvard University Press, 1988.

31 Ben-Ami Shillony, *Politics and Culture in Wartime Japan*, Oxford: Clarendon Press, 1981.

32 Shillony's example is particularly important in the light of the Western debate over European fascism because he is one of the few Japanologists to take seriously the new empirical pressure on the victor's justice definition of fascism. Liberal empirical revisionism in Europe and North America is recasting the debate that began with Ernst Nolte's *Three Faces of Fascism*. The goal today is not to deflect criticism of the German past but to make proper sense of the historical record. This is the goal of George L. Mosse, for example, in *The Fascist Revolution: Toward a General Theory of Fascism*, New York: Howard Fertig, 1999.

33 See note 18 above.

34 Tetsuo Najita and H.D. Harootunian, 'Japanese Revolt Against the West: Political and Cultural Criticism in the Twentieth Century', in Peter Duus (ed.) *The Cambridge History of Japan*, Vol. VI, Cambridge: Cambridge University Press, 1988, p. 741.

35 Peter Dale, *The Myth of Japanese Uniqueness*, London and Oxford: Croom Helm and Nissan Institute of Japanese Studies, 1986.

36 John Dower, *War without Mercy: Race and Power in the Pacific*, New York: Pantheon, 1986.

37 Ryōsuke Ōhashi, '"Kindai no Chōkoku" to Kyōtō-gakuha no Tetsugaku' ('"Overcoming Modernity" and the Philosophy of the Kyoto School'), in Niita Yoshihiro *et al.* (eds) *Datsuō no Shishō* (*Post-European Thought*), *Iwanami Kōza Gendai Shisō* (*Iwanami Course in Contemporary Thought*), Vol. XV, Tokyo: Iwanami Shoten, 1994, pp. 101–132.

38 Iwao Kōyama, 'Sekai-shi no Rinen' ('The Idea of World History'), *Shisō* (April–May 1940), quoted in Sakai, 'Modernity and its Critique', *op. cit.*, p. 106. This was the earlier version of the text that became the first chapter of one of Kōyama's most influential books, *Sekai-shi no Tetsugaku* (*The Philosophy of World History*), first published in 1942 (after appearing in various journals between the spring of 1940 and the spring of 1942) but recently republished, in the version mentioned above in note 4.

39 Jean-Paul Sartre, 'Preface', in Frantz Fanon, *The Wretched of the Earth*, trans. Constance Farrington, London: Penguin, 1967, p. 18.

40 Sakai, 'Modernity and its Critique', *op. cit.*, p. 117.

41 Yoshimi Takeuchi, 'Kindai to wa Nani-ka' ('What is Modernity?'), in *Takeuchi Yoshimi Zenshū* (*The Complete Works of Yoshimi Takeuchi*), Vol. IV, Tokyo: Chikuma Shobō, 1980, p. 130.

4 Scholarship or propaganda: neo-Marxism and the decay of Pacific War orthodoxy

1 Remark made in an article in the *New York Times*, 19 August 1969.
2 *The Mill on the Floss*.
3 Max Weber, 'Wissenschaft als Beruf', in *Gesammelte Aufsaetze zur Wissenschftslehre*, Tübingen, 1922, pp. 524–555. An English translation can be found in H.H. Garth and C. Wright Mills (eds), *From Max Weber: Essays in Sociology*, New York: Oxford University Press, 1946, pp. 129–156. The quotation from Weber is on p. 147.
4 I borrow this expression from Graham Parkes's article 'The Putative Fascism of the Kyoto School and the Political Correctness of the Modern Academy', *Philosophy East & West* 47(3) (July 1997): 305–336, where he criticises the treatment of such figures associated with the Kyoto School, broadly defined, as Kitarō Nishida, Shūzō Kuki and Keiji Nishitani by writers such as Harry Harootunian, Tetsuo Najita, Bernard Faure, Kōjin Karatani and Leslie Pincus. I initially resisted using the term 'neo-Marxist' because Harootunian does not appear to be a serious Marxist, certainly not by European or Japanese standards. Karatani's grasp of Marxism is far more confident. So is Dale's. But there is a family resemblance among these American left-wing critics of Japan that may justify this collective designation.

First, the term 'neo-Marxist' has the virtue of calling into doubt the widely held assumption that these academics are French theorists; they are not. These writers are caught in the orbit of neither Paris nor, for that matter, Frankfurt. Secondly, the American neo-Marxist seems reluctant to labour among the primary sources to justify their uncompromising attacks on some of modern Japan's greatest thinkers. See, in this connection, Parkes's review of Leslie Pincus, *Authenticating Culture in Imperial Japan: Kuki Shūzō and the Rise of National Aesthetics* (1996), in *Chanoyu Quarterly* 86 (1997): 63–70.

The work of Bernard Faure appears to be of an entirely different order. This scholar appears to be manifestly at home in Paris and the twentieth-century tradition of French thought. His *Chan Insights and Oversights: An Epistemological Critique of the Chan Tradition*, Princeton, NJ: Princeton University Press, 1996, is impressive in scale and range of reference. It lies outside the scope of my knowledge and expertise to offer a definitive judgment on his interpretation of the *Chan* tradition.
5 Tetsuo Najita and H.D. Harootunian, 'Japanese Revolt Against the West: Political and Cultural Criticism in the Twentieth Century', in Peter Duus (ed.) *The Cambridge History of Japan*, Vol. VI, Cambridge: Cambridge University Press, pp. 711–774.
6 Harry Harootunian, *Overcome by Modernity: History, Culture and Community in Interwar Japan*, Princeton and Oxford: Princeton University Press, 2000.
7 David Williams, 'America as Japan Scholar to the World', Book Review, *Los Angeles Times*, August 1999, p. 2.
8 George Steiner, *In Bluebeard's Castle: Some Notes Towards the Re-definition of Culture*, London/New Haven, CT: Faber & Faber/Yale University Press, 1971, p. 86.
9 Marius Jansen, *The Making of Modern Japan*, Cambridge, MA: Harvard University Press, 2000, was reviewed by R.T. Murphy in 'Looking to Game Boy', *London Review of Books*, 3 January 2002, pp. 32–35.
10 Herbert Bix, *Hirohito and the Making of Modern Japan*, New York: Harper, 2001.
11 Tetsuo Najita (ed.), *Tokugawa Political Writings: Cambridge Texts in Modern Politics*, Cambridge: Cambridge University Press, 1998.

12 James McMullen, 'Ogyū Sorai and the Definition of Terms', *Japan Forum* 13(2) (2002): 249–265.

13 Harootunian, *op. cit.*, pp. xxxi–xxxii.

14 The page references for quotations from *Overcome by Modernity* will henceforth appear in square brackets, [ ].

15 Gianni Vattimo, *La fine della modernità*, Garzanti Editore s.p.a., 1985. It has been rendered into English as *The End of Modernity: Nihilism and Hermeneutics in Post-modern Culture*, trans. Jon R. Synder, London: Polity Press, 1988. Harootunian uses the American edition, but the pagination appears to be the same as the British. The quotation from Nietzsche appears on p. 165 of the English translation.

16 Lesley Chamberlain, *Nietzsche in Turin: An Intimate Biography*, New York: Picador, 1996, p. 208. But on the subject of Nietzsche's descent into madness, see Richard Schain, *The Legend of Nietzsche's Syphilis*, Greenwood Press, 2002, where the author concludes that the clear and powerful nature of Nietzsche's prose, as displayed in *Ecce Homo*, the philosopher's last book, is utterly at odds with any diagnosis of a brain ruined by syphilis.

17 Vattimo, *op. cit.*

18 Graham Parkes, 'The Early Reception of Nietzsche's Philosophy in Japan', in Graham Parkes (ed.) *Nietzsche and Asian Thought*, Chicago and London: University of Chicago Press, 1996, p. 183. I have relied extensively on Parkes's invaluable discussion of this subject.

19 Vattimo, *op. cit.*, p. 164. Note that Heidegger introduced the term '*Verwindung*' into philosophy, but Nietzsche, according to Vattimo, anticipated the precise nuance of '*Verwindung*', rather than '*Überwindung*'; it is where Nietzsche, via Heidegger and French structuralism, will take us.

20 Julio Ramos, *Desencuentros de la modernidad en América Latina: literatura y política en el siglo* XIX, Buenos Aires: Fondo de Cultura Economica, 1993, has been rendered into English as Divergent Modernities: Culture and Politics in Nineteenth-century Latin America, trans. John D. Blanco, Durham, NC, and London: Duke University Press, 2001.

21 Naoki Sakai, 'Modernity and its Critique', in Masao Miyoshi and H.D. Harootunian (eds) *Postmodernism and Japan*, Durham, NC, and London: Duke University Press, p. 105.

22 These two works have recently been republished as Shigetaka Suzuki, *Yōroppa no Seiritsu-Sangyō Kakumei*, Kyōtō Tetsugaku Sensho, Dai Roku-kan, Kyōtō: Tōei-sha, 2000. Aspects of the Ōtsuka-Johnson axis in this rich hour in trans-Pacific ideas are touched upon in my *Japan and the Enemies of Open Political Science*, London & New York: Routledge, 1996.

23 Victor Farías, 'Foreword to the Spanish Edition, *Heidegger and Nazism*', in Tom Rockmore and Joseph Margolis (eds) *The Heidegger Case: On Philosophy and Politics*, Philadelphia: Temple University Press, 1992, p. 334.

24 The conventional translation of '*sōryoku-sen*' is 'total war', but given the way the idea is treated by the participants in this *zadankai* and the rapid disintegration of Japan's military position in the Pacific after the Battle of Midway (June 1942), the expression 'total war' (Carl Schmitt) can be and has been wilfully misunderstood. 'Total resistance' is a more accurate rendering. For a detailed discussion of this linguistic-ethical conundrum, see my forthcoming translation of and commentary on *The Standpoint of World History and Japan*.

25 As noted above, Chūō Kōron-sha later published a transcription of all three sessions in book form under the title *Sekai-shi-teki Tachiba to Nippon* (*The Standpoint of World History and Japan*) in April 1943.

26 One of the most useful sources on the secret political war that forms the essential background for the *Chūō Kōron* symposia is Yasumasa Ōshima, 'Daitōa Sensō

to Kyoto-gakuha – Chishikijin no Seiji Sanka ni Tsuite' ('The Greater East Asian War and the Kyoto School: The Political Involvement of Intellectuals'), *Chūō Kōron* 80 (August 1965). Perhaps even more important, both on Ōshima himself and the wider involvement of the Kyoto School in the resistance to Tojo's regime, is Ryōsuke Ōhashi, *Kyōtō-gakuha to Nippon Kaigun: Shin Shiryō 'Ōshima Memos' o Megutte* (*The Kyoto School and the Japanese Navy: On the New Historical Documents,* The Oshima Memos), Tokyo: PHP, 2001.

27 Wataru Hiromatsu, <Kindai no Chōkoku> Ron: Shōwa Shisō-shi e no ichi Shikaku (On 'Overcoming Modernity': One Perspective on the Intellectual History of the Showa Period), Tokyo: Kōdansha, 1989.

28 Wataru Hiromatsu (ed. and trans.), *Die Deutsche Ideologie, 1. Band, 1. Abschnitt by Karl Marx and Friedrich Engels,* Tokyo: Kawade Shobō, 1974.

29 Tetsutarō Kawakami and Yoshimi Takeuchi (eds), *Kindai no Chōkoku,* Tokyo: Tomiyama-sho, 1979.

30 The sole exception of which I am aware is the *fukugenban* of the relevant 1942 issue(s) of *Bungakkai* that appeared in the March 1973 issue of *Dentō to Gendai.*

31 Kawakami and Takeuchi, *op. cit.*, p. 176.

32 Kōjin Karatani (*hen, chō*), *Shinpojiumu,* Tokyo: Shichō-sha, 1989, pp. 181–235.

33 *Ibid.*, p. 183.

34 Karatani made this claim in a recent interview with Toshiaki Kobayashi: 'Nihon Shisō wa Kokkyō o Koerareru ka' ('Is Japanese Thought Exportable?'), *Shūkan Dokusho-jin,* 4 July 2003, p. 2.

35 Horio Tsutomu, 'The *Chūōkōron* Discussions, their Background and Meaning', trans. Thomas Kirchner, in James W. Heisig and John C. Maraldo (eds) *Rude Awakenings: Zen, the Kyoto School and the Question of Nationalism,* Honolulu: University of Hawaii, 1994, pp. 289–315.

36 Slavoj Žižek, *Did Someone Say Totalitarianism? Five Interventions in the (Mis)use of a Notion,* London and New York: Verso, 2001, p. 3.

5 Wartime Japan as it really was: the Kyoto School's struggle against Tojo (1941–44)

1 The title quote from Tsutomu Horio appears in his essay 'The *Chūōkōron* Discussions, their Meaning and Background', in James W. Heisig and John C. Maraldo (eds) *Rude Awakenings: Zen, the Kyoto School and the Question of Nationalism,* Honolulu: University of Hawaii Press, 1994, p. 291. I have slightly altered the translation.

2 Quoted in John Patrick Diggins, *The Promise of Pragmatism: Modernism and the Crisis of Knowledge and Authority,* Chicago and London: University of Chicago Press, 1991, p. 1.

3 As noted in Chapter 1, the three symposia, or *zadankai* (round-table discussions), were originally published in the pages of the magazine *Chūō Kōron*. Chūō Kōron-sha later published the transcripts of all three sessions in book form under the title *Sekai-shi-teki Tachiba to Nippon* (*The Standpoint of World History and Japan*) in April 1943. The first symposium and the book carry the same title, so, henceforth, the book will be cited as *The Standpoint of World History and Japan*, and the title of the symposium will be put in quotation marks.

4 Georg Wilhelm Friedrich Hegel, *The Philosophy of World History,* trans. J. Sibree, New York: Dover Publications, 1956, p. 21 (translation slightly amended).

5 The expression 'court of world history' comes from Schiller's poem 'Resignation', but Hegel gave it its philosophical meaning and weight.

6 Nishida is an absence that is a presence in this chapter. I have consciously chosen to concentrate on Tanabe and the so-called 'gang of four' of the second generation (Kōsaka, Kōyama, Suzuki and Nishitani) because they have been relatively

neglected while Nishida's stance during the war has been discussed in detail. Another reason is that despite Nishida's political involvement in the events described below and in the face of his important political writings during the period – including the essays on the philosophy of history collected in Nobuki Kagishi (ed.), *Nishida Tetsugaku Senchū, Dai Go Kan, <Rekishi Tetsugaku> Ronbun-shū (Selected Readings in Nishida Philosophy*, Vol. 5, *Essays in 'The Philosophy of History'*), Kyōtō: Tōei-sha, 1998 – I am not convinced that philosophically his heart was in this struggle. As I have explained elsewhere, I ground this position in the distinction I draw between 'subjectivist' and 'objectivist' philosophy, a distinction I find useful in understanding Heidegger's posture towards the Third Reich.

The discussion of the wartime activities of Tanabe and the 'gang of four' casts a powerful light on Nishida's role in the Pacific War, including his controversial and not entirely clear degree of involvement in the drafting of 'the philosophical principles of the Greater East Asian Co-prosperity Sphere' in 1943. See, for example, the interpretation of Nishida's wartime position elaborated by Michiko Yusa in 'Fashion and A-lētheia: Philosophical Integrity and War-time Thought Control', *Hikaku Shisō Kenkyū* 16 (February 1990): 294–281. For a major statement on Nishida's role in the Pacific War, see Christopher Jones, *Ideas at War: Nishida Kitarō and the Philosophical Context of the Co-prosperity Sphere* (forthcoming).

7 Mark Anderson has apparently prepared a partial translation, but I have been unable to locate his version of the first *Chūō Kōron* symposium mentioned in J. Victor Koschman's *Revolution and Subjectivity in Postwar Japan*, Chicago and London: University of Chicago Press, 1996, p. 142 n. 163.

8 See *Kongen-teki Shutaisei no Tetsugaku* in *Nishitani Keiji Chosakushū* (*NKC*) 1–2, as well as the essays gathered in *NKC* 4.

9 Ryōen Minamoto, 'The Symposium on "Overcoming Modernity"', in Heisig and Maraldo, *op. cit.*, p. 203.

10 Ryōsuke Ōhashi, Kyōtō-gakuha to Nippon Kaigun: Shin Shiryō 'Ōshima Memos' o Megutte (The Kyoto School and the Japanese Navy: On the New Historical Documents, The Ōshima Memos), Tokyo: PHP, 2001, pp. 25–26.

11 Questioning the relevance of Hegel, Karatani notes that Nishida suggested that the Leibnitzian idea of 'blind' monads illustrated the dynamic at work in the Greater East Asian Co-prosperity Sphere. But Tanabe and the second generation 'gang of four' of the Kyoto School were resolutely Hegelian in their approach not because Hegel offered a 'total system' but because he placed the idea of the nation-state as *the agent* of global change within the most demanding of all subjectivist frameworks: the making of world history. Nevertheless, this Leibnitzian idea is suggestive about the sources of failure of the Greater East Asian Co-prosperity Sphere during the early 1940s. For Karatani's view, see his interview with Toshiaki Kōbayashi, 'Nihon Shisō wa Kokkyō o Koerareru ka' ('Is Japanese Thought Exportable?'), *Shūkan Dokusho-jin*, 4 July 2003, p. 2.

12 Yasumasa Ōshima, 'Dai-tōa Sensō to Kyoto-gakuha – Chishiki-jin no Seiji Sanka ni Tsuite', *Chūō Kōron* 80 (August 1965): 125–143; Minamoto, *op. cit.*, p. 202 n. 10.

13 Horio, *op. cit.*, p. 290.

14 Tojo fell from power in July 1944 when Saipan was captured by American forces, but the Kyoto School's dialogue with the Imperial Navy continued. However, the focus of their discussions shifted from criticism of the Army to the question of post-war reconstruction as the end of the Pacific War drew closer.

15 Ōhashi, *op. cit.*

16 Michiko Yusa, 'Nishida and Totalitarianism', in Heisig and Maraldo, *op. cit.*, p. 122.

17 Ōhashi, *op. cit.*, p. 14.
18 *Ibid.*, p. 14.
19 *Ibid.*, pp. 14–15. But see also p. 26 n. 1.
20 *Ibid.*, p. 15.
21 For a detailed account of this affair and the background to the authority's attack on Chūō Kōron-sha, see Richard H. Mitchell, *Censorship in Imperial Japan*, Princeton, NJ: Princeton University Press, 1983.
22 Ōhashi, *op. cit.* This is a general point, rather than a specific one. Miki, for example, went to prison for helping 'a friend, who had violated the Public Peace Ordinance, evade the terms of his parole' (Michiko Yusa). The Toyotama Prison, in Nakano, Tokyo, where Miki was kept, was notoriously unhealthy, and he died from medical causes. For the details of his arrest and death, see the detailed research contained in 'Philosophy and Inflation: Miki Kiyoshi in Weimar Germany, 1922–24', *Monumenta Nipponica* 53(1): 45–71.
23 Ōshima, *op. cit.*, p. 131.
24 Ōhashi, *op. cit.*, p. 18.
25 Ōshima, *op. cit.*, pp. 13–131.
26 On Yanaihara, see Susan C. Townsend, *Yanaihara Tadao and Japanese Colonial Policy: Redeeming Empire*, London: Curzon, 2000.
27 As noted above, there was support for the war as an idea. The Kyoto School was prepared to support the use of force to break Western hegemony over Southeast Asia and the Western Pacific. The Kyoto School supported the attack on Pearl Harbour as an inevitable world-historical confrontation, as 'the event', but they were critical of the reckless strategy behind the actual assault of December 1941. Furthermore, as noted above, the Kyoto School's worries over Japan's conduct in China were profound and warranted.
28 Ōhashi, *op. cit.*, pp. 227–244.
29 Ōshima confirms this point in his *Kaisetsu* to *THZ* 7: 384.
30 On this neglected wartime discourse, see Naoki Sakai, 'Ethnicity and Species: On the Philosophy of the Multi-ethnic State in Japanese Imperialism', *Radical Philosophy* 95 (May–June 1999): 33–45.
31 Benedict Anderson, *The Spectre of Comparison: Nationalism, Southeast Asia and the World*, London: Verso, 1999.

6 Taking Kyoto philosophy seriously

1 D.S. Clarke Jr, 'Introduction', in Keiji Nishitani, *Nishida Kitarō*, trans. Seisaku Yamamoto and James W. Heisig, Berkeley: University of California, 1991, p. vii.
2 This point has been forcefully argued most recently by Shinichi Nakazawa in an interview: 'Tamashii no Kanto-shugisha: Tanabe Hajime' ('Hajime Tanabe: A Kantian of the Spirit'), *Shūkan Dokushojin*, 6 April 2001, p. 1. See also his recent book, *Philosophia Japonica*, Tokyo: Shūei-sha, 2001, which offers a revisionist interpretation of Tanabe's philosophy.
3 For a near contemporary account of the complexities and confusions of the early history of the reception of German philosophy in Japan before the rise of Nishida and Tanabe, see Yūjirō Miyake, 'The Introduction of Western Philosophy', in Count Shigenobu Okuma (ed.) *Fifty Years of the New Japan* (*Kaikoku Gojūnen Shi*), Vol. II, London: Smith, Edler & Co., 1909, pp. 226–241.
4 For a fascinating portrait of this trans-cultural encounter, see Michiko Yusa, 'Philosophy and Inflation: Miki Kiyoshi in Weimar Germany, 1922–24', *Monumenta Nipponica* 53(1): 45–71.
5 George Steiner, *Heidegger*, London/Glasgow: Fontana/Collins, 1978, p. 12.
6 'Genshōgaku ni okeru Atarashiki Tenkō', *Tanabe Hajime Zenshū* (*THZ*) 4: 17–34.

7 Graham Parkes, 'Rising Sun over Black Forest', in Reinhard May (ed.) *Heidegger's Hidden Sources: Some East Asian Influences on His Work*, London: Routledge, 1996, p. 82.

8 *Ibid.*, p. 82, for quotation from the editor of this volume of the *Gesamtausgabe*.

9 *Ibid.* See pp. 81–87 for Parkes's detailed discussion of this extraordinary episode in the Heidegger–Tanabe relationship.

10 Such empirical methods – this testing of the potential for communication, correspondence and congruencies on a case-by-case basis – provide the basis for the philosophy of comparison or the transcendental conceptual territory between any two traditions which are grounded in radically different assumptions and points of departure.

11 David Williams, 'In Defence of the Kyoto School: Reflections on Philosophy, the Pacific War and the Making of a Post-White World', *Japan Forum* 12(2) (2000): 144.

12 Graham Parkes, 'Introduction', in Graham Parkes (ed.), *Heidegger and Asian Thought*, Honolulu: University of Hawaii, 1987, p. 5.

13 For a detailed discussion of this criticism of Anglo-American philosophy, see David Williams, *Japan and the Enemies of Open Political Science*, London: Routledge, 1994, pp. 51–96.

14 Parkes, 'Introduction', *op. cit.*, p. 9. The two texts in question are Nishitani's *Shūkyū to wa Nani ka* (*What is Religion?*), published in English as *Religion and Nothingness*, trans. Jan Van Bragt, Berkeley, Los Angeles, London: University of California, 1982, and 'Reflections on Two Addresses by Martin Heidegger'. The latter essay can be found in Parkes (ed.), *Heidegger and Asian Thought, op. cit.*, pp. 145–154.

15 John Russell, *Francis Bacon*, London: Thames & Hudson, 1993, p. 109.

16 George Steiner, 'The Archives of Eden', *Salmagundi* 50–51 (Fall 1980–Winter 1981): 71. For a slightly less forceful version of this essay, see George Steiner, *No Passion Spent, Essays 1978–1996*, London and Boston: Faber & Faber, 1996, pp. 266–303.

17 Steiner, 'The Archives of Eden', *op. cit.*, p. 80.

18 *Ibid.*

19 Giovanna Borradori, The American Philosopher: Conversations with Quine, Davidson, Putnam, Nozick, Danto, Rorty, Cavell, MacIntyre, and Kuhn, Chicago: University of Chicago, 1994, p. 3.

20 See, for example, 'Gentile and Marxism' in A. James Gregor, *Givoanni Gentile: Philosopher of Fascism*, New Brunswick, NJ: Transaction Publishers, 2001, pp. 35–46.

21 See, for example, J. Victor Koschmann, *Revolution and Subjectivity in Postwar Japan*, Chicago: University of Chicago Press, 1996, pp. 89–95.

22 On this complex theme, see Curtis Anderson Gayle, *Marxist History and Postwar Japanese Nationalism*, London: RoutledgeCurzon, 2003.

23 On this contentious subject, see Graham Parkes, 'The Putative Fascism of the Kyoto School and the Political Correctness of the Modern Academy', *Philosophy East & West* 47(3) (July 1997): 305–336, and Parkes's review of Leslie Pincus, *Authenticating Culture in Imperial Japan: Kuki Shūzō and the Rise of National Aesthetics* (1996), in *Chanoyu Quarterly* 86 (1997): 63–70.

24 Risaku Mutai, *Basho no Roki-gaku* (*The Logic of Place*), ed. Kitano Hiroyuki, Tokyo: Kobushi Shobō, 1996 (originally published in 1944), and Kōsaka Masaaki, *Nishida Kitarō to Watsuji Tetsurō*, Tokyo: Shinchō-sa, 1964.

25 Masao Maruyama, 'Koten kara dō manabu ka' ('How to Learn from the Classics?'), '*Bunmeiron no Gaiyaku' o Yomu* (*Reading 'An Outline of Civilisation'*), jo, Tokyo: Iwanami Shoten, 1986, pp. 1–23.

26 Karl Löwith, 'Afterword to the Japanese Reader', 'European Nihilism: Reflections on the Spiritual and Historical Background of the European War', in *Martin Heidegger and European Nihilism*, ed. Richard Wolin, trans. Gary Steiner, New York: Columbia University Press, 1995, pp. 228–234.

27 *Ibid.*, p. 233.

28 *Ibid.*, p. 232.

29 *Ibid.*, p. 232.

30 *Ibid.*, p. 230.

31 'Zushiki <Jikan> kara Zushiki <Sekai> e' ('From "Time" to the "World" as Schemas'), *THZ* 6: 3–49. *Tanabe Hajime Zenshu, Dai Roku-kan, <Shu no Ronri> Ronbun-shu, I* (*The Complete Works of Hajime Tanabe*, Vol. 6, '*The Logic of the Species', Essays I*), Tokyo: Chikuma Shobō, 1963, pp. 3–49.

32 See, for example, the work of Eiko Hanaoka, the Japanese philosopher and student of Nishitani.

33 James W. Heisig and John C. Maraldo (eds), *Rude Awakenings: Zen, the Kyoto School and the Question of Nationalism*, Honolulu: University of Hawaii Press, 1994, p. 3.

7 Racism and the black legend of the Kyoto School: translating Tanabe's *The Logic of the Species*

1 Combined quotation from Charles Péguy, *Notre Jeunesse*, pp. 72 ff., and *Note conjointe*, p. 82, after H. Stuart Hughes, *The Consciousness and Society: The Reorientation of European Social Thought, 1890–1930*, Brighton: Harvester Press, 1979 (reprint), p. 355.

2 'Text and Context', *On Difficulty and Other Essays*, Oxford: Oxford University Press, 1978, p. 5. The last sentence has been abbreviated.

3 Peter Dale, *The Myth of Japanese Uniqueness*, London and Oxford: Croom Helm and the Nissan Institute of Japanese Studies, 1986.

4 Hajime Tanabe, 'The Logic of the Species as Dialectics', trans. David Dilworth and Taira Satō, *Monumenta Nipponica* XXIV: 273–288.

5 Dale, *op. cit.*, pp. 193–194.

6 *Ibid.*, p. 196.

7 Tanabe, *op. cit.*, p. 274.

8 For an extended discussion of this point, see Naoki Sakai, 'Ethnicity and Species: On the Philosophy of the Multi-ethnic State in Japanese Imperialism', *Radical Philosophy* 95 (May–June 1999): 33–45, esp. p. 41.

9 Tanabe, *op. cit.*, p. 273 n. 1.

10 *Ibid.*, p. 273 n. 2

11 *Ibid.*, p. 275.

12 This interpretation is confirmed by Yasumasa Ōshima in his *Kaisetsu* (commentary) on Vol. 7 of *THZ*, p. 384. James Heisig affirms this conclusion in his article 'Tanabe's Logic of the Species and Nationalism', in James W. Heisig and John C. Maraldo (eds), *Rude Awakenings: Zen, the Kyoto School and the Question of Nationalism*, Honolulu: University of Hawaii Press, 1994, p. 269 n. 39.

13 Tanabe, *op. cit.*, p. 274.

14 New York: Pantheon Books, 1986.

15 Kevin Michael Doak, *Dreams of Difference: The Japan Romantic School and the Crisis of Modernity*, Berkeley, Los Angeles and London: University of California Press, 1994, p. xxvii

16 Tokyo: Iwanani Shoten, 1942.

17 The evidence gathered by Dower is damning on this point. More interesting still, the racist idiom of combat for American soldiers has persisted into the would-be liberal post-war era.
18 Tanabe, *op. cit.*, p. 274.
19 *THZ* 7: 258.
20 Henri Bergson, *Les Deux Sources de la Morale et de la Religion*, Paris: Librairie Félix Alcan, 1932.
21 *Ibid.*, p. 345.
22 Beruguson, *Dōtoku-Shūkyō no Futatsu Gensen*, trans. Kōji Hirayama, Tokyo: Shiba Shoten, 1936, front matter.
23 I have used the Audra and Cloudesley translation, published as *The Two Sources of Morality and Religion*, London: Macmillan and Co., 1935, p. 3.
24 Bergson, *op. cit.*, p. 4.
25 Berugoson, *op. cit.*, pp. 6–7.

8 When is a philosopher a moral monster? Tanabe versus Heidegger versus Marcuse

1 For a translation of 'The Philosophy of Crisis or a Crisis in Philosophy?', see Appendix to this book.
2 Frank O. Miller, *Minobe Tatsukichi: Interpreter of Constitutionalism in Japan*, Berkeley and Los Angeles: University of California Press, 1965, p. 54.
3 Peter Dale, *The Myth of Japanese Uniqueness*, London and Oxford: Croom Helm and the Nissan Institute of Japanese Studies, 1986.
4 The pressures are evident even in critical studies such as A. James Gregor, *Giovanni Gentile: Philosopher of Fascism*, New Brunswick, NJ: Transaction Publishers, 2001.
5 The essay appeared in James W. Morley (ed.), *Dilemmas of Growth in Prewar Japan*, Princeton, NJ: Princeton University Press, 1971, pp. 489–510. Ron Dore first posed the question in the same volume.
6 For the text of The Ōshima Memos, see Ryōsuke Ōhashi, Kyōtō-gakuha to Nippon Kaigun: Shin Shiryō 'Ōshima Memos' o Megutte (The Kyoto School and the Japanese Navy: On the New Historical Documents, The Oshima Memos), Tokyo: PHP, 2001.
7 See Miller, *op. cit.* For a contrasting interpretation of the Minobe Affair, see Richard H. Mitchell, *Censorship in Imperial Japan*, Princeton, NJ: Princeton University Press, 1983.
8 Alberto Moreiras, *The Exhaustion of Difference: The Politics of Latin American Cultural Studies*, Durham, NC, and London: Duke University Press, 2001, p. 13.
9 Victor Farías, *Heidegger et le nazisme*, Paris: Éditions Verdier, 1987. In English, see Victor Farías, *Heidegger and Nazism*, Philadelphia: Temple University Press, 1989.
10 See *Die Selbstbehauptung der deutsche Universität/Das Rektorat, 1933/34*, Frankfurt am Main: Vittorio Klostermann, 1990.
11 Kiyoshi Miki was another. See his 'Haideggā to Tetsugaku no Unmei' ('Heidegger and the Fate of Philosophy'), *Serupan* (*Le Serpent*), November 1933, pp. 14–19.
12 Hajime Tanabe, 'Kiki no Tetsugaku ka Tetsugaku no Kikika', *Tanabe Hajime Zenshū* (*THZ*) 8: 3–9.
13 The 'offending' passage can be found on p. 199 of Martin Heidegger, *An Introduction to Metaphysics*, trans. Ralph Manheim, New Haven, CT, and London: Yale University Press, 1959. Heidegger was not a fool. He has set a metaphysical trap for his critics.

14 Heidegger was appointed to the rectorship on 21 April 1933.
15 'Preface to the MIT Press Edition', in Richard Wolin (ed.), *The Heidegger Controversy: A Critical Reader*, Cambridge, MA: MIT Press, 1993, p. xvii.
16 In *Heidegger's Children: Hannah Arendt, Karl Löwith, Hans Jonas and Herbert Marcuse*, Princeton, NJ: Princeton University Press, 2003.
17 *The Betrayal of the Intellectuals* (*La Trahison des Clercs*), trans. Richard Aldington, New York and London: W.W. Norton & Co., 1969, p. 27.
18 Rüdiger Safranski, *Martin Heidegger: Between Good and Evil*, trans. Ewald Osers, Cambridge, MA, and London: Harvard University Press, 1998, p. 231. Given the text that Safranski cites, how is it possible to question his interpretation? The answer lies in the problem of anachronism. Like the famous clock in Shakespeare's *Julius Caesar*, Heidegger presents us with a problem of time, sequence and history. We who come after the Third Reich find it almost impossible to make the effort to understand what Heidegger, as an heir to European Romanticism ('the largest recent movement to transform the lives and the thought of the Western world' – Isaiah Berlin), meant by primitivism. But it is the first job of the scholar to insist on understanding what Heidegger means, and then proceed to some other task (criticism, for example). Safranski has not performed this job of understanding.
19 Hajime Tanabe, *Zange toshite no Tetsugaku*, Tokyo: Iwanami Shoten, 1946, translated into English as *Philosophy of Metanoetics*, trans. Yoshinori Takeuchi, Berkeley, Los Angeles and London: University of California Press, 1986.
20 George Steiner, *Heidegger*, London: Fontana Press, 1978, p. 21.
21 Here my intention is to attempt to get the political-philosophical relationship between Tanabe and Heidegger right. But there is a metaphysical question to be answered in another context: does Tanabe get Heidegger's ontology right? One of the most important summary statements of Tanabe's response to Heidegger's thought as a whole may be found in the 'Afterword' to his long study titled *Sūri no Rekishishugi Tenkai* (*The Historicist Development of Mathematics*), *THZ* 12: esp. 330–332. Pro-Nishida anti-Tanabe critics in Japan such as Hideki Mine, in, for example, *Haidegga to Nihon no Tetsugaku* (*Heidegger and Japan Philosophy*), Tokyo: Mineruba Shobō, 2002, are particularly keen to discredit Tanabe's understanding of Heidegger, but the Japanese assessment of Tanabe needs to be approached cautiously because of the profound resentments against him among Nishida's students and supporters.
22 This text appears in the Appendix of this book.
23 I cite the translations of the letters contained in 'An Exchange of Letters: Herbert Marcuse and Martin Heidegger', in Wolin, *op. cit.*, pp. 152–164. This quotation is on p. 160.
24 See previous note.
25 Wolin, *op. cit.*, pp. 152–164.
26 *Ibid.*, p. 157.
27 *Ibid.*, p. 157.
28 *Ibid.*, p. 157.
29 Miguel de Beistegui, *Heidegger and the Political: Dystopias*, London and New York: Routledge, 1998, p. x. Beistegui wants the philosopher to weigh his conclusions more carefully. In a different way, so does the historian of ideas.
30 Wolin, *op. cit.*, p. 160.
31 *Ibid.*, pp. 160–161.
32 *Ibid.*, pp. 160–161.
33 *Ibid.*, p. 161.
34 *Ibid.*, p. 162.
35 *Ibid.*, p. 162.
36 *Ibid.*, p. 162.

37 *Ibid.*, pp. 162–163.
38 *Ibid.*, p. 163.
39 *Ibid.*, p. 163.
40 *Ibid.*, p. 163.
41 Marcuse's letter is reproduced in *ibid.*, pp. 163–164.
42 *Ibid.*, p. 164.
43 *Ibid.*, p. 164.
44 *Ibid.*, p. 164.
45 *Berlin: The Downfall 1945*, London: Viking, 2002, p. 105.
46 *Ibid.*, p. 106.
47 *Ibid.*, p. 107.
48 *Ibid.*, p. 107.
49 *Ibid.*, p. 107.
50 *Ibid.*, p. 108.
51 *Ibid.*, p. 120.
52 Wolin, *op. cit.*, p. 164.

9 Heidegger, Nazism and the Farías Affair: the European origins of the Kyoto School crises

1 Victor Farías, *Heidegger et le nazisme*, Paris: Éditions Verdier, 1987. In English, see Victor Farías, *Heidegger and Nazism*, Philadelphia: Temple University Press, 1989.
2 Published in Frankfurt by Campus.
3 Jacques Derrida, *De l'esprit*, Editions Galilée, 1987. In English, see Jacques Derrida, *Of Spirit: Heidegger and the Question*, trans. Geoffrey Bennington and Rachel Bowlby, Chicago: University of Chicago Press, 1989.
4 Also note that 'The publication in Germany of the *Introduction to Metaphysics*, the lectures of 1935 in which there appears the famous phrase "the inner truth and greatness" of the National Socialist movement, gave rise in 1953 to a fight in the press between Charles Lewalter [who defended Heidegger and had his support] and a young student from Frankfurt named Jürgen Habermas': Luc Ferry and Alain Renaut, *Heidegger and Modernity*, trans. Franklin Philip, Chicago: University of Chicago Press, 1990, p. 112. I have relied heavily on the summary by Ferry and Renaut of these French quarrels in my discussion of the pre-history of *l'Affaire Farías*.
5 'Heidegger et la "révolution"', *Méditation* 3 (1961).
6 Luc Ferry and Alain Renaut, *Heidegger et les Modernes*, Paris: Éditions Grasset & Fasquelle, 1988.
7 A summary of the complicated history of the various versions of this text, French and German, is presented in the introduction to the English translation of this essay by Richard Wolin in the volume he edited titled *The Heidegger Controversy: A Critical Reader*, Cambridge, MA: MIT Press, 1993, p. 67.
8 This is Wolin's summary in his introduction to his translation of Löwith's 'The Political Implication of Heidegger's Existentialism', in Wolin, *op. cit.*, p. 167.
9 'Preface to the New Edition', *History and Class Consciousness: Studies in Marxist Dialectics*, trans. Rodney Livingstone, Cambridge, MA: MIT Press, 1971, p. xxii.
10 Philippe Lacoue-Labarthe, *La Fiction du politique: Heidegger, l'art et la politique*, Paris: Christian Bourgois, 1987, p. 81. There is a paragraph-length quotation from this text in Ferry and Renaut, *Heidegger and Modernity*, *op. cit.*, pp. 2–3.
11 See Heidegger's lecture from the winter term of 1931/32 later published as *Hegels Phänomenologie des Geistes*, Frankfurt am Main: Vittorio Klostermann, 1980.

See, in English, *Hegel's Phenomenology of Spirit*, trans. Parvis Emad and Kenneth Maly, Bloomington and Indianapolis: Indiana University Press, 1988.

12 Wolin, *op. cit.*, and Tom Rockmore and Joseph Margolis (eds), *The Heidegger Case: On Philosophy and Politics*, Philadelphia: Temple University Press, 1992.

13 These essentialist, racial and imperialist confusions may be sampled in Rorty's contributions and interventions in Chantal Mouffe (ed.), *Deconstruction and Pragmatism*, London: Routledge, 1996.

10 Heidegger and the wartime Kyoto School: after Farías – the first paradigm crisis (1987–96)

1 Quoted in Jan Van Bragt's 'Kyoto Philosophy – Intrinsically Nationalist?', in James W. Heisig and John C. Maraldo (eds) *Rude Awakenings: Zen, the Kyoto School and the Question of Nationalism*, Honolulu: University of Hawaii Press, 1994, p. 243 n. 23.

2 *Ibid.*

3 James W. Heisig, *Filósofos de la nada: Un ensayo sobre la escuela de Kioto*, Barcelona: Editorial Herder, 2001. Translated into English as *Philosophers of Nothingness: An Essay on the Kyoto School*, Honolulu: University of Hawaii Press, 2001.

4 Take, for example, the string of impressive translations and monographs contained in the Nanzan Studies in Religion and Culture series.

5 Heinrich Dumoulin, *Zen Buddhism: A History (Japan)*, 2nd edn, trans. Paul F. Knitter, New York: Simon & Schuster, 1989, and Keiji Nishitani, *Religion and Nothingness*, trans. Jan Van Bragt, Berkeley, Los Angeles and London: University of California Press, 1982.

6 Heinrich Dumoulin, *Zen Buddhism in the Twentieth Century*, trans. Joseph O'Leary, New York: Weatherhill, 1992.

7 Honolulu: University of Hawaii Press, 1994.

8 *Ibid.*, pp. vii–viii.

9 *Ibid.*, p. vii.

10 *Ibid.*, p. 50.

11 *Ibid.*, p. 168.

12 *Ibid.*, p. 169.

13 *Ibid.*, p. 235.

14 Andrew Feenberg, *Lukács, Marx and the Sources of Critical Theory*, New York and Oxford: Oxford University Press, 1981, and Robert Pippin, Andrew Feenberg and Charles P. Weber, *Marcuse: Critical Theory and the Promise of Utopia*, Bergin & Garvey, 1986.

15 Richard Wolin (ed.), *The Heidegger Controversy: A Critical Reader*, Cambridge, MA: MIT Press, 1993, p. xi.

16 Takeuchi's essay may be found in Tetsutarō Kawakami and Yoshimi Takeuchi (eds), *Kindai no Chōkoku*, Tokyo: Tomiyama-sho, 1979, pp. 273–341.

17 *Ibid.*, p. 182.

18 This gap in understanding is painfully on display in Richard Wolin's bitter criticism of Derrida in 'Note on a Missing Text', the preface to the MIT edition of Wolin, *op. cit.*, pp. ix–xx.

19 Mexico was an Allied power, but the impact of Pacific War orthodoxy has been far less great there than among the 'White' Anglo-Allies.

20 'The Return of the Past', in Heisig and Maraldo, *op. cit.*, p. 137.

11 Nazism is no excuse: after Farías – the Allied Gaze and the second crisis (1997–2002)

1 *The Betrayal of the Intellectuals* (*La Trahison des Clercs*), trans. Richard Aldington, New York and London: W.W. Norton & Co., 1969, p. 27.
2 James W. Heisig and John C. Maraldo (eds), *Rude Awakenings: Zen, the Kyoto School and the Question of Nationalism*, Honolulu: University of Hawaii Press, 1994.
3 For a devastating attack on the neo-Marxist position, see William R. LaFleur, 'A Half-dressed Emperor: Societal Self-deception and Recent "*Japanokritik*" in America', in Roger T. Ames and Wimal Dissanayake (eds) *Self and Deception: A Cross-cultural Philosophical Enquiry*, Albany, NY: State University of New York Press, 1996, pp. 263–285.
4 In this genre of failure, the best-known text is Tetsuo Najita and H.D. Harootunian, 'Japanese Revolt against the West: Political and Cultural Criticism in the Twentieth Century', in Peter Duus (ed.) *The Cambridge History of Japan*, Vol. VI, Cambridge University Press, pp. 711–774. This essay and other examples of neo-Marxist *Japanokritik* are analysed in detail in Chapter 4 above.
5 Andrew Feenberg, 'The Problem of Modernity in the Philosophy of Nishida', in Heisig and Maraldo, *op. cit.*, pp. 151–173.
6 *Ibid.*, p. 151.
7 Naoki Sakai, 'Ethnicity and Species: On the Philosophy of the Multi-ethnic State in Japanese Imperialism', *Radical Philosophy* 95 (May–June 1996): 33–45; Graham Parkes, review of Leslie Pincus's *Authenticating Culture in Imperial Japan: Kuki Shūzō and the Rise of National Aesthetics* (1996), in *Chanoyu Quarterly* 86 (1997); Christopher S. Jones, 'Politicizing Travel and Climatizing Philosophy: Watsuji, Montesquieu and the European Tour', *Japan Forum* 14(1) (2002): 41–62.
8 For the original Japanese-language text of The Ōshima Memos, see Ryōsuke Ōhashi, Kyōtō-gakuha to Nippon Kaigun: Shin Shiryō 'Ōshima Memos' o Megutte (The Kyoto School and the Japanese Navy: On the New Historical Documents, The Ōshima Memos), Tokyo: PHP, 2001.
9 Feenberg, *op. cit.*, p. 151 n. 1. For more about the problematic nature of Dale as a source on the Kyoto School, see Chapter 7 above.
10 On Yanaihara, see Susan C. Townsend, *Yanaihara Tadao and Japanese Colonial Policy: Redeeming Empire*, Richmond, Surrey: Curzon Press, 2000.
11 Feenberg, *op. cit.*, p. 152.
12 Feenberg cites Harootunian's essay 'Visible Discourses/Invisible Ideologies', in Masao Miyoshi and H.D. Harootunian (eds) *Postmodernism and Japan*, Durham, NC, and London: Duke University Press, 1989, pp. 63–92, and 'Japan's Revolt against the West' (see note 4 above), but the inaccuracies and thin textual basis of these articles mean they do not qualify as sound empirical sources on the thought and actions of the wartime Kyoto School.
13 James W. Heisig, *Philosophers of Nothingness: An Essay on the Kyoto School*, Honolulu: University of Hawaii Press, 2001.
14 Edward W. Said, *Orientalism*, Harmondsworth: Penguin, 1985.
15 In my review in *The Japan Times*, I concluded that 'Heisig has provided us with the intellectual equivalent of one-stop shopping. *Philosophers of Nothingness* allows the curious reader to take his bearings, quickly and confidently, on the Kyoto School. The result is a formidable research resource.' The wartime Kyoto School aside, I stand by this conclusion.
16 Heisig, *op. cit.*, p. 38.
17 *Ibid.*, pp. 8–9.
18 *Ibid.*, p. 9.

19 *Ibid.*, p. 65.
20 *Ibid.*, p. 6. Italics in the original.
21 *Ibid.*, p. 122.
22 *Ibid.*, p. 122.
23 To be fair, Mark Lilla has rightly called attention to the reprehensible anti-Semitic streak in Schmitt's occasional writings in *The Reckless Mind: Intellectuals in Politics*, New York: New York Review Books, 2001. Schmitt's comments on Jews are beyond the pale. But Schmitt's anti-Semitism is not why he is admired and studied today more closely than ever by a growing army of readers worldwide. The refusal to acknowledge the power of Schmitt's philosophy explains why Lilla's summary of this great German thinker's thought and career is unbalanced and distorted. Lilla is right to be angry with Schmitt, but being angry is rarely a formula for reading a major thinker properly. Furthermore, the moral blindness of American exceptionalism and Euro-hate undermines Lilla's reading of almost all the thinkers treated in his book.
24 Heisig, *op. cit.*, p. 123.
25 *Ibid.*, pp. 314–315.
26 *Ibid.*, p. 315.
27 *Dreams of Difference: The Japan Romantic School and the Crisis of Modernity*, Berkeley, Los Angeles and London: University of California Press, 1994.
28 Robert Bernasconi, 'Will the Real Kant Please Stand Up: The Challenge of Enlightenment Racism to the Study of the History of Philosophy', *Radical Philosophy* 117 (January–February 2003): 14.
29 *Ibid.*, p. 15.
30 *Ibid.*, p. 14.
31 *Ibid.*, p. 14.
32 Richard Wolin, *The Politics of Being: The Political Thought of Martin Heidegger*, New York: Columbia University Press, 1990, and Heidegger's Children: Hannah Arendt, Karl Löwith, Hans Jonas and Herbert Marcuse, Princeton, NJ: Princeton University Press, 2003.
33 Miguel de Beistegui, *Heidegger and the Political: Dystopias*, London and New York: Routledge, 1998, pp. ix–x.
34 *Ibid.*, p. x.
35 Note, further, that while Allied conduct can be forcefully and convincingly defended in the name of nationalist or racial necessity, no defence is possible on liberal moral grounds. This is the true desolation of the case. For decades, I have written and lectured in the public sphere guided by the assumption that 'the Japanese brought the catastrophe of war on themselves'. The scales fell from my eyes only with the ugly controversy over the Smithsonian *Enola Gay* exhibition, but the groundwork for my awakening, my very own *tenkō*, had been prepared by the moral debacle of the American war in Vietnam.

12 Nothing shall be spared: a manifesto on the future of Japan studies

1 Karl Löwith, 'Afterword to the Japanese Reader', *Martin Heidegger and European Nihilism*, trans. Gary Steiner, New York: Columbia University Press, 1995, p. 233.
2 The contest between the Enlightenment and Romanticism is not an uneven struggle. See, for example, Isaiah Berlin's *The Roots of Romanticism*, where he vigorously defends the Enlightenment but concedes that Romanticism is 'the greatest transformation in modern European history'.

3 Alberto Moreiras, *The Exhaustion of Difference: The Politics of Latin American Cultural Studies*, Durham, NC, and London: Duke University Press, 2001, p. 14.
4 For details about the fate of John Davies, see David Halberstam, *The Best and the Brightest*, New York: Modern Library, 2001.
5 R.T. Murphy, 'Looking to Game Boy', *London Review of Books*, 3 January 2002, pp. 32–35.
6 *Ibid.*, pp. 32 and 33.
7 *Ibid.*, p. 32.
8 *Ibid.*, p. 32.
9 *Ibid.*, p. 34. See Marius Jansen, *The Making of Modern Japan*, Harvard, MA: Harvard University Press, 2000.
10 Murphy, *op. cit.*, p. 34.
11 Personal communication.
12 Max Weber, 'Wissenschaft als Beruf', *Gesammelte Aufsaetze zur Wissenschftslehre*, Tübinger, 1922, pp. 524–555. An English translation may be found in H.H. Gerth and C. Wright Mills (eds), *From Max Weber: Essays in Sociology*, New York: Oxford University Press, 1946, pp. 129–156.
13 *Ibid.*, p. 145.
14 *Ibid.*, p. 147.
15 The six volumes, all published by Princeton University Press, were: Marius B. Jansen (ed.), *Changing Japanese Attitudes toward Modernization*; William W. Lockwood (ed.), *The State and Economic Enterprise in Japan*; R.P. Dore (ed.), *Aspects of Social Change in Modern Japan*; Robert E. Ward (ed.), *Political Development in Modern Japan*; Donald H. Shively (ed.), *Tradition and Modernization in Japanese Culture*; and James W. Morley (ed.), *Dilemmas of Growth in Prewar Japan*.
16 Löwith, *op. cit.* Löwith's quotation reads in translation 'In fact critique is the principle underlying our progress, to the extent it dissolves and propels, step by step, whatever exists.'
17 See Friedrich Nietzsche, *Beyond Good and Evil: Prelude to a Philosophy of the Future*, trans. Walter Kaufman, New York: Random House, 1966.
18 Isaiah Berlin, 'European Unity and its Vicissitudes', *The Crooked Timber of Humanity*, ed. Henry Hardy, London: John Murray, 1990, p. 198. Berlin is writing about Marxism, but his remark can be applied to the realities of the ethnic cleansing of North America with equal force. In the second part of the quotation, the word 'this' has replaced the word 'the' in the original.
19 This argument informs much of the analysis of the war developed in Yoshimi Takeuchi's essay 'Kindai no Chōkoku', in Tetsutarō Kawakami and Yoshimi Takeuchi (eds) *Kindai no Chōkoku*, Tokyo: Tomiyama-sho, 1979.
20 John W. Dower, *War without Mercy: Race and Power in the Pacific War*, New York: Pantheon Books, 1986.
21 George Steiner, *In Bluebeard's Castle: Some Notes Towards the Re-definition of Culture*, London/New Haven, CT: Faber & Faber/Yale University Press, 1971, p. 32.
22 Honolulu: University of Hawaii Press, 1988.
23 Quoted by Henry Scott Stokes as a quotation in an essay by Yukio Mishima, in *The Life and Death of Yukio Mishima*, Tokyo: Charles E. Tuttle, 1975, pp. 224–225.
24 Frantz Fanon, 'Preface', *Studies in a Dying Colonialism* (*L'An Cinq de la Revolution Algerienne*), trans. Haakon Chevalier, London: Penguin, 1959, p. 24.
25 Tokyo: PHP Kenkyūjo, 1998.
26 See Sakai's pioneering revisionist interpretation of Kōsaka and Kōyama developed in 'Modernity and its Critique: The Problem of Universalism and Particularism', in Masao Miyoshi and H.D. Harootunian (eds) *Postmodernism*

and Japan, Durham, NC, and London: Durham University Press, 1989, pp. 93–122.

27 Tanabe Hajime, *Shu no Ronri*, *Tanabe Hajime Zenshū* 6–7, Tokyo: Chikuma Shobō, 1963; Kōyama Iwao, *Sekai-shi no Tetsugaku*, Tokyo: Iwanami Shoten, 1942; Kōsaka Masaaki, *Rekishi-teki Sekai, Zoku: Rekishi-teki Sekai, Kōsaka Masaaki Chosakushū*, 1, Tokyo: Risō-sha, 1964.

28 Frederic Jameson, 'Foreword', in Jean-François Lyotard, *The Postmodern Condition: A Report on Knowledge*, trans. Geoff Bennington and Brian Massumi, Minneapolis: University of Minnesota Press, 1984, p. ix.

29 Giovanna Borradori, *The American Philosopher: Conversations with Quine, Davidson, Putnam, Nozick, Danto, Rorty, Cavell, MacIntyre, and Kuhn*, Chicago and London: University of Chicago Press, 1994, pp. 109–110.

30 *Ibid.*, pp. 103–118. The title of Borradori's interview with Rorty is 'After Philosophy, Democracy'.

Appendix: 'The Philosophy of Crisis or a Crisis in Philosophy: Reflections on Heidegger's Rectoral Address' (1933)

1 Although published in the pages of *Asahi Shinbun*, the Tokyo daily, over three days in the autumn of 1933, the version of 'Kiki no Tetsugaku ka Tetsugaku no Kiki ka' that appears in *Tanabe Hajime Zenshū* 8: 3–9 has been used for this translation. Note that the title of this essay is Tanabe's but I have added the subtitle for a Western audience unlikely to be familiar with Tanabe's work.

2 Words in round brackets, ( ), are Tanabe's; those in square brackets, [ ], are the translator's.

Appendix: 'On the Logic of Co-prosperity Spheres: Towards a Philosophy of Regional Blocs' (1942)

1 This text was discovered among the papers left by Yasumasa Ōshima, and published as part of *The Ōshima Memos* by Ryōsuke Ōhashi in *Kyōtō-gakuha to Nippon Kaigun: Shin Shiryō 'Ōshima Memos' o Megutte* (*The Kyoto School and the Japanese Navy: On the New Historical Documents*, The Oshima Memos), Tokyo: PHP, 2001, pp. 227–244. It does not appear in *Tanabe Hajime Zenshū*. Note that the title of this essay is Tanabe's but I have added the subtitle for a Western audience unlikely to be familiar with Tanabe's work.

2 Words in round brackets, ( ), are Tanabe's; those in square brackets, [ ], are the translator's.

3 Translator's note: In *A Kant Dictionary* (Oxford: Blackwell, 1995), Howard Caygill notes that 'the idea is a concept of reason whose object can be met with nowhere in experience' (p. 236).

4 Translator's note: From 'scheme', Greek for 'form'. In this context, the term 'schema' refers to a system of abstract reasoning that proposes a decisive argument about the nature of the question at issue. But, as is so often the case in Tanabe, the meaning of 'schema' in Kant's philosophy should be kept in the back of the reader's mind: 'a rule or principle that enables the understanding to apply its categories and unify experience' (*Collins English Dictionary*). The point that should be evident throughout this piece by Tanabe is that he is heir to the metaphysical revolution launched by Fichte and Schelling that transformed the most vital metaphysical ideas from their use as precision tools of the spirit until Kant

to the dynamic forces that they become in Hegel. After Fichte, metaphysical ideas perform on the page less like machine tools and more like the characters of a novel. Hence the commonplace comparison between Hegel and Tolstoy.

5 One of the implications of Tanabe's cyclical dynamic is that given the shifting power bases of national strength, the so-called leading nation-state may over time be replaced by one or more of the so-called follower states.

Select bibliography

Abbreviations

NKC   *Nishitani Keiji Chosakushū* (*The Collected Works of Keiji Nishitani*) Tokyo: Sōbun Shuppan, 1987.

THZ   *Tanabe Hajime Zenshū* (*The Complete Works of Hajime Tanabe*), Tokyo: Chikuma Shobō, 1963.

Ames, Roger T. and Dissanayake, Wimal (eds) *Self and Deception: A Cross-cultural Philosophical Enquiry*, Albany, NY: State University of New York Press, 1996.

Anderson, Benedict, *The Spectre of Comparison: Nationalism, Southeast Asia and the World*, London: Verso, 1999.

Aoki, Tamotsu, 'Bunka no Hiteisei' ('Culture as Negation'), *Chūō Kōron*, 1987.

Asada, Sadao, 'Japanese Perceptions of the A-Bomb Decision 1945–1980', in Joe C. Dixon (ed.) *The American Military and the Far East*, Washington: Government Publications Office, 1980.

Beevor, Antony, *Berlin: The Downfall 1945*, London: Viking, 2002.

Benda, Julien, *The Betrayal of the Intellectuals* (*La Trahison des Clercs, 1927*), trans. Richard Aldington, New York and London: W.W. Norton & Co., 1969.

Bergson, Henri, *Les Deux Sources de la Morale et de la Religion*, Paris: Librairie Félix Alcan, 1932. In English: *The Two Sources of Morality and Religion*, trans. R. Ashley Audra and Cloudesley Brereton, Notre Dame, IN: University of Notre Dame Press, 1977 (reprint).

Berlin, Isaiah, 'European Unity and its Vicissitudes', in *The Crooked Timber of Humanity*, ed. Henry Hardy, London: John Murray, 1990.

—— *The Roots of Romanticism*, Princeton, NJ: Princeton University Press, 1999.

Bernasconi, Robert, 'Will the Real Kant Please Stand Up: The Challenge of Enlightenment Racism to the Study of the History of Philosophy', *Radical Philosophy* 117 (January–February 2003).

Beruguson, *Dōtoku-Shūkyō no Futatsu Gensen*, trans. Kōji Hirayama, Tokyo: Shiba Shoten, 1936.

Bird, Kai and Lifschultz, Lawrence (eds), *Hiroshima Shadows: Writing on the Denial of History and the Smithsonian Controversy*, Stony Creek, CT: Pamphleteer's Press, 1998.

Bix, Herbert, *Hirohito and the Making of Modern Japan*, New York: Harper, 2001.

Borradori, Giovanna, *The American Philosopher: Conversations with Quine, Davidson, Putnam, Nozick, Danto, Rorty, Cavell, MacIntyre, and Kuhn*, Chicago and London: University of Chicago Press, 1994

Chamberlain, Lesley, *Nietzsche in Turin: An Intimate Biography*, New York: Picador, 1996.

Clarke, D.S., Jr, 'Introduction', in Keiji Nishitani, *Nishida Kitarō*, trans. Seisaku Yamamoto and James W. Heisig, Berkeley: University of California Press, 1991.

Cohen, Mitchell, *The Wager of Lucien Goldmann: Tragedy, Dialectics, and a Hidden God*, Princeton, NJ: Princeton University Press, 1994.

Connors, Lesley, *The Emperor's Adviser: Saionji Kinmochi and Prewar Japanese Politics*, London: Croom Helm, 1987.

Dale, Peter, *The Myth of Japanese Uniqueness*, London and Oxford: Croom Helm and the Nissan Institute of Japanese Studies, 1986.

de Beistegui, Miguel, *Heidegger and the Political: Dystopias*, London and New York: Routledge, 1998.

Derrida, Jacques, *De l'esprit*, Editions Galilée, 1987. In English: *Of Spirit: Heidegger and the Question*, trans. Geoffrey Bennington and Rachel Bowlby, Chicago: University of Chicago Press, 1989.

Diggins, John Patrick, *The Promise of Pragmatism: Modernism and the Crisis of Knowledge and Authority*, Chicago and London: University of Chicago Press, 1991.

Dixon, Joe C. (ed.), *The American Military and the Far East*, Washington: Government Publications Office, 1980.

Doak, Kevin Michael, *Dreams of Difference: The Japan Romantic School and the Crisis of Modernity*, Berkeley, Los Angeles and London: University of California Press, 1994.

—— 'Nationalism as Dialectics: Ethnicity, Moralism, and the State in Early Twentieth-century Japan', in James W. Heisig and John C. Maraldo (eds) *Rude Awakenings: Zen, the Kyoto School and the Question of Nationalism*, Honolulu: University of Hawaii Press, 1994, pp. 174–196.

Dower, John W., *Empire and Aftermath: Yoshida Shigeru and the Japanese Experience, 1878–1954*, Cambridge, MA: Harvard University Press, 1988.

—— *War without Mercy: Race and Power in the Pacific War*, New York: Pantheon Books, 1986.

Dryburgh, Marjorie, *North China and Japanese Expansion, 1933–1937: Regional Power and the National Interest*, Richmond, Surrey: Curzon, 2000.

Dumoulin, Heinrich, Fr, *Zen Buddhism: A History (Japan)*, 2nd edn, trans. Paul F. Knitter, New York: Simon & Schuster, 1989.

—— *Zen Buddhism in the 20th Century*, trans. Joseph O'Leary, New York: Weatherhill, 1992.

Duus, Peter (ed.), *The Cambridge History of Japan*, Vol. VI, *The Twentieth Century*, Cambridge: Cambridge University Press, 1988.

Fanon, Fritz, *L'An Cinq de la Revolution Algerienne* (*Studies in a Dying Colonialism*), trans. Haakon Chevalier, London: Penguin, 1959.

Farías, Victor, 'Foreword to the Spanish Edition, *Heidegger and Nazism*', in Tom Rockmore and Joseph Margolis (eds) *The Heidegger Case: On Philosophy and Politics*, Philadelphia: Temple University Press, 1992, pp. 333–347.

—— *Heidegger et le nazisme*, Paris: Éditions Verdier, 1987. In English: *Heidegger and Nazism*, trans. Joseph Margolis and Tom Rockmore, Philadelphia: Temple University Press, 1989.

Faure, Bernard, *Chan Insights and Oversights: An Epistemological Critique of the Chan Tradition*, Princeton, NJ: Princeton University Press, 1996.

Feenberg, Andrew, *Lukács, Marx and the Sources of Critical Theory*, New York and Oxford: Oxford University Press, 1986.

—— 'The Problem of Modernity in the Philosophy of Nishida', in James W. Heisig and John C. Maraldo (eds) *Rude Awakenings: Zen, the Kyoto School and the Question of Nationalism*, Honolulu: University of Hawaii Press, 1994, pp. 151–173. (*See also* Pippin, Robert, Feenberg, Andrew and Weber, Charles P.)

Ferry, Luc and Renaut, Alain, *Heidegger et les Modernes*, Paris: Éditions Grasset & Fasquelle, 1988. In English: *Heidegger and Modernity*, trans. Franklin Philip, Chicago: University of Chicago Press, 1990.

Garth, H.H. and Mills, C. Wright (eds), *From Max Weber: Essays in Sociology*, New York: Oxford University Press, 1946.

Gayle, Curtis Anderson, *Marxist History and Postwar Japanese Nationalism*, London: RoutledgeCurzon, 2003.

Goldmann, Lucien, *Lukács et Heidegger*, Paris: Editions Denoël, 1973. In English: *Lukács and Heidegger: Towards a New Philosophy*, trans. Williams Q. Boelhower, London: Routledge and Kegan Paul, 1973.

Gregor, A. James, *Giovanni Gentile: Philosopher of Fascism*, New Brunswick, NJ: Transaction Publishers, 2001.

Halberstam, David, *The Best and the Brightest*, New York: Modern Library, 2001.

Harootunian, Harry, *Overcome by Modernity: History, Culture and Community in Interwar Japan*, Princeton and Oxford: Princeton University Press, 2000.

—— 'Visible Discourses/Invisible Ideologies', in Masao Miyoshi and H.D. Harootunian (eds), *Postmodernism and Japan*, Durham, NC, and London: Duke University Press, 1989, pp. 63–92. (*See also* Najita, Tetsuo and Harootunian, Harry; Miyoshi, Masao and Harootunian, H.D.)

Hegel, Georg Wilhelm Friedrich, *The Philosophy of World History*, trans. J. Sibree, New York: Dover Publications, 1956.

Heidegger, Martin, *Brief über den Humanismus*, in *Wegmarken*, Frankfurt am Main: Vittorio Klostermann Verlag, 1967, pp. 145–194. In English: *Letter on Humanism*, trans. Frank A. Capuzzi and J. Glenn Gray, in David Farrell Krell (ed.) *Martin Heidegger Basic Writings*, New York: Harper & Row, 1977, pp. 189–246.

—— *Die Selbstbehauptung der deutschen Universität*, Breslau: Korn Verlag, 1933 (see also *Die Selbstbehauptung der deutsche Universität/Das Rektorat, 1933/34*, Frankfurt am Main: Vittorio Klostermann, 1990). In English: 'The Self-assertion of the German University', trans. Williams S. Lewis, in Richard Wolin (ed.) *The Heidegger Controversy: A Critical Reader*, Cambridge, MA: MIT Press, 1993, pp. 29–39.

—— *Einführung in die Metaphysik*, Tübingen: Max Niemeyer, 1935. In English: *An Introduction to Metaphysics*, trans. Ralph Manheim, New Haven, CT, and London: Yale University Press, 1959.

—— *Hegels Phänomenologie des Geistes*, Frankfurt am Main: Vittorio Klostermann, 1980. In English: *Hegel's Phenomenology of Spirit*, trans. Parvis Emad and Kenneth Maly, Bloomington and Indianapolis: Indiana University Press, 1988.

—— *Sein und Zeit*, 7th edn, Tübingen: Neomarius Verlag (first published 1927). In English: *Being and Time*, trans. John Macquarrie and Edward Robinson, San Francisco: Harper, 1962.

—— [For Heidegger–Marcuse correspondence *see* Marcuse, Herbert.]

Heisig, James W., *Filósofos de la nada: Un ensayo sobre la escuela de Kioto*, Barcelona: Editorial Herder, 2001. In English: *Philosophers of Nothingness: An*

Essay on the Kyoto School, trans. James W. Heisig, Honolulu: University of Hawaii Press, 2001.

—— 'Foreword', in Hajime Tanabe, *Philosophy as Metanoetics*, trans. Yoshinori Takeuchi, Berkeley, Los Angeles and London: University of California Press, 1986, pp. vii–xxx.

—— 'Tanabe's Logic of the Specific [*sic*] and the Spirit of Nationalism', in James W. Heisig and John C. Maraldo (eds) *Rude Awakenings: Zen, the Kyoto School and the Question of Nationalism*, Honolulu: University of Hawaii Press, 1994, pp. 255–288.

Heisig, James W. and Maraldo, John C. (eds), *Rude Awakenings: Zen, the Kyoto School and the Question of Nationalism*, Honolulu: University of Hawaii Press, 1994.

Hime, Kiyoshi, *Tanabe Tetsugaku Kenkyū: Shūkyō Tetsugaku no Kanten kara* (*Studies in Tanabe Philosophy: From the Perspective of Religious Philosophy*), Tokyo: Hokuju Shuppan, 1990.

Hiromatsu, Wataru, *<Kindai no Chōkoku> Ron: Shōwa Shisō-shi e no ichi Shikaku* (*On 'Overcoming Modernity': One Perspective on the Intellectual History of the Showa Period*), Tokyo: Kōdansha, 1989.

—— (ed. and trans.), *Die Deutsche Ideologie, 1. Band, 1. Abschnitt*, by Karl Marx and Friedrich Engels, Tokyo: Kawade Shobo, 1974.

Horio, Tsutomu, 'The *Chūōkōron* Discussions, their Background and Meaning', trans. Thomas Kirchner, in James W. Heisig and John C. Maraldo (eds) *Rude Awakenings: Zen, the Kyoto School and the Question of Nationalism*, Honolulu: University of Hawaii Press, 1994, pp. 289–315.

Hughes, H. Stuart, *The Consciousness and Society: The Reorientation of European Social Thought, 1890–1930*, Brighton: Harvester Press, 1979 (reprint).

Ives, Christopher, 'Ethical Pitfalls in Imperial Zen and Nishida Philosophy: Ichikawa Hakugen's Critique', in James W. Heisig and John C. Maraldo (eds) *Rude Awakenings: Zen, the Kyoto School and the Question of Nationalism*, Honolulu: University of Hawaii Press, 1994, pp. 16–39.

Jacinto, Agustin Zavala, 'The Return of the Past: Tradition and the Political Microcosm in the Later Nishida', in James W. Heisig and John C. Maraldo (eds) *Rude Awakenings: Zen, the Kyoto School and the Question of Nationalism*, Honolulu: University of Hawaii Press, 1994, pp. 132–148.

Jameson, Frederic, 'Foreword', in Jean-François Lyotard, *The Postmodern Condition: A Report on Knowledge*, trans. Geoff Bennington and Brian Massumi, Minneapolis: University of Minnesota Press, 1984, pp. vii–xxi.

Jansen, Marius, *The Making of Modern Japan*, Cambridge, MA: Harvard University Press, 2000.

—— (ed.), *Studies in the Modernization of Japan*, 6 vols: Jansen, M. (ed.), *Changing Japanese Attitudes Toward Modernization*; Lockwood, William W. (ed.), *The State and Economic Enterprise in Japan*; Dore, R.P. (ed.), *Aspects of Social Change in Modern Japan*; Ward, Robert E. (ed.), *Political Development in Modern Japan*; Shively, Donald H. (ed.), *Tradition and Modernization in Japanese Culture*; Morley, James W. (ed.), *Dilemmas of Growth in Prewar Japan*, Princeton, NJ: Princeton University Press, 1965–71.

Jenkins, Roy, *Churchill*, London: Macmillan, 2001.

Johnson, Chalmers, *Blowback: The Causes and Consequences of American Empire*, New York: Henry Holt & Co., 2000.

—— 'The Looting of Asia', *London Review of Books*, 20 November 2003, pp. 3–6.

—— *MITI and the Japanese Miracle: The Growth of Industrial Policy, 1925–1975*, Stanford, CA: Stanford University Press, 1982.

—— *The Sorrows of Empire: Militarism, Secrecy and the End of the Republic*, New York: Metropolitan Books, 2004.

Jones, Christopher S., *Ideas at War: Nishida Kitarō and the Philosophical Context of the Co-prosperity Sphere* (forthcoming).

—— 'Politicizing Travel and Climatizing Philosophy: Watsuji, Montesquieu and the European Tour', *Japan Forum* 14(1) (2002).

Jünger, Ernst, 'Totale Mobilmachung', in *Krieg und Krieger*, Berlin: Junker und Dünnhaupt, 1930. In English: 'Total Mobilization', trans. Joel Golb and Richard Wolin, in Richard Wolin (ed.) *The Heidegger Controversy: A Critical Reader*, Cambridge, MA: MIT Press, 1993, pp. 119–139.

Karatani, Kōjin, 'Nihon Shisō wa Kokkyō o Koerareru ka' ('Is Japanese Thought Exportable?'), interview with Toshiaki Kobayashi, *Shūkan Dokusho-jin*, 4 July 2003, pp. 1–2.

—— (hen, chō) *Shinpojiumu*, Tokyo: Shichō-sha, 1989.

Kawakami, Tetsutarō and Takeuchi, Yoshimi (eds), *Kindai no Chōkoku* (*Overcoming Modernity*) Tokyo: Tomiyama-sho, 1979.

Kennedy, Malcolm D., *The Estrangement of Great Britain and Japan, 1917–35*, Berkeley and Los Angeles: University of California Press, 1969.

Kersten, Rikki, *Democracy in Postwar Japan: Maruyama Masao and the Search for Autonomy*, London: Routledge, 1996.

Kobayashi, Toshiaki, interviewed by Kōjin Karatani, 'Nihon Shisō wa Kokkyō o Koerareru ka' ('Is Japanese Thought Exportable?'), *Shūkan Dokusho-jin*, 4 July 2003, pp. 1–2.

Kōsaka, Masaaki, *Minzoku no Tetsugaku* (*The Philosophy of the Nation*), Tokyo: Iwanani Shoten, 1942.

—— *Nishida Kitarō to Watsuji Tetsurō* (*Kitarō Nishida and Tetsurō Watsuji*), Tokyo: Shinchō-sa, 1964.

—— *Rekishi-teki Sekai, Zoku: Rekishi-teki Sekai, Kōsaka Masaaki Chosakushū*, 1 (*The Historical World, The Historical World – A Sequel, The Collected Works of Masaaki Kōsaka*), Tokyo: Risō-sha, 1964.

Kōsaka, Masaaki, Nishitani, Keiji, Kōyama, Iwao and Suzuki, Shigetaka, *Sekai-shi-teki Tachiba to Nippon* (*The Standpoint of World History and Japan*), Tokyo: Chūō Kōron-sha, 1943.

—— 'Sōryoku-sen no Tetsugaku' ('The Philosophy of Total War/Resistance'), *Chūō Kōron* (January 1943): 54–112.

Kōsaka, Masaaki, Suzuki, Shigetaka, Kōyama, Iwao and Nishitani, Keiji, 'Sekai-shi-teki Tachiba to Nippon' ('The Standpoint of World History and Japan'), *Chūō Kōron* (January 1942): 150–192.

Kōsaka, Masaaki, Suzuki, Shigetaka, Nishitani, Keiji and Kōyama, Iwao, 'Tō-A Kyōeiken no Ronri-sei and Rekiski-sei' ('The Ethical and Historical Character of the East Asian Co-prosperity Sphere'), *Chūō Kōron* (April 1942): 120–161.

Koschman, J. Victor, *Revolution and Subjectivity in Postwar Japan*, Chicago and London: University of Chicago Press, 1996.

Kōyama, Iwao, *Sekai-shi no Tetsugaku* (*The Philosophy of World History*), Tokyo: Iwanami Shoten, 1942 (new edition, ed. Hidefumi Hanazawa, Tokyo: Kobushi Shobō, 2001).

Lacoue-Labarthe, Philippe, *La Fiction du politique: Heidegger, l'art et la politique*, Paris: Christian Bourgois, 1987.

LaFleur, William R., 'A Half-dressed Emperor: Societal Self-deception and Recent "*Japanokritik*" in America', in Roger T. Ames and Wimal Dissanayake (eds.) *Self and Deception: A Cross-cultural Philosophical Enquiry*, Albany, NY: State University of New York Press, 1996, pp. 263–285.

Lieven, Anatole, 'The Push for War', *London Review of Books*, 3 October 2002, pp. 8–11.

Lilla, Mark, *The Reckless Mind: Intellectuals in Politics*, New York: New York Review of Books, 2001.

Löwith, Karl, 'Afterword to the Japanese Reader', trans. Gary Steiner, in Richard Wolin, *Martin Heidegger and European Nihilism*, New York: Columbia University Press, 1995, pp. 228–234.

Lukács, George, *Chvostismus und Dialetik*, Budapest: Áron Verlag, 1996. In English: *A Defence of History and Class Consciousness*, trans. Esther Leslie, London and New York: Verso, 2000.

—— *Existentialisme ou Marxisme?*, Paris: Editions Nagel, 1947.

—— *Geschichte und Klassenbewusstein*, Berlin and Newied: Hermann Luchterhand Verlag, 1968. In English: *History and Class Consciousness: Studies in Marxist Dialectics*, trans. Rodney Livingstone, Cambridge, MA: MIT Press, 1971.

Lyotard, Jean-François, *The Postmodern Condition: A Report on Knowledge*, trans. Geoff Bennington and Brian Massumi, Minneapolis: University of Minnesota Press, 1984.

Macksey, Richard and Donato, Eugenio, *The Structuralist Controversy: The Language of Criticism and the Sciences of Man*, Baltimore and London: Johns Hopkins University Press, 1972.

McMullen, James, 'Ogyū Sorai and the Definition of Terms', *Japan Forum* 13(2) (2002): 249–265.

Maharidge, Dale, *The Coming White Minority: California, Multiculturalism, and America's Future*, New York:Vintage Books, 1999.

Maraldo, John C. *see* Heisig, James W. and Maraldo, John C.

Marcuse, Herbert/Heidegger, Martin, 'An Exchange of Letters', trans. Richard Wolin, in Richard Wolin (ed.) *The Heidegger Controversy: A Critical Reader*, Cambridge, MA: MIT Press, 1993, pp. 152–164.

Maruyama, Masao, '*Bunmeiron no Gaiyaku' o Yomu* (*Reading 'An Outline of Civilisation'*), *jo*, Tokyo: Iwamani Shoten, 1986.

May, Reinhard, *Heidegger's Hidden Sources: Some Asian Influences on His Work*, London: Routledge, 1996.

Miki, Kiyoshi, 'Haidegga to Tetsugaku no Unmei' ('Heidegger and the Fate of Philosophy'), *Serupan* (*Le Serpent*), November 1933.

Miller, Frank O., *Minobe Tatsukichi: Interpreter of Constitutionalism in Japan*, Berkeley and Los Angeles: University of California Press, 1965.

Minamoto, Ryōen, 'The Symposium on "Overcoming Modernity"', in James W. Heisig and John C. Maraldo (eds) *Rude Awakenings: Zen, the Kyoto School and the Question of Nationalism*, Honolulu: University of Hawaii Press, 1994, pp. 197–229.

Mine, Hideki, *Haidegga to Nihon no Tetsugaku* (*Heidegger and Japan Philosophy*), Tokyo: Minerubā Shobō, 2002.

Mitchell, Richard H., *Censorship in Imperial Japan*, Princeton, NJ: Princeton University Press, 1983.

Mitter, Rana, *The Manchurian Myth: Nationalism, Resistance, and Collaboration in Modern China*, Berkeley and Los Angeles: University of California Press, 2000.

Miyake, Yūjirō, 'The Introduction of Western Philosophy', in Count Shigenobu Okuma, *Fifty Years of the New Japan* (*Kaikoku Gojūnen Shi*), Vol. II, London: Smith, Edler & Co., 1909, pp. 226–241.

Miyoshi, Masao and Harootunian, H.D. (eds), *Postmodernism and Japan*, Durham, NC, and London: Duke University Press, 1989.

Moreiras, Alberto, *The Exhaustion of Difference: The Politics of Latin American Cultural Studies*, Durham, NC, and London: Duke University Press, 2001.

Morley, James W. (ed.), *Dilemmas of Growth in Prewar Japan*, Princeton, NJ: Princeton University Press, 1971.

Mosse, George L., *The Fascist Revolution: Toward a General Theory of Fascism*, New York: Howard Fertig, 1999.

Mouffe, Chantal (ed.), *Deconstruction and Pragmatism*, London: Routledge, 1996.

Murphy, R.T., 'Looking to Game Boy', *London Review of Books*, 3 January 2002, pp. 32–35.

Mutai, Risaku, *Basho no Roki-gaku* (*The Logic of Place*), ed. Hiroyuki Kitano, Tokyo: Kobushi Shobō, 1996 (first published 1944).

Najita, Tetsuo (ed.), *Tokugawa Political Writings: Cambridge Texts in Modern Politics*, Cambridge: Cambridge University Press, 1998.

Najita, Tetsuo and Harootunian, H.D., 'Japanese Revolt Against the West: Political and Cultural Criticism in the Twentieth Century', in Peter Duus (ed.) *The Cambridge History of Japan*, Vol. VI, *The Twentieth Century*, Cambridge: Cambridge University Press, 1988, pp. 711–774.

Nakazawa, Shinichi, *Philosophia Japonica*, Tokyo: Shūei-sha, 2001.

—— 'Tamashii no Kanto-shugisha: Tanabe Hajime' ('Tanabe Hajime: A Kantian of the Spirit'), interview, *Shūkan Dokushojin*, 6 April 2001, pp. 1–2.

Nietzsche, Friedrich, *Beyond Good and Evil: Prelude to a Philosophy of the Future*, trans. Walter Kaufman, New York: Random House, 1966.

Nishida, Kitarō, *Nishida Tetsugaku Senchū, Dai Go Kan, <Rekishi Tetsugaku> Ronbun-shū* (*Selected Readings in Nishida Philosophy*, Vol. V, *Essays in 'The Philosophy of History'*), ed. Nobuki Kagishi, Kyōtō: Tōei-sha, 1998.

Nishitani, Keiji, *Kongen-teki Shutaisei no Tetsugaku* (*The Philosophy of Foundational* [or *Primordial*] *Subjectivity*), NKC 1–2, Tokyo: Sōbun Shuppan, 1987.

—— *Nishida Kitarō: Sono Hito to Shisō* (*Kitarō Nishida: The Man and His Ideas*). In English: *Nishida Kitarō*, trans. Seisaku Yamamoto and James W. Heisig, Berkeley: University of California Press, 1991.

—— 'Reflections on Two Addresses by Martin Heidegger', in Graham Parkes (ed.) *Heidegger and Asian Thought*, Honolulu: University of Hawaii Press, 1987, pp. 145–154.

—— 'Shūkyū to wa Nani ka' ('What is Religion?'). In English: *Religion and Nothingness*, trans. Jan Van Bragt, Berkeley, Los Angeles and London: University of California Press, 1982.

Ōhashi, Ryōsuke, '"Kindai no Chōkoku" to Kyōtō-gakuha no Tetsugaku' ('"Overcoming Modernity" and the Philosophy of the Kyoto School'), in Niita Yoshihiro *et al.* (eds) *Datsuō no Shishō* (*Post-European Thought*), *Iwanami Kōza Gendai Shisō* (*Iwanami Course in Contemporary Thought*), Vol. XV, Tokyo: Iwanami Shoten, 1994, pp. 101–132.

—— *Kyōtō-gakuha to Nippon Kaigun: Shin Shiryō 'Ōshima Memos' o Megutte* (*The Kyoto School and the Japanese Navy: On the New Historical Documents,* The Ōshima Memos), Tokyo: PHP, 2001.

—— (ed.), *Kyōtō-gakuha no Shisō* (*The Thought of the Kyoto School*), forthcoming.

Okuma, Shigenobu, Count (ed.), *Fifty Years of the New Japan* (*Kaikoku Gojūnen Shi*), Vol. II, London: Smith, Edler & Co., 1909.

Ōshima, Yasumasa, 'Dai-tōa Sensō to Kyoto-gakuha – Chishiki-jin no Seiji Sanka ni Tsuite' ('The Greater East Asian War and the Kyoto School: The Political Involvement of Intellectuals'), *Chūō Kōron* 80 (August 1965).

—— *Kaisetsu* (commentary), *THZ* 7: 373–386.

—— *The Ōshima Memos,* reproduced in Ryōsuke Ōhashi, *Kyōtō-gakuha to Nippon Kaigun: Shin Shiryō 'Ōshima Memos' o Megutte* (*The Kyoto School and the Japanese Navy: On the New Historical Documents,* The Ōshima Memos), Tokyo: PHP, 2001.

Ott, Hugo, *Martin Heidegger: Unterwegs zu seiner Biographie*, Frankfurt: Campus Verlag, 1988. In English: *Martin Heidegger: A Political Life*, trans. Allan Blunden, London: Fontana Press, 1994.

Parkes, Graham, 'The Early Reception of Nietzsche's Philosophy in Japan', in Graham Parkes (ed.) *Nietzsche and Asian Thought*, Chicago and London: University of Chicago Press, 1996, pp. 177–199.

—— 'Introduction', in Graham Parkes (ed.) *Heidegger and Asian Thought*, Honolulu: University of Hawaii Press, 1987, pp. 1–14.

—— 'The Putative Fascism of the Kyoto School and the Political Correctness of the Modern Academy', *Philosophy East & West* 47(3) (July 1997).

—— review of Leslie Pincus's *Authenticating Culture in Imperial Japan: Kuki Shūzō and the Rise of National Aesthetics* (1996), in *Chanoyu Quarterly* 86 (1997).

—— 'Rising Sun over Black Forest', in Reinhard May, *Heidegger's Hidden Sources: Some East Asian Influences on His Work*, London: Routledge, 1996, pp. 79–117.

—— (ed.), *Heidegger and Asian Thought*, Honolulu: University of Hawaii Press, 1987.

—— (ed.), *Nietzsche and Asian Thought*, Chicago and London: University of Chicago Press, 1996.

Pippin, Robert, Feenberg, Andrew and Weber, Charles P., *Marcuse: Critical Theory and the Promise of Utopia*, New York: Bergin & Garvey, 1986. (*See also* Feenberg, Andrew.)

Ramos, Julio, *Desencuentros de la modernidad en América Latina: literatura y política en el siglo XIX*, Buenos Aires: Fondo de Cultura Economica, 1993. In English: *Divergent Modernities: Culture and Politics in Nineteenth-century Latin America*, trans. John D. Blanco, Durham, NC, and London: Duke University Press, 2001.

Reischauer, Edwin O., 'What Went Wrong?', in James W. Morley (ed.) *Dilemmas of Growth in Prewar Japan*, Princeton, NJ: Princeton University Press, 1971, pp. 489–510.

Rockmore, Tom and Margolis, Joseph (eds), *The Heidegger Case: On Philosophy and Politics*, Philadelphia: Temple University Press, 1992.

Roth, Michael S., *Knowing and History: Appropriations of Hegel in Twentieth-century France*, Ithaca and London: Cornell University Press, 1988.

Russell, John, *Francis Bacon*, London: Thames & Hudson, 1993.

Safranski, Rüdiger, *Ein Meister aus Deutschland: Heidegger und seine Zeit*, München Wien: Carl Hanser Verlag, 1994. In English: *Martin Heidegger: Between Good and*

Evil, trans. Ewald Osers, Cambridge, MA, and London: Harvard University Press, 1998.

Said, Edward W., *Orientalism*, Harmonsworth: Penguin Books, 1985.

Sakai, Naoki, 'Ethnicity and Species: On the Philosophy of the Multi-ethnic State in Japanese Imperialism', *Radical Philosophy* 95 (May–June 1999).

—— 'Modernity and its Critique: The Problem of Universalism and Particularism', in Masao Miyoshi and H.D. Hartoounian (eds) *Postmodernism and Japan*, Durham, NC, and London: Duke University Press, 1989, pp. 93–122.

—— 'Shakai Kagaku Hōhō Josetsu' ('Methods in Japanese Social Science: An Introduction'), *Iwanami Kōza Shakai Kagaku no Hōhō*, III, *Nihon Shakai Kagaku Shisō* (*Iwanami Course on Methods in Social Science*, Vol. III, *Japanese Social Science as Thought*), Tokyo: Iwanami Shoten, 1993.

Sakai, Naoki and Nishitani, Osamu, <*Sekai-shi*> *no Kaitai: Honyaku, Shutai, Rekishi* (*The Dissolution of 'World History': Translation, Subject, History*), Tokyo: Ibun-sha, 1999.

Sartre, Jean-Paul, 'The Respectable Prostitute' ('La Putain respectueuse'), in *In Camera and Other Plays*, trans. Kitty Black, London: Penguin, 1982.

Schain, Richard, *The Legend of Nietzsche's Syphilis*, Westport, CT: Greenwood Press, 2002.

Sharf, Robert H., 'Whose Zen? Zen Nationalism Revisited', in James W. Heisig and John C. Maraldo (eds) *Rude Awakenings: Zen, the Kyoto School and the Question of Nationalism*, Honolulu: University of Hawaii Press, 1994, pp. 40–51.

Shillony, Ben-Ami, *Politics and Culture in Wartime Japan*, Oxford: Clarendon Press, 1981.

Spector, Ronald H., *Eagle Against the Sun: The American War with Japan*, London: Cassell & Co., 2000.

Steiner, George, 'The Archives of Eden', *Salmagundi* 50–51 (Fall 1980–Winter 1981).

—— *Heidegger*, London/Glasgow: Fontana/Collins, 1978.

—— *In Bluebeard's Castle: Some Notes Towards the Re-definition of Culture*, London/New Haven, CT: Faber & Faber/Yale University Press, 1971.

—— *No Passion Spent, Essays 1978–1996*, London and Boston: Faber & Faber, 1996.

—— *On Difficulty and Other Essays*, Oxford: Oxford University Press, 1978.

Stinnett, Robert B., *Day of Deceit: The Truth about FDR and Pearl Harbor*, London: Constable, 2000.

Stokes, Henry Scott, *The Life and Death of Yukio Mishima*, Tokyo: Charles E. Tuttle, 1975.

Suro, Roberto, *Strangers Among Us: Latino Lives in a Changing America*, New York: Vintage, 1999.

Suzuki, Shigetaka, '<Kindai no Chōkoku> Oboegaki', *Bungakkai* (*Literary World*), October 1942, pp. 41–43.

—— *Yōroppa no Seiritsu-Sangyō Kakumei* (*The Formation of Europe; The Industrial Revolution*), Kyōtō Tetsugaku Sensho, Dai Roku-kan, Kyoto: Tōei-sha, 2000.

Takeuchi, Yoshimi, 'Kindai no Chōkoku', in Tetsutarō Kawakami and Yoshimi Takeuchi (eds) *Kindai no Chōkoku* (*Overcoming Modernity*), Tokyo: Tomiyama-sho, 1979, pp. 273–341.

—— 'Kindai to wa Nani-ka' ('What is Modernity?'), in *Takeuchi Yoshimi Zenshū* (*The Complete Works of Yoshimi Takeuchi*), Vol. IV, Tokyo: Chikuma Shobō, 1980.

Tanabe, Hajime, 'Genshōgaku ni okeru Atarashiki Tenkō' ('A New Direction/Apostasy in Phenomenology'), *THZ* 4: 17–34.

—— 'Kiki no Tetsugaku ka Tetsugaku no Kiki ka', *THZ* 8.

—— 'Kyōeiken no Ronri ni Tsuite' ('On the Logic of Co-prosperity Spheres') (1942), in Ryōsuke Ōhashi, *Kyōtō-gakuha to Nippon Kaigun: Shin Shiryō 'Ōshima Memos' o Megutte* (*The Kyoto School and the Japanese Navy: On the New Historical Documents,* The Ōshima Memos), Tokyo: PHP, 2001, pp. 227–244. In English: 'On the Logic of Co-prosperity Spheres: Towards a Philosophy of Regional Blocs', trans. David Williams, in Appendix to the present volume.

—— 'The Logic of the Species as Dialectics', trans. David Dilworth and Taira Satō, *Monumenta Nipponica* XXIV: 273–288.

—— *Shu no Ronri, THZ* 6–7.

—— *Sūri no Rekishishugi Tenkai* (*The Historicist Development of Mathematics*), *THZ* 12.

—— *Zange toshite no Tetsugaku*, Tokyo: Iwanami Shoten, 1946. In English: *Philosophy of Metanoetics*, trans. Yoshinori Takeuchi, Berkeley, Los Angeles and London: University of California Press, 1986.

—— 'Zushiki <Jikan> kara Zushiki <Sekai> e' ('From "Time" to the "World" as Schemas'), <*Shu no Ronri*> *Ronbun-shu, I, THZ* 6.

Townsend, Susan, *Yanaihara Tadao and Japanese Colonial Policy: Redeeming Empire*, London: Curzon, 2000.

Van Bragt, Jan, 'Kyoto Philosophy – Intrinsically Nationalistic?', in James W. Heisig and John C. Maraldo (eds) *Rude Awakenings: Zen, the Kyoto School and the Question of Nationalism*, Honolulu: University of Hawaii Press, 1994, pp. 233–254.

Vattimo, Gianni, *La fine della modernità*, Garzanti Editore s.p.a., 1985. In English: *The End of Modernity: Nihilism and Hermeneutics in Post-modern Culture*, trans. Jon R. Synder, London: Polity Press, 1988.

Wakeman, Frederic, Jr, 'A Revisionist View of the Nanjing Decade: Confucian Fascism', in Frederic Wakeman Jr and Richard Louis Edmonds (eds) *Reappraising Republican China*, New York: Oxford University Press, 2000, pp. 141–178.

Weber, Max, 'Wissenschaft als Beruf', *Gesammelte Aufsaetze zur Wissenschftslehre*, Tübingen, 1922 (a translation may be found in H.H. Gerth and C. Wright Mills (eds), *From Max Weber: Essays in Sociology*, New York: Oxford University Press, 1946).

West, Cornel, *The American Evasion of Philosophy: A Genealogy of Pragmatism*, Madison, WI: University of Wisconsin Press, 1989.

Wetzler, Peter, *Hirohito and War: Imperial Tradition and History Decision Making in Prewar Japan*, Honolulu: University of Hawaii Press, 1998.

White, Theodore H., *The Making of the President 1960*, New York: Atheneum House, 1961.

Williams, David, 'America as Japan Scholar to the World', Book Review, *Los Angeles Times*, August 1999, p. 2.

—— 'In Defence of the Kyoto School: Reflections on Philosophy, the Pacific War and the Making of a Post-White World', *Japan Forum* 12(2): 143–156.

—— *Japan and the Enemies of Open Political Science*, London and New York: Routledge, 1996.

—— 'Modernity, Harootunian and the Demands of Scholarship', *Japan Forum* 15(1) (2003): 147–162.

—— 'One-stop Shopping in the Kyoto School', review of *Philosophers of Nothingness: An Essay on the Kyoto School* by James W. Heisig, *The Japan Times*, 29 July
2001, p. 15.

Wolin, Richard, *Heidegger's Children: Hannah Arendt, Karl Löwith, Hans Jonas and
Herbert Marcuse*, Princeton, NJ: Princeton University Press, 2003.

—— *The Politics of Being: The Political Thought of Martin Heidegger*, New York:
Columbia University Press, 1990.

—— (ed.), *The Heidegger Controversy: A Critical Reader*, Cambridge, MA: MIT
Press, 1993.

Woodward, Bob, *Bush at War*, New York: Simon & Schuster, 2002.

Yusa, Michiko, 'Fashion and A-lētheia: Philosophical Integrity and War-time
Thought Control', *Hikaku Shisō Kenkyū* 16 (February 1990): 274–281.

—— 'Nishida and Totalitarianism: A Philosopher's Resistance', in James W. Heisig
and John C. Maraldo (eds) *Rude Awakenings: Zen, the Kyoto School and the
Question of Nationalism*, Honolulu: University of Hawaii Press, 1994, pp.
107–131.

—— 'Philosophy and Inflation: Miki Kiyoshi in Weimar Germany, 1922–24', *Monumenta Nipponica* 53(1).

Žižek, Slavoj, *Did Someone Say Totalitarianism? Five Interventions in the (Mis)use of
a Notion*, London and New York: Verso, 2001.

Index

Adorno, Theodor 42, 137, 172
Aeschylus 182
Afghanistan, US invasion of 5, 6
al-Qaeda 4–5, 32
Algeria 67
Algerian Revolution 44, 67, 138
Anderson, Benedict 75
Angel, Robert 48
Aoki, Tamotsu 36
Arendt, Hannah 117, 132, 145
Aristotle 90, 115, 184, 185
Aron, Raymond 135
Asada, Akira 59, 148
Asada, Sadao 14
Australia, racial demography 22
authority, and power 102, 104

balance of power 8–9
Bard, Alexander 109
Barthes, Roland 47
Beard, Charles 7
Beaufret, Jean 132
Beevor, Antony 125
Being, politics of (Heidegger) 115, 116, 119, 136, 140
Being and Time (*Sein und Zeit*) (Heidegger) 81–2, 84, 85, 86, 119, 133, 134, 135, 150
Bellah, Robert 48
Benda, Julien 115, 151
Benjamin, Walter 47
Bergson, Henri 67, 85, 90, 133, 157; 'spontaneous obedience' 102–5
Berlin, Isaiah 172
Bernasconi, Robert 161–2
'Biteki no Seikatsu Ronzu' (Chogyū) 53
Bix, Herbert 39, 49
Boas, Franz 34
Borradori, Giovanna 36

British Empire, rise and fall of 3
Bush, George H. W. 4
Bush, George W. 4, 7, 9

Calder, Kent 48, 176
Cambridge History of Japan, The 40, 47
Canada, racial demography 22
Celan, Paul 129
China 4, 39; emigration to USA 24; Japan's intervention 70
Chogyū (Takayama) 52–3, 54
Chomsky, Noam 7
Chūō Kōron 18, 21, 55, 62, 66, 69, 70, 72, 153
Chūō Kōron symposia 55–8
Chūō Kōron-sha 55
Churchill, Sir Winston 8
class tensions, Tanabe on 191–2
co-prosperity spheres 73–6, 195–9
Cold War, red purges 168
Colville, John 8
conflict, Tanabe on class tensions 191–2
Connors, Lesley 39
criticism, and good confronting evil 171–2
Croce, Benedetto 87, 90

Dale, Peter 93–4; *Myth of Japanese Uniqueness, The* 40–1, 92, 93, 103, 152; race 99
Danto, Arthur C. 36, 37
Darwin, Charles 93
Davies, John 168
De Beistegui, Miguel 162–3
De Man, Paul 33–4, 144, 147–8
death, Heidegger's treatment of 82
decolonialisation 36; anti-white resistance 31

deconstruction, de Man scandal, Farías
Affair and *Rude Awakenings* 147–9
Deleuze, Gilles 47
democracy: and imperialism 8; liberal
democracy 109–10; and terror 177
demography: racial demography 22–4;
US since WW II 15
Derrida, Jacques 42, 47, 74, 85, 131, 138,
139, 172
Descartes, René 177
Dewey, John 61, 87, 110, 177
dialectics 95
Did Someone Say Totalitarianism?
(Žižek) 60
Dilthey, Wilhelm 47
Dilworth, David 93, 95–8; Tanabe and
race 99, 100; Tanabe and
'spontaneous obedience' 102
Doak, Kevin 64, 99–100, 160
Dore, Ronald 48, 49
Dostoevsky, F. M. 172
Dower, John W. 24, 39, 64, 169; race 41,
99, 100, 173
Dreams of Difference (Doak) 100
Dresden, fire-bombing 15
Dreyfus Affair 16
Dryburgh, Marjorie 39
Du Bois, W. E. B. 29, 44
dualism, Heidegger critical of 136
Dumoulin, Heinrich, Fr 142, 143
Dunkirk, British evacuation 8
Durkheim, Emile 103–4

Eastern Europe, repression 123–6
economy, post-war Miracle 170–1
Eisenhower, Dwight D. 7
Eliot, George 46
Emerson, R. W. 177
empires, rise and fall of 3–4
essentialism 74, 154
*Estrangement of Great Britain and
Japan, The* (Kennedy) 39
Etō, Jun 10, 11–13
Eurocentrism 29; overthrown in Japan
31
'European Nihilism' (Löwith) 88
European philosophy, and Japanese
compared 85
Existentialisme ou Marxisme? (Lukács)
137

Fallows, James 48
family, Tanabe on 188–90

Fanon, Frantz 45, 67, 159, 175–6
Farías, Victor 107, 113, 114, 146; Farías
Affair 129–40, 138, 139, 147; impact
141, 144
fascism 39–40; analysis of Harootunian
55, 60; Dale's criticism of Imanishi
94; de Man scandal 147; and Gentile
106–7; Heidegger accused of
supporting 107, 113, 117, 118,
119–26, 145–6, 162–3; Italy 86–7,
106–7; nature of World War II 39–40;
nazism and humanism 139–40; and
subjectivity 138–9; Tanabe 19, 21, 86,
95, 107, 149–50, 156, 162; *Tennō-sei*
fascism 21
Faye, Jean Pierre 132
Fédier, François 132
Feenberg, Andrew 64, 145–6, 152, 153
Ferry, Luc 132, 139
Fichte, J. G. 133
Foucault, Michel 44, 47, 67, 85, 138, 150
French philosophy 85
Freud, Sigmund 14
Friedman, David 48
Fujita, Masakatsu 149

Garon, Sheldon 48
Gentile, Giovanni 86, 106–7
Germany 85; causes of defeat in WW I
11–12; Heidegger's influence on
Japanese philosophers 81–2; Löwith
88–90
Gibbon, Edward 4
Goldman, Lucien 137, 138, 139, 172
Gordon, Andrew 48
Gramsci, Antonio 45, 87
Grange, Joseph 141
Great East Asian War 22, 108; and
subjectivity 139
Greater East Asian Co-prosperity
Sphere 30, 62–3, *see also* co-
prosperity spheres
Greek philosophy: Tanabe on 183–7,
198, *see also* Aristotle; Plato; Socrates
Green, Thomas Hill 133
Gulf War (first) 4
Gulf War (second) 6

Habermas, Jürgen 42, 47, 139
Harada, Kumao 71
Harootunian, Harry 33, 40, 47, 48;
Overcome by Modernity 33, 47, 50–60
Hawaii, Japanese attack on 10

Hegel, G. W. F. 43, 44, 61–2, 67, 98, 102, 104, 133, 172, 185; on death 193
Heidegger Controversy, The (Wolin) 118
Heidegger et le nazisme (Farías) 130, 131
Heidegger, Martin 19, 34, 42, 44, 47, 108, 172; Being, politics of 115, 116, 119; 'deep ecology' 110; dualism 136; Farías Affair 129–40; and fascism 107, 113, 117, 118, 119–26, 145–6, 162–3; impact of Farías Affair 141; influence on Japanese philosophers 81–2; *Letter on Humanism* 135; and Lukács 136–7; and Marcuse, correspondence 117–26; and Nazism 150; objectivism 135–6; Rectoral Address 113–14, 115, 119, 122, 139; Sarte's debate with 134–7; *Sein und Zeit* (Being and Time) 81–2, 84, 85, 86, 119, 133, 134, 135, 150; subjectivity 135–6, 139–40; Tanabe on 112–16; Tanabe on Rectoral Address 113, 181–7
Heisig, James W. 34, 36, 60, 64, 144, 153–4; *minzoku*, translation of 159–60; on Tanabe 34–5, 155–9
Herrenvolk 160
Hidaka, Daijirō 70
Hirayama, Kōji 104
Hirohito and the making of Modern Japan (Bix) 49
Hiromatsu, Wataru, *On 'Overcoming Modernity (Kindai no Chōkoku-ron)* 57–8, 59, 148
Hiroshima, atomic destruction of 15, 33, 42, 175
historical materialism, Tanabe on 191–2
history: Hegel and the Kyoto School 62–3; nature of 44–5, *see also Standpoint of World History and Japan, The*
History and Class Consciousness (Lukács) 45, 132–3, 136
Hitler, A. 2, 8, 48, 119
Ho Chi Minh 23, 25
Hobbes, Thomas 109, 159
Holocaust 8; 'Japanese Holocaust' 14
Horio, Tsutomu 60, 61, 70, 72
human nature, Tanabe on 192
humanism 30; and nazism 139–40
Husserl, Edmund 47, 85, 135
Hyppolite, Jean 45, 67

Ichikawa, Hakugen 148

Ichikawa, Hiroshi 148
Imanishi, Kinji 41, 93–4
imperialism: and democracy 8; US challenge to 7
India, Sepoy Mutiny 3, 5
Introduction à la Lecture de Hegel (Kojève) 67
'intuition', and mediated knowledge 90
Iraq 5
Ishimoda, Shō 86
Islamic fundamentalist terrorism 32
Israel, US policy towards 4, 9
Italy: fascism 86–7, 106–7; Italian philosophy 86–7
Ives, Christopher 148

Jacinto Zavala, Agustin 149
James, Henry 20, 47
James, William 90, 133
Jansen, Marius 49, 169, 171
Japan, defense of Pacific War 18–22
'Japan critique' 33
Japan Romantic School 30
'Japanese Revolt Against the West: Political and Cultural Criticism in the Twentieth Century' (Harootunian and Najita) 47
Jefferson, Thomas 11, 177
Johnson, Chalmers 7, 48, 54, 176
Jonas, Hans 117
Jones, Christopher 152
Jünger, Ernst 11–12

Kaisetsu (Ōshima) 69
Kant, Immanuel 161–2
Karatani, Kōjin 59, 147, 148–9
Keene, Donald 49
Kehre ('turn') 19
ken'i 104
Kennedy, Malcolm 39
Kersten, Rikki 100, 169
Kimura, Motomori 70
Kindai no Chōkoku (Hiromatsu) 57–9
Kipling, Rudyard 5
knowledge: and 'intuition' 90; and philosophy 92; Tanabe on 182–3
Kobayashi, Toshiaki 149
Kojève, Alexandre 45, 67
Korea 11; Korean conflict 23
Korsch, Karl 137
Kosaka, Kunitsugu 149
Kōsaka, Masaaki 18, 19, 29, 31, 56, 61, 66, 72, 80, 87, 91, 100, 152, 176

Koschmann, Victor 64
Kōyama, Iwao 18, 19, 30, 31, 44, 45, 54, 56, 57, 61, 66, 71, 72, 80, 91, 152, 176
Kuhn, Thomas 176
Kuki, Shūzō 81–2, 84, 89
kyō-sei 104–5
Kyoto School and the Japanese Navy, The (Ōhashi) 70

Labriola, Antonio 87
Lacoue-Labarthe, Philippe 136
Lanzmann, Claude 131
Laski, Harold 110
Latin America 168; hegemony of USA 75
Lattimore, Owen 168
Lee, Homer 174
Lenin, V. I. 86
L'Etre et le Néant (Sartre) 134, 135
Letter on Humanism (Heidegger) 135
Lévi-Strauss, Claude 47, 104
Lévy-Bruhl, Lucien 104
liberal democracy 109–10
Lieven, Anatol 9
List, Friedrich 110
Locke, John 160–1, 167
Lockwood, William 48, 54
logic, dialectics 95
Logic of Social Existence (Tanabe) 111–12
Logic of the Species, The (Tanabe) 18, 19, 22, 35, 64, 69, 74, 94, 108, 111–12, 114, 116, 133, 150, 156, 157, 159, 176; race 99–101; 'spontaneous obedience' 101–5; translating 95–101
Löwith, Karl 88–90, 113, 117, 132, 167, 177
Lukács, Georg 47, 86, 114, 134; *Existentialisme ou Marxisme?* 137; and Heidegger 136–7; *History and Class Consciousness* 45, 132–3, 136
Lukács, Marx and the Sources of Critical Theory (Feenberg) 146
Luther, M. 193

McMullen, James 49
Magellan, Ferdinand 23
Making of Modern Japan, The (Jansen) 49
Malinowski, Bronislaw 34
Manhattan, as 'nerve-centre of mid-century' 37–8
Mann, Thomas 117

Maraldo, John C. 60, 64, 144
Marcuse, Herbert 107; and Heidegger, correspondence 117–26
Maruyama, Masao 88
Marx, Karl 38, 86, 134
marxism 136; and Italian philosophy 86–7
Mexico, emigration to USA 24
micro-revisionism 40
Middle East: US policy towards 9; US response to September 11 4
Miki, Kiyoshi 19, 21, 56, 72, 81, 84, 87
military expansion, Pacific War 32
Mill, John Stuart 99, 129
Minamoto, Ryōen 68, 69
Minobe, Tatsukichi 68, 106, 109, 111–12
minzoku, translation of 99–101, 159–60
Mitchell, Richard 64
MITI and the Japanese Miracle (Johnson) 48
Miyazaki, Ichisada 70
Miyoshi, Masao 64
modernisation 45; and modern 43
modernity 48; *Overcome by Modernity* (Harootunian) 33, 47, 50–60; overcoming 32
monarchy, Tanabe on 196
Monroe Doctrine 75
Moreiras, Alberto 168
multiculturalism 44
Murphy, R. T. 48, 49, 169
Mutai, Risaku 87
Mysticism and Morality: Oriental Thought and Moral Philosophy (Danto) 36–7
Myth of Japanese Uniqueness, The (Dale) 40–1, 92, 93, 103, 152

Nagasaki 33, 175
Nagata, Kiyokimi 197
Najita, Tetsuo 40, 47, 49
Nanjing, slaughter of Chinese 15
national identity 70; discourse of 93
nationalism 35, 152–3; Dale and Tanabe 93–4, 97; *Rude Awakenings: Zen, the Kyoto School and the Question of Nationalism* 34, 35, 39, 60, 141, 143–9, 151, 152, 155; Tanabe accused of 108–9, 156
Nature 104
Naulahka 5
nazism 39; and humanism 139–40, *see also* fascism

Needham, Joseph 49
neo-Marxism 33, 40, 46–60; neo-Marxist scholarship 152
'New Turn in Phenomenology: Heidegger's Philosophy of Life, A' (Tanabe) 81
New York 37
Newton, Sir Isaac 167
Nietzsche, Friedrich W. 3, 34, 47, 51–3, 79, 85, 113, 171, 172, 198–9; and fascism 115
Nishi , Amane 87
Nishida, Kitarō 5, 19, 30, 31, 34, 40, 56, 62, 71, 79–80, 83, 87, 94, 115, 133, 148–9, 150, 152, 153, 160, 176; European civilisation 89–90; and fascism 107, 156; German philosophy 81, 90; and Japanese hegemony 145; and Japan's plunge into fascism 106; positivism 145; stance during Pacific War 206–7; transcendence 155
Nishitani, Keiji 18, 19, 31, 34, 56, 61, 66, 72, 79–80, 81, 84, 85, 91, 139, 149–50, 152, 155, 156, 159, 162, 176
Nishitani, Osamu 35
Nissan Institute for Japanese Studies 92–3
Nolte, Ernst 15; deep revisionism 16
Norman, E. H. 168, 169, 170–1, 175
nothingness 193

obedience, 'spontaneous obedience' 101–5
'objective spirit' 102, 104
objectivism 146; Heidegger 135–6, 145, 146
Ōhashi, Ryōsuke 20, 42, 69, 70, 71, 72, 73, 149
Okimoto, Daniel 48
oil, US policy in Middle East 5
'On the Logic of Co-prosperity Spheres: Towards a Philosophy of Regional Blocs' (Tanabe) 188–99
On 'Overcoming Modernity' (Kindai no Chōkoku-ron) (Hiromatsu) 57–8, 148
Orwell, George 16
Ōshima Memos, The 19, 22, 69, 70, 71, 72, 73, 108, 152, 173
Ōshima, Yasumasa 69–70
Ōtsuka, Hisao 54, 176
Ott, Hugo 131
Ouchi, William 48

Overcome by Modernity (Harootunian) 33, 47, 50–60
'Overcoming Modernity' ('Kindai no Chōkoku') 31, 50, 55, 56, 57, 58, 59, 94, 133, 153, 173

Paci, Enzo 87
Paglia, Camille 147
Pakistan 4
Palestine, American policy towards 4, 9
Parkes, Graham 33, 53, 81, 83, 84, 152
Parris, Matthew 6
Pascal, B. 192
patriarchal family, Tanabe on 73–4
Patrick, Hugh 48
patriotism *see* nationalism
Pearl Harbour, attack on 10–11, 14, 17, 19, 21, 24–6, 43, 44, 61–3, 72, 80
Peattie, Mark 174
Péguy, Charles 92
Pempel, T. 48
Perry, M. G. 23
Phenomenology of Spirit (Hegel) 44
Philosophers of Nothingness 141, 153, 154, 155, 156, 158, 160
philosophy, and Kyoto School 82–5
'Philosophy of Crisis or a Crisis in Philosophy: Reflections on Heidegger's Rectoral Address' (Tanabe) 115, 181–7
Philosophy as Metanoetics (Tanabe) 34–5, 86, 121
Philosophy of World History (Kōyama) 71, 176
Pierce, Charles Sanders 85
Piovesana, G. 93
Plato 115, 116, 145, 184, 185, 193–4
politics, and assessment of philosophers 36
post-structuralism 138
power: and authority 102, 104; deconstruction of 30; US global hegemony 6, 7
Problem of Japanese Culture, The (Nishida) 153
propaganda, role of 14
Protestant work ethic 111

race: Battle of Wounded Knee to Pacific War 173–6; changing attitudes to racism 101; Dale on Tanabe and Imanishi 92–4; Heisig's translation of *minzoku* 159–60; impact of WW II

24–6; Kant, racism 161–2; nature of the Pacific War 99–101; racial demography 22–4; US justification for participation in WW II 24; and US victory over Japan 20
Ramos, Julio 54
Ranke, Leopold von 14
rationality: and Japanese war aims and means 20; rational society, Japan 110–11; and subjectivity 13; Tanabe on 186
Reagan, Ronald 25
reason, and Japanese society 110–12
Rectoral Address (Heidegger) 113–14, 115, 119, 122, 139
Reischauer, Edwin O. 108, 169, 171
religion, and objectivism 135
Renaut, Alain 132, 139
'Return to the Past: Tradition and the Political Microcosm in the Later Nishida' (Jacinto Zavala) 149
revisionism 14–26
Riehl, Alois 81
Ritter, Rana 39
Rockmore, Tom 114
Romanticism, attitude of Western scholars to Zen 142
Rome (Republic/Empire): rise and fall of 3; sack of Rome 4
Roosevelt, Franklin D. 25, 26, 110
Rorty, Richard 85, 139, 177
Rosenbluth, Frances 48
Rosovsky, Henry 48
Rude Awakenings: Zen, the Kyoto School and the Question of Nationalism 34, 35, 39, 60, 141, 143–9, 151, 152, 155
Russell, Bertrand 42
Russo-Japanese War (1904–5) 173

Said, Edward 7; *Orientalism* 33, 154
Saigō, Takamori 42
Saitō, Shō 68
Saitō, Tadashi 68
Sakai, Naoki 29, 35, 36, 37, 40, 44, 54, 64, 152, 176
Samuels, Richard 48, 176
Sartre, Jean Paul 42, 44, 45, 67, 81, 85, 159; and Heidegger 132, 133, 134–6
Satō, Taira 95–8; Tanabe and race 99, 100; Tanabe and 'spontaneous obedience' 102
Satō, Tsuji 68
satori 141

Saudi Arabia 4, 9
Schelling, F. W. J. von 133
Schmitt, Carl 109, 159
Schneider, Axel 100
Sein und Zeit (*Being and Time*) (Heidegger) 81–2, 84, 85, 86, 119, 133, 134, 135, 150
Sepoy Mutiny 3
September 11 (terrorist attacks) 4, 10, 24, 32
Sharf, Robert 37–8, 145
Shillony, Ben-Ami 39, 64, 203
Shoah 8, 113, 137–8; Heidegger-Marcuse correspondence 122–4
shu (species) 112
shutaisei see subjectivity
Singapore, siege of 19
Sioux 5
slavery, and John Locke 161
Smith, Adam 110
social determinism 103
Socrates 134, 184, 185–6
sōryoku-sen 205
Soviet Union, brutality in Eastern Europe 124–5
Spain, loss of colonial possessions 7
species 95
'species society' 41
Spencer, Herbert 103
spirit, Tanabe on 182–3
Spirit of Capitalism and the Protestant Ethic, The (Weber) 12–13
'spontaneous obedience' 101–5
Stalin, J. 125
Standpoint of World History and Japan, The (Kōyama et al) 12, 18, 19, 20–1, 22, 30, 31, 55, 57, 64–9, 70, 71, 72, 73, 75, 133, 152, 173
state: attitude of periphery and centre to 41–3; nature of imperial Japan 110–11; and reason 106; Tanabe on 74, 98, 106, 134, 183–7, 190–9
Steiner, George 37, 81, 85, 92, 173, 175
Studies in the Modernization of Japan 171
subjectivity 17, 75, 110, 138–9, 149; European subjectivity 31; and the Farías Affair 133–4; Goldman 139; Heidegger criticises Sartre's subjectivism 135–6; and rationality 13; *shutaisei* 11, 21–2, 30, 63, 68, 115–16, 175–6; Tanabe 99, 133–4, 139, 145; Tanabe on the state 99; and terror 177

Sugimura, Kōzō 197
Surrealists 67
Suzuki, D. T. 19, 31, 36–8, 40, 80, 91
Suzuki, Shigetaka 18, 19, 54, 56, 58–9,
    61, 62, 66–7, 72
Syria 4

Tacitus, Publius 25
Takagi, Sōkichi 70, 71
Takayama, *see* Chogyū
Takeuchi, Yoshimi 44, 147–8
Tanabe, Hajime 18, 19, 20, 21, 30, 31,
    34–5, 40, 43, 45, 66, 68, 69, 72, 79, 80,
    83–4, 85, 86, 91, 133–4, 135, 176;
    accused of being authoritarian 152;
    class tensions 191–2; co-prosperity
    spheres 73–6, 195–9; criticised for
    nationalism 108–9, 156; Dale's
    criticism of 93–4; European
    philosophy 89–90; family 188–90;
    and fascism 19, 21, 86, 95, 107,
    149–50, 156, 162; Heideger's
    influence 81–2; on Heidegger 112–16;
    Heisig on 34–5, 155–9; Hesig's
    translation of *minzoku* 159–60;
    historical materialism 191–2; human
    nature 192; on knowledge 182–3;
    liberal democracy 109; *Logic of
    Social Existence* 111–12; rational
    discourse 111–12; 'On the Logic of
    Co-prosperity Spheres: Towards a
    Philosophy of Regional Blocs'
    188–99; 'Philosophy of Crisis or a
    Crisis in Philosophy: Reflections on
    Heidegger's Rectoral Address' 115,
    181–7; reason 41; spirit 182–3; state
    74, 98, 106, 134, 183–7, 190–9;
    subjectivity 99, 133–4, 139, 145, *see
    also Logic of the Species, The*; *Myth
    of Japanese Uniqueness, The*
Tennō-sei fascism 21
terrorism, US reaction to 4–5, 6, 9
theōría, Tanabe on Greek philosophy
    183–4
Thomas Aquinas, St 87
Tojo, Hideki 11, 17, 20, 26, 39, 63, 68,
    75–6; Kyoto School's battle with
    69–72
Tokugawa Political Writings (Najita) 49
Tōma, Seita 86
Tosaka, Jun 19, 21, 72
total mobilisation 12
Toynbee, Arnold 175

transcendence 155
*Two Sources of Morality and Religion,
    The* (Bergson) 103
Tyson, Laura 48

UK: racial demography 22; rise and fall
    of British Empire 3; World War II 8
Umemoto, Katsumi 86
universalism, and Japanese intellectuals
    167–8
universals, Plato 194
USA: academic ascendancy 48–9;
    attitude to Asia, 4–6; Civil War 15;
    Constitution 7; demographic changes
    since WW II 15; empire in Pacific 17;
    global hegemony 6, 7, 9–10, 11;
    hegemony over Latin America 75;
    immigration 24; imperialism and
    democracy 8; neo-conservatives
    ('neo-cons') 9–10; opposition to
    American hegemony 32; race, impact
    of WW II 24–6; racial demography
    22; reaching summit of its power 3;
    revision of Pacific War history 16–17;
    White Republic 15; World Trade
    Centre destruction 4
USSR: total mobilisation 12; UK
    alliance with during WW II 8

Valéry, Paul 134
Valour of Ignorance (Lee) 174
values, universalism and Japanese
    intellectuals 167–8
Van Bragt, Jan 141, 142, 146, 150
Van der Rohe, Mies 46
Varus, Publius Quintilius 3–4
Vattimo, Gianni 52, 53, 55, 87
Védrine, Hubert 8
Vidal, Gore 7
Vietnam 5, 11, 24, 36, 44; opposition to
    war within US 25
Vietnamese/Indo-Chinese Wars 23
Vogel, Ezra 48, 54
Volpe, Galvano Della 87

Wade, Robert 48
Waehlens, Alphonse de 132
Wagner, Richard 115
Wahl, Jean 67
Wakeman, Frederic 39
war crimes 16–17; Tokyo War Crimes
    Tribunal 34
War without Mercy: Race and Power in

the Pacific War (Dower) 41, 99, 100, 173
Watsuji, Tetsurō 84, 89, 93, 94
Weber, Max 12–13, 46, 110, 111, 170
Weil, Eric 45, 67, 132
West, Cornel 30
Wetzler, Peter 39
Whitehead, Alfred North 91
Whiteness 172
Wilson, Woodrow 61
Wittgenstein, Ludwig 42, 129
Wolin, Richard 114–15, 118–19, 121, 147
Woodward, Bob 5
'World Historical Position and Japan, The' 56–7
World Trade Centre destruction 4, 17
World War I, causes of German defeat 11–12

World War II: Churchill's dilemma 8; expansion of American empire 31; revisionism 15–16; total mobilisation 12

Yamagata, Aritomo 169
Yasukuni Shrine 35
Yoshida, Kazuo 176
Young, Robert 148
Yukawa, Hideki 70
Yusa, Michiko 70–1

zaiya seishin (oppositional spirit) 42
Zen Buddhism 34, 37, 80, 89, 91; death 193; impact of Farías Affair 141–3, 148; and tyranny 145
Žižek, Slavoj 60
Zola, Emile 16